Consuming Sustainability

Critical Social Analyses of Ecological Change

Edited by
Debra J. Davidson, Kierstin C. Hatt,
and the Northern Critical Scholars Collective

Fernwood Publishing • Halifax

Copyright © 2005 Debra J. Davidson, Kierstin C. Hatt

All rights reserved. No part of this book may be reproduced or transmitted in any form by any means without permission in writing from the publisher, except by a reviewer, who may quote brief passages in a review.

Editing: Robert Clarke
Cover photo: Colin Brown, Artists Against War
Printed and bound in Canada by: Hignell Printing Limited

A publication of:
Fernwood Publishing
Site 2A, Box 5, 32 Oceanvista Lane
Black Point, Nova Scotia, B0J 1B0
and 324 Clare Avenue
Winnipeg, Manitoba, R3L 1S3
www.fernwoodbooks.ca

Fernwood Publishing Company Limited gratefully acknowledges the financial support of the Department of Canadian Heritage, the Nova Scotia Department of Tourism and Culture and the Canada Council for the Arts for our publishing program.

Library and Archives Canada Cataloguing in Publication

Consuming sustainability : critical social analyses of ecological change / edited by Debra J. Davidson, Kierstin C. Hatt and the Northern Critical Scholars Collective.

Includes bibliographical references.
ISBN 1-55266-155-5

1. Human ecology--Canada. 2. Human ecology.
I. Davidson, Debra II. Hatt, Kierstin C. (Kierstin Carolyn), 1967-
III. Northern Critical Scholars Collective

GF41.C65 2005 304.2'0971 C2005-901428-8

Contents

This book is dedicated to the planet and those who are committed to sustaining it.

Preface

As students and teachers who share an interest in the social-scientific treatment of environmental concerns, the contributors to this book have all shared in a certain frustration regarding the nature of instructional materials available. We all find environmental issues to be of increasing concern both personally and politically, and as social scientists we believe that the contributions of our respective disciplines to an understanding and treatment of the environment have yet to reach their full potential. Citizens and scholars who are concerned about these issues tend to look for answers and discussion to those disciplines that are more readily associated with environmental management in the natural sciences, and of course economics. One problem is that few social science texts specifically focused on these topics have been aimed at a broader audience: at undergraduate students being exposed to this material for the first time, at scholars outside the social sciences, or at non-academics who seek better understanding of our relationship to the natural world and the potential for social change. We decided to try to remedy that situation.

This book has followed a somewhat unusual process in that it has been written largely as a collective effort. As members of a reading and discussion group that has met regularly for several years to discuss social-scientific articles about environmental issues, we have had plenty of opportunity to vent our frustrations about the need for more social analysis in public and political discussions about the environment. We have also had the opportunity to discuss potential remedies. Our group has eleven members, including five graduate students, five professors representing five different academic departments and three universities, and one non-academic professional: six men and five women. We believe that this collective approach has been important to the success of our project, not only intellectually and socially but also because of the type of book that the collective process can produce. We wanted this to be similar to many edited books in its variety and diversity of expertise and styles; but we also wanted it to "hang together" as a coherent and comprehensive representation of social-scientific understandings on ecological exhaustion, social organization, and activism.

The vision for the book and the division of the material into chapters were developed collectively. Most of the chapters were be written by more than one author in an effort to provide a diversity of expertise, perspectives and enthusiasms both within and among the chapters. We reviewed each other's chapters, relying on two global editors to be responsible for book continuity, coverage and distribution of material, as well as for the introduction and conclusion chapters.

Acknowledgements

This book was a collaborative process in every sense of the word—it involved not only the authors but also an extensive support network of family and colleagues. Our thanks go out first and foremost to our families, who put up with several late-night and weekend meetings and writing sessions. Wayne Antony, your contributions to this book go far beyond the call of professional duty. Thank you for your insightful reviews, accessibility, and most of all your patience. Other colleagues, including Michael Clow, Harris Ali, and Cheryl Henkleman, have offered thorough reviews and constructive comments on earlier drafts. This work has also benefited from the willingness of several parties to allow us to reprint their graphics, maps, and photographs. Thank you especially to Colin Brown; your photographs are stories in themselves. The careful and skilled copy-editing of Robert Clarke improved the manuscript tremendously. Thanks also to the Fernwood Publishing production folk: Beverley Rach for design and layout, Debbie Mathers for typing the final manuscript, and Brenda Conroy for proofreading. And finally, to our illustrious, warm, and inviting meeting hosts, the Organic Roots Café in Edmonton, Alberta: your great coffee and tasty treats are directly responsible for inspiring much of our intellectual creativity.

Debra J. Davidson and Kierstin C. Hatt
Edmonton, Alberta

1. Power and Sustainability

Kierstin C. Hatt, Debra J. Davidson, and Ineke Lock

> What should be clear by now to thoughtful greens is that without social and economic justice, there can be no environmental or ecological justice, and thereby no sustainability. If one community becomes "sustainable" at the expense of another, is the biosphere better off?... Unless a significant number of humans stand actively against all degradations, wherever they occur, global sustainability simply won't happen.
> —Mark Dowie, *Losing Ground: American Environmentalism at the Close of the Twentieth Century*

Why this Book? Why Now?

An average fully grown Western man measures close to two metres tall these days. One metre of standing water would go up to that person's waist, or thereabouts. A full metre: that is the level, according to climate experts, by which the world's oceans will almost certainly rise in this century. This catastrophic scenario would displace hundreds of millions of residents in flood-prone areas, from Bangladesh and India in the South to the Netherlands and Canada's coastal cities in the North.

While much of the world's climate has warmed by one half of a degree Celsius over the last one hundred years, the Arctic regions are warming at a much faster rate: two to three degrees since 1950. For at least thirty years now, according to the Arctic Climate Impact Assessment (Spears 2004), Arctic ice has been thinning, and its area shrinking. Northern countries such as Canada, Russia, and Norway have a special interest in this melting Arctic ice: large stretches of terrain in these countries consist of frozen tundra, rivers, lakes, and seas. Although the regions are sparsely populated and rarely on the minds of the countries' urban citizens, the Northern warming has begun to threaten animal species such as the polar bear and has already had severe effects on the livelihoods of indigenous groups.

That same melting Arctic ice, combined with the melting of Greenland's glaciers and warming oceans, also poses a threat to over a billion people who live in flood-prone regions. But the threat is much more severe for people living in Bangladesh, for example, than it is for people living in wealthier countries such as the Netherlands. Millions of people in the Netherlands already live on land that is below sea level, and they are protected by dikes that are marvels of engineering technology. Faced with rising sea levels, the people of the Netherlands will most likely look to further technological solutions to protect their country. In contrast, Bangladeshi lives and possessions are already being regularly devastated by seasonal flooding. Rising sea levels are likely to displace or kill many more people in the near future.

Why doesn't the government of Bangladesh build dikes too? To answer that question—and other similar critical questions—is to raise connections between the environment and social factors, which is the reason we wrote this book. The question of whether science or technology will save us from ecological disaster is compelling, but it does not consider the whole picture. Dike-building technology is available, but poverty-stricken Bangladesh does not have the monetary resources to use this technology to protect its people. The Netherlands, a rich Northern country, does have the resources to do so. This difference in available resources has been called the "vulnerability gap," identified by the United Nation's Environmental Programme (UNEP 2002) as a disparity that places the disadvantaged at a much greater risk when it comes to environmental change and disasters.

Even so, the Netherlands' over-reliance on technological solutions to environmental maladies may not save that country's people—just as it may not save any of us in the end—when the causes of environmental degradation are deeply embedded in our cultures, economies, and political systems. Moving towards a future that is less prone to environmental catastrophe requires not just more effort in the ecological sciences and advances in engineering and technology. Our future viability demands that all of us become better critical social analysts. In this book, drawing from several social sciences—including human geography, environmental sociology, philosophy, and ecological economics—that offer key tools for conducting critical analyses, we teach you to do just that.

This book was written by a group of scholars who work and live in Canada. While issues like Arctic warming and melting Northern ice are of specific concern to Canadians, they also resonate with people in other countries. Effects of ecological change know no national boundaries, and what concerns us should concern others as well. Canada's experience is similar to that of most industrialized countries and certainly subject to the same international pressures of global neo-liberal capitalism. Many, though not all, of our empirical case studies are Canadian, but the critical analytical approach we offer can easily be applied to other contexts. The chapter themes and stories present a microcosm of contemporary ecological disruption and renewal that is being experienced the world over: from heavy economic interdependence between countries to the sensitivities of geopolitical positioning; from encroachment on increasingly remote places for resources to the insurgence of indigenous rights and values.

That human activities are having a significant, deleterious impact on the environment is no longer news to most of the people living on this planet. Warnings of imminent ecological disasters are issued with distressing regularity. One such warning came from the Union of Concerned Scientists over a decade ago, when 1,680 scientists signed a "Warning to

Humanity" concluding with no reservations that "human activities inflict harsh and often irreversible damage on the environment and on critical resources" (Union of Concerned Scientists 1992). Still, although such warnings have become regular features of our political and everyday discourse, the ensuing discussions do not appear to have fostered significant change in our ways of doing things.

Much of the discourse at the political level consists of arguments about whether we have enough proof that global warming is real; whether nature is able to absorb the pollution we generate in ever-increasing quantities; or whether resource exhaustion will magically cause science to discover a cheap, clean, and ever-lasting alternative energy source. But the case of quickly melting Arctic ice, among many other occurrences of ecological change and disruption, tells us that the irreversibility and devastating impact of ecological disruption will not offer us the luxury of waiting for such questions to be settled before we act. Nature's imposition of limits will be harsh and unpredictable and will result in severe human suffering. The real question is whether we will keep on slouching towards disaster, or whether we will take an active and informed part in changing human practices and activities to attain sustainability.

This book uses social science perspectives to, first and foremost, provide a deeper conceptual understanding of the social, political, economic, and cultural aspects of human activity and organization. Social-scientific research has provided ample evidence that our human societies are not nearly as capable of transcending ecological limits as we had once presumed. This miscalculation of human capabilities also explains why an ecological perspective is becoming increasingly important to advancing knowledge in the social sciences. Given that this perspective has until recently been absent from social-scientific scrutiny, we are only just beginning to understand the myriad ways in which our lives, both individually and collectively, affect and are affected by ecological conditions. That we are indeed a part of, rather than apart from, our ecosystems, poses critical challenges to many fundamentals of social-scientific scholarship. More contemporary scholarship shows how this "society-ecology dialectic" influences everything from settlement patterns and economic development trajectories to political mobilization and state legitimacy. This work is so compelling that ecological issues may well become a central feature of social-scientific research and teaching in the future, and young, ecologically informed scholars will be crucial to these disciplines. For this reason, while our first priority is to offer readers the tools required to become critical social analysts in their own realms, we also provide avenues for readers to dig further into these disciplines, to encourage future scholars in these important areas of inquiry.

Our aim is to provide an ecologically informed understanding of social change and, more importantly, a social science-informed understanding of ecological change, while providing a realistic mandate for personal and political action. Critical social analysis is important for anyone contemplating ecological crisis and renewal, whether that anyone is a scholar attempting to conduct academic research on the relationship between ecological systems and society, a member of an activist social organization, or simply a citizen pondering ways of reducing her or his "ecological footprint."

Approaches to Sustainability and Development

What will it take for those life-giving features of our planet—and consequently ourselves—to survive and thrive in the future? One popular possible answer to that question rests in the concept of **sustainable development**. *Our Common Future* (commonly referred to as the Brundtland Report), which represented the culmination of the efforts of a United Nations Commission headed by Gro Harlem Brundtland (World Commission on Environment and Development 1987: 43), offers this simple definition: "development that meets the needs of the present without compromising the ability of future generations to meet their own needs."

The simplicity of this definition belies its underlying ambiguity—and this ambiguity has been the source of multiple political contests since the introduction of the term. At the core of the sustainable development debate are four central areas of conflict. The first area is the conflict between the North and the South, a conflict that dates back to earlier development debates about poverty and power and the rights of the poor versus the rights of the rich. The second area is defined by conflicting priorities between, on one side, meeting the needs of current generations and, on the other, addressing the (possibly mutually exclusive) need to ensure sufficient quantity and quality of environmental resources for future generations. The Brundtland Report explicitly directed attention to the stipulation that future generations should be left with the capability of providing for their needs. In the South, however, in many instances the needs of current generations are not being met and must therefore take priority. In the North environmental organizations, and other proponents of sustainable development, tend to be preoccupied with future generations.

Third, debates regarding the appropriate means of implementing sustainable development have been defined by conflicts between anthropocentric perspectives that promote the needs of human beings over other species, and biocentric perspectives that prioritize ecosystem well-being and its non-human inhabitants. And fourth, many sustainable development dialogues have become entrenched in the heated debate between those who subscribe to the belief that human ingenuity will always allow us to resolve ecological crises without changing our (especially economic) behaviours, and those who subscribe to the notion that nature poses absolute limits on human activities, and that we must therefore alter our lifestyles to respect those limits.

While the Brundtland Report does trace the many environmental causes of poverty, the most salient—and arguably problematic—feature of the sustainable development perspective is its adherence to fundamental principles of modernization. The accumulation of scientific information on our environmental ills since the 1970s has challenged many steadfast beliefs and assumptions regarding social development and prospects for a modernized future of industrial growth and prosperity, but these beliefs have survived despite the growing counterevidence. Couched in the tenets of **modernization theory**, these beliefs translate into prescriptions for economic growth for developed and underdeveloped countries alike—prescriptions that have called for rapid industrialization and engagement in capitalist market economies in the name of improving material well-being. Modernization proponents consider capitalist economic growth—as it is now understood and measured—to be the only means of meeting the basic needs of all of the world's people and of providing the necessary funds to preserve and maintain nature's services. This formula demands energy- and technology-intensive industrialization processes, which means that large transnational corporations become dominant players due to their ability to mobilize capital and modern technologies and achieve economies of scale—or the ability to lower per unit costs by engaging in production on a large scale. The modernization paradigm also calls for the upgrading of physical infrastructure—modern electricity delivery, water management, and road networks are essential to even the most basic industrial activities if they are to be economically competitive—and the "modernization" of political and cultural structures to help that process along. Of course, given the global scale of our economic system, increased participation in the global market is also seen as critical to jump-starting emerging economies (e.g., Bendix 1967; Eisenstadt 1966; Moore 1966; Rostow 1960; Weiner 1966).

In the early 1970s, before the widespread introduction of the sustainable development concept, the modernization paradigm did in fact see its pre-eminent position threatened, if only temporarily, by a report produced by a group of predominantly physical scientists. These researchers, who have since become known as the Club of Rome, launched a full-scale attack on the tendencies of modernization theory by compiling enormous amounts of data indicating that the environment can and does pose formidable "limits to growth" (Meadows et al. 1972). Employing large-scale modelling to simulate likely future scenarios given current economic trajectories, these scientists concluded that the global economy was being supported directly through the depletion of natural resources. The authors concluded that unless there were major structural changes (including population control and drastic limitations on economic growth and pollution) the ecological limits to growth would be breached, leading to social collapse. In contrast to modernization theory, the limits to growth perspective urged that economic development planning show a greater respect for ecological limits. Suggestions included making large investments in ecological science and monitoring, and limiting the impact of economic actors on the environment through rigid, prohibitory regulations.

The Club of Rome Report generated heated debate regarding our ability to continue on an industrial economic path in the 1970s and 1980s. The Brundtland Report—albeit more ecologically informed than traditional modernization theory—once again advocated economic growth, defining it as the key means of overcoming ecological limits and social inequity. By this means the Brundtland Report took direct aim at the primary assumption embedded in the Club of Rome Report. The Brundtland Commission did not link poverty and ecological disruption to economic drivers; rather it redefined those problems as the unfortunate consequences of factors such as poor management, lack of technology, and overpopulation, all of which were presumed to be remediable through more economic development. This position, reinforced at the 1992 Earth Summit in Rio de Janeiro, continues to be the predominant paradigm driving environmental governance today.

Not surprisingly, that position is far more palatable to the political and economic power-wielders who benefit from capitalist expansion (Davidson and MecKendrick 2004). Infinite growth, after all, is by definition sustainable (at least in economic theory, if not in ecological reality). As a result environmental politics has repeatedly ignored, assumed away, or dismissed ecological limits, assuring all concerned that the scientific and technological prowess of humankind will prevail. The idea of sustainable development thus offered a welcome relief from the model of conflict that dominated limits to growth debates (Verburg and Wiegel 1997: 251). The sustainable development paradigm has been quickly and widely adopted and is now the principal approach to addressing environmental degradation.

Given modernization theory's emphasis on economic growth, industrialization, and science and technology, the environment tends to be perceived as a pool of "natural resources" that are valued according to their potential ability to provide economic benefit—and the exploitation of which will in turn finance environmental improvement. In the management of natural resources and the environment, scientific expertise and technological solutions—genetic engineering being the most recent development—are at the forefront. When ecological limits rear their imposing head, as they inevitably will, instrumental utopian thinking predominates, raising concepts such as eco-efficiency, ecological modernization, dematerialization, resource substitution, and reliance on correcting market signals through the pricing of nature's services.

Conventional environmental policies reflect this way of thinking. Seemingly unabashed by the tremendous degree of scientific uncertainty and lack of knowledge regarding environmental and ecological systems, most regulatory apparatuses rely upon technological solutions to the scientifically defined critical loads or carrying capacities of ecosystems. There have indeed been a number of success cases in which technological improvements, combined with innovative organizational strategies in environmental management, have led to dramatic increases in efficiency in the use of raw materials or to reductions in waste. Some social scientists and analysts cite these case studies as evidence that our social systems are making the necessary transitions to sustainable societies. Calling this transition **ecological modernization**, proponents are confident that the rapid development of a global governing apparatus, as well as advances in science and technology, will lead to the resolution of environmental maladies.

Ecological modernization postulates that our modern economic and political systems have undergone one of the most dramatic shifts experienced since the Industrial Revolution (Huber 1982), and that the institutions making up our contemporary societies have begun to incorporate an ecological awareness into their decision-making; ecological improvements have thus become a priority in politics and economic development. Proponents are optimistic that economic growth and environmental degradation can be reconciled through the internalization of environmental costs (Mol 1996), and that we can work within economic goals and constraints (Christoff 1996), particularly through reliance on science and technology (Spaargaren and Mol 1992). The adoption of ecological modernization, however, will require a more flexible, responsive style of management than our rigid bureaucratic organizations are designed to provide (Weale 1992; Mol 1996), particularly because many of the experts and resources needed for environmental improvement are to be found in civil society (Janicke 1997). Indeed, many observers have highlighted the extent to which new institutional arrangements are emerging all the time. Most importantly, ecological modernization theorists are confident in the capacity of capitalism to transform itself in the face of ecological crisis (Mol and Spaargaren 2000).

These concepts of ecological modernization and sustainable development (or its close associate **sustainability**) have become increasingly influential at national and international levels. The 1992 United Nations Conference on Environment and Development in Rio de Janeiro, known as the Earth Summit, played a part in this, especially with its plan of action set out in "Agenda 21." Worldwide, governments and private- and civil-sector organizations have developed, or are developing, sustainable development policies and practices.

Still, numerous scholars and activists have seen fit to critique these notions of sustainable development and ecological modernization (see Caldicott 1992; Clow 1991a; Daly and Cobb 1989; Hecht and Cockburn 1990; Redclift 1984, 1987, 1991; Sachs 1992; Shiva 1991; Vandermeer and Perfecto 1995). Both approaches first and foremost fail to acknowledge the real limits to growth. If, as the Club of Rome found, industrialization is the primary cause of ecological destruction, how can industrialization simultaneously become the primary means of ecological renewal? Critics also note that these approaches do not include considerations of how to address the significant global inequities in standards of living and capacities for change.

Furthermore, the prevailing notion of sustainable development assumes that natural resources, like all economic products and services, are divisible and controllable through the forces of supply and demand. This notion denies the intrinsic value of natural resources and avoids seeing them as interdependent parts of ecological systems that are susceptible to cumulative, permanent systemic changes. Many of these conditions and changes are so complex that we lack the ability to monitor them, much less ameliorate them. This is in part why market mechanisms fail to deal effectively with environmental goods and services.

Finally, the ambiguous definition of sustainable development allows for a virtual explosion of made-to-order variations on the theme, providing a source of intense political debate: emphasis can be placed on ecological sustainability, community sustainability, sustained economic growth, technological progress, global redistribution of resources, or sustainable companies. Practitioners of this bent can pretty much choose a meaning that fits with their intentions, whether those intentions are guided by a concern for the environment or a desire to bolster economic growth.

Many in this debate, including the authors of this book, are attempting to reclaim the concept of sustainability from those who have manipulated its meaning to serve the interests of those in power. Instead we promote an understanding of the concept of sustainability as an ever-evolving vision for humanity that prioritizes acknowledgement of and adjustment to ecological limits; supports a systems-level analysis of the dialectic relationships between the environment, economy, and society; includes a strong concern for equity, fairness, and participatory, democratic decision-making; and demands employment of the precautionary principle in our scientific and technological endeavours.

Consuming sustainability

One of the most controversial aspects of attaining sustainability is the question of overconsumption in the rich countries of the North. As Jeremy Seabrook has observed, nothing could be more threatening to the growth-dependent economic system than that "the people should declare themselves satisfied with what they have" (cited in Bauman 1998: 40). While the poor countries of the South need to provide their populations with the basics of a decent human life, and economic growth is considered the principle means of doing so, the people and organizations of the North consume far more than their fair share of the planet's resources and use more than their fair share of the world's pollutant sinks—the capacity of the planet to absorb pollution and waste. The populations of the rich

Northern countries (meaning you and I) are, in a sense, "consuming sustainability," and eliminating possibilities for a sustainable future. If we continue to do so, there is simply not going to be any way of sustaining the planet's population into the future. While this may at first have an impact on only the most vulnerable, as in the example of flooding in Bangladesh, eventually it will touch on the lives of everyone. According to many critical accounts of ecological disruption, we in North America and Western Europe have already consumed sustainability for others by appropriating the bulk of the world's resources for ourselves.

Sustainability can also be consumed in more ways than just the material sense. It is also consumed when we passively accept contemporary perspectives on sustainable development, such as the presumed need for sustainability of corporate profits as a prerequisite for environmental well-being or improvements in liveability for the poor. Sustainability is consumed when we buy, eat, and wear things that provide us with no real benefit. It is consumed when we engage in activities that harm either ourselves or others. The chapters that follow, covering a range of topics, offer analyses that show how and where sustainability is threatened, and how it can be reclaimed.

Analyzing Power and Sustainability: Using the Social Sciences as a Guide

The often simplistic prescriptions pursued in the name of sustainable development, or even of environmental activism, tend to fall flat because of the lack of a critical socio-political understanding of social change. Our relationship with the natural world is defined by culture, identity, organizational behaviour, history, and, most significantly, power. We usually think of power as an individual asset—some of us have it, some don't. But power is an institutional asset as well, and as such it is often poorly understood, or ignored altogether. It has a central importance to questions of sustainability. Institutional power not only determines access to environmental and ecological goods but is also wholly responsible for great harm associated with environmental degradation. As the following chapters make clear, power influences everything from access to clean water supplies and the exploitation of natural resources to the ability to impose technological risks upon others and the very rights to define the risks, and values, associated with environmental issues. Environmental access, then, is an equity issue, and that access has historically been characterized by sharp divisions between North and South; rich and poor; white and non-white; and men and women.

Power also influences the nature of ecological decision-making, often in deleterious ways. The tremendous complexity and uncertainty associated with many ecological and environmental phenomena have justified a variety of centralized, expertise-based management and regulatory regimes that not only serve to reinforce existing inequalities but also, in many instances, to justify the exclusion of local, experiential knowledge from decision-making.

As a result social scientists and sustainable development practitioners alike are becoming aware of the need to broaden our understanding and implementation of sustainability in a manner that incorporates both the material, ecological limits to growth and the real social limits—and potential—for change. In short, sustainable development can only be an effective means of supporting healthy, ecologically viable social systems if it is pursued in conjunction with **ecological democracy**—equal opportunities to participate in environmental decisions that impinge on our lives and values; and **environmental justice**—the equitable distribution of environmental goods and risks.

While social and ecological crises are complex and sometimes overwhelming, they are not necessarily so. When they are examined relative to daily life issues, with analyses that are holistic and interdisciplinary and lay bare power and powerful interests, they are neither incomprehensible nor hopeless—and therein lies the basis for individual empowerment. As individuals we are neither completely responsible nor completely removed from the dynamics of the system. Throughout this book we aim to identify the dynamics that underlie social and environmental crises, but without leaving readers feeling powerless. The chapters provide examples of social actions that can be implemented by average citizens in the rich, industrialized countries of the North.

From the Clothes We Wear to the Air We Breathe

The following chapters introduce several fundamental concepts in the social sciences that can be applied to critical social analysis by activist, citizen, and scholar alike. We analyze several features of our society-nature relationship: for instance, the means by which we come to understand and relate to our ecosystems; the quantity and quality of our basic necessities, including clothing, food, water, air, space, work, health, and energy; and the not-so-basic social relations that surround our access to them—social relations that in many instances can also foster the misuse or overexploitation of those ecosystems.

Chapter two, "Clothes Encounters: Consumption, Culture, Ecology, and Economy" by Ineke Lock and Satoshi Ikeda, provides a working definition and critical evaluation of consumption in modern industrial societies. By discussing the production, marketing, consumption, and environmental impact of blue jeans, Lock and Ikeda describe how clothing choices reflect culture, gender, and identity. Our consumption patterns are also influenced by larger structural factors, however—not the least of which are the multinational corporations that dominate the clothing industry. Their corporate profit levels (and our Western consumption), moreover, are enabled by their control over the production of key raw materials such as cotton, and over the labour process, which has come to be characterized by a predominantly female workforce in Export Processing Zones—a workforce that must work long hours for little pay and benefits. The authors introduce the concepts of commodification and ecological footprint as analytical tools to evaluate this and other systems of production and consumption, our individual roles in it, and the means by which we can resist.

In chapter three, "Water: A Human Right," Stephen Speake and Michael Gismondi discuss the other side of commodification—attempts to privatize the commons. Beginning with a discussion of the hydrological cycle, its central role in human livelihood, and its long-term sustainability, they highlight the means by which power dictates how social systems assume control over and determine the distribution of water to users. Speake and Gismondi introduce readers to social-scientific perspectives on globalization and present a relatively new evaluative framework—political ecology.

Chapter four, "You Are What You Eat" by Ella Haley, Kierstin Hatt, and Richard Tunstall, deconstructs the global food economy, including our dependence on many imports, by conducting a commodity-chain analysis of some of our more common foods. They outline the structure of international trade in agriculture—including alternative systems such as fair trade—and introduce two important theories of development: dependency theory and world systems theory.

The following two chapters take a perceptual turn towards a focus on the means by which our relations to the Earth's ecosystems are "socially constructed," or influenced by our interpretations of reality, which may or may not be in alignment with reality itself. Jeff Masuda and Jeji Varghese, in chapter five, "Space, the Canadian Frontier? Landscape, Identity, and Power," elaborate on the concept of social constructionism, using it as a means of describing social relations with space. Beginning with a case study of the Mackenzie Valley pipeline, they move on to focus on both urban sprawl and the challenges facing contemporary rural communities, due in no small part to contending social constructions of the landscape. In chapter six, "The Air up There," Debra Davidson and Josh Evans describe the historical expansion of, and qualitative changes in, air pollution. Introducing social theories of risk, Davidson and Evans look at Canada's role in the Kyoto negotiations and consider a recent local community controversy over sour gas emissions in Southern Alberta. They show how politics and economics define whose social constructions of risk and environmental phenomena predominate decision-making, and how these particular social constructions serve to marginalize other claims that may be more conducive to sustainability.

Chapter seven, "Economy, Work, and the Environment in Canada" by Satoshi Ikeda, Michael Gismondi, and Ineke Lock, traces the history of the fundamental relations to the natural world that humans, and eventually complex, organized societies, have forged through our economic endeavours, from hunter-gatherer societies to modern global economic transactions. Using concepts developed by Marx, and more contemporary ecological Marxists, they reveal the means by which structural inequalities supported by the global capitalist system serve to further exacerbate the potential for humans to have an overwhelming and devastating impact on the planet—and they question whether such structures are really necessary to modern social systems. They cite recent controversies, including old-growth forest protection in Clayoquot Sound, global climate change regulation, and intensive hog farming, to illustrate the growing tensions between work, economy, and environment.

Chapter eight, "Environmental Health Issues Related to Industrial Pollution" by Ella Haley and Richard Tunstall, incorporates insights from the sociology of health and illness to illustrate the many ways in which toxins and other industrial pollutants are harming human health and well-being. Using a case study of a local grassroots movement's campaign against pollution from the petrochemical and phosphate industries in Alberta's industrial heartland, Haley and Tunstall illustrate how environmental health concerns are becoming a critical new source of social movement mobilization as grassroots organizations make use of "popular epidemiology" to counter the claims of safety posed by scientific experts.

Chapter nine, "Entropic Futures" by Michael Gismondi and Debra Davidson, argues for the necessity of both realism and social constructionism in any comprehensive critical social analysis of ecological change. Beginning with a discussion of numerous important works that abide by a "Limits to Growth" perspective, the authors move on to explain how social constructionism expands upon the critical contributions made by structuralists. These conversations are posed in the context of a critical analysis of the means by which the concept of entropy can be employed to understand societies' tenuous relationships to their preferred sources of energy. As the laws of thermodynamics dictate, each advancement in social complexity comes at an enormous cost in energy supplies, even as those same energy supplies become less readily available. The authors highlight the Sydney Tar Ponds as a means of introducing the concept of "social entropy" to show how ecological disruption can spill over into social disruption.

Chapter ten, "Towards a Sustainable Future," closes the book with an evaluation of how ecological disruption and renewal have initiated social change on several levels. Debra Davidson and Kierstin Hatt outline social-scientific understandings of states and social movements in this context, as well as the important role of post-materialist cultural values and the new ecological paradigm. They offer these social scientific perspectives, in closing, not solely as a means of reflecting on the impact of society on environmental and ecological systems, but also as a guide to the real prospects for social change towards sustainability now and in the future.

2. Clothes Encounters: Consumption, Culture, Ecology, and Economy

Ineke C. Lock and Satoshi Ikeda

> We see it like this: it is as if we are all in a canoe travelling through time.
> If someone begins to make a fire in their part of the canoe,
> and another begins to pour water inside the canoe,
> and another begins to piss in the canoe,
> it will affect us all.
> And it is the responsibility of each person in the canoe
> to ensure that it is not destroyed.
> Our planet is like one big canoe travelling through time.
> —Ailton Krenak, activist, Brazilian Union of Indian Nations

The great North American pastime of shopping is spreading across the globe. As if urged on by the corporate and government mantra that increased consumption is necessary for a sound and healthy economy, more and more North Americans buy ever more "stuff" to fulfil needs, wants, and desires or to create images, lifestyles, meaning, and identity. For many people, if they think about it at all, consumer culture represents the liberal ideals of individual freedom and prosperity. In a market society the consumer is a hero of modern freedom and progress—an individual who rationally and freely chooses from a broad offering of goods and services. In Canada and other wealthy industrialized countries the average supermarket offers a selection of some 40,000 products, including many of the fifty-two possible versions of Crest toothpaste. Consumers can choose from 225 models of mobile-phone handsets and thirty-seven available configurations of a Dodge Caravan (Cristol and Sealy 2004). Proponents of neo-liberal economic theory claim that the exercise of "freedom of choice" and "consumer sovereignty" creates a dynamic and democratic society.

Since the 1980s, neo-liberal ideology has dominated thinking in most of the powerful industrialized countries and in supranational institutions such as the World Bank and the International Monetary Fund, which in turn have imposed this ideology on countries in the global South. **Neo-liberalism** is first and foremost a belief in the ability of unrestricted market forces to achieve the best possible economic outcomes for all people. Other neo-liberal doctrines include the primacy of economic growth; reduction of the regulatory capacity and size of governments; the importance of free trade to economic growth; and individual choice (Steger 2002). In this worldview, the whole notion of democracy is reduced to the freedom to choose between various goods and services in the marketplace.

Cultural analysts have taken up the themes of choice and freedom to portray most consumption as symbolic and directed at constructing self-identities and lifestyles. A Rolex watch does not just tell time, it symbolizes a privileged, wealthy lifestyle. It is a matter of self-image and social status. Since most social analysis has until recently abided by the **human exemptionalist paradigm**—the belief that nature poses no limits on human activity—the natural environment is largely absent in these discussions about consumption, as it is in the consciousness of most consumers.

Of all the factors that contribute to our world's inability to sustain itself, excessive consumption is one of the most important. Still, it gets little attention in research, policy discussions, or education campaigns, for at least a couple of reasons: first, it is among the most difficult of all human behaviours to change; second, as a policy option, reducing consumption is almost impossible to sell. Who wants to hear that instead of more, we must make do with less? As a result we keep hearing about the need to reduce resource consumption and about the production of waste to sustainable levels, but not about levels of consumption *per se*. To solve this problem of overconsumption people in wealthy Northern countries have placed their faith in future discoveries of science and yet-to-be-developed technologies—a solution that depends on the assumption that it is possible to de-materialize consumption through processes that use materials much more efficiently and that reduce waste. While this might take us part of the way to great sustainability, it does not address questions about hard limits to growth or about the just and equitable distribution of that growth.

An alternative way of thinking about consumption includes the natural environment. This view acknowledges that ever-increasing growth and high levels of consumption are unsustainable, both in terms of the natural environment and in relation to the South—the 2.8 billion people unable to meet many of their basic needs, people who live on less than $2 a day (Worldwatch Institute 2004). The world is a closed and finite ecosystem and—as chapter nine explains—there are limits to increased material utilization. Consumption levels in the North already necessitate the appropriation of resources from other places and from the future. At least three or four additional planets would be needed to supply the resources necessary for people in the South to raise their consumption levels to those of the North. For example, if the rates of Asian car ownership were to rise to the world average, another two hundred million cars would have to be added to the current total (Worldwatch Institute 2004). But as it is now, nature can no longer absorb the strains of humanity's uses and abuses: the result is global warming, loss of biodiversity, ozone depletion, and resource scarcities. The key is that too many people, in the wrong places, consume too many resources and generate too much waste and pollution.

When confronted with endless choices, we often don't know what is too much, what is not enough, what is "just right," what is sustainable, or what is fair to others. If we are to learn to live more lightly and sustainably on the Earth, we need to ask a number of difficult questions about consumption. Not only do we need to know what is consumed, by whom, and why, we also need to ask questions about the environmental and social effects of that consumption across space and time. Finally, we need to ask about the production conditions—such as sweatshops—behind the object of consumption and how the object reached us—was it, for instance, shipped halfway around the world? (See chapter four for a commodity chain analysis of Canadian banana consumption.) In other words, we need to connect the cultural, social, economic, and ecological spheres of our lives.

Clothes Encounters

> I am against fashion that doesn't last.
> I cannot accept that you throw your clothes away
> just because it's spring.
> —Coco Chanel, designer, quoted in Diamond and Diamond 2002: 1.

We can find points of contact with these four spheres by thinking about the clothes we wear. What we wear is cultural because we express our lifestyles and identities—who we are—partly through our clothing choices. What we wear is social because clothes express gender, class, ethnicity, and social group affiliations. The consumption of clothing is also a very important part of the economies of countries. In 2002 Canadians spent $21 billion on clothing and accessories (Lin 2003). In modern industrialized countries, two-thirds of the Gross Domestic Product (GDP) depends on consumer spending (DeJuan and Seater 2003). Finally, the environmental impact of clothing consumption resides in the transformation of materials and energy into **commodities**—products that are bought, sold, maintained, perhaps reused or recycled, and finally discarded in a marketplace.

Clothes are clearly more than a means of keeping warm, staying cool, "being cool," or covering our nakedness. We wear the ecological, economic, and social relations of the global economy on our backs. Are you wearing jeans today? In jeans, you can make a statement without ever saying a word. Just about anything matches with a pair of jeans, and the more you wear them, the more stylish they become. In blue jeans, you can be just about anybody you want to be—country cowboy or girl; upscale engineer working in the field; climber in the Peruvian Andes. But to focus on clothing choices only as an expression of "image" and "identity" ignores the cost to workers and the environment. The real nature of a thing is in the materials it is made of and the people who made it. With your jeans, you are also wearing one-third of a kilogram of chemical fertilizers and pesticides used to produce the cotton, you are wearing a total of 7,000 litres of water used in their production (Sustainable Cotton Project website).

The dyes used to make your jeans blue contain toxic metals to make them colourfast against light, chlorine, laundering, and mechanical abrading (Lewis and Gertsakis 2001).

Are our clothing choices environmentally and socially sustainable? Under what conditions were the textiles produced and the products manufactured? Do you know where your jeans were made, or if the workers involved in their manufacture received a living wage for their work? What were the costs in terms of ecological appropriation, low-wage jobs, and transportation pollution? What are the long-term environmental costs of maintaining your clothes and finally disposing of them? Last but not least: what are the social and environmental costs of keeping up with the latest fads, trends, and fashions?

2.1 Defining commodification

"Commodification" is fundamental to understanding the way capitalism develops. In precapitalist societies, only those things that were superfluous or that were produced by industrial processes would be sold. Under capitalism, everything can be—and according to Marx, eventually *will be*—transformed into a commodity and sold for profit. Today most people in industrialized countries address their needs and desires by purchasing goods, services, and experiences rather than by providing these for themselves. Things are no longer produced for their use value, but rather for their exchange value and their potential for the generation of profit; that is, they become commodities. Money allows all social relations and needs to become quantifiable. Nowadays many things that previously were not subject to market relations are being commodified: ideas as intellectual property rights; carbon credits; user fees for public goods; commercialization of scientific and cultural activities; privatization of government services such as education, health care, water supply, and parks maintenance; and, increasingly, ecological services.

Toxic cotton

Blue jeans, khaki's, and t-shirts are most often made from cotton—"the single most important textile fibre in the world" (Economic Research Service website). When it comes to textiles, many people believe "natural fibres" such as cotton and wool are "environmentally friendly." Although these fibres come from renewable resources, the processes of farming and manufacturing associated with them are far from friendly to the environment or to people. Worldwide, growers of cotton apply almost $3.5 billion worth of pesticides annually, more than 10 percent of the global total (Worldwatch Institute, 2004: 162). In the United States alone pesticide use in cotton production amounts to about fifty-three million pounds and 25 percent of total pesticide usage in the country. Of the top fifteen pesticides used on cotton, seven have been identified as potential carcinogens. Aerial spraying means that many are widely dispersed in the environment (Geller 2004; Lewis and Gertsakis 2001). Ironically, many cotton pesticides were originally developed as toxic nerve gases during the Second World War (Sustainable Cotton Project

2-2 Heavy Jeans

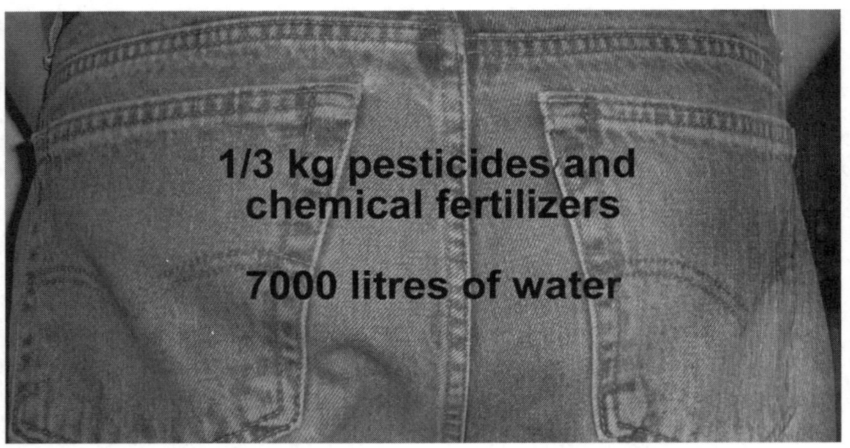

1/3 kg pesticides and
chemical fertilizers
7000 litres of water

Image by James Foufas, Vancouver.

website, "Pesticides."

The World Health Organization classifies many of the pesticides commonly used on cotton as "extremely hazardous." The nervous systems of infants and children are particularly susceptible to organophosphorous insecticides such as diazinon and parathion. The farmers who grow these crops may not be aware of the danger, much less of the proper safety procedures in handling and disposing of pesticides. According to the Worldwatch Institute (2004: 162), a survey in Benin, West Africa, revealed that 45 percent of cotton farmers "used pesticide containers to carry water and 20 to 35 percent used them to hold milk or soup."

Contaminants can enter the food chain in different ways. Cottonseed—about 60 percent of the cotton harvest by weight—is processed into cottonseed oil, used in biscuits, salad dressings, cake mixes and snacks. Cottonseed is also fed to cattle, including dairy cows (Geller 2004). Ecologists have found that cotton pesticides have done devastating harm to birds, fish, and other wildlife, and herbicides used to defoliate cotton plants to facilitate easier harvesting have destroyed wildlife habitats (Worldwatch Institute 2004).

Massive cotton production also brings other dangers. The crop depletes the soil and is extremely thirsty. In the former Soviet Union water diversion for cotton crops was the main culprit in shrinking the Aral Sea to less than half its former size (Worldwatch Institute 2004: 162).

Later, in the factory, to make the fabric and to give it colour cotton is treated to yet more chemicals. The dying process releases into the environment waste water containing metals such as chromium, cobalt, copper, zinc, and nickel. The most common chemical dye used in textiles, azo-dye, was banned in Germany after concerns were raised about it being carcinogenic (Schor 2002). It is still in use in North America.

2.3 Canada's "Anti-retailer... a business that grows more improbable by the year"

A wildly successful business that has grown steadily since 1971, does not do any advertising or marketing, makes no profit, and hosts an equipment swap to discourage its customers from unnecessarily buying new: this is Mountain Equipment Co-op, Canada's member-directed outdoor retail co-operative, affectionately known to its members as MEC, with ten locations across Canada from Vancouver to Halifax.

In 2003 MEC converted its children's wear line to organic cotton, the last step in making its entire MEC-labelled clothing line 100 percent organic cotton and part of its ongoing efforts to make its entire line of products environmentally and socially sustainable. Organic cotton farmers do not use synthetic fertilizers, pesticides, herbicides, insecticides, or defoliants on their crops. Soil fertility is maintained with manure or natural phosphates and crop rotation with nitrogen-fixing plants like vegetables. Less irrigation is needed, because organic soil naturally holds more moisture. Pests and weeds are controlled with barrier plants and natural predators. Regrettably, MEC has not yet been able to replace chemical dyes because no alternatives are available. MEC's clothes are made in factories that have been inspected and conform to the International Labour Organization's core labour standards.

According to its website, MEC's sustainability policy is based on three interdependent principles:

- the planet has a limited carrying capacity and we are all dependent on a healthy, functioning biosphere;
- individuals can best meet their needs in caring and vibrant communities;
- a just economy is dependent on an equitable society and a healthy planet.

Organized as a co-operative, MEC's 1.6 million members each paid $5 for a membership, a price that has not changed since its inception. Co-operative ownership means that the founding members' share is still worth just as much as everyone else's: $5. With the clout and loyalty of its members, this co-op may just be able to make a difference. Will it be enough?

Sources: MacQueen 2002; Organic 2003; Mountain Equipment Co-op website.

Toxic alternatives

About 30 percent of all clothing is made from synthetic fibres such as nylon, acrylics, or polyester. Are these synthetic textiles a better alternative to not-so-natural products fashioned from cotton? Not quite. The petrochemical industry makes synthetic fibres from petroleum products—based on a non-renewable resource—and globally supplies the majority of textile, upholstery, industrial cloth, cordage, and related products. Only limited information is available on the impact of making petrochemical

2.4 Selling genetically modified cotton

Biotech crops provide solutions for pest and weed control that can have added benefits for growers, consumers, and the environment, including a reduction in the number of pesticide sprays and reduced environmental exposure, reduced labour, higher yields, and compatibility with more sustainable agricultural practices, while respecting the environment as well as regional and cultural diversity.

Source: Monsanto website, "Products and Solutions."

fibres, and only a small fraction of the total oil and gas consumed for energy is used for fibre production. Nevertheless, this production is linked to all impacts of the petrochemical industry, such as airborne emissions of volatile organic compounds (VOCs). Production of polypropylene and polyethylene is relatively energy efficient and, along with polyester, relatively clean to produce. Still, according to Lewis and Gertsakis (2001: 136), the production of "nylon, a polyamide, may be responsible for emissions of nitrous oxide, a greenhouse gas and ozone-depleting chemical."

Monsanto, the leading company producing genetically modified (GM) seeds, cites GM cotton as its biggest success, because it can increase yields by up to 60 percent and reduce the need for pesticides by 80 percent. GM cotton incorporates a gene isolated from the bacterium *bacillus thuringiensis* (Bt.), which helps make the cotton resistant to the bollworm, or boll weevil, a common cotton pest. The industry argues that Bt. cotton also requires significantly less water. Scientific studies on the benefits of Bt. cotton offer mixed results. A 2003 study of field trials in India on 157 farms showed that Bt. cotton "needed 70% less pesticide and produced up to 87% more cotton than traditional hybrids. Some farmers had increased their income fivefold" (Radford 2003). The results seem to support the argument that GM crops can contribute to reducing poverty, hunger, and disease (Taverne 2004).[1] Critics point out that the production of GM crops have harmful social effects such as the dependence of poor farmers on expensive seeds monopolized by one or two giant seed-producing firms. For example, the number of small-scale South African farmers growing GM cotton rose from 7 percent in 1998 to around 90 percent in 2002. Ordinary cotton seed in South Africa costs about U.S.$57 for a bag of 25 kilograms. Bt. cotton seed costs U.S.$156 for a bag of the same size, including a "technology fee" of U.S.$106 (STAT Communications 2004).

Scientific and public concerns have long focused on the long-term effects of GM seeds. Agricultural economist Dr. Charles Benbrook, who released the first long-term study in November 2003, found that pesticide applications declined during the first three years of commercial use—as claimed by the industry—but that in the last three years of the eight-year study, biotechnologically produced cotton and corn registered small increases in pesticide use—and pesticide use on GM soybeans skyrocketed. Benbrook was not surprised by this finding: "Scientists have warned that heavy reliance on [herbicide-tolerant] crops might lead to changes in weed communities and resistance, in turn triggering the need to apply additional herbicides and/or increase rates of application.... These predictable ecological adaptations have now been documented" (quoted in Hattam 2004: 22).[2]

Other concerns focus on the broader effects of GM production on ecological systems. A British study compared biodiversity in fields growing conventional sugar beets, oilseed rape plants, and maize with those growing GM plants. The study results showed fewer seeds, flowering weeds, and insects in the GM fields—all important food sources for birds and other wildlife (Hattam 2004: 22).[3] For now, it appears that increased yields and decreased pesticide use occur in the first years of growing GM crops, but the long-term and broader effects of GM crops are uncertain and will be subject to further study.

Doing laundry...

So now you've bought your jeans, and there's nothing—environmentally speaking—to worry about, right? Surprisingly, whether your jeans and t-shirt are made from organic or conventionally grown cotton, most of the environmental impact associated with clothing—about 70 to 80 percent of the environmental costs—occurs during consumption rather than production. Activities such as washing, drying, ironing, and dry cleaning all have an effect (Walsh and Brown 1995, cited in Lewis and Gertsakis 2001: 141).

Buying an item is not the final act of consumption. Further environmental resources and services are required to maintain and, in the end, dispose of the purchased item. Such "cradle to grave" thinking has led to an initiative called **life cycle analysis**, the systematic evaluation of the environmental aspects of a product or service system through all stages of its life cycle (UNEP 2004 website). Perchloroethylene (or perc), a standard solvent used in dry cleaning, is the cause of grave environmental concern. In response, numerous dry cleaning services now offer alternative methods of cleaning: for example, liquid carbon dioxide (CO2) used in high-pressure cleaning machines; a silicone-based solvent used in modified dry cleaning machines, and "wet cleaning" with plain water in computer-controlled washing machines (Consumer Reports website).

Architect William McDonough and chemist Michael Braungart have taken the "cradle to grave" concept one step further and instead propose a "cradle to cradle" design. Guided by the biological principle that "waste equals food," they take nature itself as their model (McDonough and Braungart 2002: 92). In nature, "waste"—fallen leaves, seeds, branches—becomes a nutrient. In their book *Cradle to Cradle: Remaking the Way We Make Things* (2002) McDonough and Braungart explain how products can be designed so that, at the end of their useful lives, materials used to make the initial product can become nutrients for a different product or products and "technical nutrients" become infinitely reusable.

Cleaning out the closet: used clothes

The Garment District in New York is a hip, department-style warehouse that sells used clothes for a few cents per pound. The wholesale price of used clothing has dropped substantially over the past fifteen years, due to an enormous increase in the quantity of discarded clothing. Clothing has become so cheap and plentiful that it is getting harder and harder to dispose of surplus items (Worldwatch Institute 2004). Schor (2002) has found that throughout the 1990s, donations to Goodwill Industries increased by 10 percent or more, even though an estimated 70 percent of annual garment consumption is thrown away and ends up in landfills (*Edmonton Sun* June 4, 1995).

Some used clothing will be resold through second-hand and vintage outlets; some will be refashioned into unique "wearable art" pieces by creative individuals; some becomes rags for repair shops or factories; some will be sold to "shoddy mills" that "grind up the clothes for car seat stuffing and other 'post-consumer' uses"; and some will be sold into the global used-clothes market, where it is "given away by charitable organizations or resold by brokers" (Schor 2002). According to Hansen (1999), worldwide second-hand clothing exports increased from a value of U.S.$207 million in 1980 to U.S. $1,410 million in 1995, a sixfold increase. Sub-Saharan African countries are the largest importers of used clothing; their consumption exceeds that of all other regions. Most importers of used clothing are in the South.

2.5 "Rummaging through piles"

In the Sub-Saharan African country of Zambia, *salaula* refers to second-hand clothing imported from the rich countries in the North. In the Bemba language the word refers to rummaging through a pile of things to select something. Bales of used clothes arrive and are displayed in large piles in the streets and marketplaces, where the *salaula* sections are now much larger than the food sections. In a 1999 study, Hansen found that such practices are important interactions between "the local and the West" and that used Western clothing is important in understanding local experiences of development. Clothes are a "central token of modernity" and an expression of living better and different lives. Because of the poor quality and high prices of local textiles, Zambians from most walks of life continue to shop at the *salaula* section of the market. Thus local manufacturers are threatened by the dumping of excess clothing from the North.

Source: Hansen 2000

Clothes and labour

When used clothing is donated to charity or sold into the global market, it often returns to the places where the garments were originally manufactured. Check the labels on your clothes and you will probably find that most of your clothing is made in faraway places: China, El Salvador, Madagascar, Bangladesh, Thailand, or Indonesia, perhaps. Almost half of the clothing bought by Canadians is imported (Sheik 1999). Clothes and textiles are at the forefront of processes of transnational production, marketing, and consumption. Concerns about the effects of relocating apparel and other factories to poorer countries prompted the concept of the "new international division of labour" as early as 1980 (Fröbel, Heinrichs, and Kreye 1980). Closing factories in wealthy nations was linked to the opening of low-wage **sweatshops** in the South. Transnational firms often select young, single women workers because they tend to be willing to work long hours in poor conditions without complaining or attempting to organize unions. This gendered employment structure ensures a high representation of young women in overseas factories (Fröbel, Heinrichs, and Kreye 1980). Low wages are just one aspect of the notorious conditions in sweatshops. Many are overcrowded, unhealthy, and lack windows or fire exits. Workers sewing clothes for brand names such as The Gap, Ralph Lauren, and Tommy Hilfiger have been found locked inside the factories. Sewers are often forced to work overtime. Occasionally they are beaten and harassed and refused time to go to the bathroom. Women who become pregnant are routinely fired (Schor 2002; Klein 2000; Ross 1997).

According to Naomi Klein (2000: 201), the relocation of manufacturing is only "the most visible manifestation of a much more fundamental shift." Many apparel manufacturers now attempt to emulate the success of the athletic "shoemaker" Nike. Nike does not actually manufacture shoes—the company contributes the product design and takes care of distribution and marketing. Most of Nike's shoes are manufactured by subcontractors who produce the shoes in factories that tend to be located in one of the poorer countries, most recently Indonesia. Other manufacturers are following Nike's model. Levi Strauss, for example, closed most of its European and North American factories in 1997 and 1998, at a cost of 16,310 jobs, and began "outsourcing" production (Klein 2000: 200). Orders placed by Levi Strauss (and others) with a contractor may be turned over to numerous subcontractors. In turn these subcontractors may pass a portion of the work on to a network of homeworkers who will be paid on the basis of the number of pieces they complete. A very small amount of the total price of the clothes we buy represents the cost of labour. A study of European jeans found that a mere 1 percent of the sale price went to workers and that "brand profits" account for 25 percent of the retail price. Ironically, workers are paid so little that they cannot afford to buy clothing themselves. In most cases, even the highest wage rates meet less than half of basic survival requirements (Schor 2002).

Apparel manufacturing is still highly labour-intensive; while half of the clothes we buy are imported from other countries, Canada maintains a sizeable garment industry consisting of more than two thousand apparel and textile manufacturers (Diamond and Diamond 2002: 125). As protections for the Canadian industry were eliminated, the garment industry underwent a profound restructuring in the 1980s and 1990s. Many factories closed or laid off massive numbers of employees. Now an increasing amount of production is shifting to virtually unregulated home-based workers and small contracting shops, staffed mainly by immigrant women of colour. According to Toronto's Labour Behind the Label Coalition, sweatshop conditions are becoming the norm in Canada's garment industry, where "we are witnessing a return to conditions remarkably similar to those at the turn of the century" (Maquiladora Solidarity Network 2004). Workers get paid on a piecework basis, which seldom pays them the minimum wage. For example, a homeworker who sews an outfit that retails for $54.90 receives $2.63 for her labour (Yanz et al. 1999). Statutory benefits such as vacation pay or even contributions to federal pension and employment insurance plans are completely absent.

The social injustices perpetuated in sweatshops, both at home and overseas, have attracted a considerable amount of activism. Curiously, anti-sweatshop groups have by and large not addressed the environmental impacts of clothing. The European-based Clean Clothes Campaign provides twenty links to other organizations on its website; only one of these—the Multinational Monitor website—lists the environment as a concern. Most likely this absence can be attributed to the historic opposition between labour and environmental groups. However, the clothing industry represents an opportunity to examine corporate globalization, labour, environment, genetic engineering, social justice, and consumption in an integrated manner.

What Is Consumption?

> Only the minute and the future are interesting; it exists to be destroyed. If everybody did everything with respect, you'd go nowhere.
> —Karl Lagerfeld, fashion designer, quoted in Diamond and Diamond 2002: 24.

This look at clothing and more specifically, one popular item of clothing—a pair of blue jeans—shows us how to place consumption within a holistic framework, integrating ecological, economic, social, and political processes.

What do we mean by consumption, consumer society, and consumerism? One dictionary, somewhat surprisingly, offers this as the first of a list of meanings for the word **consumption**: "the action or fact of destroying; destruction" (Fowler and Fowler 1964). Most of the additional descriptions also use words such as "decay," "waste," "using up," "wearing out." Thus, a consumer can be described, in Zygmunt Bauman's (1998 : 23) apt words, as:

> a person who consumes and to consume means using things up: eating them, wearing them, playing with them and otherwise causing them to satisfy one's needs or desires. Since in our part of

> the world it is money which in most cases 'mediates' between desire and its satisfaction, being a consumer also means—normally means—*appropriating* most of the things destined to be consumed: buying them, paying for them and so making them one's exclusive property, barring everybody else from using them without the one's permission.
>
> To consume also means to destroy. In the course of consumption, the consumed things cease to exist, literally or spiritually. Either they are "used up" physically to the point of complete annihilation, such as when things are eaten or worn out, or they are stripped of their allure, no longer arouse and attract desire, and forfeit their capacity to satisfy one's needs and wishes—for example, an overused toy or an overplayed record—and so become unfit for consumption.

This is consumption in a very literal, "dictionary" sense. But consumption is more than this. In the book *Environmentally Significant Consumption*, Paul C. Stern (1997: 20) proposes that **environmental consumption** "consists of human and human-induced transformations of material and energy." He adds: "Consumption is environmentally important to the extent that it makes materials or energy less available for future use, moves a biophysical system toward a different state or, through its effects on those systems, threatens human health, welfare or other things people value."

This definition is helpful for considering the environmental impacts of human consumption, but it is by no means complete. It is an anthropocentric statement—consumption is only about what humans do and its effects "are seen through human eyes" (21). This viewpoint does not take other species into consideration unless their loss threatens the well-being of humans or unless they are something people value. The act of consumption is portrayed as a human-environment transaction: "Its causes are largely economic and social... but its effects are biophysical" (20). On the positive side, this approach acknowledges that all consumption is not the same in terms of its effects on the environment; that consumption also includes the indirect consumption of producers who transform materials and energy, and that consumption is affected by those "whose actions indirectly shape the purchase of consumer goods and services, for example, by setting building codes or manufacturing standards" (21).

Canada and other countries like ours often are described as consumer societies. Of course, people in all societies consume—they have to in order to exist. When we speak specifically of a **consumer society**, we are referring to the claim that modern societies are distinctive in that they are increasingly organized around consumption. A consumer society exemplifies "the modern" and stands in opposition to traditional ways of life, where production is for direct consumption. According to Bauman (1998: 24), society in its late-modern or postmodern stage "engages its members... *primarily* in their capacity as consumers." U.S. president George W. Bush urged Americans to get back to living a "normal" life and go shopping following the September 11, 2001, terrorist attacks. Shopping—consumption—is good; it is "normal." Not only that, it is absolutely necessary. Whenever economic growth slows, we are urged to do our duty and buy our way out of the slump in a "consumer-led recovery." This is known as **consumerism**: the doctrine that economic growth, even progress itself, depends on the ever-increasing consumption of material goods and services.

By this measure the world has progressed very nicely indeed. Since 1950 humanity has consumed more resources than did all the people who lived before combined (Buchholz and Rosenthal 1998: 226). By virtually any measure, consumption has grown rapidly in the industrialized countries. In Canada, personal disposable income rose by 35 percent between 1951 and 1960, ushering in the age of mass consumption. New electronic goods, for example, quickly became necessities. By 1998 most Canadian households owned a VCR, colour television, microwave oven, compact disc player, and cablevision; almost half had a computer (Williams 2000: 11). In the United States, "new houses were 38 percent bigger in 2002 than in 1975," while in about the same time period the number of people living under one roof fell from 3.2 to 2.5 (Worldwatch Institute 2004: 4, 5). Our appetites, our "needs," and our wants—and now our bodies too—continually get larger.

Globally, private household consumption topped U.S.$20 trillion in 2000, up from U.S.$4.8 trillion in 1960 (in 1995 dollars) according to the Worldwatch Institute (2004: 5). This global number masks enormous differences in consumer spending. North Americans and Western Europeans, about 12 percent of the world's population, account for 60 percent of private consumer spending, while people living in South Asia and Sub-Saharan Africa—one-third of the world's population—spend only 3.2 percent of the total (Worldwatch Institute 2004: 6). To address such disparities, **Agenda 21**—the program of action adopted at the 1992 United Nations Earth Summit in Rio de Janeiro—stipulated that rich countries should take the lead in reducing consumption. Unsustainable consumption—"the excessive demands and unsustainable lifestyles among the richer segments"—places immense stress on the environment, while the basic needs of a large section of humanity are not being met (United Nations 1992). Little progress has been made on the plan of action agreed to in Agenda 21, least of all reducing the consumption of the rich. Instead, levels of consumption have increased steadily in the industrialized countries and continue to expand. Ironically, gas-guzzling SUVs and light trucks became the best-selling vehicles in North America in the years following the 1992 Earth Summit, while warnings of devastating global climate change, resource exhaustion (including oil), water shortages, and loss of biodiversity became increasingly common.

The production of consumers

Increased consumption is the necessary counterpart to increased production and efficiency. A revolutionary system for the steadily increasing production of goods had been created by the end of the nineteenth century. Today, modern industrial workers produce the same in one week as eighteenth-century workers did in four years (Worldwatch Institute 2004: 12). This system though contains within it "the seeds of its own destruction" (Robbins 1999: 5). Fears about how overproduction would result in falling prices, falling demand, and consequently recession or depression necessitated methods to increase consumer demand.

The "consumer" and "consumer culture" were created with the help of four developments (see Robbins 1999: 14–23), the first of which was the rise of the department store. Until at least well into the nineteenth century in Europe and North America, merchants did not find it necessary to advertise or market their goods; they assumed that people would buy things when they needed them. Most goods were sold in bulk, and the first pre-packaged goods did not appear until the 1870s. In 1852 the first department store, the Bon Marché, opened in Paris, allowing people to view displayed commodities without being expected to purchase something. In North America department stores became the most important retail anchors, first in downtown areas and later in shopping malls. The shopping mall has become one of the new "spaces of consumption." George Ritzer argues that, as a consumer society, the postmodern world continuously invents new means and spaces of consumption: credit cards, malls that combine shopping and entertainment, theme parks, shopping networks. It pays more attention to this task than it does "to the more traditional course of creating new means of production." Capitalism, to remain capitalism, he says, requires "spending at ever-increasing levels.... Without ever-increasing consumerism, capitalism as we have come to know it would collapse or at least be transformed dramatically" (Ritzer 2000: 340, 341). Social spaces are organized around leisure and consumption and become central to social and cultural pursuits. Consumption becomes the basis of social relationships.

The second development consisted of advances made in advertising, marketing, and the display of goods. In 2002 global spending on advertising reached U.S.$446 billion, almost nine times more than in 1950 (Worldwatch Institute 2004:14). Some commentators of the 1950s—Vance Packard and J.K. Galbraith, for example—commented on the "false needs" created by advertising. Thorstein Veblen (1899) used the expression "conspicuous consumption" to indicate what people do when they use their purchases to increase their social status. More recent years have brought a focus on how individuals create identities and meaning through the act of consuming. Consumption is primarily a social process, and, in societies like Canada, consumption derives from symbolic and communicative motivation rather than the drive to meet basic needs (Schor 2000). Our

2.6 Buying factors

1. The Cool Factor
2. Peer Pressure
3. Advertising
4. Wishful Thinking
5. Money Matters
6. Quality
7. Entertainment
8. Supporting good businesses

Source: World Wildlife Fund and Centre for a New American Dream website, "Be, Live, Buy Different—Make a Difference."

consumption is not so much about the actual things we buy, but about the symbolic meanings, values, and images that underlie the actual objects of consumption (for example, see Baudrillard 1994; Featherstone 1991; Giddens 1991). Consumption choices become indicators of the individual's status, prestige, and fashion sense.

The marketing of identity has lead to "branding"—the idea that a specific brand of clothing, footwear, transportation, or accessory communicates a particular identity and lifestyle. Expressions of diversity, such as Black culture, are quickly appropriated and turned into the next brand. In this world of brands, identities, and lifestyles, the youth demographic is the key to market success, and "cool hunters" search for the next fad, fashion, or wave to hook into.

In addition to marketing, a third development was the notion of "consumer service," including most importantly the extension of consumer credit. It proved a successful strategy, considering that in 2002 the average American carried U.S.$12,000 in credit card debt at 16 percent annual interest. At this rate, a cardholder would pay U.S.$1,900 a year in finance charges, more than the annual average income in at least thirty-five countries (Worldwatch Institute 2004:15).

Perhaps most important was the idea of fashion, not only in clothing, ornament, or decoration, but also in broader domains such as lifestyle, leisure, sports, music, video and children's games, housing, and transportation (Harvey 1999). Canadians spent $307 billion in retail stores in 2002, with clothing purchases representing about 7 percent of the total. Of the total dollars spent on clothing needs, more than one-half went towards women's clothing and accessories. About 29 percent of clothing spending went to men's clothing and accessories, while the balance went to children and infant clothing (Lin 2003: 3). This gendered spending difference reflects the patriarchal expectation that women will invest themselves deeply in their appearance, a message trumpeted on a daily basis by advertisements and mass media. For most women, clothing has come to express meaning, and fashion creates, reveals, or conceals aspects of their identity. In recent years, pressure to consume has increasingly been put on men as well as on women to establish a certain "appearance" and "identity."

In a consumer society most material things do not wear out—they simply get replaced with goods that reflect the latest designs and fashions. Fashion cycles tend to accelerate to encourage consumption. For example, from 1971, when Nike sold its first shoe, to 1989, the average life of the company's shoe designs decreased from seven years to ten months

(Skoggard 1998: 59). Often it is impossible to repair an item because parts are no longer available; or it is simply cheaper to replace an item. People are urged to purchase goods on the basis of what others consider to be fashionable or stylish, aided by easy disposability of goods and "planned obsolescence"—goods that are designed to require replacement on the basis of changing fashions.

2.7 Becoming a conscious consumer: Thinking about personal consumption

Can you consume your way to happiness? In what ways do you consume to entertain yourself or others, not be bored, console/reward yourself, define or affirm yourself, be cool/hot/in? Did it work? For how long? What were the costs/impacts? Were they visible or invisible to you? Was it worth it? Can you think of alternatives?

Advertising in mass media has been a primary means of encouraging consumption, but perhaps just as important is the program content of television shows and movies. North American programs tend to present a middle- to upper-class and opulent view of daily life. What for many had previously been luxuries have been transformed into necessities. Earlier values emphasizing thrift, modesty, moderation, and delayed gratification fell to the wayside in favour of free spending, individual fulfilment, and ostentatious display. The idea of "the simple life" has a long history in North America; historically, values emphasizing modest lifestyles have alternated with periods of high consumer demand (Shi 1985). Belts were tightened in response to wider social, economic, and political realities: for example, wars, recession or depression, or political conditions. Pent-up consumer demand always led to times of spending and increased consumption. Our current period with its acceptance of high levels of consumption followed the lean years of the Great Depression and Second World War, when low consumption was justified by patriotic ideologies and values that emphasized sacrifice for the sake of freedom. Only recently has the realization begun to set in that high levels of consumption, consumer culture, and consumerism may be leading us down an unsustainable path to a future in which nature may not allow us much freedom to choose.

Consuming less?

Reductions in consumption—even by relatively small amounts—can have severe economic effects, such as widespread unemployment and declines in the standard of living. But it is possible that people who spend less might also want to work less. In fact, it may be necessary to have reductions in consumption accompanied by reductions in work-time (Schor 2000; Hayden 1999; Gorz 1993)—to have consumption reductions or different types of consumption (for example, increased self-provisioning) offset by work-time reductions. Whether changes in consumption patterns reduce employment also depends on what types of consumption are encouraged and how we understand the effects of different types of consumption.

Who or what is to blame?

It has long been acknowledged that the size of a population and what this population does determines the degree of anthropogenic environmental change. Paul Stern and his colleagues (1997) summarize the international policy debate as a "frustrating exchange" that puts the blame for environmental disaster either on global population growth, concentrated in the poor countries—a position taken primarily by the rich countries—or on "overconsumption" in the rich countries—a position taken largely by the poor countries. While both sides agree on the importance of action to prevent environmental collapse, strategies proposed to reduce consumption flow from polarized starting positions. Reducing consumption means either reducing the number of people in the world or finding a way for those who consume more than their fair share to consume less. The first position is problematic, considering that a child born in North America will consume on average ten times the resources and produce ten times the pollution of a child born in Bangladash or Bolivia (Stern et al. 1997: vii). In the rich countries efforts are underway to reduce the material and energy inputs of production with strategies such as ecological modernization (see chapter one).

Noteworthy in this debate is the "either-or" framing of the disagreement. Is it really only a simple matter of reducing population growth or reducing overconsumption? A more complete conception of the contributors to ecological exhaustion and degradation takes into account the relationship between the factors of population and level of consumption and adds a third factor: the impact of technology. In 1971 Paul Ehrlich and John Holdren conceptualized this relationship in the so-called IPAT formulation: I = P x A x T. In this formula *I* represents environmental impact, *P* stands for population, *A* represents affluence, or levels of consumption, and *T* stands for technology. The formulation is useful as a means of showing that we need to have some idea of the size of the population, "some measure of activity per person, and some measure of the average impact of each unit of activity on the environment" (Stern et al. 1997: 3). As many critics have pointed out, the *A* of consumption has long been ignored in discussions about sustainability, and all of the elements must be discussed in relation to each other. Despite the usefulness of this formulation, though, a closer look reveals a number of shortfalls. The most important is that it ignores economic and political power. As Michael Maniates (2002a) points out, following the formula to its logical end means that if we simply encourage the developing countries to control their population growth, the developed nations to control their consumption, and everyone to use green technology, all would be well with the world. But this simple prescription fails to take into account the economic and political factors that stand in the way of implementation. Citizens are continually pressured to consume more, and public discussions are dominated by discourses that ignore issues of distribution and domination.

Donella Meadows concluded, "IPAT may be physically indisputable. But it is politically naïve" (quoted in Maniates 2002a: 61).

Consumption Matters

In terms of sustainable development, we need to ask *what* is to be sustained, for *whom* and *why*. Sustainable development is understood in many and often contradictory ways (see chapter one). To begin with, our current ways of doing things are clearly unsustainable—so much so that in the rich countries our consumption levels require that we borrow from the future. Analyses show that by the late 1970s or early 1980s, total consumption levels exceeded the planet's capacity to regenerate. By 1997 this impact exceeded regenerative capacity by 30 percent (Rees 1998; Wackernagel and Rees 1996; see also chapter nine).

The products we buy tend to be grown or manufactured in faraway places. Many of the fruits and vegetables consumed in Canada are imported from countries with warmer climates. The cotton for our jeans is grown in the United States or in Africa, and our clothing is often made in developing countries. Thomas Princen (2002a) argues that, under these circumstances, costs are displaced over space and time and feedback loops are severed, a process he calls **distancing**. Consumers have no way of knowing the ecological and economic impacts of their consumption. In simple terms the goods that are produced—and how and by whom they are produced—are usually separated by long distances from those who consume them, so that consumers know little about the social and environmental impacts of their behaviour.

The increasingly globalized nature of trade makes these connections even more difficult to see or uncover (as in the example of blue jeans). This disconnection allows "modern society to lead the dangerous life of an ecological invader" (Wackernagel et al. 2002: 107).

Green consumerism and eco-labelling are two initiatives that try to overcome the problem of incomplete information. Green products are produced in an environmentally friendly manner; green consuming is simple, much more immediate than the political process, and satisfying—it gives consumers the feeling that they can do their part to "save the Earth" (MacKenzie 2000). By the late 1980s the impact of this approach on consumer behaviour was evident in the sellout success of *The Green Consumer Guide*. During the 1980s a flurry of activity occurred in this area, including the introduction of toilet paper made from recycled or post-consumer waste paper, CFC-free sprays, and many more products, often with confusing labels and claims. By the 1990s this confusion had given way to efforts towards a more exact manner of communicating the environmental impacts of certain products (Gray 1997).

Eco-labelling, or eco-certification (ECL), is a much more organized attempt to convey information to consumers. According to the Global

Ecolabelling Network (GEN), eco-labelling is a voluntary method of environmental performance certification based on lifecycle consideration (Global Ecolabelling Network website). The use of ECLs has expanded in the past two decades, "driven largely by health, safety and environmental concerns about the consequences of industrial approaches to production" (Gale 2002: 277). Environment Canada launched its eco-label "Environmentally Friendly Products" in 1987. Canada's eco-label resembles a maple leaf formed from the wings of three interlocking doves, symbolizing the co-operation between government, industry, and society. To obtain permission to use the Canadian eco-label manufacturers must apply for testing through the independent Canadian Standards Association, often at great cost to industry (Losch 1990). Much of the push behind eco-labelling comes from environmental organizations, which often develop their own standards that later become internationally recognized.

The development of ECLs in the forest industry is particularly interesting. Started in the United Kingdom by Friends of the Earth as a proposal to study the feasibility of eco-certification and labelling in the tropical timber industry, the proposal met with heavy opposition from industry and the producing countries, most of them developing nations. The project was broadened to examine incentives for sustainable forest management and was later taken on by the World Wildlife Fund. This effort culminated in the establishment of the Forest Stewardship Council in 1993, now a global player in forest certification (Gale 2002: 278, 279). Canada, with its heavy reliance on exporting wood products, is particularly vulnerable to international actions such as boycotts and demands for eco-certified forest products, and many forestry companies operating in Canada are now pursuing certification with one of the many certification bodies that have emerged in the past decade.

Where eco-labelling exists, it can be a helpful tool in decision-making. But it only tells us whether the product itself harms the environment during or after its use. It does not give us any information about the method by which it was produced or processed and whether this had harmful effects on the environment (World Trade Organization 2003). Furthermore, labelling and certification still rely on "market forces to achieve environmental objectives and is based on voluntary participation by producers and consumers" (Terra Choice website). In addition, the explosion of interest in green consumption has encouraged the establishment of multiple certification institutions, most of them sponsored by business or government organizations and all of which have developed their own standards for certification. Ultimately, many environmentalists argue that "green shopping" will do little to bring about the more fundamental social and economic changes necessary to protect the biosphere. Green marketing still encourages consumption, and green consumerism is not necessarily related to decreased material and energy throughput.

Disproportionate levels of consumption between rich and poor means that people in rich countries also expropriate from distant others. Most importantly, "the process through which we enlarge our choices, and reduce those of others, is largely invisible to us" (Redclift and Woodgate 1997: 57). It is not just the process that is invisible, or even that our reduction of the choices of those distant others is invisible to us (see chapter four). No piece of clothing or food item has a label on it that says how much we took from a far-off piece of land in the form of ecological degradation. Nor is there a label that indicates the labour conditions of production: whether the workers are allowed to organize, go to the bathroom, or get paid enough to provide for their families.

To grow or not to grow?

The struggle over the meaning of sustainability includes intense disagreement about whether, and to what extent, economic growth should be encouraged or restricted in order to attain sustainable and equitable development. Since the 1972 United Nations Stockholm Conference on Development and the Environment, the poorer nations have argued that they want global equity, access to resources, and control over their own destinies. They emphasize that their people's basic needs are not being met and that before they can make any progress on improving or protecting the environment they will need to achieve economic growth and increased wealth to ensure a decent level of well-being. At international forums, especially those of the United Nations, speakers for the developing countries consistently emphasize that the rich need to scale back their consumption levels both to allow a decent life for the rest of the world and to preserve the environment for future generations. The arguments of the rich nations follow a different logic. Economic growth is seen as necessary to ensure that sufficient capital is available to attain increased environmental protection and remediation and an equitable distribution of wealth. One side touts consumption as "the solution" for attaining sustainability and the other sees it as "the problem." How do we make sense of these different approaches?

One explanation rests in the social construction of the idea of progress. In Canada, as in other rich nations, the idea of economic progress is generally connected to stable and continued economic growth. Gross National Product (GNP) measures economic performance and consists of the value of all goods and services produced and traded in a country's market over one year. One of the problems with the GNP is that it only measures monetary transactions. Marilyn Waring (1988, 1999) points out that most women's productive and reproductive work does not count, because no money changes hands. Another problem is that the GNP measures all monetary activity—whether positive or destructive—like a calculator that can only add and not subtract (Cobb 1992). For example, the cleanup expenditures associated with the massive 1989 Exxon Valdez oil spill increased GNP, but no mechanism exists that would deduct the destruction of wildlife and ecosystems from the account. Conventional economics accounts for neither ecological costs nor the value of nature itself—an oversight that seriously distorts notions of progress.

The United Nations' Human Development Index (HDI) is a different and much broader way of thinking about progress. The HDI concentrates on three dimensions of human development—longevity, knowledge, and a decent standard of living. According to the UN's 1998 *Human Development Report:*

> Consumption clearly contributes to human development when it enlarges the capabilities and enriches the lives of people without adversely affecting the well-being of others. It clearly contributes when it is as fair to future generations as it is to the present ones and when it encourages lively, creative individuals and communities. But the links are often broken and when they are, consumption patterns and trends are inimical to human development. Today's consumption is undermining the environmental resource base. It is exacerbating inequalities. And the dynamics of the consumption-poverty-inequality-environment nexus are accelerating.... For more than a billion of the world's poor people increased consumption is a vital necessity and a basic right. (iii)

In other words, the environmental resource base already is threatened by today's consumption levels. The necessary increases in consumption for the world's poor consist precisely of those needs that have a material dimension, such as food, shelter, and clothing. Is this increase possible within ecological limits?

Ecological footprints

The goal of global equity demands economic growth in the South. The difficult question is whether equity and growth can be achieved without reductions in Northern consumption levels. An innovative concept—the **ecological footprint**—developed by William Rees and Mathis Wackernagel (1996), calculates the land and water area (usually expressed in hectares per person) necessary to sustain current levels of resource consumption and to assimilate wastes discharged by a population. Rees and Wackernagel (1996: 89) found that if the total area of ecologically productive land was distributed equally among the world's population, each person's "fair earthshare" would consist of 1.5 hectares. The calculation does not take into account the space needed by other species. Yet by the mid-1990s the ecological footprint of an average Canadian was nearly 4.3 hectares. In other words, Canadians appropriate three times their fair share of available productive space (see also chapter five).[4] People in the United States have a somewhat higher ecological footprint—5.1 hectares—while people in India have a modest ecological footprint at 0.4 hectares (85). Any reasonable conception of fairness would insist, then, that consumption in the wealthier nations must be reduced.

Reducing Consumption: Power and Structural Barriers

Our clothing and other consumption link us directly to global conditions of inequality and ecological devastation. Mainstream understanding of consumption considers consumer phenomena as isolated acts, divorced from questions about where products come from, how things were grown or made, and under what conditions. It is only by ignoring the organization and conditions of production and the social, ecological, and power relations embedded in products that we can think of all consumption as constructive acts and positive expressions of image, identity, or even freedom.

The study of consumption as an act of using up, wasting, and even destroying the environment as well as of perpetuating conditions of inequality, requires an analysis of what happens at the level of the structures and institutions of society. What is it in the organization of our societies that influences and promotes environmentally destructive and inequitable consumption? Given that a capitalist organization of production and consumption is dependent on economic growth, the resulting gains in and efficiency must be offset by increased consumption productivity—all of which places societies firmly on the **treadmill of production**. But increased consumption does not just happen. It needs to be encouraged, and the conditions that support it must be created. The phenomenon of fashion links the creation of identities to the purchase of consumer goods and services; and fashion as an ideal is perpetuated through enormous amounts of advertising expenditures and the modification of intellectual and spiritual values.

The increased distancing of production from consumption and the accompanying severing of ecological and social feedback loops mean that the costs associated with production become ever more invisible. This problem is further exacerbated by the failure of measurements of progress not only to account for certain costs, losses, and destruction but also to consider the distribution of the fruits of progress. The concept of ecological footprint in turn illustrates how the maintenance of consumption patterns requires the appropriation of resources from distant others and future generations. (See also chapter nine, which further develops the notion of appropriation using William Catton's concept of "ghost acreage.") When we look at the sustainability challenge from the point of view of consumption we can consider the core issues of sustainable development: how big is the economy in relation to the biosphere's regenerative capacity—the question of scale—and who gets what and at whose cost—the question of distribution (Wackernagel 2000).

If we want to work at changing the destructive and pathological

2.8 What gets our attention?

Imagine, some of the brightest people in the world are looking to develop stain-resistant, wrinkle-free pants. If you had taken that team's intellect and applied it towards addressing even one simple social problem, chances are we'd make tremendous progress. — Rahul Raj, Founder and Executive Director, Meal Exchange.

Source: Johnson 2004: 10.

nature of consumption patterns, where would we place responsibility for making changes? Most thinking about consumption assumes that it is directly caused by households and individuals. For affluent countries this assumption is incorrect. The bulk of environmentally significant consumption—energy and material use, releases of water and air pollutants, for example—results directly from organizational behaviour, specifically from the acts of corporations and governments (Stern et al. 1997). In Alberta, for example, 78 percent of water is used by industry and agriculture (Henton 2002). In industrialized countries, municipal waste accounts for less than 5 percent of daily totals (Stern et al. 1997), and consumer goods represent a small fraction of material use. Production processes, marketing, distribution, infrastructure, and public provisioning use a much larger amount of material goods.

Of course, most industrial and agricultural production is eventually destined for consumer markets. But the processes and impacts of production are mostly invisible to individual consumers, who furthermore lack—or at least perceive of themselves as lacking—the power to make decisions about production processes, what is produced, and how, where, and for whom it is produced. The argument that consumers vote with their dollars and that the market simply responds does not hold as a theory of social change. Individual consumers may have a choice between a white toaster and a stainless-steel toaster, but many of the truly necessary choices are simply not available—products that are long-lasting, easily repaired, and easily reused or recycled are few and far between. Technological choices influence the availability of certain goods. Industrial infrastructure, for example, is tooled for the use of virgin materials, making the use of recycled materials difficult. By one estimate, the vast majority of materials are used only once in industrial societies and then disposed of (Gardner and Sampat 1998). Technical progress is directed towards increasing the amount, variety, and availability of consumer goods and services for sale, not the reduction of materials.

Political decisions also have an impact on the available choices. In Canada, for example, tax rates for recycled materials are on average 27 percent compared to 24 percent for virgin materials, resulting in a $367 million disadvantage to the recycling industry (Gardner and Sampat 1998). We need to ask why this is so.

Responding to the consumption challenge

So far an important part of the wealthy nations' response to the consumption problem has been to talk about the need to lower material and energy throughput. At the production level the main strategy is ecological modernization. At the consumption end the burden is primarily placed on the individuals, who are encouraged to save the planet by reducing, reusing, and recycling. This approach implies "environmental degradation as the product of individual shortcomings" and that, therefore, solutions also depend on individual action (Maniates 2002a: 45). Maniates argues that this **individualization of responsibility** undermines our collective ability to challenge structures, institutions, the distribution of political and economic power, and our capacity to respond effectively to threats (45). For example, the province of Ontario decided in 1977 that 75 percent of all beverage containers should be reusable, putting the responsibility to keep bottles and cans out of landfills on the container industry. In 1985 the industry lobbied hard and negotiated to support recycling in return for a reduction of the refillable quota to 30 percent. It is now up to individual consumers to return bottles and cans (Toronto Environmental Alliance website).

Automobiles are the world's leading mass-produced durable good (Freund and Martin 1993). The sheer volume of automobiles produced raises questions regarding high environmental resource use. Schrecker (1996: 80) notes that reliance on the automobile is "one of the most conspicuous unsustainable aspects of human activity in North America almost regardless of how sustainability is defined." The automobile industry is interconnected with many other industries, providing a dominant industrial presence to everyday life. Pushed well beyond its utility as a means of transport, the psychological value of the car now includes themes such as self-expression and the ownership of a status symbol. In North America, and increasingly in other parts of the world, car ownership is viewed as an indicator of prosperity and modernity.

> The reproduction of space, in which the built environment has been destroyed, reconstructed, and rearranged in a dispersed fashion, creates social costs in the form of ecological destruction of the landscape, social segregation, and privatization of social space.... The consumption of auto-centered transport has material consequences for both the environment and social relationships, as well as for the reproduction and expansion of capitalist economies. (Freund and Martin 1996: 10–11)

Although automobiles are individually consumed, they are dependent upon a collective infrastructure. Infrastructures that once supported people who did not have cars have shrunk or vanished. Cities are designed to accommodate cars, with far-flung suburbs separated from the spaces where most people work and stores located on the fringes.

As Ursula Franklin (1999: 95) suggests, automobile users have the "impression that they are entirely free to accept or reject a particular technology and its products. But when a technology, together with the supporting infrastructures, becomes institutionalized, users often become captive supporters of both the technology and the infrastructures." And so it turns out that often we are consumers of cars and distances driven not because we choose the car but because the structures and infrastructures put into place to facilitate the use of the car exclude alternatives—for example, bicycle paths or stores close to home—and force dependency on the automobile (Franklin 1999). Our seemingly individual acts—in this case dependence on the private use of automobiles—must, then, be placed within a structural framework.

To think structurally means that, for example, rather than focusing solely on recycling all the cardboard that arrives unasked along with your purchase (although it is a good idea to put it in the curbside recycling), you might also pay attention to the "producer's acts of packaging, processing and distribution" (Maniates 2002a: 58). In several European countries, lifecycle analysis and "cradle to grave" thinking have resulted in so-called "anti-packaging" and "take-back" laws requiring producers to take back products at the end of their useful lives. That particular obligation encourages producers to design goods for reuse, repair, and recycling. Since 1991 packaging in Europe has been reduced by 17 percent, and the recycling rate has increased from 12 to 86 percent (Myers 2000: 10).

Consumption decisions, as we've seen, are made not only at the moment a finished product is purchased but also all along the "various stages of extraction, manufacture and final use, embedded at every step in social relations of power and authority" (Princen, Maniates, and Conca 2002: 12). This state of affairs requires political action.

Confronting consumption requires an approach that questions consumption decisions and expressions of power at every stage of the process. At its most basic level, consumption is reproduction—we must consume to stay alive. While social reproduction requires consumption beyond the fulfilment of basic needs, many of us do not actively participate in decisions regarding what, and how much, consumption is appropriate. Instead, our consumption choices are heavily influenced by social and cultural forces that we are often not cognizant of, such as advertising, television, and fashion. At a deeper level, structural forces such as distancing, the perceived need for continuous economic growth, the invisibility of social and ecological costs, and specialized forms of infrastructure shape our consumption patterns. Ironically, consumption is no longer about *ensuring* survival. Consumption levels that are too high and too damaging to the natural environment, ourselves, and distant others now *threaten* our survival. At risk is the integrity of biophysical systems that are vital to all life on Earth.

Also at risk are "habits of citizenship essential to democratic forms of governance.... Ultimately, the challenge is not just to confront consumption but to transform the structures that sustain it" (Princen, Maniates, and Conca 2002: 317, 328). To reclaim consumption as a life-sustaining and life-affirming activity will not be simple. A response may have to include rethinking what share of total economic activity should be devoted to the production of more consumer goods and services and what share of economic resources should be dedicated to collective provisioning. The U.S. inventor Thomas Alva Edison said, "If we did the things we are capable of we would astound ourselves." Whether what we are capable of is directed towards positive or negative ends is our collective choice.

What Can We Do?

So, how is it that you brought home social inequalities, environmental pollution, chemicals, pesticides, and a boatload of guilt, when all you wanted was to buy a new pair of jeans? As we have seen, numerous factors influence how and under what conditions a thing is produced. In addition, many factors and processes are invisible to us, often hidden by design. Our individual actions must be placed within a structural and institutional framework that often limits our choices, hides the social and environmental costs, and forces dependency on choices that no informed and concerned citizen would freely choose. We may be offered a choice of numerous brands and styles of blue jeans, but we are not given a choice of jeans that are produced in a socially and environmentally responsible manner.

Regrettably, this means that—while you should be informed and thoughtful about your purchases—you will not be able to "save the Earth" simply by your individual actions. Nor will you be able to purchase your way to an improved planet. That is the bad news. The good news is that whatever action you choose to take individually will help and is important.

To be effective, what you can do must consist of a combination of individual and collective actions. The first step is simply becoming a conscious consumer. The next time you get the urge to "shop," think about what needs your shopping is fulfiling, and if these needs can be filled in non-material ways. Next, think about what companies and business principles you are supporting with your purchases. Are there other companies that produce similar products but have produced them according to social and environmentally responsible business ethics? Finally, when you do consume, the basic principles of ecology suggest a creative framework for decision-making in every day life:

- take only what you need
- use it until it is no longer useable

- repair rather than replace
- refashion to provide variety (Schor 2002).

The other bit of good news is that by the end of this book you will be much better equipped to ask difficult questions about economic organization, the nature and distribution of power, ways of changing the distribution of wealth, and the impact of all of these factors on nature. The second part of what you can do is political—be aware, get involved, and never underestimate the power of a group of committed individuals.

Useful Websites

International Institute for Sustainable Development
<www.iisd.org>
United Nations Sustainable Development Commission
<www.un.org/esa/sustdev>
Center for a New American Dream
<www.ibuydifferent.org/>
World Wildlife Fund
<www.panda.org>
Maquiladora Solidarity Network
<http://www.maquilasolidarity.org/>

Notes

1. For a long time others have pointed out that the problems of hunger and malnutrition are not due to lack of food; rather the problem is one of poverty and distribution (see, for example, Lappé and Collins 1977, and other works by Frances Moore Lappé).
2. For Benbrook's complete study, see <www.biotech-info.net/technicalpaper6.html>.
3. For the British study, see <www.defra.gov.uk/environment/gm/fse>.
4. For calculating your personal ecological footprint, see lead website or Mountain Equipment Co-op website.

3. Water: A Human Right

Stephen Speake and Michael Gismondi

> Humans consume water, discard it, poison it, waste it, and restlessly change the hydrological cycles, indifferent to the consequences: too many people, too little water, water in the wrong places and in the wrong amounts.
> —Marq de Villiers

Water is life-sustaining. It has no substitute. Not surprisingly, as shortages begin to emerge the issues surrounding water have become many and complex. In very general terms humans across the world suffer from two basic problems related to water: overuse and pollution. Millions of people live in deserts or arid regions with little access to surface waters, while millions of other desert dwellers swim in backyard pools and play golf on manicured lawns. Some people are separated from water sources by political borders, some by race or class. Others find their water sources contaminated by the wastes of agro-industry, manufacturing, or other humans. Still others have their access blocked by social planning and powerful interests. The problems are at once social and ecological. Whether water should be considered a common good and human right or simply another increasingly scarce commodity to be priced and traded in the marketplace has become a key question of the age.

3.1 The state of Canada's water resources

- 20–25% of the world's fresh water is in Canada.
- 9% of Canada's land area is covered by freshwater lakes, ponds, and rivers.
- 30% of the Canadian population rely on groundwater for domestic use.
- 21 Canadian cities dump about 3.25 billion litres of untreated sewage into our waters every day.
- Adults drink 1.5 litres of water per day, including water used in drinks such as coffee, tea, and juice.
- Canadians drank an average 21.4 litres of bottled water in 1997.
- Canadians used an average of 343 litres of water per day inside their homes in 1998.
- During the summer months, 50% of all municipally treated water is used to water lawns.
- 20% of all municipal drinking water is lost to leaks.

Source: Wood 2002.

Waterscapes

Most of us have access to water systems that are no longer natural, but part of what Henri Lefebvre (1991) called **second nature** and what Neil Smith (1984) later described as "the production of nature"—that is, natural systems that have been altered or disrupted by human societies' choices over time, and in this process stamped with changing human meanings (political and symbolic). For example, when Canadians think of the hydrological cycle, they think of water in Canadian ways—as clean, free, fresh, tumbling from mountainsides, and always there. There is less recognition of the history of alterations of water flows by engineers, planners, politicians, and business interests and how those interventions in natural processes are reflected in Canadian consciousness and attitudes towards water and even in scientific claims about water management. As environmental historian John McNeill (2001: 150) explains:

> States and societies regarded adjustments to nature's hydrology as a route to greater power or prosperity.... Since 1850, hydraulic engineers and their political masters have reconfigured the planet's plumbing. They did so to accommodate the needs of the evolving economy, but also for reasons of public health, geopolitics, pork-barrel politics, symbolic politics, and no doubt to satisfy their vanity and playfulness.

For social critics, then, it is not enough to understand water politics solely in terms of hydrological processes that are assumed to have persisted since time immemorial. Hydrological flows are hybrid phenomena. Rivers, lakes, and streams of water moving into and out of human settlements (and our bodies) are better seen as what geographer Erik Swyngedouw calls **waterscapes**—a combination of material and ecological processes and "discursive and symbolic representations of nature" (Swyngedouw 2003: 95; 2004). Swyngedouw (2003: 95) explains: "Hardly any river basin, hydrological cycle, or water flow has not been subjected to some form of human intervention, or use, not a single form of social change can be understood without simultaneously addressing and understanding the transformations of and in the hydrological process." For him, waterscapes throughout the world are "socionatural" hybrids, "part natural and part social." They embody "a multiplicity of historical-geographical relations and processes."

A waterscape approach avoids simple oppositional thinking about ecology and society. It reorients questions about how citizens should organize a politics around water access and quality by asking questions of **political ecology**. Political ecology understands the economy as comprised by physical and social systems that draw upon energy and material flows, create wastes and pollutants, and are embedded in social institutions such as the "distribution of property rights, power and income, gender, ethnic and class inequalities; territorial divisions and barriers," which in turn give rise to social conflicts around the uses of nature (Martinez-Alier 1999). Political ecologists pose questions such as: why are some people excluded from access to water? Is water a common property? Is water access a human right necessary for survival, or is water simply another resource to be mined and sold as a commodity? Is the best way of distributing water through privatized companies or publicly? What is the role of social power in all these questions?

Water and Life

On a blue planet, water appears abundant. Over 97 percent of the planet's water, however, is salt water, unavailable for human use. What remains, about 2.5 percent, is potable freshwater. Most of this is frozen at the polar ice caps, in glaciers, or trapped in underground aquifers too deep to access. Only 0.6 percent is available in its liquid state ready for human use, and most of that is situated in aquifers both shallow and deep (Malkia-Pykh and Pykh 2003). As Marq de Villiers puts it, "if all the earth's water were stored in a 5-litre container, available fresh water would not quite fill a teaspoon." Moreover, the amount of water has "not changed since geological times" (de Villiers 2000: 31, 29). What has changed is the intensity with which water is being used.

Is water a renewable resource? Yes and no. According to some writers, the amount of water renewed through the hydrological cycle is more than enough to support the world's population, if both the water and the people were evenly distributed around the globe (Clarke 1993; de Villiers 2000; Mawhinney 2002). The hydrological cycle depicted in science textbooks suggests a continuous recycling and refreshing of water over time, but that cycle varies according to location. Surface waters, subject to evaporation, return to earth as rain or snow in about eight days. Rivers renew, roughly speaking, every sixteen days. Soil moisture is renewed yearly. Small lakes renew every seventeen years. Underground water may take up to fourteen hundred years to renew (Clarke 1993).

Most water used by humans comes from surface water in the form of runoff, the water flow of rivers and lakes that would normally empty into the oceans or seep back down into aquifers. Watersheds are catchments or drainage basins where water flows collect on the way to oceans. Canada has five drainage basins: the Arctic or Peace-Athabasca-Mackenzie basin in northwest Canada drains to the Arctic Ocean; the waters of the Pacific watershed flow from the Rocky Mountains to the Pacific Ocean; the Hudson Bay drainage system (the largest watershed in Canada in area) drains waters from Alberta in the west to Quebec in the northeast of the country; the Atlantic watershed, including the Saint Lawrence River, empties the Great Lakes region to the Atlantic Ocean; southern Saskatchewan and parts of southeastern Alberta have some internal drainage, and in the far southern regions of Alberta and Saskatchewan water flows south towards the Gulf of Mexico (Linton 1997). Some 60 percent of Canada's freshwaters flow north, while 90 percent of Canada's population live within 300 kilometres of the U.S. border (Environment Canada 1987). Further, about 25 percent of Canada's population live in the Great Lakes region, with about 45 percent of Canada's industrial activity occurring there. However, only 1 percent of the Great Lakes' volume is renewed each year; human use exceeding that amount represents an overuse of the resource (Natural Resources Canada 2002). Harnessing water resources is difficult without interfering with the hydrological cycle. The main method of securing access for surface waters is to build dams, irrigation systems, and canal projects. Canadian naturalist David Suzuki (in Suzuki and McConnell: 1997: 72) argues, "No species has been as imaginative and as demanding in its use of water as human beings."

Engineering water

Efforts to harness water have involved some of the industrial world's most spectacular engineering feats. The planet has more than 40,000 large dams over fifteen metres or taller. Of these, 5,000 were built prior to 1950. China has about 19,000 and the United States 5,500. Another 96,000 smaller dams are spread across the U.S. landscape (Rothfeder 2001). The large Glen Canyon and Hoover dams in the United States divert water from the Colorado River to irrigation systems for use by agribusinesses in the southwestern United States. Although ecologically unsound, agribusiness in this semi-arid region produces much of the United States' and most of Canada's consumer fruits and vegetables. Diverting water into the southern region of the United States required the combined efforts of federal and state governments, as well as the U.S. Army Corps of Engineers, to move water many hundreds of miles and then store it for agricultural uses and, to a lesser extent, for cities (Rothfeder 2001; Biro 2002). Andrew Biro (2002) argues that such diversion projects were linked to the historical growth of capitalist agriculture in California, which today draws over 70 percent of the flow of diverted waters. Agribusiness is huge in California, and so too are its supporting industries such as transportation, shipping, and agricultural hardware implements, yet big growers pay some of the lowest prices for water.

In Canada dam-building has also been widespread but little of that work has been directed to agriculture. By 1991 Canada had 650 large dams higher than fifteen metres—the average height of dams built since 1940 is well over thirty metres, according to the World Commission on Dams (2000). Some 71 percent of Canadian dams are used to generate hydroelectricity, 9 percent for irrigation, 7 percent for water supplies, and 4 percent for flood control (Government of Canada 1996). Dam projects are seen as clean, low-cost alternatives to fossil fuels. Hydropower conserves an estimated 4.4 million barrels of oil per day based on recent oil production levels, or roughly 6 percent of total global oil production (World Commission on Dams 2000). The James Bay Hydro-Québec project will generate 27,000 megawatts of electrical power, the equivalent of about thirty-five nuclear power plants (McCutcheon 1991).

Nevertheless, the damming and engineering of waterscapes have harmed both hydrological cycles and Aboriginal peoples in northern

Quebec, where dam projects are transforming aquatic and land ecosystems, displacing Native people, and altering traditional ways of life (McCutcheon 1991). Around the world, environmental damage from dams has resulted in loss of wetlands, loss of habitat, salinization of the soil, soil erosion, desertification, and exhaustion of water sources. Millions of people have been displaced and their livelihoods lost (World Commission on Dams 2000)—all of which is justified as a trade-off to provide flood control for downstream cities, controlled water flows for agriculture, and hydro-power for urban dwellers.

The social and ecological impact of each dam varies. Perhaps the starkest example of the misuse of environmental science to justify the social and environmental impacts of dam building is the Three Gorges Dam in China, which was approved by a Canadian environmental review (Fearnside 1994). Begun in 1993 and due to be finished in 2009, the Three Gorges Dam will create a reservoir over 600 kilometres long and displace hundreds of thousands of people. The project will submerge 13 cities, 140 towns, and 1,350 villages (Lang 2002). In Canada, similar political justifications (hydro-power or irrigation for agribusiness) of dam projects can be found in the stories surrounding Phase 2 of the James Bay Project in Quebec, the Kemano Completion Project in British Columbia, and the Rafferty-Alameda Dam and Oldman River dam projects in Western Canada. Each of these dam stories juxtaposes questions of consumptive needs versus long-term sustainability, pitting the rights of industrial users and urban consumers against the rights of Aboriginal people, future generations, and nature itself (Niezen 1993; Hood 1994; Christensen 1995; Glenn 2000).

Our cup runneth over?

Perhaps no other engineering effort has better provided humans with the deception that we can control nature than has our ability to harness water; so much so that the lack of water is rarely seen as a constraint to development. To the contrary, this powerful belief system has justified a model of excess that is expanding quickly across some of the driest regions of North America, including Southern California, New Mexico, and Arizona. Las Vegas, the quintessential city of excess, sits at the centre of this Southwest desert basin. Per capita consumption in Las Vegas is "360 gallons daily versus 211 in Los Angeles, 160 in Tucson, or 110 in Oakland. In a desert basin that receives only four inches of annual rainfall, irrigation of lawns and golf courses, not to mention artificial lakes and lagoons, adds the equivalent of another 20 to 30 inches per acre." The whole region is a "house of cards" according to Mike Davis, who predicts growing water shortages caused by expanding agribusiness and highly consumptive operations such gambling casinos (Davis 1994).

While engineering feats may give the impression that water can be created through human ingenuity, what these have really accomplished is

> **3.2 Mexico City**
>
> Mexico City sits on top of a large aquifer. The city is now pumping water out of that aquifer at a rate of fifty to eighty times faster than the aquifer can be recharged.
>
> Source: Rothfeder 2001.

an extraordinary increase in our **drawdown** of water supplies. Given that most freshwater is not held in dams, but in underground aquifers that must be accessed with pumps, and take many years to recharge, the overuse of those aquifers raises social and ecological concerns. About a third of the world's people (two billion) are dependent on groundwater aquifers, and human beings are now using groundwater supplies faster than the supplies can be recharged (Malkia-Pykh and Pykh 2003). West Asia and the Arabian Peninsula are both dependent upon aquifers for their water. For all practical purposes, water in these regions is a non-renewable resource. Continued human overuse will eventually cause aquifers to simply run out. China, India, and the United States all run annual groundwater deficits (Postel 2000).

In Alberta, the oil industry's use of surface and groundwater clashes with environmental goals. A report by the Pembina Institute records that the Alberta government allocated 380 million cubic metres of surface water to the oil industry, or about 4 percent of Alberta's total surface water. A third of that allocation will be used for oil-field injection, a practice that permanently removes water from the hydrological cycle by forcing water deep into oil wells as means of bringing oil to the surface. In support of the industry the Alberta government has granted a further fifty-eight million cubic metres of Alberta's groundwater, resulting in a net loss of water. For every barrel of oil produced Albertans lose one barrel of potable water. The oil and gas industry has been allocated twice as much water as the city of Calgary will use in one year (Griffiths and Woynillowicz 2003).

How long can these consumption rates continue? Canada has 20 percent of the world's fresh water; only about a third of that amount is accessible for use by its thirty million inhabitants (Environment Canada 2004). In contrast, more than one billion people in the developing world do not have enough water to maintain proper health conditions, and 2.9 billion people have no access to sanitation services (de Villiers 2000; Rosegrant et al. 2002). Some thirty-one countries—with about 8 percent of the world's population—face chronic freshwater shortages. By 2025, forty-eight countries with 2.8 billion people, or 35 percent of the world's growing population, will face chronic shortages. The countries most at risk are Ethiopia, India, Kenya, Nigeria, and Peru (Hinrichsen et al. 1998). The Middle East is also running out of water: the amount that can be distributed to each person there is already declining, yet by 2025 the population of the Middle East is expected to increase by 15 percent, to 350 million people, and the region will need twice as much water as it did in 1975 (Rothfeder 2001).

Inequality and Water

Technological optimists suggest that one way of making up water deficits is to open more desalination plants to take advantage of abundant ocean waters. More than 7,500 desalination plants already exist worldwide. Much of that capacity—57 percent—is concentrated in the Middle East, with 12 percent in the Americas, concentrated in the Caribbean and Florida (Malkia-Pykh and Pykh 2003). Unfortunately desalination remains an inefficient process; it converts only 25 percent of saltwater into drinking water (Rothfeder 2001). As well, the technological process causes pollution and uses non-renewable fossil fuels. It is entropy costly (see chapter nine).

Just as the focus on technology can mislead, we need to consider carefully how certain other ways of seeing the problem of water access can also mask contradictions. The use of aggregate statistics, or certain terms like "population pressure" or "industrial use" to describe water consumption, for example, masks inequalities in water access:

> "Population" pressure in general abstracts from… the stark division between rich and poor: the richest one-fifth of the world's population accounts for 86 per cent of global consumption. More specifically, the richest one-fifth accounts for 45 per cent of meat and fish consumption, 58 per cent of energy consumption, 84 per cent of paper consumption, and 87 per cent of vehicle consumption. These are all water-intensive goods, and that exacerbates the imbalance already suggested by the fact that 1.3 billion people continue to lack access to clean water. (UNDP 1998)

Estimated per capita averages of water consumption can be equally misleading. In Mexico less than 10 percent of the land area accounts for usage of more than half of the nation's annual runoff, while the other 90 percent of the nation remains arid and chronically short of water (Clarke 1993; Hinrichsen et al. 1998). Not only does Mexico have considerably less water than the U.S. and Canada, but the water it does have is also very unevenly distributed. National per capita estimates are therefore suspect. Mexico's national per capita averages give the impression that the country has sufficient water resources, but this finding distorts the country's extremes.

In an important study of water and development in rural Mexico, David Barkin (2001) found that many peasant communities had been forced onto marginal farming lands but were nevertheless located in areas with sufficient water. Still, for a number of reasons they remained unable to gain access to water for productive uses such as farming: the rigid social structure of land tenure limits access; state mismanagement and corruption favours the wealthy over the poor; and class power and ethnic stratification marginalizes rural peasants and Indians, keeping them on the outside of the political process.

Table 3.1 Water Use in NAFTA countries

Country	Year	Domestic (%)	Industrial (%)	Agricultural (%)	Estimated 2000 per capita withdrawal
Canada	1990	11	80	8	1431*
USA	1995	12	46	42	1688
Mexico	1991	6	8	86	785

* cubic metres per person per year.
Source: Gleick 1998.

Peasants who migrate to cities are seldom better off. At local scales in all Latin American cities, many neighbourhoods and social sectors are excluded from water access or sewage removal. A recent study of water access in Mexico City showed that "60% of all urban potable water is distributed to 3% of the households, whereas 50% of the inhabitants make do on 5% of the water" (Swyngedouw 2004: 30). The poor lose out twice: once in the countryside, and again in the city. Swyngedouw found inequalities in water distribution in every major Latin American city. The poor are "systematically excluded from many of the basic services, including piped potable water," while "a tiny minority of urban residents consume the bulk of available potable water" (53, 55). In areas of water stress, socially and economically marginalized populations often do not have access to water because of non-existent or deteriorating water delivery systems. This situation is closely tied to their lack of social status.

Canada's urban issues are not nearly so dramatic. Most Canadians, whether rich or poor, have access to potable water in their homes. But northerners in Nunavut pay more for water than for gasoline, many rural hamlet dwellers have poor water quality, and city water is noticeably processed. Many of Canada's urban centres generally allow untreated waste water back into the hydrological system. In Canada and Australia major cities such as Victoria and Sydney dump human and other urban sewage wastes directly into oceans with little or no secondary treatment—an approach that seems unwise given that most communicable diseases associated with water come via contamination with animal or human feces (Malkia-Pykh and Pykh 2003). Like Victoria, Sydney uses ocean outfalls—pipes designed to disperse raw sewage into ocean currents and tides—based on the notion that dilution works to eliminate pollution. A 1989 study of Sydney's ocean sewage outfalls—*Toxic Fish and Sewer Surfing*—by Australian engineer and ecologist Sharon Beder found high amounts of heavy metals and toxins in fish around the outfalls; contamination was spreading along Australia's famous surfing beaches. Studies of Canadian lakes also identify many industrial pollutants in freshwater drinking and recreational sources. Freshwater pollution concerns include acid deposition, the migration of organochlorines and heavy metals from the industrial south to remote northern lakes and river beds, declining freshwater fisheries, climate change and wetland reduction, and more (Schindler and

Bayley 1990). Together these factors indicate that human economic systems are altering the hydrosphere and adding pollutants at rates faster than the hydrological cycle can purify and filter out this contamination. Solutions cannot rest solely with individual consumer uses of water, but require political reassessment of our industrial and social institutions and practices.

Political ecology is the study of inequalities in the use of nature, such as water access. In developed countries, it is not individuals or municipalities but industry that is by far the largest user of water (see Table 3-1). Often the new knowledge society and its computer-based economy is heralded as an example of **dematerialization**: that is, a technological society that does not have a heavy ecological footprint compared to older forms of industrial society. In reality, the society is a material hog. In her book *Water Wars* Vandana Shiva (2002) shows that to produce one six-inch silicon wafer used in personal computers requires 10,340 litres of water. This usage amounts to 18 million litres of water per day worldwide and 1.5 trillion litres per year. It generates 300 billion litres of waste water annually (McKenzie 2002). Not only is computer technology water-intensive, but also many of the world's computer chip companies are located in California, the home of agribusiness, where water is already in limited supply.

Industrial and agricultural consumption figures are radically different from other estimates of how much water is necessary for the daily sustenance needed for basic human survival. Several international agencies have suggested fifty litres per person per day as an appropriate level of water use per person for drinking, sanitation, bathing, and food preparation. Yet even at those very low levels, in 1990 more than a billion people were subsisting on less. Given the differences between industrial and agricultural use and domestic use the question becomes: is a political focus on individual use really the most significant way of dealing with water shortages?

In Canada 64 percent of water is used for industrial cooling, 14 percent for manufacturing, and about 1 percent for mining. As well, some 42 percent of Canadian manufacturers continue to release untreated wastewater into Canada's freshwater system (Environment Canada 2004). Significantly, wastewater generated by these practices places additional demand on freshwater **ecosystem services** to transport, dilute, or process industrial waste, which in turn reduces total available freshwater supplies. In the United States 40 percent of all surface waters are unfit for bathing or fishing, and 48 percent of all lakes are eutrophied and clearly not potable without treatment (Hinrichsen et al. 1998).

Water is also crucial for food production. Some 15 percent of the world's cropland is irrigated, accounting for 40 percent of the world's harvests (de Villiers 2000). Clearly, although irrigation raises food production, it also increases pollution and is wasteful. In 1996 in Canada's

3.3 Bottled water: A commodity bonanza

The largest consumers of bottled water—Britain, France, Germany, Japan, and the United States—spent nearly $6 billion in 2000, or about 20 percent of worldwide sales. Canada is now second only to France in exporting water to the United States, growing its market share from 2 percent in 1988 to 30 percent in 1998. Some 140 bottling, distribution, and equipment companies are regulated by Canada's Food and Drug Act; they produce 85 percent of the bottled water sold in Canada.

One of the driving factors in Canada's water sales is the image of "pure" water sources. But the country's bottled water generally comes from municipal sources, which have been treated by a public utility, or from other underground sources, usually labelled "spring" or "mineral" water.

Companies have access to water through licensing agreements. Bottling companies can take water for free, so long as they have a licence. In Ontario, about 5,300 such water-taking permits allow companies to take an estimated 160 billion litres daily from the province's lakes, rivers, and underground sources.

To encourage participation in this market the Ontario government gave the water company Echo Springs the right to withdraw 176 million litres of spring water at no charge for two years in Artimesia Township. Ontario has in fact issued permits to commercial bottlers to take, free of charge, 18 billion litres of water per year from underground sources. A casual glance at store shelves reveals that bottled water sells for more per litre than gasoline, without the overheads.

Coca Cola's Dasani brand is just filtered water from Calgary's municipal water system. In Britain Dasani recalled all its bottled water because it contained overly high levels of bromide—a cancer-causing agent that is a derivative of calcium chloride, which was added to tap water taken from the Thames water main supply and bottled at the Coke plant in Sidcup, southeast London. The calcium chloride was added to meet the minimum calcium levels required by British law for bottled waters.

Sources: Agriculture and Agri-Food Canada 2001; Brooymans 2004; de Villiers 2000; France 2004; Mittelstaedt 1999; Rothfeder 2001; *Sault Star* 2004.

agricultural sector, farmers and ranchers were responsible for about 9 percent of all water withdrawals. Of that 9 percent, 85 percent was mainly used for irrigating croplands in Alberta, Saskatchewan, and British Columbia; and 15 percent was used for watering livestock, especially in Alberta and South Saskatchewan (Environment Canada 2004). Western Canada is home to many large concentrated feedlot operations. Cattle in the prairies in 1994 were producing waste equivalent to 220 million people annually (Linton 1997). Surface waters are not sufficient to dilute and transport this problem. Most of Canada's irrigation occurs in southern Alberta and Saskatchewan. In 1990, 64 percent of all of Canada's irrigation occurred in Alberta (Statistics Canada 1994, cited in Linton 1997). As water is diverted for irrigation, it becomes less available for the remaining wetlands and river systems. In addition, the chemical fertilizers, herbicides, and pesticides used in the production of crops for human and animal consumption and the manure from livestock either seep into

underground aquifers or are washed away in the surface water system (Environment Canada 2004).

This water abuse cannot easily be dismissed. Is it possible to reduce or eliminate our society's "chemical addictions" and stop irrigation practices and still meet the world's food needs? Some say yes, if we become more efficient technologically; others say no, or not unless we reduce the scale of production and explore appropriate technologies (Beder 1993). Still others are exploring the traditional water management systems of indigenous peoples and farmers in Asia who have used irrigation techniques that have worked within ecological limits for centuries.

The ecological management of water resources globally, regionally, and locally is an important issue fraught with difficulties. Many of the international problems surrounding water may be beyond the Canadian government's direct sphere of influence. However, Canada will be implicated in many of these debates; its access to large quantities of freshwater will result in pressure to export its water. Although water is used disproportionately by industry and agriculture, many of these uses directly benefit Canadians in general. Irrigation allows Canada to maintain a measure of food self-sufficiency, while hydroelectric power provides much of the power used in Canadian homes and businesses. The problem of inequality of access and distribution, then, is never as simple as denying access. It is a question of balancing competing interests. Canada's water problems are not as yet severe, but the decisions that are made now will have an impact on future generations of Canadians.

Common pool resources

Groundwater aquifers, lakes, rivers, and watersheds are **common pool resources**—a resource from which it is hard to exclude others and which is subject to degradation as a result of overuse. On the one hand, even though everyone benefits from the hydrological system of water movement that maintains soil moisture, provides drinking water for human and animals, and dilutes household, municipal, and industrial wastes, no one owns it. We effectively treat water as a free good—an entitlement. On the other hand, when a person or company pollutes or overuses water that is meant for everyone, that loss hurts all of us equally. Because of that sense of entitlement and the problem of ensuring equal access to clean water, it has been difficult to come up with a proper means of regulating its use.

There are two classic problems associated with common pool resources. The first, called **subtractability**, refers to a situation in which one person's use subtracts or "takes away" from another person the benefits of using that resource, either through overuse or degradation. For example, the owners of industry and manufacturing benefit economically from the relatively free use of lakes and rivers, not only as a resource, but also as sites for disposing waste, yet everyone, not just corporations, pays the price for these actions, which result in the degradation of ecosystems, ecosystem services, contaminated drinking water, loss of species and habitat, and the ruin of the recreational and aesthetic properties of lakes and rivers. A resource may be characterized by subtractability across the number of users as well, in that too many users will cut back on the use of each individual, and over time the overuse of a finite resource will limit users in the future.

The second dilemma, called the **free-rider problem**, refers to the near impossibility of preventing, through regulation, access to and use of a resource by those who have not "paid" their fair share of the costs. For example, the resources spent by the federal and Ontario governments to clean the Great Lakes will benefit Detroit, regardless of whether Detroit helps to pay for such efforts. In the worst-case scenario, the free-rider does not act unless everyone can be made to act. This dilemma proved to be a major challenge in attempts to clean up the Great Lakes over the last two decades, and remains a challenge today.

This is the same dilemma that Garrett Hardin (1968) was grappling with in his now famous treatise *The Tragedy of the Commons*. Hardin believed that people would have no vested interest in managing land unless it was privately owned; therefore, he argued that we need to commodify common property like Crown forests to ensure their good management. Hardin assumes that people act only when the benefits to themselves can be maximized. While this utilitarian assumption about human behaviour is highly contested, it is also the underlying assumption of **neo-liberal economics**. As a consequence, neo-liberals argue that we need to commodify waterworks to ensure the social good. Alternatively, critics have argued that Hardin and neo-liberals may have underestimated the potential for organized social behaviour to lead to effective management of common pool resources at the local level. It is these grassroots organizations, along with the activism of organizations like Greenpeace, that oppose the continued neo-liberal agenda of commodification. Oppositional social movements are engaged in debates that try to recover access to the **commons** for the public and reject as lip service corporate claims about global commons management, which they perceive as ways of disguising continued economic growth and the increased use of nature by a select few. Josee Johnson (2003) argues, in opposition to government and corporate sustainable development discourses, that new meanings of the commons are democratic:

> A turn to the commons cannot suddenly or magically ameliorate ecological exhaustion, but it can suggest ways of life regulated by participatory democratic communities, instead of corporate marketeering or top-down managerialism. As such, the commons discourse represents a direction for human-nature interactions that is more egalitarian, democratic, and oriented towards ecological survival across generations.

Similarly, James Goldman (1998: 14) in *Privatizing Nature* argues that a new oppositional politics is emerging around recovering the commons as public property and public space: "We find that the commons are increasingly becoming a site for robust and tangible struggles over class, gender, nation/ethnicity, knowledge, power and, of course, nature." In other words, people are becoming increasingly aware of the importance of regaining and preserving public ownership as a means of securing the future of their communities. Likewise, in *Nature's Revenge*, the authors use the concept of "democratic control of common resources" to reassert and prioritize forms of ecological sustainability as an alternative to perpetual, growth-centred economic models of sustainability. For them, the concept of the commons operates across geographic and temporal scales and comprises both common rights and common property: not only groundwater and food or atmosphere and oceans, but also the civil sphere of "traditions of democratic participation, public services, and cultural heritage that serve to protect and regulate access to natural commons" (Johnson et al. 2005). They argue that we must begin to think globally and act across many scales from the local, regional, and national to the planetary.

We have only recently begun to contemplate water in terms of the global commons, as we realize the extent to which and rapidity with which pollution and overuse are altering the global environment. The global commons refers to parts of the planet that fall outside national jurisdiction, including freshwater aquifers and hydrological systems, oceans, atmosphere, outer space, and the global gene pool. As with the notion of global risk, contemplating a global commons is a distinctive feature of modern society as advances in scientific knowledge encourage a growing awareness of the global reach of certain environmental and ecological processes that humans depend upon for life. But we are not all in this together. Powerful forces are at play in defining global commons issues and their possible solutions. In *The Water Manifesto*, Petrella (2001) argues that water is life and that we need a democratic world water contract to protect freshwater access for billions of humans, as well as to protect the ability of hydrological ecosystems to recover. His work, which falls within the democratic commons perspective, is critical of the "water lords" (those privatized companies and interests) who want to privatize and make water a commodity. He is critical of the inequality of power amongst nations and between classes and social groups and genders. He rejects simple notions of global resource management and is exploring a world parliament for water. (See also Monbiot 2004 for similar arguments for a democratic world parliament. These democratic interventions challenge the corporate approaches to global commons issues proposed by the G8, the World Bank, and the United States, which are seen to maintain inequalities between nations and among social classes and genders.)

Water: A Commodity or a Right?

In Dublin, Ireland, in January 1992 the International Conference on Water and the Environment (ICWE) suggested four principles for dealing with the problems associated with water use and distribution. Known as the "The Dublin Water Principles," they have since influenced most political discussions about water:

Principle 1:	Fresh water is a finite and vulnerable resource, essential to sustain life, development, and the environment.
Principle 2:	Water development and management should be based on a participatory approach, involving users, planners, and policy-makers at all levels.
Principle 3:	Women play a central part in the provision, management, and safeguarding of water.
Principle 4:	Water has an economic value in all its uses and should be recognized as an economic good.

Controversy surrounded principle number four, which essentially called for the commodification of water as a solution to the world's water problems. In this sense water, normally thought of as a necessary resource for the survival of life, ceases to be part of the commons and becomes a commodity, traded in the marketplace. Corporations buy and sell it for profit. This principle changes how people relate to a necessary resource.

Commodification is a necessary element in the accumulation of wealth within a capitalist economic system. To facilitate it, international regulations restricting the transnational flow of capital around the globe have changed in favour of trade liberalization, which emphasizes the "free" movement of capital and commodities. These changes resulted in an intense era of commodification of the commons over the last decades of the twentieth century, and the privatization of the commons (the trading of greenhouse gas emission permits, for example) is a part of **globalization**. As a consequence the social connections that people traditionally form in local communities are breaking down. Individuals are being reconstituted as independent consumers within a vast market system. The doctrines of **privatization** and **deregulation** have become mantras for all levels of government as they seek ways of developing and modernizing their economies, which they believe will raise the standard of living for all peoples. The creation of the World Trade Organization (WTO) in 1995 was one step in the institutionalization of this neo-liberal ideology.

3.4 Right versus need

A **right** is an entitlement that cannot be denied without sanction.
A **need** is something that is necessary and desired, but is not guaranteed.
Source: Rothfeder 2001.

The WTO acts to ensure the **principle of non-discrimination** (Mol 2001), which decrees that all member nations must treat all commodities equally and give corporations equal access to their internal markets. What is at issue is whether neo-liberal economic practices are leading to universal economic development or whether trade agreements and regulations favour some interests at the expense of others—favouring, to be specific, corporate interests at the expense of the basic needs of a large portion of the world's poor and marginalized. Existing trade deals, including the North American Free Trade Agreement (NAFTA), also regulate trade using this same ideological framework, and were forerunners to the WTO.

The fourth Dublin Principle now runs through many treatises on sustainability and the future management of water. At the World Water Forum, held in The Hague, Netherlands, in 2000, the debate again took the view that water is a need and not a right, and that to conserve water we should make a commodity of it—all in the belief that when people pay for something they are most likely to look after the resource. Putting a price on water will let the market take care of it, and conserve dwindling supplies, or so the argument goes.

The World Water Development Report, released by the United Nations in March 2004, continues to suggest that nations need to "move towards pricing water services to reflect the cost of their provision" (UNESCO 2004: 20). The Canadian government's Fresh Water Policy (1987) endorses a five-point strategy for managing and sustaining Canada's access to potable water—science and technology, integrated planning, legislation, public education, and water-pricing (Environment Canada 1987). This policy is enacted through a variety of provincial legislation, resulting in a patchwork of different laws in different jurisdictions. In Alberta, for example, the Water Act is still based on the legal concept of "first in time, first in right" (Mallet 2004). This is an outdated legal principle that grants the right of ownership to whoever gains access to a resource first. That principle will become increasingly problematic as demand increases for water from different sources.

3.5 Coal-bed methane extraction: A necessary evil?

A relatively new commercial venture in Canada, the extraction of methane from coal beds, involves removing large volumes of water from underground aquifers. In Alberta this activity puts the oil industry in conflict with agriculture over access to scarce sources of water. The ecological problem is that the water released has a high saline content that may also contain heavy metals. Aquifers could become contaminated, reducing the amount of water available for use by municipalities and agriculture in the area. As of yet, businesses have not "figured out what to do with the water pumped out of the ground, who will use it, and how it may pollute the landscape if it contains any impurities." Nevertheless, commercialization is moving ahead. In Alberta in 2003 twenty-five pilot projects were examining the economic potential of coal-bed methane extraction (CBM). By April 2004 there were about 1,000 coal-bed sites, but still no rules to protect the environment.

Sources: Brooymans 2003; *Edmonton Journal* 2004.

In the meantime, the privatization of resources has emerged as a central theme of globalization. The World Bank and the International Monetary Fund (IMF) often tie their loans to developing countries to the implementation of **public-private partnerships** (P3s), which have become euphemisms for the privatization and commodification of public utilities providing such services as water treatment and supply in addition to energy distribution. The water itself may also become a commodity. In a political climate characterized by rising costs, debt hysteria, and crumbling infrastructure due to neglect, the privatization of delivery systems is held out as a source of new money. It is touted as offering efficient, cost-effective, technical expertise and health monitoring. While privatization does guarantee profits, the evidence that P3s serve the best interests of the public remains debatable. While the privatization of water services will guarantee profits for the businesses involved, the public has no reciprocal guarantee that it will retain its right to have access to water or its democratic right to demand accountability from those using national resources.

Critics argue that P3s are a purposive economic plan promoted by the World Bank to create opportunities of capital investment, while the actors involved can ignore opportunities to improve existing public systems (Shiva 2002). Efforts to install P3s have resulted in considerable resistance in the communities affected, led in the global South by the poor and the marginalized. In Moncton, N.B., the community finally rejected P3 plans, finding that the partnerships were not delivering the promised savings. The province's auditor general found that the plans would lead to much higher costs. On the whole, New Brunswick's experience with P3s was for the most part negative (CUPE 2002).

The May 2002 disaster at the small, southwestern Ontario town of Walkerton demonstrates the effects of government withdrawal from its responsibilities to ensure public access to safe water. The town's water supply was infected by the deadly E. coli bacteria, killing seven people and making another 2,300 sick. The source of the E. coli at Walkerton was thought to come from animal waste seeping into the groundwater, and the Ontario government's privatization program is often blamed for the tragedy. The government used privatization to divest itself of public testing facilities after 1996, while the public continued to trust that its water would continue to be safe. Others have used the tragedy to argue that privatization will lessen environmental risks by bringing new investments in water infrastructure. There may also be policy problems on how changes in water quality are monitored and reported (McKenzie 2002). The tragedy eventually led to the enactment of Ontario's Safe Drinking Water Act in 2002. Passed more than two and a half years after the Walkerton tragedy, the act states that all Ontarians are entitled to expect safe drinking water, and it builds on existing laws of treatment and distribution. Whether privatization solves these problems is still open to debate, but it is becoming more common as municipalities that have not invested in new infrastructure seek capital investment to make up shortages.

Walkerton exemplifies how the Canadian public can be marginalized in its relationship to government officials and technical experts. Harris Ali (1997), after investigating the role of trust in the relationship between the public and those experts and public officials who are responsible for managing potential environmental risks, concluded that a certain amount of distrust was necessary in a democracy to ensure political accountability. In a taken-for-granted world, environmental threats are excluded until an event like Walkerton shatters the public's sense of security. Ali suggests that Canada's government uses a paternalistic approach to managing environmental risks, while the U.S. relies on the participation of various interest groups to spotlight ecological issues. As a result, unfortunately, Canadians tend to be less involved in the process of managing environmental risks.

In the United States, private water delivery systems now make more than $80 billion in annual revenues (Rothfeder 2001). Canada too is exploring these public-private partnerships as a part of its infrastructure strategy. The privatization of water and sewer systems has now been expanded to include our national parks in Banff and Jasper. The Council of Canadians argues, "P3 privatization coupled with the disciplines of trade agreements can result in our water systems being run by foreign countries as for-profit businesses" (Council of Canadians 2004b). Some countries, like Kenya, are now finding it cheaper to import water from Canada than to update and repair their own delivery systems (Rothfeder 2001). A French corporation, Lyonnaise des Eaux, is the world's largest water company, servicing sixty-eight million people in some thirty countries, including Canada, where it provides water to a half-dozen municipalities (de Villiers 2000). These trends raise an important public concern. Are corporations using scarcity arguments and the lack of public financial resources as an opportunity to commodify water for the sake of profits?

Can we trust corporations with our drinking water? Murray Dobbin (1998) argues that their citizenship record is weak; corporations have often been cited for fraudulent practices that result in court cases. He notes that in Britain, Prime Minister Margaret Thatcher's privatization of water in 1990 resulted in a series of prosecutions of water companies for not fulfiling their contracts to provide affordable, efficient services. An average of three successful prosecutions per week had occurred by 1996, and more than 250 since 1990. Moreover, water rates increased by an average of 85 percent in Britain, with some areas exceeding 300 percent. Many poor people had their water cut off when they could not afford to pay their bills.

Elizabeth Brubaker (2002), executive director of Environment Probe, a Toronto-based environmental think tank, sees it differently. She argues in *Liquid Assets* that privatization will make it easier to enforce environmental standards. For Environment Probe, the privatization of water delivery systems is an economic necessity. Brubaker notes that the costs of upgrading and expanding water utilities are prohibitive; therefore, municipal governments are turning to private companies for practical reasons rather than ideological ones. The Federation of Canadian Municipalities estimated in 1985 that over 30 percent of the municipal water infrastructure was already thirty years old on average (Brubaker 2002). Environment Probe takes the position that governments should stop subsidizing the water needs of their populations because it will force the public to conserve water. Canada, of all the nations of the Organization for Economic Co-operation and Development (OECD), pays the lowest municipal rate for one cubic metre of water, at thirty-one cents; while the United States pays about forty to eighty cents and the Germans, at the other extreme, are paying $2.15 (Environment Canada 2004). Reviewing the British case, Brubaker (2002) argues that utility bill increases were more in the range of 67 percent after water was privatized.

Unfortunately, when she promotes the market as mechanism for conservation, Brubaker does not differentiate between those who can afford the increases and those who cannot. She is also silent on questions such as why should the public subsidize the profits of companies with public resources. Her strongest reason for implementing P3s is that governments do not have the financial resources to pay for upgrading public systems, and she does not talk about alternatives. For example, why couldn't the conservation and financial goals of municipalities be achieved using the same market mechanisms as businesses? Perhaps the introduction of a sliding fees scale for domestic and business could be implemented as a way of raising capital for public upgrades. Fees would be tied to use: here excessive use would be more heavily penalized, while basic domestic use remains accessible and affordable.

Public services such as water treatment are usually breakeven utilities; sewage systems and sewage treatment infrastructures are costly and run deficits. In Canada, since the crisis at Walkerton, water treatment costs have increased, especially for smaller communities, due to increases in health protection standards. Governments interested in downsizing and cost savings argue that they can no longer afford to upgrade or replace aging water treatment systems. Businesses, especially large engineering firms with the necessary staff, flexible workforces of expert consultants, and large sums of capital to invest see an opportunity to profit from a worsening municipal situation. In water treatment they see profits from combining design and engineering and construction—processes previously tendered out to many individual firms—with management and administration of the system previously run by municipalities. One critic argues that privatization appears to be an action to create investment opportunities for business (Shutt 1998). Others point out that government is downloading the tax burden onto the backs of individuals through privatization, while corporations earn a profit and benefit from reduced taxes (because of tax and royalty holidays). Brubaker concludes that private-sector and government-run programs can co-exist in Canada, as they do in much of the rest of the world.

In contrast, Erik Swyngedouw, in *Social Power and the Urbanization of Water* (2004), studies the relationship in Guayaquil, Ecuador, of public water providers and private water vendors (*tanqueros*) who hold monopolies over the sale of water to urban sectors where municipal piped water is not available. He uses this case study to show inequalities between rich and poor and ask broader questions about water and social control, class and lifestyle, privatization, influence in municipal planning and provision, the ecological costs of capitalist production and consumption, and the social construction of the concept of water scarcity itself.

Access to water is more than an economic issue. It is social necessity. Communities generally organize around access to their most basic needs. Commodification forces human relationships to be organized according to an economic ideology rather than human needs. This nexus is also gendered because women, as the Dublin principles note, are most likely to collect and use water resources. Decommodification or preserving the commons does not guarantee sound ecological practices, but is a necessary condition for implementing effective environmental practices as they become necessary. What is inevitable under the current system is that the scarcity of water, for whatever reason, will result in people with money having the financial ability to buy as much water as they want, while people on fixed or low incomes will have to go without.

Resisting water commodification

Patrick Bond (2004), working in South Africa, describes the struggle over water commodification as the new global apartheid. Looking at all the major world summits, including Cancun and Kyoto, he traces the role of popular groups, unions, and non-governmental organizations in resisting the privatization of water—having seen this resistance as well at the community and neighbourhood levels in Soweto, South Africa, and other places in the global South. South Africa is one of the world's most water-stressed nations, and there he finds that "commodified water is failing to deliver the goods, or even the profits" and is being resisted by "those who would decommodify water" (Bond 2004: 25). In the Black townships, where water is scarce, water companies require end-users to buy debit cards in advance; they then have to use the cards to get water. Locals fought back by digging up water pipes and taking the water. Commodification has turned human beings in need of water into deviants, accused of stealing privately owned property.

In Canada large-scale resistance to the commodification of water is being led by the Council of Canadians, who are themselves part of a larger international water security movement. Together these critics see access to water as a basic human right. They also attack head-on the new ideology that sees the global water shortage as an economic opportunity for Canada, as Andrew Biro says, to spin our extra water resources into "blue gold." "Canada takes up its traditional position in the global economy as a staples exporter and 'excess' is converted effortlessly into profit as the thirsty masses rush to buy our disproportionate share of the world's fresh water" (Biro in Johnson, Gismondi, and Goodman 2005). Maude Barlow and Tony Clarke's book *Blue Gold* (2002) traces the way in which corporate strategy and rhetoric are trying to turn the "water commons" into a marketable good, playing on our fears about water scarcity and water depletion and on the market ideology of greed. Those closest to the ground, the men and women in communities, have identified social inequalities and power over the flow of water as the causes of water shortages. Biro explains that "water scarcity" is as much a socially constructed reality as any other reality:

> Like all ideologies, the fantasies circulating around notions of "water scarcity" have a material basis. For the dominant discourses (efficiency-minded economics and conservation-minded mainstream environmentalism) that are conjoined in what Karen Bakker terms "market environmentalism" (Bakker 2003), scarcity is taken to be a natural fact and marketization the best way to deal with it. Another view, however, which I will argue is at least partially visible in resistance to the commodification and export of Canada's water supply, posits "scarcity" as socially and politically produced and thus emphasizes the intensely political character of the market. Each view presents its own political project, or "fantasy," and claims its sustainability based on a particular perception of "reality." Sustainability, however, is itself political, not just scientific. It is not just a matter of objectively assessing differing perceptions of reality, but also of assessing which fantasy can provide a more meaningful form of human existence. (Biro in Johnson, Gismondi, and Goodman 2005)

Biro concludes that that we need to organize an alternative discourse and practices of resistance. But nowhere in the United Nations Declaration of Human Rights is water explicitly mentioned. Article 25 states that "everyone has the right to a standard of living adequate for the health and well-being of himself and of his family, including food, clothing, housing, medical care and necessary social services." If water is just a need, then by implication it can be denied (Rothfeder 2001). One strong counterclaim is forming around the notion of a people's "water revolution" and a World Water Contract that would defend the right to life and water, recognizing that water is the basis of all life (Petrella 2001). As if to underscore this basic right, workers, peasants, and citizens of the barrios of Cochabamba, Bolivia, took to the streets to fight against and protest, some at the cost of their lives, the privatization of their water system in 2000 by the multinational Bechtel Corporation. That event has been described as the "la guerra del agua" or "the water wars"—and that type of resistance is occurring worldwide.

What Can We Do?

In his keynote address at the Parkland Institute's Water Conference in June 2004, Tony Clark of Canada's Polaris Institute identified six clear and provocative ways of seeing what is at stake (Polaris Institute website).

1. *Water sovereignty*. Whoever owns water, controls water. He suggested that activists take the position that water belongs to the people and to nature.
2. *Water conservation*. He suggested vigilance over the guzzlers—agribusiness and oil and gas and industry, and to lesser extent municipal users. Individual conservation is important but not the main structural or political challenge.
3. *Water quality*. We need to reduce and eliminate contamination. There are regional and neighbourhood issues of equity here.
4. *Water equity*. Access to sufficient water is a universal human right. Environmental racism must be confronted everywhere, for example, the disparity between water quality in mainstream and First Nation's communities.
5. *Water democracy*. Access requires political systems to guarantee this right; government and corporations cannot guarantee human rights. We need global democratic forums.
6. *Water spirituality*. Water is part of all of us, making up over 65 percent of our bodies, which raises issues of privatization and human nature.

Issues around water scarcity cannot be solved by pointing the finger at household use. Home based actions to reduce water use, like low-flow toilets, showering instead of bathing, retrofitted shower nozzles, and arid gardening (xeroscape) are important but not sufficient responses to what is at stake. Given the patterns of water use, industrial and agricultural excesses need controlling. Collective action and planning at the political level is what is most needed, and that requires the political involvement of the citizenry. Some may think that political action is not for them, but it is in the end the strongest, most influential process we have in Canada for voicing public concerns. A good place to start is to familiarize yourself with political-ecological issues in your local region. Does each of us know the civic plans that are in place for the upgrade or replacement of water treatment, distribution, and sewer systems? Are some P3s being explored in your municipality, as they were in cities such as Moncton? Find out what local plans and actions are being proposed for your local city or town, or for the region or province in which you live, and fight back.

Here's an exercise you can try. Using your own region or city as a case study, try bringing together cultural, historico-geographic, political, and spatial understandings—all in the same analytical moment—of water ecology and use in your home place. Reflect on your own lifetime or ask your relatives and elders about changes—physical or attitudinal—about water.

Key questions might include:

- How has the waterscape been altered for human uses? Are there some remnants of historic uses still visible as ruins or functioning components of the water flow?
- How has housing and suburban growth altered streams and surface-water flows in your neighbourhoods?
- How else has the flow and management of water into and out of the city changed?
- If you live in a rural area, ask what changes have taken place to surface water with roads, or to streambeds with government projects to "improve" natural areas and wetlands?
- Identify the headwater region of your watershed. How has forest loss or agricultural expansion and urban growth changed water flow? What changes are happening underground with water removal from the aquifers? Have wells changed over the years? Or septic systems? Does your region have plans for major projects that would divert or supply water to other regions? Industrial uses?
- How has thinking and rhetoric around water issues changed?
- Identify the flows of power in these water patterns and water discourses.

Some actions include creating a local water watch group. This group could develop programs of education and action at the municipal level to increase local discussion and create debate and community politics around water. Water watch means more than drinking and waste waters. Most municipalities also control considerable portions of wetlands and watercourses and watershed headwaters within their boundaries. A good source of information and organizing skills is your local public service worker and their organization (see CUPE website, "Rebuilding Strong Communities").

Useful Websites

Alberta. Industrial Use of Water Committee
<www.waterforlife.gov.ab.ca/html/removed.html>

Alberta Water law
<www.nawmp.ab.ca/AlbertawetlandsGuide.pdf.>

Blue Planet Project

<www.blueplanetproject.net>
Bolivia's Water Wars
<www.democracyctr.org/waterwar>
Canadian Council for Public-Private Partnerships
<www.pppcouncil.ca>
Canadian Union of Public Employees. Water Marks: National Drinking Water report card
<www.cupe.ca/www/privatizationwater/4051>
Coal bed methane
<www.energy.gov.ab.ca.com/Gas/NGC-CBM/default>
Council of Canadians water campaign
<www.canadians.org>
Moncton P3s discussion
<www.cupe.ca/www/ARP2002Moncton>
National Aboriginal Health Organization. Water issues
<www.naho.ca/firstnations/english/pdf/health_issues_information_sheets_canadas_enviro.pdf>
Polaris Institute. Operation Water Rights
<www.polarisinstitute.org/polaris_project/water_lords/water_lords_index.html>
Public Citizen (U.S.)
<www.citizen.org/cmep/Water>
Public Services International Research Unit
<www.psiru.org>
Sharon Beder
<www.uow.edu.au/arts/sts/sbeder>
Thirst. VHS video
<www.bulldogfilms.com>
UNESCO
<www.unesco.org/water>.
Water and oil. An Overview (water use for injection in Alberta)
<www.waterforlife.gov.ab.ca/html/technical_reports.html>
Water Page
<www.thewaterpage.com>
Water under Fire. Video Series
<www.waterunderfire.com>
World Commission on Dams
<www.dams.org>
World Water Council
<www.worldwatercouncil.org>

4. You Are What You Eat

Ella Haley, Kierstin C. Hatt, and Richard Tunstall

> And before you finish eating breakfast in the morning, you've depended on more than half the world. This is the way our universe is structured; this is its interrelated quality. We aren't going to have peace on Earth until we recognize this basic fact of the interrelated structure of all reality.
> —Martin Luther King

We all think we know what we're eating. But what we eat has global effects—environmental, socio-cultural, political, and economic. The breakfasts we eat offer in particular a prime example of how agriculture has become industrialized and food has become a **commodity**—how the production, processing, and marketing of food is largely controlled by huge **transnational corporations**. As a result of this control the growing conditions, including agricultural working conditions, are often unsustainable.

Still, not all has been lost: despite these problems, concrete actions can be taken, both individually and collectively, to protect the quality of food, foster sustainable local agriculture, and ensure safe work and adequate wages for workers in food-related occupations.

Breakfast

Breakfast is a simple meal ... or is it? Think about your breakfast today. What did it cost? Where did it come from? How was it produced? Who produced it? What was in those simple foods? Answering these questions might seem simple enough, but when we dig into it, take a close look at our food choices, it turns out to be not quite so straightforward.

Breakfast 1: Wheat cereal with milk and banana

Wheat: a basic human food source, an excellent source of fibre, vitamin B, and iron. But with the increasing industrialization of agriculture, and the treatment of wheat as just another commodity, the security of this critical food source has come under threat. According to the Ontario Public Health Association (2005), a number of factors have an impact on "the security, safety, accessibility, affordability, acceptability and nutritional value of the food supply itself. These systemic aspects of the food supply ... are dependent upon environmental, economic and social policies at every government level."

Canada is the second-largest wheat exporter in the world (Wilson 2002)—which might be good for this country, but not necessarily so good

Table 4.1 Key Sources of Toxins in Fertilizers

Rank	Industry	Pounds of Toxic Waste Sent (1990–1995)	% of Total
1	Steel Works and Allied Processes	79,932,179	30%
2	Electronic Components and Accessories	52,812,315	20%
3	Industrial Organic Chemicals	23,538,608	9%
4	Coating, Engraving, and Allied Services	21,690,344	8%
5	Secondary Smelting and Refining of Nonferrous Metals	20,261,853	8%
6	Rolling, Drawing, and Extruding of Nonferrous Metals	19,444,463	7%
7	Industrial Inorganic Chemicals	7,915,093	3%
8	Soap, Detergents, and Cleaning Preparations	7,653,790	3%

Source: Savitz, Hettenbach, and Wien 1998: 21

for the many countries receiving our wheat. The economic base of small farmers in those countries has often been destroyed when locally produced grains are replaced by imports from other countries (Garcia 2003). Importing cheap Canadian wheat tends to drive local prices down, undermine local markets, and change cultural diets, depriving rural peoples of their livelihoods. This occurs whether the grains are imported or received as "development aid" (McMichael 2000; Shiva 1991).

There is growing evidence about the buildup of contaminants in food crops. For example, there is evidence that cadmium has accumulated in our wheat crop (Wilson 2002). How does a toxic heavy metal like cadmium get into wheat? One main route is via phosphate rock that is processed into fertilizer. Phosphate rock contains cadmium and other contaminants (uranium, fluoride, and other heavy metals). In addition, the chemical fertilizer industry routinely "recycles" industrial waste into fertilizer (Wilson 2002). In the United States "more than 600 companies in 44 different states sent 270 million pounds of toxic waste to farms and fertilizer companies between 1990 and 1995" (Savitz, Hettenbach, and Wien 1998: 1). Information on the chemical fertilizer industry in Canada is not as readily available, but phosphate-processing factories that make fertilizer and cattle-feed supplements have routinely accepted "spent" (waste) sulphuric acid from other industries. This acid, used to break down phosphate rock, contains many kinds of contaminants (Haley 2002).

Duff Wilson (2002) reports that a large number of metals were found in fertilizer: arsenic, cadmium, cobalt, mercury, molybdenum, nickel, lead, selenium, and zinc. When Washington state environmental authorities tested for dioxins in industrial waste used as fertilizer, they found very high levels in steel-mill smokestack ash, in "Bay Zinc" fertilizer, in the

"Bay Zinc" brand of tire ash fertilizer, and in cement kiln dust for farm use (Wilson 2002).

Agricultural crops are also routinely fertilized with the by-products of industrial and human sewage. Municipalities encourage this practice, it offers a cheap way of "recycling" sewage waste, and farmers are led to believe that it is a safe practice. But sewage sludge routinely contains a range of toxins: polychlorinated byphenols (PCBs), chlorinated pesticides, chlorinated compounds such as dioxins, polynuclear aromatic hydrocarbons, heavy metals, bacteria, viruses, protozoa, parasitic worms, fungi, and miscellany such as asbestos, petroleum products, and industrial solvents (Stauber and Rampton 1995). Why do farmers use sludge? In *Toxic Sludge Is Good for You* John Stauber and Sheldon Rampton (1995) document a massive public relations campaign to get U.S. farmers to accept sludge, including a name change to "biosolids." The plot thickens with "a murky tangle of corporate and government bureaucracies, conflicts of interest, and a cover-up of massive hazards to the environment and human health" (Stauber and Rampton 1995: 101). Milwaukee's sewage sludge, marketed as "Milorganite," contains such high levels of cadmium that the fertilizer bag carries a warning, "Do not use on vegetable gardens, other edible crops or fruit trees" (97).

Milk: one of the basic food groups, according to Canada's Food Guide (Health Canada, Office of Nutrition Policy and Promotion 2005), but the family dairy farm is quickly becoming a nostalgic memory. Although most of Canada's milk is supplied locally—only 4 percent of Canadian milk is exported (Laidlaw 2003)—control over the Canadian milk industry is increasingly being concentrated. In the early 1960s, 125,000 milk and cream producers operated in Canada, but by 1979 the number had fallen dramatically to around 60,000 producers, and in 2002 to only 18,673 producers (NFU 2004). The producers' milk is marketed by just three dairy conglomerates: Parmalat (of Italy), Saputo (of Montreal), and Agropur (of Granby, Quebec) (NFU 2004; Ram's Horn 2003–4). Parmalat had $12.95 billion in revenues in 2003. Parmalat brands include Beatrice, Lactantia, Astro, Black Diamond, Balderson, Cheestrings, Sargento, Olivina, and Parkay (Parmalat website). While some might argue that the smaller farms were not efficient enough to compete with larger producers, research supports a different picture. According to the National Farmers' Union (2004: 6):

> Canadian farmers are generating wealth, but they are not benefiting as much as they should be from their efforts.... Canadian farmers are among the most efficient and technologically-advanced sectors of the economy, yet their economic gains are being captured on the one hand by input suppliers and on the other hand by processors and exporters.

The domination of the milk industry by a few global dairy corporations has increased pressures for the further industrialization of milk production. Small producers are finding that rules governing milk production are stacked against them. One example is having minimum transportation charges applied to low levels of milk shipped, which means that smaller operations pay a higher transportation bill, per litre, than do larger players. While milk marketing boards were originally set up to ensure a fair milk price for farmers, the price of the milk quota[1] has skyrocketed, making it basically unaffordable for young farmers to start dairy farming. The end result may be that more and more family farms will be bought up by larger agribusinesses, driving families off the land and hurting rural areas economically and socially. As well, existing free-trade agreements threaten the supply management system that Canadian dairy farmers now have and prohibit Canadians from expanding supply management to cover other commodities (NFU 2004).

Canadians have so far been willing to pay slightly higher prices to ensure that farmers receive a consistent and fair price for their product. That pattern could change, given ongoing World Trade Organization (WTO) talks that may determine the fate of milk marketing boards in Canada. The United States argues that the marketing boards are unfair (Kneen 2004), that they stop foreign (namely U.S.) imports of milk from entering Canada and protect artificially high prices for Canadian producers. In the United Kingdom, where in 1994 the Milk Marketing Board was abolished, prices paid to farmers have declined. Previously farmers were paid twenty-four pence per litre of milk, while the cost of producing the milk was eighteen to twenty-two pence. In 2001 farmers were paid nineteen pence per litre, less than their production costs. At the same time, milk was selling for seventy-two pence per litre at the supermarket (Pretty 2001).

Another consequence of a more corporatized milk industry may be the increasing use of growth hormones and chemicals, which are banned in Canada. In the early 1990s the United States approved Monsanto's recombinant bovine growth hormone (rBGH or rBST[2]), a synthetic hormone designed to push cows' physiological abilities to produce more milk. The aim is to increase the "productivity" of the dairy cow by as much as 40 percent (King 1986; Kneen 1999; National Dairy Council 2005).

Although clearly aimed at increasing profits, the "increased productivity" associated with rBGH comes at a harsh price to small farmers and to cows' and humans' health. Cattle given rBGH are physically overworked and develop health problems such as "cystic ovaries, udder infections, digestive disorders, foot and leg ailments, body sores and reproductive problems" (Lee, Liffman, and McCulligh 2002: 42). The cows develop mastitis, a painful infection of the udder that requires antibiotics. Residues of the antibiotics find their way into the milk, encouraging the growth of bacteria—"superbugs" that are antibiotic resistant (Mateu and Martin 2001).

With respect to human health, rBGH milk differs from natural milk chemically, nutritionally, pharmacologically, and immunologically. The rBGH milk triggers the production of a hormone, Insulin-like Growth Factor 1 (IGF-1), which causes "uncontrolled cell division in humans" and has been linked to various cancers (such as colon and prostate cancer). Elevated IGF-1 levels are also one of the leading "known risk factors for breast cancer" (Epstein 1998: 612).

In Canada, Monsanto and industry-funded researchers have defended rBGH,[3] while at the same time acknowledging that small farmers will not survive (Kalter 1985, cited in Kneen, 1999). In 1999 Canada prohibited the use of rBGH because of the health problems for humans and cattle. The decision was not made easily (Health Canada 1999). During their evaluation of rBGH, Health Canada scientists revealed that they were unduly pressured by Monsanto to declare the drug safe (Standing Senate Committee on Agriculture and Forestry 1999). Canadians cannot afford to be complacent, however. Although legally banned in Canada, rBGH milk products are imported regularly from the United States, and reports indicate that illegal rBGH use by Canadian dairy producers is booming (Canadian Federation of Humane Societies 1999). Further, it is not clear whether mechanisms such as NAFTA and the WTO could be used to pressure Canada into accepting rBGH and rBGH products.

Bananas. Canadians love their favourite fruit, which represents 25 percent of all fruit consumed in Canada. Some $250 million worth of bananas were imported into Canada in 1996 (Lee, Liffman, and McCulligh 2002). Nutritionally, a single banana contains high levels of B vitamins, vitamins A and C, magnesium, calcium, very high levels of potassium, and yet only has around 140 calories. Bananas are easily digested, and many doctors and baby books recommend bananas as a baby's first solid food.

Although a banana may seem very "at home" on your cereal, it has probably travelled thousands of kilometres to arrive there. The journey of the breakfast banana began far away and long ago: tracing the origin of banana industry exports to North America means going back to the original "Banana Republic" of Costa Rica. The banana industry in Costa Rica established the plantation model for banana production worldwide.

Tropical forest originally comprised 99.8 percent of Costa Rica (Tropical Science Center 1982). With the formation of the United Fruit Company in the late nineteenth century, almost 20,000 hectares (50,000 acres) of bananas were planted, which meant deforesting 20,000 hectares of land (Adams 1914: 171). Tropical forests are very species-rich in Costa Rica, and the widespread cultivation of bananas significantly altered the ecology of Costa Rica's Atlantic zone, destroying ecosystems and the habitats of numerous species, and thus reducing biodiversity. Deforestation also

4.1 Bananas in Latin American Culture and Literature

A number of different works of literature have expressed the strong subjective experience associated with the banana industry, offering details of how cultural identities were shaped by banana production. Colombian novelist Gabriel García Márquez and Chilean poet Pablo Neruda, both of them winners of the Nobel Prize for Literature, provide examples.

> He tried to reconstruct in his imagination the annihilated splendor of the old banana-company town, whose dry swimming pool was filled to the brim with rotting men's and women's shoes, and in the houses of which, destroyed by rye grass, he found the skeleton of a German shepherd dog still tied to a ring by a steel chain and a telephone that was ringing, ringing, ringing until he picked it up and an anguished and distant woman spoke in English, and he said yes, that the strike was over, that three thousand dead people had been thrown into the sea, that the banana company had left, and that Macondo finally had peace after many years.
> — Gabriel García Márquez, *One Hundred Years of Solitude* (1970)

> When the trumpets had sounded and all
> was in readiness on the face of the earth,
> Jehovah divided his universe:...
> the most succulent item of all,
> The United Fruit Company Incorporated
> reserved for itself: the heartland
> and coasts of my country,
> the delectable waist of America. ...
> Then in the bloody domain of the flies
> The United Fruit Company Incorporated
> unloaded with a booty of coffee and fruits
> brimming its cargo boats, gliding
> like trays with the spoils
> of our drowning dominions.
> —Pablo Neruda, "La United Fruit Co." (1961)

led to topsoil loss, the sedimentation of waterways, and an increase in malaria (Janzen 1983; García, Chacón, and Isabel 1995; MIRENEM 1990, 1992; Tropical Science Center 1982; UICN 1995; Hatt 2000).

Costa Rica now has over 40,000 hectares of bananas in production. Banana companies sometimes use lands that were previously deforested by cattle ranches. Throughout the 1990s banana production pushed into the Sarapiquí region, a richly biodiverse area containing 50,000 hectares of biological reserves (Corporacíon Bananera Nacional [CORBANA] documentation; Vandermeer and Perfecto 1995).

The United Fruit Company held a monopoly on banana production in Costa Rica until 1956. The U.S.-based company so dominated Costa Rican development patterns that it was known pejoratively as "El Pulpo"—"The Octopus"—with one tentacle in virtually every aspect of life (Fallas 1954; Cerdas Mora 1976; Hatt 2000). In the first decade of the twenty-first century, three U.S. transnationals dominate the Costa Rican banana industry: Chiquita Brands International (formerly the United Fruit Company), Dole Food Company, and, to a lesser extent, del Monte Corporation (López 1988; Bulmer-Thomas 1987; CORBANA 1990–97; Hatt 2000).

4.2 Banana Stickers

All day, sixteen-year-old "Maria" puts stickers on chemical-drenched bunches of bananas. Asked what is sprayed on the bananas and sends fumes drifting out of the receptacle beside her, she responds "liquid." She is not aware that the chemical she inhales and which soaks into her unprotected skin contains a combination of fungicides to keep the bananas from rotting before they reach their markets. The fungicides include chemicals that are moderately to highly toxic and that can lead to skin lesions and nervous system disorders. Although some banana plantations provide worker protection, it is not mandatory.

Sources: Hatt 2000; Mata and Mata 1993; Hilije, Castillo, Thrupp and Wesseling 1987; Soto 1992; Sierra 1993; WHO cited in MIRENEM 1992.

The banana transnationals have greatly influenced both policy and practices within the industry. One example was the active suppression of an extremely critical report on the banana industry that cited deforestation, chemical use, solid waste, pollution of rivers and soils, unemployment, migration, and higher land prices as direct consequences of the expansion of banana production. The report was produced by well-qualified, respected Costa Rican and international academic and technical experts. It was suppressed for years due to criticism and pressure by the banana industry (MIRENEM 1992; Gallagher and McWhirter 1998; Hatt 2000).

In the mid-1920s the United Fruit Company implemented science-based production techniques that included a substantial shift to the Cavendish variety of banana, immune to Panama disease but delicate and vulnerable to Sigatoka disease and nematodes (microscopic worms). The result was chemically intensive banana production employed on enormous monocrop plantations designed to maximize profits (Pérez et al. in Soto 1992; Vandermeer in Janzen 1983; Soto 1992; Sierra and Eduardo 1993).

Chemical control is the favoured practice for nematode-vulnerable Cavendish bananas. However, two commonly used chemical nematicides, DBCP (1,2-dibromo-3-chloropropane) and Aldicarb, were banned because of their harmful effects on human health. Despite these legal bans, about U.S.$12.5 million was spent in Costa Rica between 1989 and 1992 importing prohibited agrochemicals, including several classified as part of the "Dirty Dozen" by the Pesticide Action Network (García, Chacón, and Isabel 1995). All of the nematicides in current use are considered either highly or extremely toxic (MIRENEM 1992; Sierra and Eduardo 1993).

Costa Rica competes on the world market with high quality bananas, and because of global oversupply the banana industry is very competitive. Quality control is paramount to maintaining market share and quality standards are largely maintained through chemical control. Chemicals are used throughout the production process, from chemical-impregnated bags, which cover banana stalks as they grow, to the application of fungicides, herbicides, and pesticides (Soto 1992; Sierra 1993; López 1988; Hatt 2000).

Worker protection from these toxic chemicals varies from moderate to non-existent. The default practice is to cut production costs by minimizing environmental and worker protection measures. As a consequence of the chemicals used to attain high-quality standards, banana production regions have ten times the number of chemical poisoning cases compared to the rest of Costa Rica. Of all cases of chemical poisoning on banana plantations, 40 percent were attributed to the Aldicarb and Paraquat chemical products alone. Aldicarb has been banned, and Paraquat, one of the most widely used herbicides in the world, has acute levels of oral toxicity (Mata and Mata 1993: 47).

The massive amount of waste created by banana production and the toxic nature of this waste have a significant environmental impact. Substantial environmental degradation originating from chemical, liquid, organic solid, and nonorganic solid waste has occurred far from production sites. Studies have detected chemical residues in the outflow of rivers that pass through plantations, in more distant rivers, and in local groundwaters. These residues have a disastrous impact on wildlife that previously thrived in and around these waterways. Banana wastes have polluted both waterways and soil and present a significant threat to animal and plant biodiversity in Costa Rica's most species-rich regions (Tropical Sciences Center 1982; Chacón et al. 1994; MIRENEM 1992; Hernández 1997; Hatt 2000).

Banana production is labour-intensive, and labour control has always been a volatile component of the industry. The powerful banana transnationals have actively repressed union activity through-

4.3 Banana Workers Fight against Dibromochloropropane (DBCP)

One of the most infamous nematicides is DBCP, produced by Dow Chemicals. Because it is extremely toxic to humans and causes male sterility, DBCP was banned in the United States in 1977 and in Costa Rica in 1978. However, Dow Chemical continued supplying DBCP to Costa Rica after the U.S. ban. In 1996 banana workers were successful in having their case heard in a Texas court. Companies were charged with negligent use of DBCP. In 1997 Dow Chemical offered a U.S.$22 million out-of-court settlement, to be divided among 981 complainants, with 40 percent deducted for lawyers' fees. This paved the way for a legal victory in 2002 in which a Nicaraguan judge ordered three U.S. companies—Dow Chemical, Shell Oil, and Standard Fruit (Dole Food Company)—to pay U.S.$490 million in compensation to 583 banana workers injured by DBCP.

Sources: Jansen 1998; Gallagher and McWhirter 1998; EIU documentation.

out the history of the industry (CORBANA 1990–97; López 1988; Hatt 2000). Despite the relatively high wages paid to banana workers, questionable and even illegal working conditions are common. Banana workers are frequently laid off, and large numbers of them move from plantation to plantation every three months. This practice keeps benefits and severance payments low and effectively prevents workers from organizing or resisting management in any significant way. Because they also function as marketing companies, the transnationals also directly and indirectly control labour practices on so-called "independent" plantations.

Quality control, transnational power, labour control, and profitability are inextricably linked. In Canada, these characteristics of the industry manifest themselves as low-cost, high-quality bananas readily available year-round (López 1988; Hatt 2000).

Banana transnationals have come under increasing pressure, particularly from European consumers and non-governmental organizations, to address the environmental issues associated with banana production. To maintain export markets the companies have developed glossy publicity programs and hired environmental co-ordinators to give banana production a "Green Sheen." They have also participated in several programs to improve environmental conditions on plantations (for example, The International Organization for Standardization's ISO 14000 certification, and Chiquita's "Better Banana" or "ECO-OK" program). These programs have contributed in some areas to worker protection from the effects of chemicals and solid waste recycling. But none of them include any attempt to reduce the amount of chemicals used in production or to adopt less toxic chemicals. Although the certification process requires sampling for chemical residues in water outflows from plantations, effective testing for pesticides is not always available. Spot checks are sporadic, and managers are often informed in advance of the test so that they can not only "facilitate scheduling arrangements" but also prepare for the testing. Participation is voluntary, and the corporations both pay for the programs and set the standards. Test results are not available to the public, and truly independent testing is prohibited (Gallagher and McWhirter 1998; Hatt 2000). A corporate environmental co-ordinator explained, "Once you open the door a crack, and researchers get a foot in the door, in the end they're into everything and you can't do production" (quoted in Hatt 2000).

Certification may help North American and European consumers feel better about the bananas they eat, but it neither ensures any change in the types or amounts of chemicals used nor speaks to how "environmentally friendly" the bananas may or not be. As the environmental co-ordinator for Chiquita pointed out, "ECO-OK [Better Banana] certification is for the production processes only and not for the fruit itself.... The Chiquita name itself implies quality and care for the environment" (CORBANA documentation; Hatt 2000).

Breakfast 2: Coffee and a donut

Okay, so you prefer coffee and donuts, eh? Not only does this breakfast have questionable nutritive value, but it also includes two products—sugar and coffee—that have a seamy past and present.

Coffee: In the 1970s international development agencies encouraged coffee growers in Central America to replace traditional coffee varieties with faster growing plants and to cut down forest overhang to encourage faster growth of "sun" coffee. Between 1978 and 1997, the U.S. Agency for International Development provided $80 million to Haiti, El Salvador, and Guatemala, and coffee production in these countries quadrupled (Dicum and Luttinger 1999). In the 1990s the World Bank and Nestlé financed coffee production in Vietnam; as a result coffee flooded the markets and lowered prices (Garcia 2003).

The backers of sun coffee did not foresee the input costs of more fertilizers, pesticides, and water. These costly inputs overburdened struggling farmers, and the soil lost fertility from the chemical inputs and excessive water used. Cutting down shade trees, including fruit and hardwood trees, also eliminated the habitats of 150 species of migratory songbirds (97 percent), and their populations went into a drastic decline (Ryan and Durning 1997; Dicum and Luttinger 1999). Farmers also lost a secondary source of food and income from the shade trees as well as soil replenishment and habitat for the beneficial insects that control the pests that harm the coffee plant. Although production increased fourfold, the cost per acre was $704 for the sun coffee and $109 per acre for the traditionally grown coffee—translating into fifty-six cents per pound of sun coffee produced versus thirty-nine cents per pound of shade coffee produced. While traditional coffee yields fewer beans per acre, it is more ecological and economic than the non-shade, high-input coffee (Dicum and Luttinger 1999).

Farmers receive little compensation for coffee that requires expensive imputs and arduous work. In Nicaragua only 4 to 7 percent of the value of the final price stays in the country (Pesonen 2004). Internationally, coffee is the third most pesticide-sprayed crop behind cotton and tobacco; pesticides banned in the United States, such as DDT, malathion, and benzene hexachloride are still used in its production (Dicum and Luttinger 1999). Smaller-scale coffee growers prefer growing organic coffee because many of them cannot afford chemical pesticides. They benefit from the premium prices paid for certified organic coffee.

Donuts: Traditionally high in refined carbohydrates, fat, and sugars, a donut has roughly three hundred calories (Calorie-Counter.Net website), about 15 percent of an adult's daily caloric intake. The prime ingredients of fast foods tend to be sugar, fat, salt, and refined carbohydrates: ingredients that are high in calories, hydrogenated or animal fats, and excess salt,

4.4 Obesity

People in the United States consume on average the equivalent of fifty-three teaspoons a day of sugar, two-thirds of it in the form of processed foods. Using the Body Mass Index (BMI) as a measurement—it estimates the percentage of body fat by using height and weight—researchers have found that one in five children in the United States is overweight—and this figure is climbing. Over the last two decades there has been a 50 percent increase in the number of overweight children. The introduction of new mostly sugar-containing foods climbed almost identically over the last thirty-five years. Eric Schlosser argues: "Today about 44 million Americans are obese.... No other nation has got so obese so fast. The number of people with very high body weights where disease risk is extreme (BMI>40) has tripled in the last decade."

Sources: Duffy (2003: 46); Brownell and Horgan (2004); Schlosser (2001: 240).

and low in minerals, vitamins, and fibre. The eating of excessive refined carbohydrates and sugars can contribute to obesity.

When it comes to sugar, a main ingredient in donuts, "The rules of the game are rigged" (Garcia 2003). "Aside from killing us, sugar destroys reef and rainforests, traps southern farmers in poverty, is supported by an insecure subsidy regime in the U.K. and makes a few companies very, very rich" (Smith 2003: 48). Runoff from sugar-cane plantations into rivers feeding the Great Barrier Reef is a key cause of the decline of coral species due to pollution from chemical fertilizers. There are reports of water pollution from sugar-cane plantations in places such as Brazil, the Philippines, and Florida.

Cane sugar accounts for 75 percent of processed sugar; the rest is made from beet sugar (Smith 2003; Garcia 2003). The bulk of beet sugar is produced in the European Union (E.U.). Pesticide use is also very high in the production of sugar beets. In the United Kingdom beet farmers use on average 10.5 herbicide-active ingredients each year—"more than double the amount used for any other crop" (Smith 2003: 48).

World sugar crops are controlled by large sugar refineries, which benefit from domestic subsidies, protective tariffs, and overproduction. All of these factors combine to keep global sugar prices low, affecting the livelihoods of farmers and workers in the sugar industry in developing countries (Garcia 2003).

The E.U. market is protected by subsidies that lower sugar prices on the world market (Garcia 2003). "The E.U. sugar regimes' subsidies are worth £1 billion a year and ensure a guaranteed E.U. price for sugar that is more than three times the world market price" (Smith 2003: 48). This ensures fair wages for European farmers (Garcia 2003).

The overproduction of sugar represents a huge problem. In 2001 sugar production from sugar beets was seven million tonnes over the ten million tonnes of the E.U. quota. The excess sugar floods markets overseas with underpriced product, which negates any advantage that local sugar farmers have (Garcia 2003; Smith 2003). Poorer sugar producing countries are also slapped with import tariffs by the E.U., Canada, the United States, and Japan (Garcia 2003). In addition, large British-owned corporations control the world sugar refining industry. In the United Kingdom, the British Sugar Company has a 100 percent monopoly on processing beet sugar. In addition, the Tate and Lyle Company in Britain is the largest cane sugar refinery in the world (Smith 2003: 49). These companies enjoy guaranteed minimum prices for their sugar in the E.U. and influence global sugar prices (Garcia 2003; Smith 2003). In contrast, sugar workers in the South (for example, Brazil, Dominican Republic, and Mozambique) earn poverty level wages. "If sugar workers in the South were paid the same as workers in the North, costs would be ten times higher than they are now" (Smith 2003: 48).

4.5 Economies of Scale

Bigger farms are not necessarily economical. When food analysts Frances Moore Lappé and Joseph Collins examined the net income per acre by farm size in the United States between 1960 and 1973, they found that modest-sized family farms generally had higher net incomes per acre than did very large farms. Poorer countries in the South reflect a similar tendency.

Sources: Lappé and Collins 1977; Harper and LeBeau 2003.

Sugar is also a monoculture crop that takes up huge tracts of land in poorer countries (Mozambique, Vietnam, and Nicaragua) that could be used to grow produce for local consumption, but instead is used to feed people in wealthier countries, usually at great distances from where the food is produced (Ribas 2004).

Breakfast 3: A better breakfast?

Perhaps you think you could do better than the average Canadian breakfast. How about starting with organic, whole-wheat toast covered in organic tahini (sesame seed butter) with a fair-trade-labelled banana sliced on top, and bottled spring water to drink. At first it may seem relatively healthy and even politically purposeful with its organic and fair-trade content; but after a closer look, we find that even the better breakfast has its problems.

The label on the plastic bread bag lists a number of ingredients—organic whole-wheat flour, purified water, sea salt, molasses, pure canola oil, and yeast—and indicates that the loaf was baked at a local bakery in town. That seems all to the good: you are not only supporting a local small business but also eating what appear to be healthy ingredients. Still, the bag does not indicate where the ingredients came from, or even what country they were grown in. Although the wheat, water, yeast, and oil may could been grown locally, you have no way of knowing for sure, and the salt and molasses would definitely have had to travel a long distance to get to you. The molasses would probably have been produced by some large sugar conglomerate. What, you might find yourself thinking, is "pure" canola oil? It could mean that the product is in its raw state and not hydrogenated. It could also mean that it was the healthier cold expeller-pressed oil, meaning that the oil was not heated during processing. Could it mean that the canola is not made from genetically engineered or modified (GE or GMO) seeds, or that it is organically grown? The label probably provides no answers to these questions.

Maybe you're also a little unsure of what the "purified" in the bottled water means. Does the water come from a municipal tap-water source or from a spring? What type of filter if any, was used? Was the filtering done through reverse osmosis or by using a carbon-based filter, or was the water passed through an ultraviolet light, or ozonated, or a combination of all these? Some bottled water has fluoride added, and so too does some municipal tap water, and there is evidence that an excessive accumulation of ingested fluoride can cause detrimental health effects such as mottled teeth or brittle bones, which can lead to fractures and suppression of the immune system (Flouride Action website; Waldbott, Burgstahler, and McKinney 1978: 295–305).

You also have to consider the packaging. It is a small amount compared to more processed foods, but all plastics have a huge environmental impact. In one study, researchers at the University of Plymouth found microscopic plastic in every sample they collected from the sandy shores to the sea beds (Thompson et al. 2004). Millions of tons of plastics are produced annually, and the product takes from a hundred to a thousand years to disintegrate. Toxins from plastics that contain xenoestrogens may well be passed up the food chain. Xenoestrogens can alter hormone levels and are linked to cancer, especially breast cancer (Kaur 2000).

All of these questions arise from a simple loaf of bread and bottle of water, without even without taking the tahini and banana into account. The sesame seeds used to make tahini were probably grown in the Middle East and shipped to Canada to be processed and packaged. A lot of oil would be consumed in transporting these goods such a distance, contributing to the greenhouse gas effect and global warming. With the banana perhaps you're wondering: what exactly does "fair trade" mean? Does it also mean organic? By checking with the store you might discover that the banana was, in fact, organically grown. But who certified it and what are their standards?

The better breakfast, while much more nutritious, still involves the transportation of food over long distances. Nevertheless, compared with the first two breakfasts, it has a less harmful impact on the environment, the health of workers, and the health of consumers. Can you imagine an even better breakfast?

The three different breakfast choices have multiple environmental, social, and health impacts. Although we might think we know what we eat, more is going on than meets the palate. Although our individual food choices are important, these choices are influenced, and limited, by global factors and conditions; and our food choices also have global ramifications for workers and the environment.

Why We Eat What We Eat

To gain a better understanding of the consequences of breakfast choices, we need to unravel the processes that bring food to the table. Doing this can also point the way to figuring out how to reduce the negative impacts of food choice. Many factors influence food choices, including class, gender, culture, personal tastes, and availability. These factors are not one-directional, nor do they occur in isolation. They are like a web of interconnected strands—increasingly organized and structured around the commodification of food.

Commodification and commodity chains

In recent years, food in all industrialized countries has become increasingly commodified: food has been made into marketable products rather than something grown for personal consumption (Harper and LeBeau 2003). In the past, most food was sold in its raw form—unprocessed meat, fruit, and vegetables, for example—with a fairly direct connection between the farmer, the marketplace, and the consumer. With increased globalization, food products become part of a global production system: they become products of a **global assembly line**.

The global assembly line is a dynamic rather than fixed system. As transnational corporations shift production locales to take advantage of changing conditions the system is constantly being reorganized (McMichael 2000; Esteva 1992). Given that systems of food production are ideally suited for generating corporate profits, global assembly lines are associated with the growth of **corporatization**. For corporations, global assembly lines:

1. provide a standardized product and allow maximized **economies of scale**;
2. allow business to be carried out anywhere in the world at the lowest possible cost (due to factors such as lower wages, fewer environmental regulations, fewer unions, and lower tax levels);
3. reduce the vulnerability that comes from depending on a single source of supply for a specific component; and
4. provide better access to both global and local markets.

One technique for analyzing the global assembly line is to outline a commodity chain identifying the linkages between production and consumption. The chain links consumers to a broad range of effects: environmental, social, economic, or political. The exercise of following each item of food, or indeed each ingredient, through its own commodity chain back to its production can illustrate the potential consequences associated with consumption. For example, in one commodity chain Deborah Barndt (2002) traced tomatoes from where they were grown in Mexico, to their

4.6 Commodity Chain Steps for Tomatoes

Production (Mexico)	step 1	Struggle for Land
	step 2	Monocultures Led by U.S. Industrial Agriculture
	step 3	Transnationals Control the Technological Package
	step 4	Selecting and Packing the Perfect Tomato
	step 5	Agro-Exports
	step 6	Processing for "Value-Added"
Transport & Distribution (U.S.)	step 7	Trucking North
	step 8	Checking for Quality: Appearance Matters
	step 9	The Line Is Drawn: Border of Inequalities
	step 10	Keeping Pests and Pesticides at Bay
	step 11	Exporting/Importing: Brokers and Wholesalers
Consumption (Canada)	step 12	A More Permeable Border: Slipping into Canada
	step 13	The Morning Zoo: Food Terminals While We Sleep
	step 14	Designer Supermarkets and Multicultural Labels
	step 15	High-Tech Tomatoes and Computerized Cashiers
	step 16	Fast Food: Homogenized Tomatoes
	step 17	Waste or Surplus: Compost or Charity?

Source: Adapted from Barndt 2002.

transportation through the United States, and eventually to the point where they were consumed in Canada.[4]

Competing perspectives: Comparative advantage and world systems theory
Most of the world's peoples are now, no matter the country, integrated into global markets. The rise in the commodification of food and of global assembly lines has been justified as part of the neo-liberal economic model by extending David Ricardo's early nineteenth-century concept of **comparative advantage** to a global scale (Sapsford 2002: 71). Following this logic, every nation should specialize in and export what it can produce most efficiently or cheaply relative to other goods; and it should import products that it cannot efficiently produce. In this way every country plays its role in an increasingly complex and interdependent world trade system. For this reason, lesser-developed countries tend to specialize in producing commodities such as sugar, coffee, cocoa, and tropical fruits for export to wealthier countries. Canada's comparative advantage for food exports includes beef and wheat (McMichael 2000; Department of Foreign Affairs and International Trade website).

From a neo-liberal economic perspective, the introduction of the global assembly line and the corporatization of food are positive developments. An alternative perspective, **world systems theory**, views the global commodification and corporatization of food systems as a massive, and harmful, concentration of power and control over vital food systems. For example, by the year 2000, with fifty-five thousand transnational corporations in the world, the top three hundred were controlling around one-quarter of the world's productive assets (Greer and Singh 2000). Just four companies— Nestlé, Kraft, Proctor and Gamble, and Sara Lee—now control about 50 percent of the coffee market (Pesonen 2004). From a world systems' perspective, the power relations of exploitation form the basis of the environmental and social exploitation that is a prime feature of the breakfasts we eat every day.

World systems theory connects the economic development of "First-World" countries (referred to as the "**core**") to the underdevelopment of "Third-World" countries (referred to as the "**periphery**"). Core countries exploited peripheral countries (often as colonies) by taking over and extracting their labour and raw food materials and at the same time using the peripheral countries as markets for processed goods. The peripheral countries were actively restructured for the core countries' benefit. The peripheral countries become dependent on the core countries, and in the process they also became under-developed.

According to world systems theorists, then, the relationship between the core and periphery is a matter of exploitation and **dependency** rather than of comparative economic advantage. Products and wealth are extracted from the periphery and concentrated in core countries, which have all the power in the relationship. The global assembly line thus reflects and perpetuates global inequalities (Baran 1957; Frank 1969, 1971; Wallerstein 1974, 1979).[5]

Although not originally intended for this purpose, world systems theory can effectively identify the global power dynamics that result in environmental degradation. In this view, the increasing dis-

4.7 Say What?

First World, Third World, developed, developing, lesser developed, underdeveloped, North, South, the West, G-7, prosperous, backwards, have, have-nots, core, periphery: all these terms represent attempts to define a people, a country, a state, a status, or a condition; each has negative or positive connotations, and subtly hints at their causes. Some terms are more political and some are more geographic. Most are normative in that they suggest a desirable outcome.

For instance, Gustavo Esteva reports that on January 20, 1949, in his inaugural speech, U.S. President Harry Truman announced: "We must embark on a bold new program for making the benefits of our scientific advances and industrial programs available for the improvement and growth of underdeveloped areas." Esteva responds: "By using for the first time in such context, the word, 'underdeveloped,' Truman changed the meaning of development and created the emblem, a euphemism, used ever since to allude either discreetly or inadvertently to the era of American hegemony.... Underdevelopment began, then, on January 20, 1949. On that day, two billion people became underdeveloped. In a real sense, from that time on, they ceased being what they were, in all their diversity, and were transmogrified into an inverted mirror of others' reality: a mirror that belittles them and sends them off to the end of the queue, a mirror that defines their identity, which is really that of a heterogeneous and diverse majority, simply in the terms of a homogenizing and narrow minority."

Sources: Esteva 1992: 6–7.

tance between production and consumption results in an increasing likelihood of environmental and human exploitation. Transnational corporations and consumers in core countries can exploit the environment of the periphery for their own benefit simply because they have the necessary power to do so—and they do not suffer the consequences of this exploitation. Given the economic power of core-based transnationals, they can marginalize and undermine local development initiatives and systems that would protect the environment. All too often, local people suffer the consequences; often they have no option but to degrade their own environment in order to survive (Gill and Law 1988; Shiva 1991; Mies 1986; Clow 1989, 1991a, 1991b; Sachs 1992).

World systems approaches challenge the positions of ecological modernization and Brundtland-style sustainable development (see chapter 1), which argue that environmental protection can be built into current models of economic development. According to world systems theory, ecological modernization and sustainable development theories do not address the underlying issues of power, inequality, and exploitation, which are the root causes of environmental degradation. Still, while ecological modernization and sustainable development tend to reduce the environment to "natural resources for economic growth," world systems theory tends to reduce it to "objects of power relations." Both positions assume that natural resources are divisible and controllable. Both deny that natural resources have intrinsic value and are part of ecological systems that are interdependent and can undergo permanent systemic changes (Clow 1991a; Daly and Cobb 1989; Redclift 1984, 1987, 1991; Sachs 1992; Shiva 1991).

Costa Rica and Canada in the world system of food

The neo-liberal principle of comparative advantage fails, then, to capture the deeper consequences of exploitation and dependency associated with corporatization and global assembly lines. Instead, using the framework of world systems theory, we can take another look at the cases of Costa Rica and Canada, which brings us back to at least one, if not more, of our breakfast foods as well.

Costa Rica's dependence on the banana industry continues today: the product represents 38.6 percent of the country's agricultural exports and almost 9 percent of its total exports. Of Costa Rica's nearly four million inhabitants, 40,000 are employed directly and 100,000 indirectly by the banana industry. The annual export value of bananas is U.S.$700 million (*La República*, May 5, 2004; CORBANA documentation). Costa Rica's dependency on the banana industry presents a challenge for controlling its development path independent of the transnational corporations. The country has no government agency or department that deals directly with development issues related to the banana industry. When they face any official pressure the banana transnationals can always threaten to pack up and move production to another country.

But bananas are only one among several agricultural exports in Costa Rica: coffee, pineapples, beef, palm oil, and sugar are others. Agriculture in general accounts for 11 percent of the country's Gross Domestic Product (GDP) and 70 percent of its exports. The economy is dominated, then, by the principle of so-called comparative advantage: supplying richer and more developed (core) countries with agricultural exports—as well as with pleasant tourist destinations (Bulmer-Thomas 1987; López 1988; Hatt 2000). Due to the encroachment of transnationals on land previously used for growing local food, Costa Rica has been required to import beans and rice, staple foods.

Food exports are a key source of foreign exchange for many countries. Coffee, for example, "is the second most valuable item of legal international trade (after petroleum)" (Dicum and Luttinger 1999: x). Unfortunately, the economic benefits of food commodities typically do not "trickle down" to actual farmers. The coffee, sugar, and bananas enjoyed in Canada have ties not only to the rural poor in underdeveloped countries, but also to the rich transnational corporations. This search for comparative advantage in a context of corporatization impinges on local food security and farmers' survival in peripheral countries (Bulmer-Thomas 1987; López 1988; Hatt 2000). As one Costa Rican explained, "we're making desserts, and people can't live on desserts" (Hatt 2000).

According to world systems theory, Costa Rica's status as a peripheral nation explains why Costa Rica is greatly exposed to toxic chemicals, environmental degradation, heavy influence from foreign transnationals, and increased dependence—while at the same time Canadians enjoy relatively inexpensive bananas year-round.

As for Canada's place in this world food system, the country exports mostly staple foods and imports mostly foods that increase variety in the Northern diets. In this respect Canada is a developed core country that peripheral countries depend on as a market. Then, too, Canada has a tendency to fall into the **staples trap** because of its economic dependence on primary resources (see chapter seven). Canada also maintains dependency relations in its economy and through NAFTA, in which Canada's role is secondary to its more powerful partner to the south. Economically developed but dependent and exploited, Canada is often termed a **semi-peripheral** country because it shares attributes of both the core and periphery.

Corporate power and the food trade

The corporate involvement in food constrains and shapes the kinds of choices we can make. Transnational corporations lobby national and international bodies to ensure that international trade rules favour them. They spend millions of dollars on marketing to create consumer demand. They work at developing **genetically modified** or **engineered** seeds and foods. The reaction to GM or GE technology is influenced by the relations among transnational biotechnology corporations and various national and international government regulatory agencies.

Again, the banana industry offers a prime example of the power of corporations and their influence in food trade. Over decades Chiquita has worked hard at maintaining a political-economic context that supports its business. The so-called "Banana Wars" involving the United States and the European Union directly—and Chiquita indirectly—were all about profits, power, and market control. By the early 1990s Chiquita, anticipating an opening of European markets with the formation of the European Union, had invested millions of dollars in plantation development. When that opening did not occur, the United States, on behalf of Chiquita, took the European Union to the World Trade Organization to complain that not opening its markets to bananas produced in Latin America constituted unfair trade practices (CORBANA documentation; Hatt 2000). On the surface, Americans pursuing trade sanctions against the European Union over bananas seems rather odd. The United States does not export bananas, and only seven thousand of Chiquita's 45,000 employees are in the United States (Sexton and Banana Link 1997).

One part of the explanation for this rests in the story of Carl Lindner, the man at Chiquita's helm. Lindner, his son Keith (also a Chiquita executive), and Lindner's companies own 40 percent of Chiquita's stock. Lindner is well known for his wealth, his leadership of the company, and his massive political donations. Since 1991 Lindner and Chiquita have donated U.S.$41,600 million to the Republican Party and $1.3 million to the Democratic Party: an average of over $600,000 a year in political contributions. In 1993 their contributions made them the second-largest contributor to both political parties of soft money—broadly, any contribution not regulated by federal election laws. In the 1997–98 election campaign in Ohio, Chiquita Banana was the top soft money contributor; its chair, Lindner, was second. These figures do not include $250,000 given to the Democratic National Committee in 1994 and $500,000 provided to finance President Clinton's corporate jet. Further, direct communications and donations originating with Lindner and Chiquita coincide with key events in the Banana Wars (Gallagher and McWhirter 1998; Barlett and Steele 2000).

In 1999 a WTO panel found in favour of the United States and Chiquita, ruling that the E.U. banana import regime contravened the trade organization's rules (EIU 1999, 3: 19–20; 4:19–20). This result represents an example of corporate power of unprecedented proportions to influence national and international governance.

Individual consumption and corporate power

As individuals, all of us, then, are integrated into a global food system dominated by corporations and power relations. The system, extending from production to marketing to consumption and based on the neo-liberal economic model, has resulted in an unsustainable food economy and comes with a high price: reduced nutrition, hazardous production conditions, exploited workers, plus depleted soil and contaminated water, soil, and air.

Wealthy consumers tend to eat too much, and they especially eat food that is detrimental to their health. Humans in general are still subject to the primitive instincts of survival: the instinct to store calorie-rich food against a time when food might not be plentiful. Our taste buds search out foods that are sweet, salty, or fat. In the past these foods contained high fibre and were rich in the vitamins and minerals necessary for survival. Today, however, food-processing companies capitalize on our primitive instincts and offer us good-tasting, cheap, calorie-loaded food that is devoid of many essential nutrients. The corporations that produce this food admit that they have no moral obligation to monitor diet, and, indeed, they do all they can to promote consumption and increase profits (Terhune 2004).

Popular culture and corporate marketing provide conflicting values, images, and messages. Despite drastic increases in obesity, food companies continue to target us with TV ads to consume. Yet "at the same time, the idea of overeating as a sin persists, pushed by the multibillion dollar a year diet industry" (Olsen 2004). As one writer points out, "Weight dissatisfaction is so common among women that it is called normative" (McKinley 1999:106). Feminists have long identified the negative effects of social pressures to be thin, particularly on younger women. Naomi Wolf (1995) argued in *The Beauty Myth* that society places impossible aesthetic standards on women, reinforced through the media, which has led countless women to an obsession with exercise, dieting, and being thin. This trend is reflected in the increasing popularity of cosmetic surgery and increased eating disorders such as bulimia and anorexia. Corporations, preying upon consumers' self-image, present media images of thin bodies next to fast-food ads. Dietary products and weight-loss clubs have become a multi-million-dollar industry.

Our food choices are constrained then, not only by the global food assembly line but also by the power of marketing, advertising, and packaging. When you buy an apple, or cookies, many factors shape your actions, and you can be sure that marketing agencies have studied these factors so that they can target their advertising dollars most effectively. Given that 75 to 80 percent of all brand decisions are made in the store in about seven seconds, eye-catching packaging is of crucial importance (Lee, Liffman, and McCulligh 2002). For example, PepsiCo spent $1.24 billion in advertising alone in 1997 (Lee, Liffman, and McCulligh 2002: 13).

Corporations are creating wants as needs. For example, you need or "deserve a break today" because hectic lifestyles leave no time to cook and McDonald's can provide a quick, inexpensive, and easy alternative. McDonald's 1998 advertising budget was U.S.$1 billion, compared with the National Cancer Institute's U.S.$1 million budget aimed at promoting increased fruit and vegetable consumption (Brownell and Horgan 2004). Focused on getting lifelong converts to their products, large corporations increasingly target children. At McDonald's, 40 percent of advertising directly targets children, and in general marketing to children has doubled since 1992 (Brownell 2004). The spending clearly pays off, because "the number of hours of TV viewed each week is correlated with what children ask their parents to buy, what parents do buy, and calorie intake" (Taras et al. 1989: 176–80).

E. Neville Isdell, the CEO of Coca Cola, summed up the attitude of the fast-food industry: "We can't answer to what's out there philosophically. We have to respond to what consumers want" (quoted in Terhune 2004: B8). But the fast-food industry itself plays a strong role in influencing consumers' wants.[6]

Many individuals are unaware of these consequences of the food they consume. One reason for our lack of awareness is due to distancing. Increasingly, food products (especially packaged and processed goods) travel large distances to the supermarket from where the food was actually produced, leaving most of us quite unaware of the source of our food. Multinational corporations would argue that distancing provides us with a greater variety of foods, but distancing occurs even with locally available foods. In 1996 Britain imported 114,000 metric tons of milk and exported 119,000 metric tons of milk, all in the search for higher profits (Norberg-Hodge, Merrifield, and Gorelick 2002).

Stuart Laidlaw (2003) provides another extreme example of distancing. A Pennsylvania farm with a single owner ended up being divided into two, with the original farmer's grandsons now each having a piece of the property. One grandson operates a dairy farm and the other has an adjacent ice cream and yogurt-making business. Oddly, though, the cousins do not do business with each other because they receive better prices elsewhere. As a result, every day milk is trucked from the dairy farm, past the neighbouring farm to another dairy hundreds of kilometres away. Meanwhile different trucks travel a similar distance to deliver milk to the ice cream and yogurt-making business.

Consumer protection versus corporate power

Industries involved in producing and selling sugar and fast foods have powerful lobbies that influence government policies regarding dietary guidelines. Marion Nestle, professor of nutrition at New York University, documented changes in U.S. government dietary guidelines between September 1999 and May 2000 and the role of corporate influence. The initial dietary advice, drawn up by corporate, government, and nutrition professionals, was to "Go easy on beverages and foods with *added* sugars." Investigative reports reveal fierce industrial lobbying to change the wording to "choose a diet moderate in sugars" (Dalmeny, citing Nestle 2003: 52–53).

4.8 How Far Did Your Food Travel?

The travel distance for a traditional English Sunday lunch

Chicken from Thailand	10,691 miles by ship
Runner beans from Zambia	4912 miles by plane
Carrots from Spain	1000 miles by truck
Mange tout from Zimbabwe	5130 miles by plane
Potatoes from Italy	1521 miles by truck
Sprouts from Britain	125 miles by truck
Transport of imported goods from port of entry to distribution centre	625 miles
Transport from distribution centres to supermarket	360 miles
Total	26,234 miles

If you choose seasonal products that are bought locally, you can reduce the total distance to 376 miles or one-sixty-sixth of the miles travelled in the meal above.

Sources: Adapted from Michaels, and the Agriculture Project at Corporate Watch (2002: 20).

In April 2003, the sugar industry demanded that the U.S. government end its $406 million funding of the World Health Organization (WHO) unless it scrapped healthy eating guidelines that limit sugar to no more than 10 percent of dietary intake. The sugar industry cited its own "scientific" evidence indicating that 25 percent of a person's intake could safely consist of sugar. According to the report (Boseley 2003: 8), WHO insiders describe the threat as "tantamount to blackmail" and "worse than any pressure exerted by the tobacco lobby." At the WHO the industry reproaches made little impression. After taking into account comments from various stakeholders the organization "felt no need to reconsider the recommendations." According to its director of non-communicable diseases and health promotion, "Denouncing a WHO report as unscientific is a standard procedure if big commercial interests are at stake" (quoted in Hagmann 2003: 469–70).

Corporate power and GE foods

During the 1990s the Canadian government used public tax dollars in a joint venture with **biotechnology** giant Monsanto to develop and test **genetically engineered** (GE) Roundup Ready wheat in "secret test locations" (Rempel 2004). Genetic engineering (GE) involves cutting parts of DNA out of one organism and inserting them into another, using a virus to enter the cell membrane, and an antibiotic gene marker. Genetic technology produces unpredictable results and is "the largest biological experiment humanity has ever entered into" (Chapela in Garcia 2003). As filmmaker Deborah Koons Garcia (2003) puts it, "Whoever controls the seeds controls the food."

Spring wheat was genetically altered to be resistant to Roundup, a herbicide manufactured by Monsanto. Farmers who grow this wheat become dependent on Roundup because they spray their crops with the herbicide to control weeds without damaging the wheat (Rempel 2004). Roundup belongs to the family of glyphosate herbicides, and exposure to it is associated with an increased risk of miscarriages, premature birth, and non-Hodgkin's lymphoma (Cox 1998).

GE crops and products are more accepted in the United States than they are in Canada—perhaps because U.S. regulators seem to be more in the hands of the GE multinational companies. Key personnel from these companies move through a "revolving door" between positions in U.S. regulatory agencies and the biotech companies (Garcia 2003). Garcia also documents how Monsanto funded the political campaigns of influential U.S. politicians.

Neither the Canadian government nor Monsanto were fully prepared for the opposition to GE wheat. Farmers in general questioned the need for GE wheat when, as Nadège Adam of the Council of Canadians reported, there was "no evidence that GE crops have higher yields and are in any way beneficial for farmers." According to a study from the University of Saskatchewan (a key institution in the research and development of GE crops in Canada), growing GE wheat could cost Canadian farmers $185 million per year in lost sales (Inouye 2003). Many of the seventy countries that import Canadian wheat have stated they would refuse Roundup Ready wheat or any wheat contaminated by GE wheat through pollination and seed contamination. Organic wheat farmers were particularly concerned about GE wheat contaminating crops and ruining the organic wheat market.

The concerns of farmers are backed by the problems relating to GE canola. In January 2002 the Saskatchewan Organic Directorate filed a $14 million class action suit against two biotechnology transnationals, Monsanto and Aventis, because of crop contamination by GE canola (Council of Canadians Feb. 23, 2003). In 2004 Saskatchewan farmer Percy Schmeiser lost his six-year legal battle with Monsanto over GE canola crops that Monsanto found in his fields. The Supreme Court ruled that Schmeiser had "infringed Monsanto's patent for a genetically altered canola gene when he used and re-used the company's seed without permission after claiming they blew on his field" (Tibbetts 2004: A5). The case sparked an international controversy between traditional farmers and environmentalists opposed to GE food and biotechnology. One dissenting Supreme Court judge argued that this court decision indirectly allows Monsanto to "acquire patent protection over whole plants" (Tibbetts 2004: A5). Other critics argue that this ruling makes it difficult for farmers to engage in organic or conventional farming because they have "no recourse" to stop GE seed contamination of their crops (Kleiss 2004: A5). As research scientist George Neville explained, "The court has failed to address the right of growers of conventional canola and mustard to cultivate their crops free of patented genetic contamination. This ruling constitutes a landmark for licensing corporate irresponsibility" (Neville 2004: A18).

Monsanto is, of course, the same company that, in the case of milk, put tremendous pressure on Health Canada scientists to approve rBGH and other drugs considered unsafe (Standing Senate Committee on Agriculture and Forestry 1999). In the United States, the Federal Drug Administration (FDA) based its approval of rBGH on inaccurate or falsified safety data provided by Monsanto rather than on independently collected data that indicated the grave dangers of the growth hormone.

The documentary film *The Corporation* (Achbar and Simpson 2003) offers yet another example of Monsanto's corporate pressure in the case of Jane Akre and Steve Wilson, a Florida husband and wife team who made a film revealing human health concerns related to rBGH. After Monsanto pressured the television station where the journalists worked, they were asked to "water down" the story. They refused, and were then offered a bribe "in exchange for their resignations and a promise to remain silent about rBGH" (Lee, Liffman, and McCulligh 2002: 42). Again they refused, and the station fired them. Their documentary was never aired. Despite the health effects, the FDA does not require appropriate labelling on hormone-enhanced milk products, which means that Americans unknowingly consume dairy products that may contain high levels of the dangerous hormone Insulin-like Growth Factor-1 (IGF-1). Nonetheless, the United States, through the WTO, continues its campaign to dismantle milk marketing boards in Canada, which would open the way to selling its milk in Canada.

North America lags behind Europe in both the regulation of GE crops and the

4.9 Where's The Beef? Mad Cow Hits Canada

The economic impact on Canada and the United States has been devastating, since bovine spongiform encephalopathy (BSE) was discovered in Canada early in 2003. The cost to Canada alone has been over $5 billion. Health Canada scientists have stated that safety measures such as the removal of "spinal cords and brains from slaughtered animals" have not gone far enough in protecting public health. Canada still allows cattle to feed on non-ruminants such as pigs and chickens, and North Americans are still reluctant to test every cow as they do in Japan and France. According to William Leiss, "It all boils down to idiot economics, where billions of dollars later, Canadians are still told we still can't afford to spend on necessary and cost-effective tests to restore confidence in our animal health programs." BSE can be transmitted to humans and attacks the brain and nervous system with a disease known as Creutzfeldt-Jakob disease (CJD). Researchers suspect a link with Alzheimer's disease. Transmission of disease between animals and humans may be a disturbing trend—recently avian flu in chickens has affected humans. Critics argue that factory farming, with its crowded conditions, mass international transportation, and production facilities, only compounds the spread of infection, and again distances us from our food supply.

Sources: Leiss (2004: 1); Bueckert (2004); Nordberg-Hodge (2002: 61); Halweil (March 8, 2001).

proper labelling of its products in food markets. There are a few reasons for these differences. The U.S. Environmental Protection Agency (EPA) initially had no clear authority to regulate GE crops, whereas the European Union has had the statutory authority to do so since 1990. Further, European governments follow the **precautionary principle** and apply stricter criteria for proving that GE seeds and food are safe (Levidov 1999). Some fifteen countries in the European Union now require the labelling of GE foods (Garcia 2003).

In Canada the labelling of food containing GE ingredients is optional, despite a strong public lobby seeking obligatory labelling. Food manufacturers that use GE ingredients oppose mandatory labelling, arguing that consumers could be "misled" into believing that non-GE foods are safer. The biotechnology industry prefers "voluntary" labelling, but when one biotechnology company, Calgene, labelled its GE tomato, "It was quickly rejected by consumers—and no other biotechnology company has since decided to voluntarily label GE foods" (Lee, Liffman, and McCulligh 2002: 43). Without labelling, there is no way of tracing GE foods to investigate health effects (Garcia 2003).

The widespread cultivation, processing, and export of GE foods and food products make this a particularly difficult issue to deal with. No single country can avoid genetically modified food and crops without bucking the system of free trade. If a government seeks to delay or challenge the introduction of GE food, it faces opposition from the food giants, who want uniform standards to apply across the world—but only if those standards favour them. The degree of corporate control in national food systems raises serious doubts about the sovereignty of national politics and the limits of that sovereignty when it comes to our food supplies (Beck 1999; NFU 2004; Norberg-Hodge et al. 2002).

What Can We Do?

> "Every choice we make can be a celebration of the world we want."
> —Lappé and Lappé 2003: 315.
> "The choices we make determine the future of food." —Garcia 2003.

Our agricultural and food system as it is now suffers from a host of serious problems:

- the use of chemical fertilizers and pesticides (which create immediate exposure issues and contaminate soil, water, air, and food);
- a heavy dependence on non-renewable resources used, for example, in the production of chemical fertilizers, especially nitrogen;
- the distancing of food supplies;
- the severe environmental and health dangers of GE crops and foods;

- low returns for most farmers, particularly in the Third World;
- poverty wages and poor working and living conditions for farmworkers;
- the "cruel treatment of livestock" and food safety issues related to intensive livestock operations (Magdoff, Foster, and Buttel 2000: 11);
- the lack of access to food for poor people; and
- the decreasing food value of processed food (such as empty calories, fast food, sugar).

These problems result in environmental damage, the destruction of peasant and small-scale agriculture, the dispossession of rural land, the dehumanization of work in both North and South, and a lack of healthy and affordable food choices.

Individuals tend to perceive that they choose what they eat. But these decisions are heavily influenced by biology, the media, culture, and corporate power. Still, people are working individually and collaboratively to challenge the shift towards corporatization and globalization and to regain control of food systems. They are actively seeking to learn how their food is produced to ensure that it is healthy, eco-friendly, and non-exploitative at the local, international, and global levels. They are working to build a more sustainable society from the ground up.

Canadians in general are also becoming increasingly vigilant, wanting to know more about the origins of their food, particularly with all the recent publicity about mad cow disease, avian influenza in chickens, and genetically modified foods. Individuals can make a difference. Each choice we make adds to choices by others, and our individual choices can influence other people near to us.

On an individual level we can take a number of steps to reduce the ecological footprint of our food choices, and to protect workers (see Halweil 2002; Lappé and Lappé 2003; Ritzer 2000).

- Eat lower in the food chain to decrease our impact on the Earth, including a plant-centred, whole-foods, organic diet.
- Grow our own gardens and make preserves.
- Eat what is in season in our areas.
- Encourage schools to stock vending machines with healthier food options.
- Avoid taking children to fast-food restaurants—if there are no other choices (for instance, if you are travelling, "consider blindfolding your child until the ordeal is over") (Ritzer 2000: 230).
- Buy locally (produced within 400 kilometres or a day's drive of your home), directly from producers, and from local family farms.
- Shop at farmers' markets or buy a contract or contribute labour to local farmers who guarantee the delivery of produce all summer and early fall.
- Form a food policy council to help guide decisions involving your

local food sources. Produce and/or distribute a local-food directory for your area.

- "Buycott" by buying fair-trade products and supporting the fair-trade practices of local businesses (co-ops, cafés, markets) and encourage local businesses to do the same.
- Educate yourself and press elected leaders to redirect subsidies and tax policies to encourage sustainable family-farm agriculture.
- Support initiatives to make the rules that govern trade, air, and gene-and-seed patenting consistent with protecting workers, consumers' health, local culture, and the environment.
- Encourage the recycling of clean food wastes to gardens and farms.
- Try getting sewage sludge cleaned up by lobbying your local community to prevent the contamination of sewage with toxic wastes from industries and homes.
- Write your member of parliament stating that you want transparency in the labelling of GE foods.
- Support the anti-GE movement.

On a collective level, powerful resistance movements are challenging the agribusiness and food corporations. The transformation of our food system requires the concerted effort of many different interests (consumers, farmers, farmworkers, environmentalists, sustainable agriculture groups).

The anti-GE/GMO movement

The fight against GE foods is "the leading edge of a struggle by farmers and the general public against complete corporate control of the food system" (Magdoff, Foster, and Buttel (2000: 17).

Canadians have been more successful than Americans in challenging GE products, rallying to prevent the approval of GE wheat and milk. Lobbying efforts by scientists, farmers, anti-GE activists, and the public in Canada and Europe have pushed government authorities to take a more precautionary approach with respect to GE wheat and milk. These coalitions include scientists who share information with the public about the uncertainties and health effects of these products, including the flawed findings associated with rBGH.

Similar public resistance to GE products has occurred around the world in different ways. Some countries (such as Thailand and Sri Lanka) have banned the growing of all GE crops, while others have banned the import of GE food products. China banned the growing of GE rice, corn, soy, and wheat for fear of losing its export markets, while some anti-GE campaigns have targeted corporations that use GE ingredients in their products (Starbucks coffee, Campbell Soup, Kellogg's cereals, McDonald's, Burger King, and Pizza Hut) (Clarke and Inouye 2002). Biotechnology corporations have responded to these pressures by "moving their GE crops and foods to other markets, or developing new GE product lines" (Clarke and Inouye 2002: 49; Garcia 2003). Meanwhile, the anti-GE movement has continued to advocate global solidarity and to pressure governments to regulate GE technologies through labelling, moratoriums, and bans. Labelling in Canada, unlike some other countries, is voluntary and is a contentious issue.

The fair-trade movement

The fair-trade movement (sometimes referred to as "Trade Not Aid") attempts to challenge the effects of distancing to ensure that consumers participate in the betterment of workers' lives in distant places. Thriving fair-trade products and distribution outlets have been developed, for example, from concern about the working conditions of tea, coffee, and chocolate labourers in developing countries.

Fair-trade distributors ensure that their products are purchased from democratically organized groups of small farmers listed and monitored by an international registry. The certified "fair trade" logo guarantees that producers of their coffee, tea, and cocoa follow specific criteria, which promote many of these goals: 1) decreasing the number of "middlemen" between workers and consumers; 2) ensuring fair and living wages; 3) providing social and educational benefits for workers; 4) eliminating or reducing the use of toxic and polluting substances; 5) protecting workers from exposure to toxins; 6) providing stable markets for small producers; 7) ensuring workers' right to organize unions or co-operatives; and 8) facilitating advance payments or credit (Transfair Canada 2004). Transfair is the only affiliate of the Fairtrade Labeling Organization (FLO) in Canada. In contrast, Europe has over 130 brand names of FLO products on the market (Robb 2004).

The fair-trade and green consumerism movements aim at substituting fair-trade or "green" products for conventional consumption. Yet while they promote better wages and working conditions for workers in the Third World, and more ecological practices, they do not address issues such as distancing or overconsumption in rich countries.

Local food movements

A vibrant local foods movement is in place throughout the world, geared to meeting local food needs and to keeping farming communities alive by strengthening and diversifying local markets. Contrary to the logic of modernization theory and neo-liberal economics, organizing economies around local consumption carries numerous benefits. Rather than working to further impoverish developing countries by exploiting their labour and best agricultural land for foreign consumption, producers keep more of the country's resources, labour, and production at home, to be used to meet basic needs and satisfy local consumption (Norberg-Hodge et al. 2002). Canada, as a semi-peripheral country, would also benefit greatly from this strategy.

At the international level, nations have united to force governments to renegotiate trade treaties that orient the economic system to free trade and globalization rather than towards local consumption. In one case the U.S. government tried to use the World Trade Organization to force GE foods and crops on other countries. A group of 135 countries formed "The Like-Minded Group of Nations" and successfully opposed this motion, reinforcing nations' ability to control their own food systems (Norberg-Hodge et al. 2002).

The food system can also be redirected through action at the national level. Hidden and direct government subsidies that now favour industrial farming and corporate agribusiness could be rechannelled to support smaller diversified farming, as well as food products that are produced locally (Ribas 2004).

Eating local foods does not eliminate all trade, nor does it undermine the economies of countries. Instead, it reduces the unnecessary transport of foods that can be purchased in or near local communities (Norberg-Hodge et al. 2002). It also addresses some of the exploitation associated with participation in the global market, and it can break cycles of dependency.

Brian Halweil (2002) demonstrates the value of keeping money in the community. When that is done in West Africa, in Niger, for each dollar of new farm income the contribution to the local economy is doubled. In Burkina Faso, the contribution is almost tripled. Further, this money circulates within the local economy instead of profiting foreign food suppliers. These types of benefits to local communities apply just as much in Canada as they do elsewhere in the world. The basic message from the local foods movement is that eating locally benefits local communities.

Global coalitions

The World Social Forum (WSF) is an example of a broad global coalition of citizens that is addressing the transformation of society and working towards a just and ecological food system. This forum is committed to non-violent social resistance through open meetings to foster coalition-building among movements. These are movements that oppose neo-liberalism and corporate control of trade and the key aspects of our lives. They are critical of government and international institutions serving corporate interests (for example, the Canadian government's support and funding of research on GE crops, subsidies that benefit multinational agrifood corporations). The WSF is intent on fostering a different form of globalization—one that promotes "social justice, equality and the sovereignty of peoples" (World Social Forum 2004: 1).

Walden Bello (2003), a key anti-globalization thinker, argues that we need to de-globalize or "change the rules of the global economy," that we need to re-embed the market in society so that it operates to strengthen local and national economies, and so that it is "governed by the overarching values of community, solidarity, justice, and equity." He points out that "the forces representing human solidarity and community" must provide alternatives quickly in order to "convince the disenchanted masses" that there are humane and just alternatives to corporate-driven globalization. Otherwise he worries that "corporate-driven globalization" will embitter many, and the vacuum will be "filled by terrorists, demagogues of the religious and secular Right, and the purveyors of irrationality and nihilism" (Bello 2003: 1).

Bello works closely with Francis Moore Lappé through the Food First/Institute for Food and Development Policy. Lappé and her daughter Anna Lappé (2003) elaborate on the "embedding" theme by providing examples of alternatives of how capitalism can evolve and become democratized. Various authors (for example, Glasbeek 2002; Bello 2003; Magdoff, Foster, and Buttel 2000) call for more radical changes—changes that cut at the heart of capitalism. "The job of creating a just and environmentally sound food system cannot be separated from the creation of a just and environmentally sound society ... hunger is only a symptom of a larger problem—inequality and poverty" (Magdoff, Foster, and Buttel 2000: 20).

4.10 Thoughts from the Agriculture Forum, People's Summit, Quebec City, April 2001

"Trade agreements must guarantee the food sovereignty and security of the peoples."
"Food is a basic human right."
"Food must be safe, accessible, and provide a fair and adequate return to its primary producer."
Agricultural policies "must limit the export and import of foods that destroy our local economies" and place our health and environment at risk.
"Governments should promote organic agriculture and prohibit the use of transgenic food products."
"We should seek equitable development rather than free trade."
Source: Barndt 2002: 241–43.

Via Campesina is an example of efforts to deglobalize the economy. This "international movement of small farmer and peasant organizations" promotes the replacement of neo-liberal economic policies with food democracy (or sovereignty) and stresses the "right of communities to protect and regulate domestic agricultural production and trade to achieve sustainability, guarantee a livelihood for farmers, and ensure the members of that community are fed" (Tulip and Michaels 2004). For example, in Brazil the Landless Workers' Movement (MST) is showing how land redistribution is helping to "end hunger." Even the World Bank is acknowledging that land reform plays a key role in the improvement of economic and social health (Lappé and Lappé 2003).

In addition, U.S. and French farmers are now involved in a mammoth anti-trust lawsuit against the major agri-chemical companies, charging "Monsanto—and 'non-indicted co-conspirators' including Novartis, Dow and Du Pont—with using biotech patents to seize monopoly control of world agricultural markets" (Lappé and Lappé 2003: 303–4). The farmers' goal is to prevent Monsanto from selling patented GE seeds.

What you eat for breakfast, then, ends up being a big issue—from how our food is produced to issues of food safety to the political economy of food, agriculture, and ecology—how agribusiness and food corporations are focused on profit, not on sustaining people, communities, or the ecosystem. Our food system creates economic disparities, harms the environment, and poses a number of health risks. Yet people around the world are organizing on a number of fronts against the negative impacts of the corporate agriculture-food system. They are working individually—in making their own food choices—and as members of organizations, coalitions, and movements. All of the actions taken, though, must ultimately address the underlying causes of the problems, and at the heart of that problem is the capitalist economy with its key focus: profit above all else.

Notes

1. A key aspect of Canada's supply management system for milk includes the concept of "quota"—the right to sell a certain volume of milk to a provincial milk board each day. Each unit of quota permits a farmers to sell a certain amount of milk at top market value. The original intent of the milk marketing system was to provide stability for the domestic milk market. The problem is that the quota itself became a commodity. This could have been avoided had the quota system been owned by the milk marketing board, which could have operated a quota pool. When farmers retired, their assigned quota could go back to the pool and be reassigned fairly (Kneen 2004).
2. Bovine somatotropin.
3. In the United States, rBGH is also known as rBST (recombinant bovine somatotropin).
4. For commodity chain analyses for commonly consumed products, such as computers, hamburgers, fries, cola, bicycles, and newspapers, see *Stuff: The Secret Lives of Everyday Things*, by John C. Ryan and Alan Thein Durning (Northwest Environment Watch, 1997).
5. Other important contributors to analyses of dependency include the following: Amin 1974; Baran and Sweezy 1966; Cardoso and Faletto 1979; Chase-Dunn 1989; Furtado 1964, 1971; Prebisch in Meier and Seers 1984; Prebisch 1964; Sunkel and Paz 1979).
6. See Eric Schlosser's *Fast Food Nation: The Dark Side of the All-American Meal* (2001); or the documentary films *Supersize Me*, directed by Morgan Spurlock, or *The Cola Conquest*, by Irene Angelico.

5. Space, the Canadian Frontier? Landscape, Identity, and Power

Jeff Masuda and Jeji Varghese

> Human beings have persistently searched for the ideal environment. How it looks varies from one culture to another but in essence it seems to draw on two antipodal images: the garden of innocence and the cosmos.
> —Yi-Fu Tuan

The surface area of planet Earth is just over 500 million square kilometres, of which only 148 million square kilometres (29.3 percent) is land. With a population now reaching six and a half billion people, Earth has less than 230 square metres of available land per person—which translates into a plot that is only 150 metres long and 150 metres wide. Of that land, less than a third is considered arable.

In Canada, things are slightly different. With 7 percent of the world's landmass, or almost ten million square kilometres and only thirty million people, Canada's allotted share of the planet works out to over 330 square metres for each Canadian. China has a comparable land mass of just over 9.5 million square kilometres, but with a population of over 1.2 billion people, China is left with about eight square metres for each person. What are the implications of these differences for how Canadians think about, utilize, and change the physical environment? Does having so much **space** in Canada mean that we are more wasteful in our land uses? How does this relative abundance of space influence who were are, our attitudes, and our relationship with the **landscape**? Who has the power to decide who or what goes where on the Canadian landscape?

Imagine all of the "things" that you own, use, eat, drink, and entertain with on a daily basis—your breakfast cereal, coffee, and newspaper, and the gasoline that gets you to work in the morning and back home at the end of the day. Can you estimate the amount of land area that was required to produce those goods? Then too, don't forget that you have to set aside a certain amount of land for the plants that are needed to soak up the carbon dioxide that you produce with every breath you take. Are you beginning to think that the world's available land may not be sufficient to meet your demands along with the other six and a half billion people? And yet, chances are, your demands *are* being met. Inevitably this must mean that others are sacrificing a part of their entitlement to the Earth's space in order to accommodate your excesses.

In this chapter, we focus on *space itself* as a site of consumption, and who has the power to decided who gets what space. Everybody uses space in their daily lives—space in which to live, travel, do business, shop, entertain yourself, grow, and breathe, as well as produce all of the resources that we consume. In putting down this ecological footprint—the space that we require to sustain ourselves—the "steps" that we take occur at a number of **scales**. As individuals, we take up space to satisfy our needs, wants, and habits. Our use of space is both made possible and constrained by social, political, economic, and cultural factors. For example, those of us who can afford it live in large houses with big backyards and additional space for two or more cars. We eat fresh fruits and vegetables grown in exotic places, importing them year-round. For fun, we enjoy the "great outdoors" in campsites and national parks during spring break or summer getaways. These same luxuries are more often denied to the majority of people living in lesser developed nations. Their "allotted" space is limited by geographic disadvantage—there is little room for luxury in the global economic periphery (the so-called Third World).

As communities, we partition space in ways that facilitate economic growth (industrial and commercial space), quality of life (neighbourhoods, schools, churches) and recreation (parks, shopping malls, ski hills). The affluent create communities that are spread out into the relative peace and safety of the city suburbs, alongside car-friendly, pedestrian unfriendly city streets without sidewalks and amidst the convenience of shopping in big box stores that can meet every material need. In contrast, the poor are often marginalized in substandard housing in decaying, inner-city cores or along busy freeways or near industrial areas.

At the highest scale, as societies, nations draw boundaries around space in order to protect the economic opportunities that accompany the land base that is within their political control. One country will guard its boundaries against those who would have alternative political agendas for the same space. Those nations with more power are better equipped to preserve their own way of life, and often impose their control over others. The U.S. occupation of Iraq is but one example of the economic territorialization of one nation over another. Whether it is in the name of freedom or oil depends on one's position.

At the same time, through international trade and travel we are connected to and often in conflict with the spaces of other individuals, communities, and societies. Likewise, the interests of those even at a far distance can have an impact on us in our local space (Massey 2004). Returning to the Middle East example, a disruption in the political environment of one country has ripple effects on both our pocketbooks (at the pump) and our entire national economy. To mitigate such negative effects and promote our own vision, powerful Western societies draw up international trade agreements to ensure that the costs of our consumption can be externalized—passed from our own backyards to other places in the world where we can offload our unsightly polluting industry and import material goods such as exotic food products and cultural artifacts.

A spatial lens, then, proves to be useful on a myriad of issues related to consumption and sustainability. Space acts as a common denominator across all forms of human activity. It is also one means by which power is projected by one group over another from the individual to the global scale (Cresswell 1996). Geographer Yi-Fu Tuan thus talks (1974: 248) about the human preoccupation with creating an ideal environment for ourselves. On the one hand, the cosmos represents our wish to create a civilized world to set us apart from the Earth from which we come. But whose world will it be? Transnational economic development, large-scale urbanization, and cultural imperialism (in the shape of Wal-Mart and McDonald's, for instance) have been the most recent attempts by the powerful to usurp the natural resources of this world to fulfil our desire to "civilize." On the other hand, the garden of innocence represents our desire to find security and comfort within a supportive and nurturing "Mother Earth." Tuan's symbolism parallels the mythology of Judeo-Christian theology in which the Garden of Eden is seen by adherents as the foundation of all humanity, a symbolic umbilical cord that must be preserved and protected to sustain us. The profound irony between resource exploitation and natural sustenance is not easily reconciled.

Social Constructionism

Tuan's "antipodal images" thus represent our central thesis here: the idea that space is socially constructed (Dunn et al. 1995). The term **social constructionism** covers a variety of approaches, but a common theme is the premise that social phenomena are not universal but are rather agreed-upon social conventions (for more on social constructionism, see also chapter nine). The traditional view is that space is always characterized by a fixed set of features and will always evolve according to the same formula. Alternatively, a social constructionist approach does not focus on the features of the environment itself (that is, the river is polluted, the suburbs are decimating natural landscapes), but rather on the various claims that are made about environmental features (who is being polluted, who is doing the polluting and why; what is a natural landscape and why should it not be replaced by suburbs?), and how the proponents of those claims interact and negotiate with others who may hold differing constructions (Best 1989, 1993; Burmingham and Cooper 1999).

A social constructionist approach provides a way of exploring the social and cultural factors that underlie decisions made about space, including land use, development, transportation, and environmental preservation and conservation. For example, Malcolm Spector and John Kitsuse (1987: 38) argue, "Social problems are products of particular constructions of social reality, rather than, necessarily of actual physical conditions." Constructionists have played an important role in showing how actors, from the individual to the organizational, develop alternative meanings of "real" world phenomena (McLaughlin 2001).

The physical appearances of places in Canada such as the North, the city, or national parks are a direct result of decisions made about what is and is not appropriate land use by individuals, groups, and society. For example, is the North a barren physical landscape or an economic frontier for mining and oil and gas development? Do our images of cities encompass pedestrian-friendly parks and streets like in downtown Montreal, or are they vast roadscapes where the car-less are socially and economically excluded? Are national parks a refuge for the preservation of untouched wilderness, or a playground for urban weekend tourists? It is when we realize that these images of Canada are social and cultural constructions created by those who have interests in propagating them as such that we can see that different views of Canada may be construed more as myths than reality. Then too, differing ideas about appropriate land use have led to a number of contemporary problems. When we examine these problems within the scope of social science, the myths can be dispelled, revealing a much more complex, contradictory, and contested reality.

The social constructionist approach does not deny the existence of environmental problems (see, for example, Benton 1994; Dunlap and Catton 1994; Dickens 1996). Rather, the practice of employing both social and physical perspectives provides a more comprehensive view. For example, Paul McLaughlin (2001) suggests that we think of human actions as occurring within a "socially constructed adaptive landscape." On the one hand, environmental contexts limit the avenues available for us to take part in the activities we desire (for example, we all need gasoline to fuel our vehicles); on the other, our constructions of these contexts (it is better to live in the suburbs and commute to work) help to determine the decisions that shape that structural/environmental context (continued oil and gas exploration), either opening up or closing off potential future avenues.

Following these ways of thinking about environmental problems and social theory, we can look at space to answer certain fundamental questions about our decisions related to various land-uses in Canada. These include:

- What is so important about Canada's North in an increasingly globalized world?
- What forces are shaping the look and feel of Canada's cities?
- How are Canada's rural areas changing as urbanization continues?

One key geographic idea suggests that people's lived experience within a particular place can build into a sense of belonging or an emotional bond (Relph 1976). It is from our everyday interactions with the places where we live, work, and play that a **sense of place** develops. A sense of place not only is a "hard-to-define-attitude, value or belief" created in individuals, but also includes "the social, historical processes by which place meanings are constructed, negotiated and politically contested" by groups, communities, and entire societies (William and Stewart 1998: 20). This is particularly important to our understanding of contested space because it identifies motivations on the individual or community level for protecting or mobilizing around local landscapes.

5.1 One "Space," Many "Senses of Place"

The Prince Albert Model Forest (in north-central Saskatchewan) includes three different communities (resort village, First Nations reserve, and national park). Research within each community has revealed three very different views of the forest ecosystem, demographic profiles, histories, goals, and community aspirations (Parkins, Varghese and Stedman 2001). The residents of the resort village see the forest as a place of relaxation. Reserve members view it as a close-knit, economically viable place of community sustenance. Residents of the national park community view the forest as a place in which they can foster ecological integrity.

Source: Parkins, Varghese, and Stedman 2001.

By understanding perceived place differences, resource managers can contextualize the impacts of decisions on communities. A decision to intensively manage the forest (as in the case of the Prince Albert Model Forest, may lead to employment opportunities for the First Nations reserve, but the jobs come at the expense of the peace and quiet priorities of the resort village and create increased concern about ecological impacts among the park community. This type of social science research helps us to anticipate issues—before they reach the stage of protests, blockades, or public hearings—and enables resource managers to proactively consider appropriate steps and propose alternative visions. In the case of Prince Albert, for example, they might propose that 1) Aboriginal contractors be used for the work; 2) cutting takes place during off-peak tourist seasons; and 3) harvest rates are kept at levels that are low enough to avoid cumulative ecological damage. The knowledge gained about each place can also be shared with each of the communities within it—which will in turn assist in community empowerment such that each community can envision its future on a shared natural landscape and work in partnership with resource managers to articulate its vision. The challenge is in negotiating between different visions and ensuring the transparency of which trade-offs are being made and why. Despite these challenges, the identification of contested meanings of place is a critical first step in natural resource decision-making.

The concept—and reality—of space has been categorized in many different ways (for examples, see Lefebvre 1991; Strassoldo 1987; Simonsen 1996; Soja 1996). Geographer Edward Soja's (1996) three-part conceptualization of space—material space, symbolic space, and lived space—provides a means of evaluating the consumption of space. The material inner-city spaces of the poor and the suburban spaces of the more affluent become symbolic space when they are represented in popular culture as places of either crime and poverty or safety and luxury. In their lived space the inner-city residents may experience gang turf wars, prostitution, and drug-trafficking in their daily lives; the middle-class, predominantly white suburbanites schedule block parties, dog walking, and recreational activities. What matters most is to identify not only how these places come to be as they are, but also who is deciding that it should be that way.

Here we use three Canadian landscapes as a means of illustrating this approach. We begin with a journey to Canada's North, with the competing images of the "North as a frontier" versus the "North as a homeland." We use the issue of the Mackenzie Valley Pipeline as a case study to examine these two competing images. Our next stop will be the Canadian city and an investigation of the spatial impacts of automobiles as a dominant form of consumption of urban spaces. Our final destination is the rural countryside, where we look at rural spaces as either "playgrounds" or "dumping grounds" (Whitson 2001).

Canada's Northern Landscape: Frontier or Homeland?

> The western arctic and sub-arctic region of Canada, encompassing the Yukon and Northwest Territories, are among the most extensive relatively intact ecosystems remaining in the world. For Aboriginal peoples, this region had been a homeland for millennia. To many people, the North is a refuge in the world's shrinking reservoir of landscapes not yet marked by industrial development.
> —Canadian Arctic Resources Committee (CARC), 2001.

The Mackenzie Valley Pipeline Proposal and the Berger Inquiry

Controversies over the role and scale of industrial development in Canada's North always reveal different constructions of space—and this is particularly true of the long-standing pursuit of a Northern oil and gas transportation corridor. In the 1970s, in the midst of the energy crisis, natural gas was discovered in the Mackenzie Delta. In 1974 the Arctic Gas Consortium first proposed a $7 billion project to build a pipeline to run across the Mackenzie Valley, where it could collect gas from the Beaufort/Delta regions and transport it to markets in the United States. This proposed development scheme would be the largest Canadian project undertaken by private interests in Canada. Much of the controversy revolved around determining who had a legitimate voice in determining what was appropriate land use: the proponents or those directly affected by the decision.[1]

In 1974 the federal government appointed a B.C. Supreme Court justice to examine the issues surrounding the proposal to construct the pipeline. From 1974–76, Justice Thomas Berger conducted the Mackenzie Valley Pipeline Inquiry (known as the Berger Inquiry). In a desire to assess Northern Aboriginal views of the issue, Berger traveled to thirty-five Northern communities and ten Canadian cities stretching from Halifax to Vancouver. He heard from nearly one thousand northerners speaking in seven different languages. According to Justice Berger (quoted in CARC 2001: 4):

> We are conducting an inquiry about a proposal to build a pipeline along the route of Canada's mightiest river; a pipeline costlier than any in our history; a pipeline to be built across our northern territories, across a land where four races of people (white, Indian, Métis and Inuit) live, where seven different languages are spoken; the first pipeline in the world to be buried in the permafrost. The inquiry is being asked to see what can be done to protect the people, the environment and the economy of the North if the pipeline goes ahead. The pipeline companies say that the impact of the pipeline will on the whole be beneficial to the North. That may or may not be true.

Social impact assessments involve a "systematic analysis in advance of the likely impacts a development event will have on the day-to-day life of persons and communities" (Burdge 2004: 2). They are now far more common than they were at the time of the Berger Inquiry, which was the first time in which the social impacts of a development on indigenous peoples was intensively probed in Canada. It was also the first case in which the decision not to proceed was based on an assessment of the social impacts (Gamble 1978; Berger 1983). Indeed, the Berger Inquiry is often considered the quintessential social impact assessment.

In many ways the process of the inquiry and the subsequent recommendations changed the face of Northern development, but not in a manner one would expect when large corporations come knocking on the door. At the heart of

5.2 Contested Constructions of the North

We look upon the North as our last frontier. It is natural for us to think of developing it, of subduing the land and extracting its resources to fuel Canada's industry and heat our homes. Our whole inclination is to think of expanding our industrial machine to the limit of our country's frontiers. In this view, the construction of a gas pipeline is seen as the next advance in a series of frontier advances that have been intimately bound up with Canadian history. But the native people say the North is their homeland. They have lived there for thousands of years. They claim it is their land, and they believe they have a right to say what its future ought to be....

The choice we make will decide whether the North is to be primarily a frontier for industry or a homeland for its peoples.

Source: Berger 1977: 1–2.

much of the debate was the political power of the Northern peoples to determine their own fate. The views of the proponents and opponents illustrate, respectively, the antipodal images of cosmos versus garden. The proponents advocated a view of the North as a frontier; the opponents advocated a view of the North as a homeland.

Impacts of development on the Mackenzie Valley

Most Canadians view the North as a largely unspoiled wilderness, a large, near-empty space waiting to be developed by whatever means necessary. Non-governmental organizations involved in the development of the North reasoned that the pipeline proposal provided a unique opportunity for appropriate development from the onset. One of them, the Canadian Arctic Resources Committee, was formed to give a voice to Northern people and to push for fair technical and socio-economic assessments of the proposal. In 1974 CARC (2001: 3) stated:

> The intent of CARC's intervention is not to stop the pipeline but to ensure that all the long-term social, economic and environmental consequences of a pipeline are brought to light and carefully considered by regulatory agencies in a manner that will enable Canadians to decide the many important issues that are involved.

Among other things, the inquiry raised issues around the pipeline's probable detrimental impact on caribou herds, birds, and other wildlife in the region and on the people who have relied on this wildlife for generations. The inquiry raised questions about the energy corridor's new infrastructure, which would have an impact on what had been until that time fairly isolated peoples. One reporter captured the sentiments of the day: "Some dismissed the impact of a pipeline, saying it would be like a thread stretched across a football field. Those close to the land said the impact would be more like a razor slash across the Mona Lisa" (O'Malley 2002).

Homeland

> I discovered that people in the North have strong feelings about the pipeline and large-scale frontier development. I listened to a brief by northern businessmen in Yellowknife who favour a pipeline through the North. Later, in a native village far away, I heard virtually the whole community express vehement opposition to such a pipeline. Both were talking about the same pipeline; both were talking about the same region—but for one group it is a frontier, for the other a homeland.
> —Thomas Berger, 1977.

The Berger Inquiry concluded that the Northern Aboriginal peoples were largely opposed to pipeline development occurring before their land rights were settled. The first volume of the inquiry's report, *Northern Frontier: Northern Homeland* (Berger 1977), called not only for a moratorium on development in the valley for ten years to enable the settlement of Aboriginal land claims but also for a permanent ban on pipeline development along the Yukon North Slope due to environmental and cultural issues. The second volume (Berger 1978) set forth terms and conditions for the future building of a pipeline in the Mackenzie Valley, after Aboriginal land claims were settled and the local peoples were in a better position to determine for themselves whether or not to go forward with the proposal.

The process of the Berger Inquiry set in motion an expanded process of self-determination. This has led to a number of factors that have changed the Northern socio-economic and cultural context. For example, most land claim matters have been settled, and communities have become less dependent on the land and/or more reliant on modern technology when on the land, increasing their need for monetary income. Combined with an increasing Northern population, there are now much stronger locally driven pressures to develop Northern resources to provide economic opportunities. According to one view, Northern governments have also gained in both power and experience, which has fostered greater Aboriginal influence on the nature of a new pipeline proposal and enhanced local community capacity (CARC 2001). In contrast, other groups, like CARC, believe that the time and events since the Berger Inquiry have created a dependency relationship, with oil and gas development especially excluding the possibility of alternative forms of development (which would include not developing the pipeline). As is the case in many impact assessments, the question had become when rather than if to build the pipeline.

By the turn of the century many of the Aboriginal groups who were key opponents of the initial proposal had changed their positions to be in favour of oil and gas development. In October 2001, in a Memorandum of Understanding (MOU), an Aboriginal Pipeline Group (APG) comprising Native communities along the proposed pipeline route joined four major Canadian oil and gas companies, called the Producer Group, which includes Imperial Oil Resources Ventures, Shell Canada, ConocoPhillips Canada, and Exxon Mobil Canada Properties. The MOU outlined principles for land access and benefit agreements, a negotiation process, and the right to acquire up to one-third ownership in the proposed pipeline. In June 2003 APG became full partners in the project. The consortium, including APG, Producer Group, and TransCanada Pipelines, brought forth a new proposal to construct a 1,200 kilometre pipeline to tap reserves in the Mackenzie River delta and then carry the gas up the Mackenzie Valley into Alberta and south to the United States. The mandate of the APG is to maximize ownership and benefits of a Mackenzie Valley pipeline so that Northern communities could take part in long-term socio-economic benefits rather than simply short-term cash (Inuvialuit Regional

5.3 Proposed Mackenzie Valley Pipeline

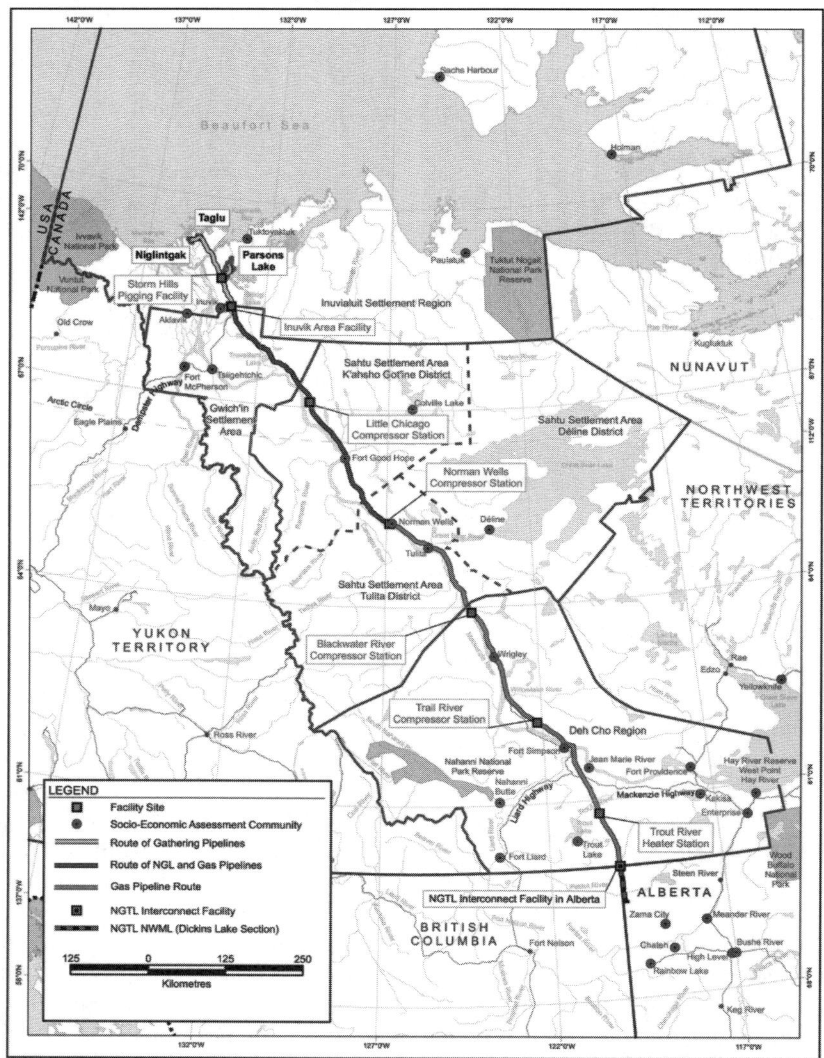

Source: Mackenzie Gas Project Regulatory Filing, Environmental Impact Statement in Brief. Available at Mackenzie Gas Project website.

Corporation 2002). The APG anticipates a number of potential benefits to Aboriginal peoples, including training, education, and employment and business opportunities; these are seen as means of supporting greater Aboriginal independence and self-reliance (APG 2004). Factors that led to the renewed interest in the pipeline include favourable market conditions—particularly increased demands for natural gas given diminishing conventional supplies, improved technological and construction methods, the settlement of the majority of Aboriginal land claims in the 1990s, and increased support from interested Northern parties.

Not everyone is pleased with this turn of events. Critics of the pipeline believe that the delay in the pipeline merely gave time for the communities to be exposed to a market economy and to become dependent upon that economy rather than on their subsistence economies. The shift in the social and cultural construction of the North by Aboriginals in response to developmental pressures has led to the real possibility of irreversible changes to the Northern landscape. CARC and other groups voice a number of outstanding concerns. For example, some Aboriginal land claims and self-governance issues are not yet settled, leaving these groups without an effective means of expressing their views. The terms of reference of the new proposal have limited the ability of the various First Nations groups to work collectively because those terms were discussed behind closed doors with limited representation from each community. For example, negotiation to have access to lands that fall with individual First Nation traditional territories were kept off the public record, and the public does not have access to the information in order to assess the equity of the negotiations from community to community. In addition, the proposed pipeline project remains a large and invasive industrial development that would introduce potentially great and cumulative risks. The impacts of increased patterns of development in the North have already fragmented and degraded some of the world's largest wilderness areas and in some places greatly damaged the health and well-being of Northern peoples.

What is the origin of this demand for the construction of the Northern landscape as a frontier? Both the North and South have the potential to gain from it, but the North will undoubtedly bear the costs. One of the reasons for the renewed interest in the pipeline is the increased demand for energy. Since the Free Trade Agreement of 1988 the United States has sought a continental energy market. Combined with the continuing U.S. desire for a stable domestic energy supply (from Alaska, for example) and in the face of a post-9/11 world of global terrorism, Canadians may face additional pressures to meet the demand. In the United States, in May 2001, a few months before the APG signed a MOU with the Producer Group, the National Energy Policy Development (NEPD) Group recommended that the U.S. president engage in dialogue to develop closer energy integration with Canada. A section of the document related to Canada mentions how the "private sector is poised to develop the continent's northern gas reserve, with pipeline linkages between both countries" (NEPD Group 2001: 8–8). The proposed Mackenzie Valley pipeline development, which advocates a construction of Northern landscape as frontier, is a result, then, of the pressures of increasing consumptive activities concentrated in the South (given higher population pressures and the desire for a secure energy supply) usurping space in the North, and thereby compromising the place-based lifestyles of the people living there (in particular, the Dene).

The frontier image of Canada's North is both justified by and legitimates the increasing consumptive patterns of Western, urban societies, particularly those south of the border. Canada "needs" to develop these Northern resources to foster its competitive place in the international economy. At the same time images of frontier limitlessness allow for rampant consumption and waste without concern for scarcity. As more accessible reserves are depleted, and as we need to penetrate ever further into the North to meet the demand, the economic rationale of constructing the Mackenzie Valley pipeline could again be reconstructed, this time in a manner that outweighs the social and environmental costs. Critics of the pipeline argue that this one-dimensional construction of the landscape closes off alternative visions of Northern development.

The Urban Landscape as Roadscape

Urban centres in Canada, as elsewhere, have historically been built up in economic transportation corridors, first alongside rivers and later alongside the railroad. The spatial structure of early cities reflected this economic reliance on water and rail transport. But perhaps the most profound change in this pattern occurred in the twentieth century with the advent of the automobile.

Automobile impacts on material space

The growing North American dependency on the automobile has made that vehicle one of the main contributors to the ecological footprint on the urban landscape. Between the 1950s and the 1990s the number of cars worldwide increased from just over fifty million to over four hundred million (Baird 1993). In the United States the automobile infrastructure (Freund and Martin 1993), encompassing millions of hectares of agricultural land, forests, and urban areas, now takes up at least 10 percent of arable land. Up to 60 percent of the land of some inner-city areas is paved over for use by cars (Baird 1993). But in addition land is required to dispose of used automobiles and automobile parts such as tires and batteries, which are not recycled; these waste disposal sites often damage local air and groundwater quality. All told, the "transformation of urban space by the auto and all of its accoutrements had profoundly reconfigured social life in the twentieth century" (Freund and Martin 1996: 111).

Automobiles have greatly contributed to the reorganizing of urban space, with **urban sprawl** the most notable evidence. Urban development traditionally focused upon public transit lines—trolleys, streetcars, buses, subways—but automobile use has led to an increased pace of **suburbanization** as people move away from city centres (Baird 1993). Rather than living in communities close to their places of work, great numbers of people have settled in suburban landscapes further and further from city centres, creating high densities of commuter traffic. Given that cities historically were located near good farmland, urban sprawl results in the consumption of what was often the best farmland. As South Coast Liveable Communities (2002) points out, sprawl not only devastates natural areas, including using up prime agricultural lands, woodlots, and wetlands, but also increases the demand for greater infrastructure, placing an increased burden on cities to fund and maintain growth that extends ever further from the urban centres—which in turn leads to the social and cultural decay of urban centres. Vehicles going in and out of the city tend to have single drivers, which results in a highly inefficient use of energy and limited road capacity, increased traffic congestion, and higher vehicle emissions and deteriorating air quality.

In 2001 more than half of Canada's population was concentrated in four broad urban regions: the extended Golden Horseshoe in Southern Ontario; Montreal and its adjacent region; the Lower Mainland of British Columbia and southern Vancouver Island; and the Calgary-Edmonton corridor. In the twenty-five year period between 1971 and 1996 Canada's cities and towns steadily expanded to an area equivalent to more than twice the land area of Prince Edward Island, representing an increase of 77 percent in urban land (Hofmann 2001). Declining average population density in Canadian cities (1,030 persons per square kilometre in 1971 to 799 persons per square kilometre in 1996) is another indicator of the increasing space consumption in urban areas. Since 1971 urban uses have consumed 12,000 square kilometres of land, half of it is considered dependable farmland or Class 1-2-3 land as classified by the Canada Land Inventory (Hofmann 2001).

Auto-centred transport systems also contribute to the increased homogenization of landscapes. Box malls (also known as big box retailers, superstores, or hypermarkets) are only possible in auto-centred communities. Consumers associate these stores, normally situated on the edge of urban areas, with lower-cost goods and greater convenience. Advocates argue that box malls provide much-needed money to sustain local infrastructures and provide local jobs. Anti-sprawl activists, also known as Sprawl Busters, argue that box malls not only use up valuable open space and contribute to traffic congestion and energy use, but also change a community's character. They place smaller, family owned or locally owned stores at a disadvantage. You usually have to own a car to get to them (Allison 1979; Norman 1999). Then too, when big box stores are abandoned as a result of economic competition or economic incentives to move to an even larger location, they leave behind them giant, unsightly, and useless "carcasses" (Weiss 2004).

Automobile impacts on social spatiality

Social spatiality refers to how space is intertwined with social practices and social processes. Automobiles and auto-centred transport systems have a huge impact on social spatiality, creating tension in land use in at least four ways: the increased individualization of social space; the reconfiguring of social spatiality spheres; shifts in time-space scapes; and the creation of spatial differences.

Individualization of social space. Social space adapts to the needs of the individual rather than to the needs of groups (Beckenbach 1989). Social space has been privatized and dispersed—examples are toll highways and the very expanse of roads across a landscape. The focus on auto-centred transportation systems results in a decreasing emphasis on public transportation systems. Rather than public transport, in which various social factions mix and mingle, we have public road spaces filled with individually driven automobiles that prevent interaction, enabling individuals to focus on individual needs (Freund and Martin 1996). Automobiles become a global form of "quasi-private" mobility subordinating other "public" mobilities (Sheller and Urry 2000).

Reconfiguring social spatiality. Social space becomes transformed into auto-dominated space. In the past public spaces featured coffee shops or small family-owned restaurants, with green spaces accessible by foot; now auto-centred transportation systems are dominant. Residential garages have replaced front porches. Highways, box malls, and drive-through fast-food restaurants overwhelm our community landscapes. The change is not simply a matter of rerouting people; the privilege accorded the automobile has done nothing short of reshaping citizenship and the public sphere (Sheller and Urry 2000). This form of mobility alters socio-spatial practices in many ways, including a decrease in walking and hence interacting with other community members. Immense subdivisions with massive lots per house result in less neighbour-to-neighbour contact, while fast-moving cars make the streets unsafe for children to play outdoors (Crawford 2002). The ideal of democratic citizenship—in which community members have ample opportunity to discuss contemporary concerns and formulate ideas for what is best for the community—is consequently in jeopardy (Project for Public Spaces n.d.).

Shifting time-space scapes. Auto-centred transport systems transform the urban/suburban dweller's time-space scapes (Sheller and Urry 2000). The notion of time becomes ambiguous, subjective, and desynchronized (in contrast, for instance, to the objective timetable of train travel). Social practices become fragmented and spatially stretched. The ability—and increasingly the need—to cover large distances in a short amount of time has increased the pace of contemporary life in North America. This capability has fragmented our lives into a series of interspersed moments of travel. Lives become segmented between moments of travel between home, work/school, recreational facilities, shopping. In the past, by comparison, there was less physical and temporal delineation between work and home. The increasing obsession with being "on time" adds stress to hurried lives and can work against a sense of community. One study showed that for every ten minutes that a person spends driving to work, there is a 10 percent drop in involvement community affairs (South Coast Liveable Communities 2002).

Geographer David Harvey (1990) coined the term **time-space compression** to describe the process by which space is reorganized in a way that reduces the constraints of time and time reduces the constraints of space. Time-space compression involves shortening time and shrinking space. The next time you get into a vehicle, think about how this technological innovation has altered your sense of time and space. In auto-centred cities it takes less time for goods and individuals to span great distances (unless you're in the middle of a traffic jam, of course). Another example is how the innovations of telecommunications have brought us the "global village." News that took months to travel halfway around the world now arrives instantaneously. Our conception of space-time shifts as a result of this time-space compression, which has implications for the types of experiences that we expect in day-to-day living (such as eating strawberries in mid-December).

Creating spatial differences. Increasing the space between the haves and have-nots: the massive suburbanization fostered by automobiles has resulted in significant changes in human ecological and social relationships with cities. The new cityscape, whether downtown or in the new subdivisions, is an environment in which it is difficult to walk or cycle, due to the long travel distances or the unsafe/unavailable walkways and bikeways. The increasing dependency on the automobile perpetuates a class system, marginalizing people, including the poor, who cannot afford the growing costs of automobile ownership; and the young, disabled, and elderly who are not capable of operating a vehicle. These people then have limited access to jobs, contributing to a cycle of poverty. Spatial segregation increases with auto-centred city planning, as zoning laws that support demands by the affluent for "cleaner, quieter neighbourhoods" on city outskirts leave less money to support the maintenance of city cores. Housing options for poor and minority residents are often limited to decayed urban cores. According to Peter Freund and George Martin (1996: 25), "There is differential access to the advantages (e.g., individual mobility) and disadvantages (e.g., exposure to polluted air)."

Given the impact of automobiles on social spatiality, we need to ask how our social practices and processes led to the domination of our landscapes—and particularly our urban landscapes—by roadscapes. Was this development the planned or unintended consequences of larger factors? Whose social construction of space is satisfied by urban roadscapes? People's dependency on automobiles in their day-to-day lives is often a result of policies that privilege the automobile over other means of transportation. Ted Schrecker (1996) argues that public policies influence transportation decisions and that these policies are influenced by a lack of vision and an overreliance on technology, which blinds political leaders from creating a more sustainable equitable transportation system. For example, income and property tax systems have made parking lots a highly lucrative form of land use in many Canadian cities. Road construction, defunding public transportation, mandatory liability, abandonment of downtown shopping areas, and failure to invest in renewable fuel alternatives are not personal choices (Beckenbach 1989); they are political and economic choices made by corporate and state actors working in concert to promote a particular development path to promote specific narrow interests. Shifting the investment of capital from rail to rubber-wheeled vehicles and the trends towards individualization and privatization impoverish the public sector, and yet require the public provision of infrastructure to function (Freund and Martin 1996). Auto-centred transport is thus a mode of consumption organized as a socially subsidized system of private consumption. The vehicle itself is a private cost, yet the infrastructure is a public cost (Freund and Martin 1996).

Rural Space: Playgrounds and Dumping Grounds

Despite the drastic changes that many of us have become accustomed to in our urban centres, when it comes to visions of our rural landscapes the garden myth continues to be especially strong in the collective cultural identity of Canada. Canadians put mythic places of nature, wilderness, and pristine landscapes at the centre of our sense of identity—as seen, for instance, in tourist advertisements to international audiences. To visitors from around the world, Canada is largely viewed as a land of natural beauty and abundance, of untouched wilderness. Names such as Clayoquot, Jasper, Hecla, Saguenay, Thousand Islands and Kejimkujik evoke a special sense of place to people in both Canada and the outside world.

Because of the established importance of nature, we have accomplished much as a society to protect our rural areas against harmful human activities. For example, Canada's land mass contains thirty-nine designated natural regions, each having a unique physical, climactic, and biotic makeup. Federal policy mandates that a portion of each of these regions be protected, and twenty-three regions now contain at least one of Canada's forty national parks and reserves. Despite such progress in setting aside these protected areas, their size remains minuscule relative to Canada's land mass as a whole.

The sense of national identity is so wrapped up in pride about rural places that Canadians often fail to realize how much the historic land-use decision-making and practices have contradicted the rural idyll that is valued so much in contemporary culture. For example, only 2 percent of Canada's territory is under the protection of national parks. The other 98 percent is left open to a myriad of human land uses, including agriculture, industry, resource exploration, and residential development. While most of Canada's land base is not occupied by human settlement, few places are untouched by human activities of some sort. Indeed, although rural change has been an integral part of our national development since the arrival of the first Europeans to Canada, the country's rural landscape is now changing at a faster pace than ever before.

5.4 Let the Love of Outdoors and Discovery Be Your Guide

Canada offers outdoor experiences like nowhere else on earth—pure, rugged and unspoiled. From mountains to coastlines, glaciers to secluded forests and lakes, there's so much to see and do that you could set out on an adventure all year round.

Canada is home to one of the world's largest networks of national parks and protected areas. Whether you're on the high Arctic, Pacific or Atlantic coasts, crossing the Canadian Shield, traveling the Great Lakes, or riding the prairie foothills or mountains, you'll experience extraordinary nature and true wilderness.

Canoe lakes and rivers, hike mountains and prairies, or watch polar bears in their natural habitat. Stay at a remote ski-lodge, sleep under the stars at a full service campsite, or relax at a luxurious resort. No matter what you choose you'll wake up to another day of adventure.

Source: Canadian Tourism Commission 2004.

The dumping ground: Dirty industries in the hinterland

Odds are, if you are a Canadian university student, you come from an urban part of the country. Since the 1930s Canada's urban population has surpassed our traditional rural heritage, and this gap has been steadily widening. To understand the impact of this demographic shift, we must travel outward from the city, past its sprawling subdivisions and into what might be considered the "rural countryside." In many places throughout the country, traditional land uses such as agriculture are being displaced by "dumping grounds"—waste incineration plants, flare stacks of industrial plants, intensive livestock operations, strip mines, oil sands operations, to name a few. Many of the worst elements of the cityscape—and especially air pollution and residential sprawl—are colonizing formerly agricultural and natural rural landscapes at an ever-increasing rate. The increasing pressures of our growing population and a host of economic, political, and cultural forces associated with globalization are the forces creating these new rural dumping grounds across the country.

At the outset of Confederation, Canada's federal government instituted a National Policy that encouraged new European immigrants to settle the West in order to boost the nation's agricultural capacity and in turn stimulate national productivity. Invoking exaggerated assurances about the productivity and opportunities of the West, as well as providing nearly free land and a newly constructed Canadian Pacific Railway, the government encouraged hundreds of thousands of immigrants to move to the West with high hopes for a prosperous future (Rollings-Magnusson

2000). In so doing, the government quickly succeeded in transforming the rural western landscape into an agricultural periphery that provided food and resources to the industrialized core. According to **staples theory**, this reliance on the export of natural resource "staples" for economic development has defined Canada's history and represents market and state power over the rural hinterland, virtually guaranteeing that future economic development will follow the same path (Innis 1930; see also Dunk 1991).

Since the beginning of the twentieth century Canada's rural landscape has been undergoing considerable changes with improvements in technology and the substitution of capital for labour in agricultural production. Beginning in 1921, as Canadians followed job prospects in our newly industrialized cities, more people lived in cities than in rural areas for the first time in our history, and this trend of urban migration has been steadily growing ever since (Bollman and Beshiri 2000). In the meantime the population of rural areas levelled off at about five million people. As farm sizes increased with the use of new technologies, farming communities declined; fewer employment opportunities in rural areas forced people in successive generations away from the land (Winson and Leach 2002).

Today agricultural productivity continues to increase with the rising global demand in international marketplaces created by trade agreements such as the North American Free Trade Agreement. But the modern, superindustrialized agri-businesses that now dominate the landscape offer few permanent, well-paying employment opportunities and have managed to outcompete formerly self-sufficient family farms (Singelmann 1996). As corporate farming continues to take over the countryside, and the populations of once-thriving agricultural communities continue to decline, there are few left who have the willingness and ability to resist the further transformation of the rural landscape from a way of life into a place to "do business" (Machum 2001).

In response to this demographic shift, many planners and decision-makers embarked upon a massive program of **rural restructuring**, attempting to locate manufacturing facilities in rural regions to absorb the workers who had become unemployed by capitalization in agriculture. The new jobs have proven to be equally unstable, and many of the income opportunities now available in rural communities that do not have a natural resource industry, such as a pulp mill, are low-paying, part-time or seasonal, and lack benefits (Winson and Leach 2002). Social changes that have accompanied rural restructuring include a massive **youth exodus** from rural areas, leaving the next generation of the agricultural community in peril.

Increasing communications and transportation technology in other sectors have further transformed rural regions as places to "do business." Our increasingly connected world no longer relies on spatial proximity to the marketplace or to the places where resources are obtained—which has

5.5 Population Trends: Rural minority in Canada in 1931

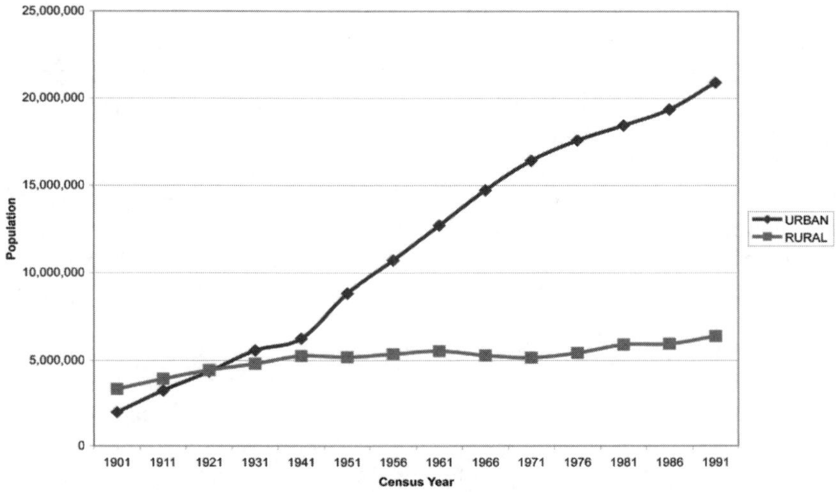

Source: Statistics Canada, Census of Population 1851–1996

led to industrial in-migration to the countryside with its often cheaper land and lower tax rates. Again, we are witnessing a time-space compression (Harvey 1990; Nelson 2001) that makes it possible to locate facilities in more remote locations where motivations such as cost, safety, and quality of life become factors into decision-making.

These transformations have not only transformed the physical landscape but also changed the social and cultural context of the communities that inhabit them. The changing economic priorities have led to conflict between agricultural land uses and industrial development. While the increased activities in rural areas create local jobs, those jobs are often transient and low-paying. In addition, transient workers and unstable jobs create tenuous local economic conditions in combination with the well-known **boom-bust cycle** that is an inherent part of industries located in rural areas (such as forestry and mining). In addition, natural resource-based companies exploiting the traditional lands of Aboriginal communities have disrupted trap lines, thereby destroying cultural ties to the land. The risks associated with industrial activity have created widespread concern about the health and safety of rural residents.

The playground: National parks in Canada

Urbanized Canadians do not easily relinquish their sense of rural identity. Although most Canadians now live in cities, they still look to the countryside to fulfil much of their cultural and recreational needs. For over a century now, Canadians have endeavoured to create special places in which to preserve nature. Many like to believe that a national parks system is a

5.6 Alberta's Industrial Heartland

In Alberta's Industrial Heartland a clash over space became abundantly obvious to community members who encountered a major industrial development proposed by local governments. In 1998 the region's economy was clearly on the cusp of attracting new major international petrochemical processing and manufacturing firms. Planners decided to prepare the political, economic, and physical landscape for the impending arrival of these facilities.

Within the Heartland a diverse community of farmers, retirees, and families has lived side by side with large-scale industrial facilities for decades. As an economic boon to the region, industries such as Dow Chemical and Shell Canada have contributed to the economic well-being of these communities and have invested considerably in promoting positive relationships with their citizen neighbours.

The prospect of further industrial development coupled with a declining agricultural sector contributed to conflict between local governments and citizens. Each has their own ideas about appropriate land use within the region. During the planning phase of the Heartland, this created conditions for a power struggle over whose vision for the landscape would prevail. On the one hand, development was seen as a social and economic opportunity—a means of sustaining a rural way of life through off-farm employment, and an industrial tax base to support the local economy. For example, one local politician made it clear that the economic benefits of the Heartland would prevail.

> Why should there be more industry? Well, I really can't understand why they would not want to see growth and development. And I guess I come from wanting to see growth because it can't stand still. If you stand still you go backward.... So where's our growth? Well, we're gonna grow from the petrochemical industry, because we have the feed stock here. Oil and gas. We have agricultural industry but that's really not a large part of our growth. Our large part of our growth and our future growth is oil and gas related.

On the other hand, many community members saw industry as incompatible with rural living and industrial development as a threat to the rural way of life and to people's health and safety. One older resident of the Heartland had concerns about the impact of the land-use changes on his life.

> That makes us feel increasingly anxious because we don't know what's in our future, you see, in the years that we have left. And it would be very difficult for us to leave the house boarded up or dismantled and not get any compensation for it. And then face the fact that we have to buy a new house, either a condominium or a senior citizen situation or whatever. You know. So that's our special problem because of our age.... I never thought that at my age I would find myself in a situation where I can't sell my house, and where I must buy another one to continue our life.

Tensions in the region were exacerbated by a lack of unity within the community. Economic restructuring within the region has resulted in a decline in the agricultural community and an increase in non-farm communities in rural areas. One local woman who had lived on a farm all of her life shared a personal poem about this tension.

A ride in the country on a summer day
Was a joy to the urban folk, so they say.
The calves were romping, the deer at play,
The geese were looking for a place to lay,
Do you think that the farm folk would care,
Or do you think they'd be willing to share?
It would just be an acre or three
Where the animals roam and the birds fly free.

For the urban folk a suggestion I make,
open both eyes for your own sake.
Look around before that move you make,
country living is not a piece of cake.
So beside a farm you choose to live,
the odours here, you have to forgive.
For we've been here a very long time,
Working the earth trying to make a dime.

So come and join us, the life is great,
But quit your grumping at our gate.
The deer and the birds now stay away,
because of the people, have come to stay.
The cow, the bird's friend is next to go.
On waste land they eat the growth down low,
so the young plants have a chance to grow,
and the weak seeds don't get a chance to blow.
—excerpts from "Friend or Foe," by Fran Kampjes

Despite differences between farmers and non-farmers, the local community came together to voice its concerns about industrial development in the Heartland. However, their struggle was curtailed by limited opportunities provided to them to be effectively included in decision-making before final plans were approved in 2001. In the wake of their frustrations, many community members vowed to continue the fight to prevent more industry from occupying the places they call home.

Source: Research by Jeff Masuda, 2004.

means of setting aside a part of our rural landscape from human economic development. According to Roderick Neumann (1998: 24), "A national park is the quintessential landscape of consumption for modern society." However, the physical environment within national parks rarely lives up to the mythic landscapes that exist in our imaginations.

The primary purpose of Canada's national parks is to protect natural areas for "public understanding, appreciation and enjoyment, while being maintained in an unimpaired state for future generations" (Parks Canada 2004a). In 1885 the government of Canada created the country's first national park in Banff, Alberta. Over the course of the next hundred years Banff National Park became the crown jewel of the national parks system. Beginning with a mere twenty-six square kilometres centred on the Banff hot springs, Canadian national parks now total nearly 250,000 thousand square kilometres (6,641 square kilometres in Banff National Park alone) or 2.5 percent of the entire area of Canada.

Despite the current conservationist ideals, in the beginning national parks were basically a means by which the government could assert its claim over natural resources that it deemed economically advantageous to hold for itself. In Banff the discovery of the Cave and Basin mineral hot springs by employees of the Canadian Pacific Railway compelled the government to create the original small reserve of land in order to exploit the region as a health resort for the public travelling through on the newly established railway (McNamee 1993). With this new impetus to profit from "natural areas," in 1887 the government passed the Rocky Mountain Park Act to extend Banff to nearly 700 square kilometres. For the first half-century of its existence, Banff National Park was actively used not only for recreational activities, but also for timber and other natural resource development.

By the early twentieth century Banff National Park (and by this time several others) was growing in popularity so much with the Canadian population that the economic value of the park's tourism activities far outweighed its natural resource endowments. In 1911 the federal government, through the Dominion Forest Reserves and Parks Act, shifted parks policy away from "places to do business" to places in which "there will be no business except such as is absolutely necessary for the recreation of the people" (McNamee 1993). According to the first commissioner of the newly established National Parks Branch, the designated areas "should exist in order that every citizen of Canada may satisfy his soul-craving for Nature." Indeed, over the next fifty years this new craving for nature became an increasingly powerful lobby in Canada, and the tourist economy of the national parks paved the way for a whole new set of values around recreation, camping, and outdoor leisure as a staple of the average Canadian family. By 1930 Parliament had passed the National Parks Act to reorient the philosophy of parks to reflect these changing values. From then on, natural resources development was discontinued, and timber and

5.7 Since October 2000, members of the Kwelkwetwelt Protection Centre have defended Aboriginal rights against expansion of the Sun Peaks ski resort in B.C.

Photo: Colin Brown/Artists Against War

wildlife protection and management became a new priority.

Beginning in the 1960s, the appreciation for and use of national parks gained a further boost through massive public mobilization connected with the environmental movement. A growing discontent with the government handling of national parks led to the establishment of an independent watchdog organization, the National and Provincial Parks Association of Canada (now the Canadian Parks and Wilderness Association of Canada) to ensure that public values figured prominently in park decision-making and management (McNamee 1993). Between the 1960s and 1980s, the national parks system became more fully integrated into federal government policy, and with the leadership of Jean Chrétien, Minister of Indian Affairs and Northern Development between 1968 and 1974, a massive expansion of national parks took place across Canada.

With the renewed federal interest in promoting national parks, the promotion and development of new park initiatives was no longer under the purview of localities. The expansion of national parks came under fire in many communities, especially Aboriginal, as opposition cemented around lack of attention to local concerns about land use. The situation took a serious twist when the federal government forced the relocation of communities that were within the proposed boundaries of new national parks. For example, in Kouchibouguac National Park in New Brunswick, some twelve hundred residents were removed from their communities as a means of restoring the natural "landscapes." In other cases efforts to remove any semblance of human activity denied the age-old existence of Aboriginal relationships with the land. The idea that "nature" must preclude human occupancy was, and still is, naive and can be counterproductive to progressive land-use management. The presence of national parks has also made life difficult for adjacent communities because certain forms of development are foreclosed (Fortin and Gagnon 1999).

Are national parks in Canada, then, a legitimate effort to preserve nature, or just another "resource" exploited by urbanites seeking refuge in the unspoiled countryside? Then too, why do Canadians feel, now more so than ever, that nature is so important that it should be protected? What are the implications of the growing pressure being put on Canada's national parks? The use of recreation areas in Canada has been increasing at a faster rate than is the ability or will of government to maintain, refurbish, and improve national parks within funding limits (Van Sickle and Eagles 1998).

Banff National Park, for instance, is on offer as one of Canada's finest "resources" in the international tourism marketplace. Each year more than four million visitors come to Banff to participate in a myriad of recreational activities that impinge on the natural landscape (Parks Canada 2004b). The park has more than 2,400 campsites available for tourists, which means that small "cities" of campers occupy the park in summer months. Many campers use large recreational vehicles, which impose a much larger environmental burden than smaller trailers and tents (Parks Canada 2003). The result is an increased demand for camping areas with serviced hookups and more paved roads, electricity, and sewage disposal. The town of Banff alone has over 4,500 hotel rooms available. The human impact on the regional landscape in the form of pollution, commercial and residential development, and population growth has become a major threat to natural ecosystems.

In general, park boundary concerns such as logging, industrial development, and hunting are isolating national parks so much that many have reached the point of being fragmented pockets of "wilderness" in an otherwise very non-wild landscape. Transboundary pollution and other effects are harming the ability of park managers to maintain the ecological integrity of the parks.

The idea of national parks as special refuges for "nature" to exist untouched by human activity is, then, a myth. The efforts that Canadians have taken to create, develop, and maintain natural parks are under threat in many areas of the country. Responsible human activity has a role to play in the maintenance and preservation of these important areas, but the demand for access to "nature's playground" is far outstripping the ability of government resources to prevent our parks from becoming very "unnatural" places subject to significant ecological and environmental pressures.

5.8 Consuming Nature in Jasper National Park

photo credit: Jeff Masuda

A Landscape under Pressure

In Canada our sense of national identity is deeply connected to our mythic landscapes. If these mythic landscapes disappear, so too will our national identity as we know it. Canada, a land of vast space, is increasingly becoming urbanized, fragmented, and depleted of the resources that provided, among other things, our initial identity as a nation. For many Canadians this trend is deeply troubling.

Urbanization has transformed the landscape. Cities are turning into concrete jungles: increasingly downtown cores are tearing up historic sites; green spaces are on the decline in favour of residential and commercial development. New pressures on the rural landscape have transformed large areas of Canada into "dumping grounds" and "playgrounds" for our growing urban population.

An airplane ride over any part of the country provides a clear visual picture of the impact of human activity on the landscape. The airport liftoff reveals the intricate network of buildings, housing, power lines, and roadways—and all they bring with them—extending into the countryside. From the pleated-quilt appearance of much of southern Quebec, Ontario, and the Prairies to the fragmentation of the boreal forests by seismic lines, oil and gas development, and forestry, we can see fewer and fewer rural places that have been left untouched by our increasing economic appetite.

The pressures have led, for example, to the B.C. forest fires, which resulted from the oversuppression of fires, and to the Red River disaster, which resulted from flooding in areas in which increased human populations encroached on areas unsuitable for occupation. As industrial and recreational land use pressures continue to rise in rural Canada, and in some locations population pressures as well, such disasters will only continue to increase in their rate and seriousness.

What Can We Do?

On an individual level, we could certainly benefit by using less space. We could consciously reflect on our use of space and adopt changes in lifestyle to use less space and reduce our ecological footprint. As we walk from place to place in the city, we could think why space has been constructed in the way it has. Are there alternatives? For example, how many parking lots can you count in a typical commercial district in your neighbourhood? What is the bus service like to that same place? When you eat, think about the geography of the food on your plate. Where has it come from? What resources were required to transport it from its origin to your local market? As an alternative, you can shop at the farmer's market (you'll be supporting local producers and reducing transportation needs), eat locally grown (apples, not bananas, for instance) and in-season fruits and vegetables (carrots, turnips, potatoes are available in the winter).

At the community level, you can choose to live in areas that encourage less space-intensive practices. Either live close to work or work close to home, so that you can more easily bike or walk between the two. To reclaim land from asphalt, actively support mass-transport systems. Next time you're planning to move, include a spatial analysis in your decision-making. You can also work with your neighbours to take back the streets in front of your homes, making them safe for children to play on and people to congregate on, by posting signs that urge drivers to slow down and by campaigning for speed bumps.

At the societal level, you can help to promote alternative visions of space. Search out activities and social movements that are aimed at reclaiming space. A few examples:

1. **International Car Free Day**. Join the over one hundred million people from over fifteen hundred cities around the world to promote alternatives to an auto-centred transportation system by leaving your car at home on a set day in September (usually around the 22nd). (See Car Free Day website).
2. **Place Jamming**. Involves reinserting nature into our perception as a counter-image to contemporary urban space being used to promote consumerism; essentially it involves reclaiming urban spaces for nature. Consider how ivy growing on the side of buildings or billboards

5.9 Critical Mass Vancouver

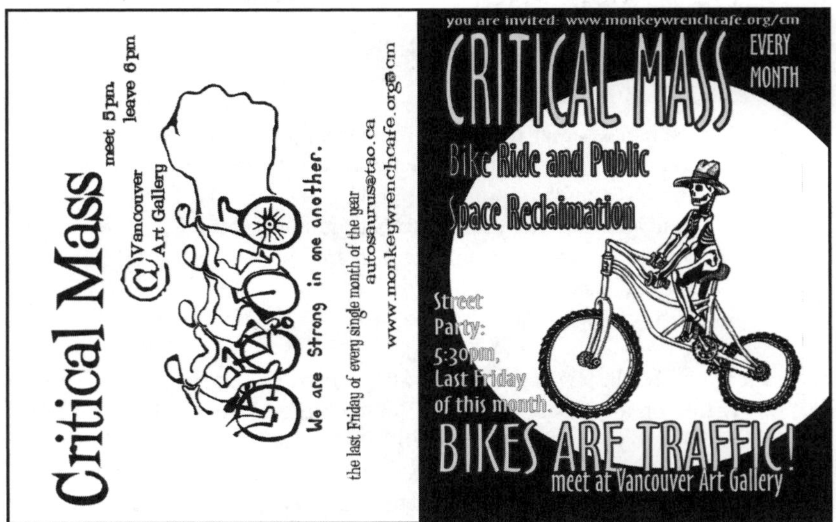

juxtaposes the built environment against the natural environment. Such an image captures the sense of nature reinserting itself into a landscape otherwise devoid of nature's touch. Jeremy Lundholm (n.d.), a Ph.D. student at the University of Guelph, provides a number of examples of place-jamming activities, including "guerrilla gardening, restoring native plant communities, media-free space, quiet zones, dark zones, car-free areas, and green mapping."

3. **Critical Mass**. A grassroots movement, spreading around the world, that aims at reclaiming public space by cycling (see Critical Mass website).

Note

1. Accounts and analysis of the Mackenzie Valley Pipelines inquiry are drawn from a number of sources, including CARC 2001; Struzik 2004; Pearce 1974; Helwig n.d.; and O'Malley 2002.

6. The Air up There

Debra J. Davidson and Josh Evans

> I asked him whether there was a great fire anywhere?
> For the streets were so full of dense brown smoke
> that scarcely anything was to be seen.
> "O dear no, miss," he said. "This is London particular."
> "A fog, miss," said the young gentleman.
> "O indeed," said I.
> —Charles Dickens, *Bleak House* 1881.

As readers of Charles Dickens know, air pollution is nothing new. But our ways of thinking about air pollution have changed over time. The pollution-infested smogs of nineteenth-century London, although a nuisance, were often seen as a sign of progress given their intimate association with advancing industry. Smog was also only perceived of as a local phenomenon, a "London particular." The working classes of London had no escape from the dirty air, but wealthy Londoners could at least relieve their senses of sight and smell by escaping the nuisance—by leaving the city for the pastoral landscapes of England's hinterlands.

Today we recognize air pollution as a serious health risk, and we know that many of the toxins in our air, unlike the dark fogs of old London, are undetectable. Consequently, although exposure to air pollutants is still in many ways influenced by class, ethnicity, and other social inequalities, our human senses do not serve as a reliable detection system. We instead rely on scientific expertise, civil servants, and elected politicians to warn us of danger. The question for many people at risk today is: can we rely on our expert scientists and government representatives to provide us with all of the information we need to make informed choices about our health?

Air pollution is now a central focus of the scientific and policy communities in Canada, with six issues dominating political conflict and debate: climate change, stratospheric ozone depletion, acidic deposition, smog, suspended particulate matter, and hazardous air pollutants (Munn and Maarouf 1997). The complexity of each individual issue is magnified because the six are interrelated; policy solutions for one may not necessarily improve the whole.

Thinking about air pollution can tell us much about how the relationships between our societies and environments have changed over time. Air pollution today is still an issue raised and addressed at the local level, but in many respects it has simultaneously become a global phenomenon, connecting industrial activities and citizenry around the globe. Activities undertaken on a distant continent can, for instance, have ramifications for a rural community in British Columbia, and vice versa.

Air Pollution in Contemporary Society

Urban airsheds

The sources of pollution have certainly expanded since Dickens's time. As Dickens's colourful depictions of nineteenth-century London suggest, air pollution has historically been associated with urbanization. The first sites of industrial production were concentrated in communities close to transportation routes, and those regions quickly attracted numerous people who migrated from the hinterlands to work in the new factories, forming densely populated urban areas. The new residents, as well as the factories, were reliant on coal for heat, and during the Industrial Revolution rapidly growing cities quickly became the locales, not just of serious sanitation problems, but also of overhanging clouds of pollutant-rich air. Few efforts were made to remedy the situation; dirty air was simply considered a price to pay for industrialization and the jobs that came with it.

Today urban areas are still the main sites of air pollution, as they remain the centres of industrial activity. Long-term exposure to poor air quality is a hazard to public health, even, as many scientists suggest, at concentrations below currently accepted standards. The concentration of health risks in urban areas is called the urban health penalty (Greenberg 1991), referring to how the confluence of poverty, unemployment, lack of housing, lack of services, and environmental pollution culminate in a health crisis of growing proportions. As industrialization extends to developing countries, so too does the process of urbanization. About 40 percent of the world's population now lives in cities, and in twenty-five years it is anticipated more than 60 percent of the world will call the city home (Brockerhoff 1996). Cities in low-income and middle-income countries are now among the most populated—and most polluted—areas on the globe.

Other aspects of air pollution have changed more dramatically. Since the Second World War, one of the primary culprits causing urban air pollution has been the private automobile, a virtual non-factor in the first half of the twentieth century and now no longer seen as a luxury good but as a necessity of life. Many people who live in urban areas must drive considerable distances to get to their jobs, often because the neighbourhoods they work in are either prohibitively expensive to live in or have become so dilapidated that safe and comfortable housing is no longer available. At the same time many of the neighbourhoods people live in have no amenities, such as grocery stores, hardware stores, coffee shops, and movie theatres, within walking distance. Our cities have become compartmentalized living spaces; we live in one region, work in another, and shop in yet another area.

We often hear the comment, "that's just the way it is," but these features of modern living are the result of decisions made, and still being made, among the political and economic elite who are closely involved in

6.1. Economics of Private Automobiles

The annual driving costs for someone who drives a subcompact for 12,000 kilometres a year on average is about $8,377 (with fixed annual ownership costs of $6,997 and a variable annual operating cost of $1,380). There are also significant hidden costs that we all pay for regardless of whether we even own a vehicle. These costs come in the form of health care, air pollution, highway and road building and maintenance, and ambulance and police services and can amount to several thousand dollars per year.

Sources: CAA, "Driving Costs" website; Gomberg 1996.

policy-making. Our dependency on automobiles is an outcome of policies that privilege the automobile over other means of transportation (Schrecker 1996). A different set of historical decisions could have created very different cities. Cities planned in a more integrative fashion, for example, can be more easily traversed on foot or bicycle, as are many European communities that were settled before the predominance of the private automobile. The millions of dollars spent each year on highway expansion could be spent on rapid transit. City planners could limit urban sprawl through zoning, ensuring the availability of housing near areas where most people work.

Road construction, the de-funding of public transportation, the abandonment of downtown shopping areas, and a failure to invest in renewable fuel alternatives are political and economic choices made by corporate and state actors working in concert to promote a particular development path. The enormous infrastructure needed to support automobiles, furthermore, comes from public coffers that we all replenish with our taxes. While vehicles themselves represent a private cost, the infrastructure is a public cost (Freund and Martin 1996). Within this system, many individuals simply have no choice but to rely upon a private automobile. Access to jobs is often conditioned by access to an automobile (Kasarda 1989, cited in Freund and Martin 1996). Particularly as the costs of automobile ownership continue to rise, those living in poverty end up facing additional burdens as limited public transportation options constrain the ability of people living without a car to seek and maintain employment.

Our car-dependent societies are fostered by other factors as well. The cultural propensities of consumers play a large role. Despite campaigns in several urban regions across Canada to support carpooling, only a small percentage of Canadian commuters take up that option. Apparently they prefer the comfort, privacy, and identity offered by their own vehicles, and many of those vehicles are large, inefficient Sport Utility Vehicles—so fitting to Western cultural identities that consumers are willing to pay over $50,000 just to own one of them. As a result, residents of places like Toronto are paying the price with their own health.

The interplay between structural influences such as policy-making, corporate advertising, and mass media coverage, and our own influence, or "agency," as individual citizens and consumers is called **structuration**

(Giddens 1993): individuals are neither hapless pawns in a world defined by larger, immutable structures and institutions, nor are they completely immune to the influences of those institutions. Structures, such as city planning policies, shape who we are and what we do, but those policies are nonetheless social artifacts, and we in turn have the ability to (re)shape those structures. Social change is thus defined by this interplay between structure and agency. (See also chapter nine, "Structural Explanations."

6.2 Automobiles and Health

In Southern Ontario summer is affectionately known as "smog season." Why? First, Ontario has three coal-fired power generating plants, where production has been increasing rapidly since the mid-1990s. Second, many Toronto residents actually live in the many suburban neighborhoods dotting the urban outskirts, and they drive into the downtown core to work. Some people commute from over 100 kilometres away. Finally, much of Ontario's smog migrates from other locales in the Great Lakes region. Because of the confluence of water-based transit routes, many heavy industries dependent on shipping their goods to Europe and other parts of the West have been belching out effluents for nearly two hundred years. The communities bordering the Great Lakes make up one of the most heavily industrialized regions in the world on both sides of the border. And the outcome for Toronto? A medical research study on the effects of air pollution on Toronto residents found that between 730 and 1,400 premature deaths and 3,300 to 7,600 hospital admissions each year can be attributed to poor air quality. Other estimates place these figures at over 2,000 and 14,000, respectively.

Source: Pengelly et al. 2000.

Rural airsheds

Air pollution is also not solely an urban issue. While urban residents with the means to do so used to be able to escape the dregs of the city by heading for the idyllic, pastoral landscapes of the country, that rural landscape is now no longer free of air pollution. Given the falling costs of shipping over the past fifty years, many manufacturing companies have taken advantage of cheap rural land prices and, frequently, lower labour costs. Even when industrial production methods have been refined so that less pollution is emitted per unit of production, the increase in intensity has led to several instances of heavy pollution in rural areas. As well many traditional farming activities—especially the livestock industry—have also themselves become sources of pollution due to the intensification of production. The sheer volume of waste product in a concentrated area leads to the pollution of both airsheds and watersheds. A rural community with livestock operations, for example, can produce greater levels of sewage than do many cities—yet this sewage does not undergo treatment in the way that municipal sewage does. Rather, it is usually simply dumped on the land.

People living in rural areas also often show less resistance to pollution because, like the residents of London over a century ago, they see dirty air as "the sweet smell of money" (Gould 1991)—and this is especially true in rural towns that are highly dependent on a small number of industries to provide jobs to local residents. Many companies resort to what social scientists call **job blackmail** (Kazis and Grossman 1982)—arguing that the costs of complying with strict environmental regulations will force them to cut their workforces—and as a result local residents often side with their employers in opposition to stricter environmental regulations. When rural regions become more diversified, residents often challenge these economic interests (as we will see in the story of a conflict over sour gas drilling in rural communities surrounding Edmonton).

No borders

One of the most important features of our contemporary understanding of air pollution has to do with the geography of that pollution, which tends to ignore our politically defined borders. At least to the extent that nineteenth-century observers were aware, the causes and effects of air pollution happened in one place. The brown London fogs were caused by London factories and residents, and the effects were felt by Londoners. Today cause and effect are no longer geographically contained: air pollution experienced in Toronto is in part due to activities in Detroit, and vice versa. On another scale, chlorofluorocarbons—used, for example, in the air conditioners and refrigerators of North America—have led to the depletion of the ozone layer.

Airsheds represent a classic common pool resource (see chapter three). On the one hand, even though everyone benefits from the air we breathe, no one owns it, and we have all effectively treated clean air as a free good. On the other hand, one person's—or country's—degradation of air hurts us all. The United States benefits economically from its production of CO2 emissions; yet everyone, not just Americans, pays the price because the resultant global warming harms all other parts of the world. Air is also subject to the free-rider problem. The resources spent by Ontario to clean its airshed will benefit Detroit, regardless of whether Detroit helps to pay for such efforts. In the worst-case scenario, no one acts unless everyone can be made to act. Airsheds have consequently been used throughout history as a **pollutant sink**. We have externalized the costs of economic development onto our public goods. Those paying the highest costs in personal health and quality of life as a result of air pollution are in many cases the very groups of people who had no part in the decision-making that led to the production or perpetuation of pollution, and they are least likely to reap the rewards (Bullard 1993; Cole and Foster 2001; Szasz 1994)—the impoverished urban residents, who also tend to be Black, Latino, or Aboriginal, living in neighbourhoods closest to heavy industry, for example. Some social scientists and activists provide evidence of **environmental racism**, or the tendency for racial and ethnic minority groups to face greater risks of pollution, regardless of their socio-economic status. Mohai and Bryant (1992) found that minorities are four times more likely to live within one mile of a hazardous waste facility than are white residents in the metropolitan region of Detroit.

Once they reach global risk status, however, environmental hazards become quite democratic, threatening everyone regardless of race or class because there is no escape. The global village becomes a global village of victims (Beck 1995, 1999). Given the impossibility of containing pollutants once they are in the air, the victims of air pollution can in many cases live far downwind from the source. When the Chernobyl nuclear power plant exploded in 1986, people were hurt not solely in the towns surrounding the plant but also as far away as Western Europe—and including citizens who received no benefits from the existence of the power plant

The Risk Society

Canada, the United States, and most of Western Europe, among other countries, have entered a "speculative age" dominated by the heightened awareness of environmental risks. Increasingly, risks such as the pervasive toxins and contaminants in our food, water, and air that evade easy detection and stay in the environment for generations, or catastrophes posed by the potential for accidents at facilities such as nuclear power plants and oil refineries, are sources of anxiety, insecurity, and feelings of dread. Global climate change, a result of the multiple technological developments that have polluted our airsheds, has become one of the most significant global risks. Whereas in the past technology was seen as the cornerstone of progress, in many cases modern technologies are now approached with fear, anxiety, and even dread, which is in some cases so acute that it becomes the source of psychological strain (Freudenburg 1997) and social conflict (Couch and Kroll-Smith 1985; Beck 1995), particularly among residents living near high-risk facilities.

Sociologists such as Ulrich Beck and Anthony Giddens (Beck 1992, 1999; Giddens 1990, 1991) argue that the primary source of conflict in late-industrial societies has now become the unintended harmful consequences of technological progress—the "bads." These **negative externalities** of modern industrial society have opened up new social cleavages. While the steadfast moral questions of old centred on the appropriate allocation of wealth, new moral questions centre on the allocation of dangers, hazards, and threats (Beck 1992; Douglas 1992). One of the key qualities of the threats that are transforming our world into this **risk society** is that in most cases we are not capable of detecting the risks with our human senses. Most forms of chemical contamination, radiation, ozone depletion, and even climate change are only detectable through science. As a result, the average person depends on science and scientists when it comes to identifying risks. Modern risks are not only invisible, but also irreversible, potentially globally catastrophic, and ambiguous. They are thus subject to multiple causal interpretations (Beck 1992).

What is risk?

Risk is a curious creature. Risks are future-oriented in the sense that they have yet to occur, yet they exert tremendous influence on the present. Open any newspaper, turn to any television channel, and you are bound to read or hear the word "risk." Although anxiety, fear, and danger have always been part of the human experience, only recently have these elements been expressed through the concept of risk.

Risk also implies a desire to *control* the future, however, and this may be the crucial difference between our contemporary risk society and social systems of the past: having grown up in a secular, proto-scientific society, to a greater extent than ever before many of us have come to expect a certain amount of personal control over our futures. Risks are pervasive, powerful social constructs that are increasingly becoming part of the everyday vocabulary that people use to make sense of uncertainty, insecurity, and danger (Wilkinson 2001). Speaking of the Western world, Iain Wilkinson (2001: 5) states, "It is now understood that we have become culturally disposed to express our anxieties in the language of risk, or conversely, it is through the cultural production of a new knowledge of the risks we face that our lives are conceived as having a new quality of insecurity."

Environmental risks are becoming a source of societal disruption and conflict not only because of a growing awareness of the risks themselves but also because our expectations for increased control and security are being met with just the opposite: uncertainty, insecurity, and growing unease regarding the ability of responsible institutions in government, science, and industry to do their job.

Institutional responses to risk

One source of this growing unease is the increasing scepticism that many of us have come to hold for the predominant strategies that modern institutions employ to manage risks. Called techno-scientific management (Beck 1992), this approach conceptualizes risks and hazards as being subject to scientific reduction and control. Risk assessments involve elaborate calculations to quantify the chance of an undesirable event, usually expressed in terms of mortality. Techno-scientific management consists of varying combinations of toxicological and epidemiological identification methods, combined with control mechanisms, such as probabilistic risk assessments, pollution control devices, and waste disposal technologies, all based on modern engineering. By anticipating potential harm to human beings, generalizing these events over time and space, and estimating the probability of an accident occurring, these approaches hold powerful sway among politicians and other decision-makers; they make risks appear to be controllable either by eliminating hazards altogether or through technological management practices that mitigate the harmful effects. Central to this approach is the belief that a certain level of risk (for example, in releases of a toxin from a chemical factory) exists that can be accepted in exchange for the benefits that accrue. Assessing this risk-benefit tradeoff is one way of making complex decisions around hazards (Leiss and Chociolko 1994); the chance of loss and the potential benefits associated with a particular risk are typically reduced to a single metric—a common unit for the purposes of making comparisons across qualitatively different items. Given that the benefits in question are usually economic, and the losses are usually compromises in the form of health or fatalities, this measurement often requires putting a dollar figure on lives. Decisions in favour of risky activities are often premised on the logic that if the economic benefits outweigh the economic risks, the activity should be permitted. In the case of risks such as air pollution, the notion of **acceptable risk** is grounded in the belief that biological and ecological systems can tolerate a certain level of pollution; the environment has an assimilative capacity within which no observable effects are present (Thornton 2000).

Do they work?

This techno-scientific model presents a number of problems when it comes to modern risks. According to Vincent Covello and Jerry Mumpower (1985), modern technological hazards are characterized by science's inability to accurately assess either their potential magnitude (before or after the event) or the underlying cause-effect relationship that led to the occurrence.

Many of the risks we face are relatively new: new pesticides, new energy sources, new industrial processes are developed all the time. Even nuclear power is a relatively new phenomenon. While the standard formulas of probabilistic risk assessment may be quite useful for assessing the probability of incidents for which we have plenty of historical data (such as the probability that a sixteen-year-old male Mustang driver living in Toronto will get into an accident), the lack of historical experience with new technologies means that we don't really have enough information to calculate the probabilities of hazard.

Unanswerable questions also exist around cumulative exposures and their synergistic effects on humans. Achieving any certainty in relating a person's health condition to one chemical in his or her environment is extremely difficult because of the impossibility of isolating that chemical from all the other chemicals the person has been exposed to over the course of a month, year, or lifetime (cumulative exposure) and the uncertainty of the effects when a "toxic cocktail" is mixed together in the body (synergistic effects). Our ability to assess dose-response relationships also tends to fall short when we consider long-term, low-level exposures (chronic exposures), due to the difficulty of conducting research over the entire course of a human lifetime.

Then too, many of the technologies in regular use in our lives are so complex that we ought to think, more realistically, of accidents as "normal" occurrences rather than as anomalies that with a little diligence we can learn to avoid. Charles Perrow (1984) analyzed several modern technological-industrial systems, illustrating that they are interactively complex. A single operating system consists of several interconnected components that interact in a non-linear fashion and are tightly coupled. A problem with one component will instigate a ripple effect throughout the system, moving with such speed that minor mishaps—even something as simple as a burned-out warning-light bulb—can quickly become major systematic failures. Such analyses ultimately raise the question of whether we should come to accept such risks or avoid adopting these complex technologies at all.

Those institutions that we rely on to operate in flawless fashion are filled with humans, after all, humans who are subject to institutionally prescribed behavioural norms (what sorts of activities are condoned, what types of issues are okay to bring up in meetings, what behaviours get rewarded) just like the rest of us. A number of empirical studies have shown how the very institutional norms and procedures that characterize complex organizations are the source of catastrophe (Vaughan 1990; Clarke 1993). According to these studies, members of these organizations, just like the rest of us, find it hard to believe in the possibility of, much less prepare for, the worst possible catastrophe. Fire drills, for example, are designed to prepare us for responding to building fires. But think of the last time you were involved in a fire drill. Did you review the location of all exits? Check closed doors for heat before opening? Take the elevator? That same tendency to disregard the real possibility of a fire, and thus prepare yourself for its occurrence, is exhibited in employees working in a chemical-processing plant or on an oil tanker. In general, scientists, bureaucrats, and company employees tend to develop a sense of confidence in and support for the technologies over which they have responsibility, so that they tend to disregard information (and the residents, scientists, and others who bring forth such information), or entertain in their own imagination, notions that their convictions may be wrong.

In the past we have depended on our government institutions and expert systems to protect us from the harmful effects of toxic substances in our communities, homes, and bodies. But as overconfidence leads to mishap time and again, we begin to lose trust in the ability of those institutions and systems to protect us. It is sometimes not the magnitude of the risk that fuels conflict; instead it is the lack of complete trust in the institution. William Freudenburg's use of the concept **recreancy**, "the failure of institutional actors to carry out their responsibilities with the degree of vigor necessary to merit the societal trust they enjoy," goes a long way in explaining why concern levels can remain high even when evidence of hazard is lacking (Freudenburg 1993: 909).

Techno-scientific approaches fail, then, to account for the organizational dynamics operating in technological systems, and they tend to lose resonance when applied to the problems of low probability–high consequence hazards (Freudenburg 1992). By reducing risks to statistics of physical harm or mortality, the techno-scientific approach excludes other ways in which risk is experienced and selected for attention (Douglas 1986, 1992). Despite these criticisms, technical approaches are attractive to policy-makers because they provide substantive foundations for direction in the form of comparable numbers.

The politics of air: Beyond objectivity

In risk cultures techno-scientific approaches to risk assessment, and scientific knowledge more broadly, stand at the centre of the growing conflict over environmentally induced illness and disease. Scientific knowledge about the effects of toxic substances in the environment is rarely objective; it is influenced by a number of factors, including politics. Expert rationalities are never truly objective; they are embedded in social and institutional settings that shape the assessment of risk.

This "situatedness" is often overlooked, though, most importantly by scientists themselves. Science, after all, carries with it an aura of certainty, value-neutrality, and status, and it is often used as a source of authority in environmental health controversies. In many instances, this authority only serves to mask the tremendous uncertainty and lack of knowledge associated with complex technologies, such as nuclear power, as power wielders overstate the degree of certainty that exists in an effort to avoid controversy (Wynne 1982).

As many citizens' groups and environmental organizations have also come to regularly employ science to support their claims, risk controversies are replete with experts and counter-experts, evidence and counterevidence, which only exacerbates the level of uncertainty and distrust experienced by individuals. Sociologists have found evidence of a direct relationship between the degree of uncertainty associated with certain scientific "expert" accounts, and public trust in the legitimacy of official accounts of danger, risk, and potential effects. In essence, we live in an era of "manufactured uncertainty"—in many instances, increases in knowledge generated about a particular threat only generates more uncertainty (Beck 1999). Special interests vie for control over the generation of and access to information regarding risks, over the ability of citizens to voice their concerns, and ultimately over the regulatory agencies that set the standards of precaution.

These controversies are exacerbated when ordinary people come into contact with air pollution in a way that is far removed from the techno-scientific ways of assessing risk. Ordinary people experience air pollution in their everyday lives and through the senses of their bodies— the smell of hazardous pollutants and the sight of polluting sources such as smoke stacks, for example. Just as important as these local ways of knowing are our methods of assessing risk: what many of us define as risky includes not only probabilities of injury or death but also threats to our families, cultural values, ways of life, and autonomy. We also consider other factors not included in the techno-scientific approach, like the level of dread associated with the risk, and our individual abilities to control our exposure to risks. In other words, while scientific experts tend to assess risks as a matter of objective and quantifiable variables (Fischoff et al. 1978, 1981; Slovic, Fischoff, and Lichenstein 1980), the rest of us employ a far more complex approach that includes, for example, the use of **heuristics**, which serves as a means of associating the risk to other experiences that may be more familiar (Kahneman and Tversky 1979).

In the face of scientific authority, these local ways of knowing and assessing risks are often devalued and ignored. Concerned citizens are framed as ignorant, perhaps even paranoid, people who at best must be educated about the wonders of science, and at worst must be excluded from decision-making.

Community responses to air pollution: A NIMBY syndrome?

While many risks we face today are global in nature, air pollution frequently manifests itself as an issue at the local level, which is where many of us are more likely to experience it—and reflect upon it and respond—because our communities are where we live, work, and play. The ways in which individuals and communities respond to hazardous technologies have been of keen interest to social scientists for several years (Edelstein 1988; Lazarus and Folkman 1984; Giddens 1990; Elliot et al. 1999; Wakefield et al. 2001; Luginaah et al. 2002; Wakefield and Elliot 2000); and the political nature of risks such as air pollution is evident in those responses. Individuals and communities react to disruptions in the environment in several ways, from direct confrontation to pragmatic acceptance of the risk conditions, sustained optimism regarding its alleviation, or cynical pessimism and chronic psychological stress (Giddens 1990; Luginaah et al. 2002). When confronted with environmental risks, some people re-evaluate their lifestyles, while others make intentional proactive changes. Those individuals who feel sufficiently empowered and capable may embark upon individual civic action and/or join or form groups to carry out civic actions (Wakefield et al. 2001), but these activities can be extremely time-consuming and sometimes require skills and resources that many communities lack.

One typical community response, often referred to as **NIMBY** (Not-In-My-Backyard) comes as a reaction to the environmental risks associated with proposed industrial projects such as waste incinerators or intensive livestock operations. Given what is often limited access to information about project sites, risks, and benefits community residents tend to espouse a local point of view and, as many critics like to highlight, can (understandably) hold highly emotional views of the issue (Smith and

Marquez 2000). Community conflicts reveal the incentive and equity problem associated with the distribution of risks and benefits: risks are imposed on one group while the benefits or incentives accrue to others (consumers, stockholders, residents of other communities, and particularly to privileged interests such as the owners of the facilities in question. The NIMBY label is indiscriminately used, often to discredit resistance and to portray residents as either selfish or irrational. In actuality, local opposition to risky facilities or practices are prudent efforts by citizens to define what is acceptable, right, and appropriate for their community. As technocratic risk definitions and associated experts are privileged in political decisions around risk, risk definitions made by the public are devalued and written off as unscientific or irrational.

This politicized context of risk, in which numerous powerful interests stand to make substantial gains through the imposition of technologically induced risks onto society, has generated tremendous upheaval in an arena that Beck (1999) calls **sub-politics**: political activity that occurs outside the traditional political institutions of modernity. Despite attempts by industrial and government institutions alike to discredit citizen's groups, their number and effectiveness continue to grow. In this sphere of sub-politics—also called "direct politics" or "the shaping of society from below"—"economy, science, career, everyday existence, private life," according to Beck (1999: 39), "all become caught up in the storms of political debate." Concerned citizens become increasingly driven not only by the risks they face but also by the declining legitimacy they attribute to those institutions espousing "expert rationalities." At the centre of sub-politics is the tension between those expert knowledge systems of science and the everyday "lay" knowledge networks and community norms and beliefs.

In some aspects, what comprises society today is a loose network of "reflexive communities" confronting the consequences of modernity (Beck 1999; Lupton 1999).

Global Risks: Climate Change

While sub-politics has had an impact on controversies at the local and regional levels, the actions taken can also at least indirectly influence a global phenomenon such as global climate change—the quintessential global environmental risk. Not only scientists, but also politicians have begun to discuss this risk. Then too, with the help of the popular press, global climate change is now also being discussed among members of **civil society**: those institutions, organizations, and activities that function in the realms that lie between the state and our personal and business lives.

Also referred to as global warming or the greenhouse effect, the issue of global climate change refers in particular to predicted increases in average temperatures, ranging between three and eleven degrees Fahrenheit over the next several decades—temperature increases caused by the growing concentration in our atmosphere of industrial pollutants such as carbon dioxide and sulphur oxides. These compounds become trapped in the lower levels of our atmosphere, effectively turning the planet into a large greenhouse. While that may not seem like a bad idea to the majority of people living in places like Canada, climate change implies far more than warmer winters. The impacts of greenhouse gases are not limited to climate warming; the rapid changes in our atmosphere will alter everything from weather patterns to trade winds and ocean currents. The results will include rising sea levels, shrinking ice packs in the circumpolar regions, increased frequency and intensity of droughts, forest fires, and storms—in general, a highly unpredictable future climate. All of these phenomena will have significant implications for humans as well as for every other living thing on the planet.

As some critics point out, the Earth's atmosphere has experienced such changes in the past; scientists have, for example, attributed the extinction of dinosaurs to climate change. The key difference now, however, is the pace of change. Whereas the climate shifts that caused increases in the Earth's temperatures in the past occurred over several millennia, today temperature increases can be measured in terms of decades.

Another problem is that greenhouse gases come from numerous sources around the world—whether industrial agriculture, coal-burning power plants, or automobiles—and we have yet to figure out how to regulate all these human activities. Some social scientists, including ecological modernizationists (chapter one), are confident that the rapid development of a global governing apparatus, as well as advances in science and technology, will lead to the resolution of this and other environmental maladies. But is this realistic? The difficulties experienced in the ratification, much less implementation, of the Kyoto Protocol indicate otherwise—and the difficulties arise not from a lack of science and technology or even of ecological awareness, but simply from the nature of modern, complex political institutions.

Canada and Kyoto

During the 1980s and early 1990s Canada played a leading role in international environmental circles and was among the nations strongly supporting an international accord on climate change. By the mid-1990s, as negotiations regarding the Kyoto Protocol began to heat up, that position had shifted rapidly. In the more recent years of negotiations Canada took a strong role along with Australia, Japan, New Zealand, and the United States, in attempts to weaken the protocol. Indeed, the international environmental organization Climate Action Network awarded Canada repeated "Fossil Awards" as the country judged to have made the worst input to the negotiations (see Vevatne and Olmos 2000). The final protocol included many compromise features. One of the most important was a so-called clean development mechanism, whereby industrialized nations can minimize the amount of emissions reduction required in their home country by getting credit for financially supporting emission-reduction projects in other, usually less developed countries.

Canada was also instrumental in convincing negotiators that countries should get credit for the amount of forests that they have because forests can act as "carbon sinks"—absorbing carbon from the atmosphere, which is called carbon sequestration. Arguing that such a proviso would encourage sustainable forestry, Canada put forth efforts that ended in the inclusion of Article 3.3 of the protocol, which provides that the amount of allowable emissions assigned to each country should be increased by that amount of carbon that can be expected to be absorbed by its forests. In other words, countries engaged in planting trees, or "afforestation," would get an increase in their carbon rating; by the same token, countries engaged in deforestation would see that "carbon credit" reduced. The catch is, the emissions associated with harvesting are *not* counted (harvesting in timber production areas is not seen as deforestation because it is assumed that the trees will be replaced). As some critics have pointed out, this approach is a bit like keeping track of the deposits you make in your bank account, but not the withdrawals.

The Chrétien government lobbied yet another modification to the protocol—the inclusion of emission credits for exporting natural gas to the United States—on the grounds that providing the United States with cleaner fuels would lead to the lowering of emissions there. The other negotiators refused to accept this option, but that didn't prevent Canada from again trying to introduce it at the United Nations climate change conference in Milan in December 2003. The Canadian efforts in this regard again came to nothing.

On December 17, 2002, Canada announced ratification of the Kyoto Protocol. The move was supported in Parliament along strictly party lines, with the former Alliance and Progressive Conservative parties voting against it, and since then the country has remained sharply divided along traditional left and right lines, complicating implementation efforts. In nearly all of the political discussions, Canada's neo-liberal, export-based economic policies continue to dominate, with supporters of the protocol trying to convince the nation that implementing Kyoto will not hamper its economy, and opponents arguing to the contrary. This approach ensures that in the debate around Kyoto concerns for the economy come first, and that proposed methods for reducing emissions are limited to voluntary, individualistic approaches and a reliance on yet-to-be developed technological improvements.

Before leaving office, Chrétien presented a $1 billion plan to cut Canada's greenhouse emissions. The proposal includes subsidies for homeowners who upgrade the energy efficiency of their dwellings, support for hydrogen fuel technology, expanded ethanol production, and cleaner fossil-fuel technology. But the package is expected to cut Canada 's emissions by only 12 to 20 megatonnes (one megatonne = one million tonnes), less than one-tenth of the country's ultimate target under Kyoto, which will require a 240-megatonne reduction by 2010.

The plan also depends on the ability of the provinces to achieve a consensus on the means of implementation, and that consensus is notably lacking given the variability in not only the extent to which regional economies benefit economically from high emission levels but also the extent to which regions are at risk from the consequences of climate change. The difference in positions of the premiers of Alberta and Nunavut provide a case in point. As the premier of a province dependent upon energy production and on coal as a primary source of electricity, Alberta's Ralph Klein was a key opponent of Kyoto. He even went so far as to directly lobby Russian Federation president Vladimir Putin, urging Russia not to sign. Paul Okalik, Nunavut's premier, strongly urged Canada to sign, citing the many ways in which climate change was already hurting Northern communities. Manitoba and Quebec sided with Nunavut; the remaining provinces were opposed to the federal proposal.

In the end the actions of the Chrétien government—or any actor involved in the Kyoto negotiations for that matter—have much to do with the role of institutions, including the economy and civil society.

The role of the economy

Much of the CO2 emissions for which Canada—the second-largest per capita greenhouse gas producer in the world—is responsible are associated with features of this country that will be difficult to change: we live in a cold climate and have a large land mass requiring long-distance transport of goods. As the fifth-largest energy producer in the world, Canada is also economically dependent on extractive industries that are energy-intensive. Even just producing energy requires a large amount of energy (for more on this, see chapter nine). The processing of Western oil sands, as well as of clean-burning fuels such as natural gas, is largely dependent on coal-burning electricity. Indeed, in Alberta—a province replete with oil and gas reserves, as well as wind-energy potential—90 percent of the electricity is generated through coal-fired plants, which is now the cheapest way of producing electricity. Cheap electricity means lower costs for industry—not only the energy industry but also all other industrial ventures that keep the province's economy growing. Most of those industrial actors (with a few notable exceptions), not only in Alberta but across Canada, were active political opponents of Kyoto and able to exert significant pressure on provincial and national state actors.

More importantly, Canada's economy is directly tied to that of the United States, its most important trading partner, particularly since NAFTA went into effect in 1994—about the time when Canada's shift in position on international climate regulation became clear. Canada's position as a semi-peripheral, or middle-power country, in the global political-economic system limits its options. As a semi-peripheral country, it shares the economic productivity and comfortable quality of life of globally dominant nations, but its ability to continue to do so directly depends upon maintaining its good standing with certain dominant nations, in particular its southerly neighbour. The country's economic dependence thus spills into the realm of politics—not only must our political position on Kyoto not deviate too far from that of the United States, but our politicians are likely to avoid any effort to implement domestic policies—whether in health care, education, or environment—that will seriously disadvantage our ability to attract U.S. investors and to export our products to the United States.

Canada is not alone with this dilemma. According to a quantitative analysis by Timmons Roberts and his colleagues (2003) the richest and poorest countries (the United States excepted) have the lowest emission intensity; those in the semi-periphery are the biggest polluters because they have enough industry to compete in the world economy but the nature of their economies and their infrastructure do not allow them to invest in efficiency measures. The cheapest fuels are usually used for energy in these countries in order to maximize economic returns (Grimes and Kentor 2003). Further, these countries are also the sites of lowered costs for raw materials and labour, which means that foreign investment has relocated many significant emissions sources from wealthy nations to these semi-peripheral countries.

These internal constraints become factors in international negotiations. When, on March 28, 2001, the Bush administration officially withdrew from the Kyoto negotiations, many doubted that Canada would go on to sign the protocol. This doubt persisted until Chrétien announced Canada's ratification at the World Summit on Sustainable Development in Johannesburg in August 2002. Although Canada remained in the debates, the government made its position known—it would be unwilling to implement any agreement that imposed actions that would hamper its economic relationship to the United States. Its concerns were listened to by other Kyoto nations because with the withdrawal of the United States, Canada's signature was the linchpin to the Kyoto Protocol going into effect at all.

The role of civil society

Although environmental organizations have had global climate change on their agenda for years, and many surveys showed public support for Kyoto in Canada, the scientific complexity of climate change, combined with the elusiveness of its impacts, has kept many people from putting global warming high on their list of concerns. Repeated social surveys have found that many people in Western countries rank global climate change comparatively low, even among the gamut of environmental issues they face (Dunlap 1998; McDaniels et al. 1996). As one Canadian mine worker interviewed by the Canadian Broadcasting Corporation said, "When I look at the problems we have in Canada in our own backyard... global warming doesn't rate in the top ten" (CBC News website). Without strong public support, even the active voices of environmental organizations are not enough to push through tough legislation to the implementation stage. Elected officials are concerned first and foremost about getting re-elected, which means they pay attention to voter support.

Why don't the scientists' proclamations cause alarm among the public? The issue of climate change does not come with any graphic visual image to grab the public—no birds dying from pesticide ingestion, no children eating toxic apples—nor does it indisputably lead to any dramatic events—plant explosions, tanker spills. Social scientists studying this disconnect between the concern expressed by scientists and the seeming lack of concern among most non-scientists have focused on the impact of **framing** in political debates, and how those frames subsequently shape how people view certain issues. Framing describes attempts to present an argument in a manner that is designed to persuade listeners to see that argument in a particular way, while downplaying any potential evidence to the contrary. A public debate on the topic of the environment can be dominated by interests that limit it to a narrow set of perspectives. Environmental social scientists adopting a constructivist perspective focus on the framing that characterizes environmental discourse in contemporary society—how understandings of nature and environmental problems are crafted, contested, and legitimated (or not) (Hannigan 1995; Buttel and Taylor 1994).

Even though those frames are often carefully disguised, nearly all environmental issues are subject to them in public debates. When different groups have opposing views on a particular issue, they will inevitably frame that issue in a manner that supports their own interests. Environmental organizations, for example, may use tactics designed to alarm members of the public about the risks of climate change; corporations, seeking to avoid more environmental restrictions, may emphasize the extent to which the science of climate change is uncertain and argue that many jobs will be lost if, for instance, the country implements Kyoto. In many cases special interests play a central role in shaping environmental concerns.

The position of the Alberta government on climate change provides a clear example of an organized effort to frame the debate. In an effort to solicit support for its anti-Kyoto position, the provincial government paid for numerous newspaper advertisements and public opinion surveys during the Kyoto negotiations, encouraging citizens, as well as the prime minister, to support a "Made in Canada" alternative approach. The central feature of this alternative is a focus on the intensity of greenhouse gas emissions relative to Gross Domestic Product, meaning the proportion of emissions for each unit of economic output. If the goal is reduction in

6.3 Open letter from Ralph Klein to Prime Minister Jean Chrétien, September 3, 2002

Dear Prime Minister:

Alberta does not believe the Kyoto Protocol is the best way to go. Specifically, Alberta's concerns are four-fold:

1. With Canada producing only two percent of the world's greenhouse gases, the commitment called for in the protocol to reduce emissions by about six percent below 1990 levels by 2012 (equivalent to a 30-percent reduction in Canada) will have little discernible impact on global warming, but will result in the unnecessary loss of thousands of Canadian jobs, and an overall slowdown in Canadian economic growth. Because countries such as the United States and Australia are not signatories to the protocol, Canada will be put at an untenable disadvantage in the global marketplace. Canada is the only country in the western hemisphere with a reduction target, putting the nation at a further competitive disadvantage.
2. The Kyoto Protocol will not result in substantive reductions in greenhouse gases around the world, but will see simply a shift in where the gases are produced and in billions of dollars from nations such as Canada to other countries.
3. As the principal supplier of Canada's energy, Alberta will be especially hurt by federal ratification of Kyoto. There have been reassurances from your government that no region or sector will be unduly affected by implementation of the protocol, but there has as yet been no plan from your government on how this commitment can be met.
4. Canadians in all parts of the country will be affected. While Alberta produces most of Canada's energy, it is all of Canada that consumes that energy. Therefore, Canadians will feel the effects of Kyoto—at the pump, on their utility bills, at the workplace, and on their ability to find jobs.

Alberta believes that a made-in-Canada approach to climate change can be developed that would achieve the intent of the Kyoto Protocol, but on different timelines and in ways that would not hurt the national economy or individual Canadians' jobs. Alberta has detailed ideas—already demonstrated to be effective—that could form part of that plan. Other provinces and other Canadians have other ideas. If your government fails to give other options a fair hearing, if it disregards the many voices of honest, profound and informed concern about Kyoto, if it proceeds with ratification of the protocol, then it will do a disservice to the country and to the cause of addressing climate change.

Sincerely yours, Ralph Klein

Source: Alberta government website. "Open letter from Ralph Klein to Prime Minister Jean Chrétien, September 3, 2002."

intensity per GDP, growth is purportedly not threatened; we can continue to grow so long as the intensity of emissions declines. The catch is that this reduction in intensity can be achieved while the real output of greenhouse gases continues to grow.

Local Risks: Sour Gas Flaring

Air connects us as individuals not only on the global level, in the context of concerns such as climate change, but also, and perhaps even more acutely, at the local level. Citizens have demonstrated that through collective action they have the power to resist industrial technologies that are the source of hazardous air pollutants.

Alberta has a long and tumultuous history of conflict around the hazardous air pollutants associated with its bread and butter, the oil and gas industry. The best example is natural gas production, a lucrative Alberta business, which also happens to be associated with a rather nasty environmental effect: sour gas flaring. Natural gas, a fossil fuel whose main ingredient is methane (CH4), is used throughout North America as an energy source to heat homes, generate power, and refine petroleum products, and it is a key ingredient for the manufacturing of plastics. Natural gas extraction is a significant portion of the energy-based economic backbone of Alberta. The Alberta oil and gas industry grew from 70 oil and gas companies in 1974 to more than 1,500 in 2002 (Alberta Energy and Utilities Board 2003). The Alberta Energy and Utilities Board (AEUB), the province's quasi-judicial regulator of energy resources, now oversees more than 317, 000 kilometres of pipeline, about 110,000 gas wells, and more than 700 gas plants (AEUB 2003). Much of this explosive growth has been generated since 1999.

The extraction of natural gas involves drilling wells to tap the gas reservoirs trapped between layers of sand and rock below the surface. After wells are drilled, the gas is drawn to the surface, compressed, and sent through a pipeline to a processing facility. Sour gas, a form of natural gas common throughout Southern Alberta, contains a hydrogen sulphide (H2S) content of 1 percent or greater. H2S gas is poisonous and invisible, and acute exposures to it induce nausea, headaches, and eye irritation. Prolonged human exposure, even to very low concentrations, can be fatal. Little is known about long-term, low-level exposures to H2S, but some studies suggest that they can result in neurological damage in humans and animals (Kilburn 1997; Scott 1998).

About 30 percent of the natural gas produced in Canada is sour, and 85 percent of that sour gas is processed in Alberta (Petroleum Communication Foundation 2000).

Sour gas contains impurities that must be removed before it is used. As a result the gas is routinely combusted at well sites and sour gas plants in a process called "flaring." In rare cases sour gas is released directly to the atmosphere through a process called "venting." Structural failures at pipelines or sour gas facilities can result in accidental releases of sour gas, sometimes referred to as fugitive releases. Sour gas flaring and venting have been blamed for a number of health problems, including spontaneous abortions in cattle and humans, lung disease, skin rashes, and abnormal rates of neurological diseases in certain regions of Alberta (Nikiforuk 2001).

Not surprisingly, over the past ten years the siting of sour gas developments in Alberta has evolved into a highly controversial environmental risk issue. The complexity and uncertainty of managing the risks and impacts of sour gas development, coupled with several recent high-profile sour gas incidents, have cast a shadow over attempts to introduce new developments and have contributed to a growing polarization among the general public, industry, and provincial regulators.

6.4 Sour Gas Impacts

Incomplete combustion of sour gas can produce a number of releases and related health effects:

- sulphur dioxide (SO2)—an emission linked to acid deposition, irritation of upper respiratory tract, increased susceptibility to respiratory infection, chronic respiratory disease, and death;
- nitrogen oxides (NOX)—an emission associated with acid deposition, ground level ozone, and fine particulate matter;
- volatile organic compounds (VOCs)—an emission including known carcinogens such as Benzene and contributing to the formation of particulate matter and ground level ozone;
- hydrogen sulphide (H2S)—an emission associated with tearing of the eyes, headaches and loss of sleep at concentrations as low as one part per million and death at concentrations of one hundred parts per million;
- carbon disulphide(CS2)—a poison that can attack the central nervous system of humans and animals; and
- polycyclic aromatic hydrocarbons—a highly toxic organic emission.

Sources: Marr-Laing and Severson-Baker 1999; Strosher 1996.

Techno-scientific management at work

Industry and government define the side-effects of oil and gas extraction and production in Alberta in much the same way: as a necessary and acceptable part of energy development. From their point of view the development of the province's energy resources is a public good, and it is in the public's interest to exploit the full economic potential of those resources. In this context the energy industry's regulators are also its promoters: the stated mission of the AEUB is to ensure the discovery, development, and delivery of Alberta's energy resources and utilities services. Energy development is, after all, the linchpin in the Klein government's "Alberta Advantage," a term used to connote the province's ability to combine an industry-friendly environment with comparative geographic advantage to its economic benefit. Not surprisingly, then, any provincial assessment of the risk-benefit tradeoff of sour gas production and its side-effects ends up simply justifying further development.

The AEUB has embraced a series of risk management approaches designed to ensure public safety in the handling of sour gas hazards. One such approach, ambient air quality guidelines, delimits acceptable minimal levels of safety and environmental protection. In addition the AEUB employs a series of guidelines for establishing safe distances—setbacks—between facilities and human populations. The guidelines were deter-

6.5 Minimum Setback Distances for Sour Gas Facilities

Type of Sour Gas Facility	Minimum Setback Distance (m)
Level 1	100
Level 2	500
Level 3 and 4	1500

Source: AEUB 1994.

mined using purely technical factors such as past occurrences of accidental releases, H2S content and pressure, pipeline size, and other existing mitigation measures (AEUB 1994). Both ambient air quality guidelines and setbacks, then, were determined using scientific evidence and risk analysis.

The AEUB has also come to rely upon standardized scientific tools to make decisions about the location of sour gas facilities—to mathematically define and characterize public safety risks associated with the industry. In the early 1990s the AEUB designed a simplified approach called GASCON 2, which it believed could estimate the individual and societal risks of potential uncontrolled sour gas releases (AEUB 1994). Quantitative risk assessment tools such as GASCON 2 were used to estimate the level of risk associated with the "worst-case-scenario"—how many casualties can be expected if the worst accident occurs, and what are the chances of this happening? Oil and gas companies are then required to devise contingency plans called emergency response plans (ERPs), which are a recipe for protecting the public in the event of an accidental release of sour gas. The area of land covered by the ERP is called the emergency-planning zone, which is also calculated by a mathematical formula. The size and shape of the planning zone are related to the distance that a chemical release could travel, the anticipated average response time of emergency response units such as ambulances and firefighters, and the availability of various protective action options such as shelter and breathing apparatuses. The formula also takes into consideration the maximum and cumulative release rate of H2S, local landscape characteristics, and population density.

Normal accidents, normal reactions

Despite the regulators' and industry's attempts to improve the safety of sour gas operations, a number of disturbing accidents have occurred, with an equally disturbing frequency. One of the biggest sour gas releases in the history of Alberta happened in 1982 in Lodgepole, where an explosion at a sour gas well caused the deaths of two workers and resulted in the continuous release of highly toxic H2S for sixty-seven days (Gephart 1993, 1997; Nikiforuk 2001). In 1994 another accidental release of sour gas forced the evacuation of residents in Sundre. Some three years later a similar release forced the evacuation of workers and residents at Rainbow Lake. In 1998, 30,000 cubic feet of 18 percent sour gas was accidentally released from a drilling site 50 kilometres northeast of Nordegg (Marr-Laing and Severson-Baker 1999).

The position taken by energy companies, and the Alberta government, is that the risks associated with sour gas production are outweighed by the economic benefits. This position is, of course, premised on the ability of these proponents to convince the Alberta public that those risks can be kept under control. But what if they are wrong and what if scientists like Charles Perrow, who argue that accidents are normal occurrences and not anomalies, are right? What if these accidents are inevitable and not just incidences of "human error" that can be avoided? As public awareness and concern mount, sceptical local residents have more and more come to agree with Perrow.

In Alberta, rural communities, landowners, and concerned citizens are mobilizing at an increasing rate in an attempt to stop or change the path of oil and gas development in and around their respective localities. Mobilizations have taken the form of anti-sour gas campaigns, community action groups, public hearings, and, as in Grande Prairie, highly publicized cases of industrial sabotage and murder (Nikiforuk 2001). Events such as these, coupled with the uncertainty of the scientific evidence on the human health impacts of chronic exposures to flaring, venting, and fugitive emissions, have contributed to growing conflict between citizens, industry, and regulators over how the environmental risks and impacts of the oil and gas industry are to be defined and the appropriateness of sour gas development in close proximity to human populations. Such conflicts include:

- the 1981–82 court battle between Zahava Hanen and Imperial Oil over the expansion of a sour gas extraction and processing facility in the Turner Valley Region (Keeling 2001);
- the 1994 confrontation between the Lubicon Cree and Unocal Canada over a proposed sour gas plant outside of Little Buffalo (Gibson, Higgs, and Hrudey 1998);
- the 1998 murder on a ranch near Rimby of Calgary oil executive Patrick Kent of KB Resources after a two-year dispute over a contaminated well (Laird 2002);
- the 1999 siting conflict around Canadian 88's proposal to drill a sour gas well northwest of Calgary;
- the 2000 siting conflict around Shell Canada's proposal to drill a sour gas well outside of Rocky Mountain House;
- local opposition in 2004 to Compton Petroleum Corporation's plan to drill a sour gas well southeast of Calgary.

Perhaps the most famous case of sour gas controversy began in 1996 in the Grande Prairie region in northwestern Alberta. A series of oilfield bombings rocked the oil and gas industry. A local farmer named Weibo Ludwig and an accomplice named Richard Boonstra were eventually charged and convicted of some of the bombings (Nikiforuk 2001; Laird 2002).

6.6 Postcard Protest in Alberta

Dear Premier Ralph Klein:

Over the last few years fuel prices and profits of the gas and petroleum companies have soared. More gas wells are being drilled and more gas is being exported. Scientific evidence shows that flaring of poisonous sour gas at the well sites is incomplete releasing thousands of tons of toxic chemicals into our environment every year including deadly hydrogen sulfide. These toxic chemicals are causing "spontaneous" abortions in cattle and people, lung disease, neurological damage, crop and forest damage and other health problems. In some other jurisdictions, including California, governments do not allow such flaring and pollution. They require the companies to scrub the stack emissions or to pipe the toxic emissions to a central location for treatment. If the companies can afford to do it in other places, they certainly can afford to do it here.

Regarding our situation in Alberta:

- ❑ Please legislate measures to curb pollution from sour gas stack flaring to protect public health and the environment of Alberta.
- ❑ Please do nothing. Let the companies continue to flare and ignore the health hazards. We must put up with a little pollution to have a viable industry!

Please register my opinion. Let me know what action you are going to take.

Name (please print)__________

Address__________

Signature__________

Published by:WCWC - Alberta Branch, 301-10168 100A Street, Edmonton, AB T5J 0R6 Ph: 780-420-1001

47 cents postage

Premier
Ralph Klein
307-Legislative Buildings
Edmonton, AB
T5K 2B6

Phone: 780-427-2251
Fax: 780-427-1349
E-mail: premier@gov.ab.ca

Source: Western Canadian Wilderness Foundation, 2003. Reprinted with permission.

A closer look at the power of protest

The local actions of concerned citizens have had significant consequences on a number of levels. On July 15, 1997, for example, the Canadian 88 Energy Corporation applied to the Alberta Energy and Utilities Board for a well licence to drill a sour gas well about sixteen kilometres northwest of Calgary. The well would determine the existence of a lucrative sour gas pool, and if successful it would add millions to company earnings. One thing stood in the corporation's way—a surrounding acreage community of residents bitterly opposed to any plan for sour gas development in their backyards. What transpired in the following two years was one of the most highly publicized disputes over sour gas development in recent Alberta history. A number of community groups made up not just of ranchers and retirees but also oil executives and geologists worked to intervene and prevent the drilling. These groups questioned the safety of a sour gas development sited in close proximity to acreage homes, ranches, and the city of Calgary. After one of the longest public hearings ever relating to such an application, the Alberta Energy and Utilities Board gave Canadian 88 Energy Corporation approval provided that it comply with eighteen conditions. Despite the community's apparent defeat, by early 2005 Canadian 88 had still not fulfiled all eighteen conditions and had not started drilling.

In summer 1999, as Canadian 88 Energy Company tried to meet the eighteen conditions needed to obtain its well licence, Shell Canada applied for a well licence to drill a similar well directly adjacent to farmland and an unrestricted community development lining the Clearwater River, eight kilometres south of the city of Rocky Mountain House. Just as in the case of Canadian 88's proposal two years earlier, Shell Canada met with opposition from residents living in the immediate vicinity. Despite Shell's attempts to mediate the conflict and reach a compromise, the opposition was steadfast. The case went to the Alberta Energy and Utilities Board, which held a public hearing to consider evidence for and against the well before reaching a decision. The hearing itself attracted national media attention. The AEUB's eventual position illustrates the power of protest. After hearing testimony from landowners and experts, the Board exerted a rare but significant degree of autonomy from the company, denying Shell Canada the well licence needed to drill.

These actions at the local level not only prevented more air pollution in the communities involved but also had effects at an institutional level by inducing shifts in policy. The AEUB has since taken actions to ensure that it does not find itself in the uncomfortable position of having to prevent future development. The Board embarked upon several public involvement programs to address issues and concerns, and in January 2000 it formed the Advisory Committee on Public Safety and Sour Gas to review the regulatory system as it relates to public health and safety. The end result of an extensive consultation process with industry, experts, and the general public was a report released in December 2001 detailing eighty-seven policy recommendations. The following month the AEUB unveiled the Appropriate Dispute Resolution Program, a framework designed to resolve disputes concerning the Alberta energy industry before they deteriorate to the point requiring a public hearing (and the further denial of permits).

The AEUB has made significant attempts to build public confidence by establishing local multi-stakeholder groups operating throughout the province (AEUB 2003). The Clean Air Strategic Alliance (CASA), for example, consists of industry, government, and community representatives. These stakeholders work together at the local level to establish regional, consensus-based airshed management systems, including designing strategies to monitor, analyze, and report on air quality within the regional airshed (AEUB 2003). Another organization, the Cumulative Environmental Management Association (CEMA), brings together regional stakeholders to manage the environmental impacts of the oil sands developments in northeastern Alberta (AEUB 2003). Time will tell whether these organizational efforts result in Albertans being convinced of the tremendous benefits and minimal risks of sour gas development, or in Albertans convincing industry and the state that the risks are simply too high, but we can be assured that the outcome will depend on who is able to control the resulting political discourse.

Both of these organizations are artifacts of the recent trend in Western societies towards the devolution of environmental management, or the decentralization of environmental management responsibilities in local, multi-stakeholder arrangements. Traditionally, environmental management has been the purview of a centralized state agency. For example, Environment Canada is the Canadian federal environmental agency; the equivalent in Alberta is Alberta Environment. Environmental management decisions are made from the top down. In an era of underfunding and growing responsibility, environmental bureaucracies are moving closer towards a "bottom-up" approach. While some scholars praise such decentralization tendencies for their reflexive, localized approach to environmental management, others view such trends as another means by which our governing institutions are shedding their responsibilities to citizens.

What Can We Do?

At stake is the question of who has the right to what sort of quality of life. Consider the debates between developed and developing countries in the Kyoto negotiations. The greenhouse gases in the atmosphere have accumulated from the past 150 years of fossil-fuel-based industrial development in a small handful of nations, including a number of Western European countries, Canada, and the United States. Yet the Kyoto negotiations are all about how many emissions each country has a right to in the *future*—to what extent should residents of industrialized nations have to compromise their opulent lifestyles, and to what extent should developing nations be exempt so they too can industrialize? Several researchers have speculated that if everyone in the world shared the same standard of living as a typical Westerner, we would need the resources of several more planets. As noted by Thomas Princen and his colleagues (2002: 124), our ecological feedback loops have been largely severed in contemporary society—the phenomenon called **distancing** (chapter two). Since we as consumers are not fully aware of the ecological consequences of our consumption, the rights related to resource use have become separated from the responsibilities of that use. Perhaps Kyoto negotiators should be debating how responsibility for curbing greenhouse gas emissions will be shared among those countries that share the greatest responsibility for past emissions. How many tonnes of greenhouse gases are you responsible for? Do you have a greater right to this emission level than does a woman your age living in Uganda today?

At the personal level we need, first of all, to confront our consumption. Each of us can start by taking just a few steps:

6.7 No Speeding /One Less Car, Use alternative transportation. RideAway from the Indy/Wholesome Undie protest, Vancouver Art Gallery, July 18, 2004.

Photo: Colin Brown/Artists Against War

1. Use alternative transportation as much as possible. Many urban areas already have organizations to help support residents who want to reduce their dependency on private automobiles. For example, Edmonton Bicycle Commuters Society, operating since 1980, supports alternative means of transport: not just cycling, but also public transport and car-sharing. This organization provides information and support for those interested in environmentally sound transport alternatives. BikeWorks, a bike repair shop that allows you to repair your own bike with help from experts, also serves an important role for members of this society.
2. Give your home an environmental audit. Any abode, from a dorm room to a mansion, can be made more environmentally efficient, and efficiency measures, such as replacing light bulbs and sealing door and window cracks in winter, can be relatively low cost. Some measures, such as adopting alternative energy sources, can involve larger investments that will nonetheless pay for themselves in reduced energy costs over time. You can get information on residential energy efficiency from your local energy provider, on the Internet, or from numerous books on the subject. Professional "environmental audi-

tors" are now working in many cities and can come to your home and show you how to improve your energy efficiency for a nominal fee.

3. Purchase your electricity from an alternative provider if available. Citizens can sometimes choose from a number of providers, many of which have varying percentages of power produced by renewable energy sources. In Alberta, for instance, a government website lists the various options available (Alberta, "Customer Choice" website).
4. In many cases, as individuals we do not have as much choice as we would like in determining our impact on the environment. So even in those instances in which we may feel we have little control (very few of us can sit down and negotiate an international agreement, for example), it is important to stay informed.

At the political level, despite the constant pressures of time, ample opportunities do exist for involvement in organizations working for environmental improvement. The good thing is that the time commitments called for can often vary depending on your own schedule. Although we may all need to accept that global change happens one increment at a time, you can make a difference through activism at the local level.

In 2003, for example, a student organization at the University of Waterloo called the Sustainability Project received $25,000 from the Climate Change Action Fund to initiate a campaign aimed at both their campus and the broader community. They used the funds to support education and action campaigns on sustainable transportation, energy efficiency, renewable energy, and the science of climate change, and they support a web page with an extensive resource list.

Useful Websites

Canadian Association for Renewable Energies
<www.renewables.ca>

The David Suzuki Foundation
<www.davidsuzuki.org>

Environment Canada
<www.ec.gc.ca/>

Intergovernmental Panel for Climate Change
<www.ipcc.ch/>

United Nations Environment Programme
<www.unep.org/>

7. Economy, Work, and the Environment in Canada

Satoshi Ikeda, Michael Gismondi, and Ineke Lock

> Capitalism as a system devoted to accumulation without end is inseparable from a capital-intensive, energy-intensive economy and thus necessitates growing throughputs of raw materials and energy, along with the creation of excess capacity, surplus labor, and economic and ecological waste. This should be differentiated from the basic needs of the broad majority of people, which have to do with the availability of steady and worthwhile employment and an improving quality of life, and therefore have no inherent link to an intensive process of ecological degradation.
> —John Bellamy Foster.

Partial arguments about the economy appear throughout this book. Our focus here is on the place of nature and the environment in economic change and globalization—on the political and sociological challenges of regulating our capitalist economy for sustainability, for sustainable work and employment, and for alternatives in work and leisure in Canada.

In the early years of Canadian history, most jobs for Canadians were based upon natural resource exploitation and agriculture. A landscape of forests, lakes, plains, and rivers provided the raw materials for labour and the natural spaces for recreation for those working people seeking to replenish their energies. A vast wilderness spurred the Canadian imagination and stamped itself on our identity as northerners. Today that Canadian identity still includes a sense of nearness to nature, land, and climate, but it has changed too. Few Canadians still farm or work directly in resource-based jobs. Outdoor jobs are fewer too, and workers have developed different sensibilities to atmosphere, light, and weather than did previous generations. Most remaining resource jobs have been deskilled and mechanized (a process called **Fordism** after the automobile assembly and production line) in order to increase output with fewer costly workers, especially well-paid and well-protected unionized workers. Canadian manufacturing jobs have disappeared too, often moved to other countries. New jobs in service and government sectors have picked up the employment slack. But those controlling today's **post-Fordist economy** seek smaller production sites and fewer workers, shedding and rehiring cheap and casual labour worldwide to increase profits and meet consumer demands. This so-called flexible economy is not only dismantling the social gains of past workers but also consuming resources and creating wastes at alarming rates. Even recreation and leisure have become businesses that consume nature; our national parks are overcrowded with visitors, and wild places are disappearing (see chapter five). As Canada's air, lands, spaces, and waters become polluted, overextended, and exhausted, and turned into market commodities, Canadians have begun to question the natural limits of our economy and society.

The resulting conflicts around natural limits are sociologically messy. Simple dichotomies describing conflicts as between environmentalists and multinational corporations, for example, capture only part of the picture. We begin by exploring three contemporary Canadian environmental controversies.

Three Stories

Each of the following stories shows how local environmental conflicts nest within global patterns of economic expansion and how economic growth speeds up the consumption of nature in contradictory ways. Each story shows how groups of people analyze environmental and socio-economic problems, how they may develop solidarities with other communities suffering similar pressures, and how local environmental conflicts can jump scales from the local to national or international levels.

The three stories also show that not everyone agrees on what is to be done. Some people want to keep on with business as usual. Others fear that our industrial activities and ways of life are exhausting nature—that they are violating ecosystems and breaking down nature's ability to provide ecosystem services, such as the ability to sequester carbon, replenish groundwater, regenerate forests, dilute wastes, and provide jobs. They question whether our capitalist economy can be changed, whether its impacts can be reduced or certain practices phased out or replaced by greener ones, or whether wholesale change in the system is needed to bring about ecological sustainability and job security.

No matter where it stands on these issues, a politics of opposition must, by necessity, find ways of reaching across divisions within communities. It must forge common cause, develop a shared language of concern, and imagine alternatives that speak to people and for nature at the same time.

Old growth and logging jobs in Clayoquot Sound

Canada is a forest nation. Some 10 percent of the world's forests can be found here, including one-fifth of the world's temperate rainforest and over one-third of its boreal forest (Global Forest Watch 2004). About 94 percent of our forests are publicly owned or Crown lands. Forests are crucial to nutrient recycling, controlling climate warming, and maintaining biodiversity and cultural diversity. Forests are also crucial to the Canadian economy. The wood and paper products industries "employ over 350,000 Canadians directly and over 770,000 indirectly. They generate over $58 billion in total sales annually, making a net contribution of $34 billion—more than half of the country's annual trade surplus" (National Forest Strategy 2003). Yet, according to Global Forest Watch (2004), less than 8 percent of our forest lands are protected from logging. Most Crown lands are under some sort of logging tenure agreement with corporations, and our forests have been fragmented by previous logging, roads, and the cut lines of the oil and gas industry. According to Global Forest Watch, "Development activities increasingly extend into Canada's northernmost forests, which have fragile soils and slow growing conditions. Over 60% of tenured forestlands face severe productivity limitations or moderate limitations." Over 60 percent of Canadian old-growth forests—that is, forests sustaining trees between two hundred and one thousand years old within complex and biologically diverse ecosystems—have already been cut (Global Forest Watch 2004).

In summer 1993, environmentalists gathered in Clayoquot Sound on the west coast of Vancouver Island to block the logging of the last remaining pristine temperate rainforest in Canada (Wilson 1993a). The blockaders were protesting the B.C. provincial government's April decision to allow logging of the old-growth rainforest. Although the allowable cut was lower than what industry had asked for, the decision was not welcomed by environmentalists.[1] People in the communities where workers resided were also unhappy with a reduced cut. They feared job losses and community decline (Matas 1993a). Some four months of direct confrontations between environmentalists, the companies, the loggers (and their families and supporters) led to the one-sided arrests of seven hundred environmentalists; many were given jail terms (Wilson 1993b, 1993c, 1993d). Meanwhile the provincial government established a panel to settle the issue. Almost two years later, in May 1995, the panel recommended ending clear-cutting in Clayoquot Sound (*Globe and Mail* May 30, 1995: A2; Lush 1995), although some limited and selective logging could be permitted (Friends of Clayoquot Sound).

Over the last two decades, similar protests against the politics and practices of clear-cutting have occurred across Canada, including protests led by First Nations peoples in Temagami, Ontario, and Meadow Lake, Saskatchewan. Canadian writer Brian Fawcett used the image of a *Virtual Clear-cut* (2003) to express his dismay with forest practices around Prince George, British Columbia, a leading centre of Canadian pulp and paper production and his hometown as a youth.

In British Columbia social divisions based on forest operations have been complicated not just by pro and con views on logging, but also by different visions of the economy held in the public and government. For example, the economic survival of many small communities in rural and northern British Columbia depends on the permanent and seasonal wages of loggers, on logging-related jobs such as trucking and heavy equipment operations and repair, and on the economic spinoffs created when these wage-earners enter the local marketplace in search of consumer goods, food, and housing. Many of the women and mothers who defended logging jobs lived in small B.C. logging communities. In *Taking Stands in the Forest,* Maureen Reed (2003) explains how the experience of community frames the actions of women in forestry towns: "Women's social relations to the environment are made and reinforced through daily activities in specific localities." Other readings of women's roles in the Clayoquot protests focus on women environmentalists (most, but not all, of them urban and from outside the region) and their equally important demands to protect the forest as a commons and an ecological and spiritual place. Reed (2003: 12, 13–14), who interviewed women who took a stand to defend logging argues "'responses' of residents to protect their way of life can be classified not by the dichotomy of 'anti' and 'pro' environmentalism but as social phenomenon that is more plural and complex." Most people in these communities pin their hopes for the resilience of community life and local economies on the exploitation of forests.

In the Clayoquot case, similar divisions exist in the Aboriginal community. Native community leaders expressed sympathy, for spiritual and ecological reasons, with environmentalists and their conservation aims. Yet they also took a social justice position that supported limited logging as an important source of jobs and revenue for their people, many of them economically marginalized (Matas 1993b). Other Aboriginal groups held their ground against exploitation and differed with the elders on the destruction of nature. Even other industries such as tourism were opposed to further logging in Clayoquot, but for competing economic reasons: "No one industry should be favoured at the peril of others" (Tofino Town Council website).

In 2003, the Nuu-Chah-Nulth Central Region Chiefs and the province of British Columbia signed the first of twelve watershed management plans under the Clayoquot Sound Interim Measures Extension Agreement. Developed by a joint Aboriginal and non-Aboriginal local management board, "The plan guides site-level forest planning and forest harvesting by identifying reserved areas, which are excluded from logging, and harvestable areas, where forestry operations will be implemented in accordance with the Science Panel's vision, goals and objectives for sustainable ecosystem management" (British Columbia Ministry of Sustainable Resources 2003). The forest management plan acknowledged "special management areas, including culturally significant areas identified by First Nations, where practices will be subject to additional restrictions and conditions in order to safeguard sensitive values." It also specified "the rate-of-cut limits that apply in pertinent watersheds and drainages based on the scientific studies." The joint board's perspective on forest management suggested that humans can work within natural processes and achieve economic growth at the same time. More subtle than old models of forest management that resulted in clear-cut destruction, the new ecosystem or adaptive management perspective, called **sustainable ecosystem management**, assumes that by patch-cutting and consuming smaller percentages of the annual forest growth, we can protect for other forest values and live, as they say, on the annual natural interest and not draw down the **natural capital** of a forest ecosystem.

Unfortunately, the B.C. government rejected these watershed plans in June 2003, approving instead a proposal put forth by the forest company Interfor that included a ten-year plan for roads and fifty-seven proposed cut blocks (areas designated for logging). Aboriginal activists subsequently began a boycott against Interfor.[2] Environmental movement critics see the new ecosystem-based forestry as inconsequential, because forest industries continue to increase production and expand into previously untouched forest regions—a process Jeremy Wilson (1998) characterized as "talk and log." The future of jobs and communities remains unclear.

7.1 Protester at the trial of Betty Krawazk, 75-year-old grandmother, jailed for defyng injunctions against logging road blockades, Vancouver Law Courts, 8 September 2003..

Photo: Colin Brown/Artists Against War

The battle between tree loggers and tree huggers is simply cast. It is not merely a battle between those who favour environmental protection and those who support economic growth; there are more divisions, more contradictions, and more values at play. The range of conflicting voices on local issues reflects different definitions of development, different preferred scales of use, and even different temporal visions (for example, some people want immediate increases in jobs and incomes; others argue that putting the ecosystem's needs first will guarantee future jobs). Anthropologist Terre Satterfield (2002: 4) argues, "These social forces are expressed culturally"—that is, "The forests dispute has everything to do with imagined worlds... that reflect their quests for change." We must be careful, then, to examine the words and images used in forest disputes

(Sherman and Gismondi 1997). But imagined worlds have powerful roots too. John Bellamy Foster (2002), who has worked in the Pacific Northwest logging communities of the United States, argues that there are structural obstacles to change. He recognizes a kind of class struggle between the forest industry and forest communities. His appraisal of the forestry situation in the U.S. Northwest rings true for the B.C. case. Arguing that "the environmentalist cause has been impeded by the executive arm of the state acting in tandem with the large corporations, while workers and endangered species are being forced to bear the main costs of the crisis," he concludes:

> It would seem to be eminently sensible for environmentalists and workers to join forces around a common platform. A progressive class-oriented response to the old-growth crisis would have to focus on an ecological conversion program that can be enacted at the level of the state. As Victor Wallis has argued, the term conversion has traditionally referred to the switch from a military to a civilian economy but can be applied more broadly to the socially planned redirection of the economy necessary to create a sustainable society. (Foster 1993)

For Foster, government and corporations have exercised both social and ecological tyranny and their projects are incompatible with conservation and job creation. He supports workers and their families forging alliances with urban environmentalists in favour of conservation, jobs, and strong communities. But this step requires both of these parties to think through the economic contradictions of capitalism and imagine what Foster calls a **conversion economy**—in which ecocentric critics of forestry operations combine with forestry workers (and their families in forest-based communities) to form an alliance against corporate capitalists and pro-growth sectors of government. This alliance will require a more democratic and egalitarian alternative social order, forged upon a new ecological ethic that asks humans to consider all of their actions in the light of what is good for the environment. Aldo Leopold calls this a **land ethic**.

Kyoto Protocol versus the economy

Unlike the local jobs–environment tradeoffs in the Canadian forests, tradeoffs between employment and global warming follow the reverse pattern, with the definitional stage emerging at the global regulatory level. As the implications of international global climate change regulation and the Kyoto Protocol of 1997 became more clear, or perhaps more accurately *un*clear, its impacts moved from a global to the national and regional levels, and then ultimately to local workplaces and communities in Canada and elsewhere.

The Kyoto Protocol to the United Nations Framework Convention on

Climate Change set up an agenda to reduce emissions of greenhouse gases, such as carbon dioxide and methane, that cause global warming. Canada's assigned goal has been to reduce emissions by 6 percent from our 1990 level by the year 2010 (Greenspon 1997). Since the December 1997 Kyoto Environmental Summit, Canadians have been split into at least two positions: one supporting the Protocol; the other rejecting it as unnecessary and promoting business as usual.

Opponents raise economic arguments about the negative impact on the Canadian economy and job loss—both existing and future jobs. Almost 80 percent of Canada's trade is with the United States. One of the strongest opponents of the Kyoto accord, the United States produces over 30 percent of the world's CO2 and has refused to sign the treaty. In 1998 a U.S. corporate think tank announced, "The Kyoto Protocol would cause a significant reduction in US employment, somewhere between 1.8 and 3.13 million people and a decline in GDP ranging from \$179 to \$318 billion"(CONSAD Research Corporation 1998). Likewise, Canadian companies in the oil, gas, chemical, and utility sectors voiced opposition to the Protocol, insisting that its implementation would reduce the competitiveness of Canadian goods and therefore reduce employment (Mittlestaedt 2000; *Globe and Mail* 1998). Adopting Kyoto, so say the critics, would increase manufacturing and distribution costs for Canadian producers, making our products uncompetitive in the U.S. market and U.S. products more competitive in Canada. All of this would lead to economic crisis and unemployment. In 2002 the Association of Canadian Manufacturers and Exporters published and promoted a "Kyoto Alert" predicting job losses in the oil and manufacturing sector of over 450,000 by the year 2010 and stating that "net job losses across the Canadian economy as a whole would be even greater." The CME argued that as a result of Kyoto, Canadians would have to "drive less," use "smaller cars" and pay more for all forms of energy—a lifestyle and economic change the organization characterized as "Pain without Gain" (CME 2002).

Spearheading opposition to the Kyoto Protocol in Canada alongside the Canadian business community were the government of Alberta and its premier, Ralph Klein, whose Conservatives put \$1.5 million of tax dollars into an anti-Kyoto ad campaign. With an economy based on oil and gas, coal-fired power, and tars sands conversion to synthetic oil, Klein and his government declared they would defend their province from Kyoto and the federal government (Alberta produces more CO2 than any other province in Canada). Likening the Kyoto Accord to another federal government initiative—Trudeau's National Energy Program of the 1980s, which set the Canadian price of oil below the world market price and created Petro-Canada, in turn causing a backlash from U.S. oil companies, which pulled out of Alberta—Klein played on Albertans' fears of another Ottawa-inspired economic downturn and wave of unemployment (Government of Alberta 2002; Baumgarten 2002).

At the opposite end of the debate, labour unions and the environmental movement countered industry and government claims. Some environmentalists argued that a 6 percent emission reduction from 1990 levels was too little. TV personality and ecologist David Suzuki argued that the application of available technology (such as better insulation and hybrid cars) would easily allow Canada to achieve 50 percent reductions (MacKinnon 2000). The Canadian Labour Congress supported the Protocol, insisting that no jobs would be left if the planet became dead from the business as usual approach (Yusuff 2000). Energy and sustainability consultant Ralph Torrie argued that the industry's calculation of job losses did not include the economic benefits of conserving energy and the health benefits of cleaner air. For example, slowing greenhouse warming would protect jobs. Efficiency saves energy, leads to some new jobs (in construction and insulation, for example), and prolongs traditional jobs by reducing their energy costs. As well, new jobs would be created in the alternative energy sectors such as the wind, water, solar, and fuel cell industries. *Making Kyoto Work*, a study by the Canadian Centre for Policy Alternatives (Marshall 2002), agreed that greening the economy would cause job loss in some sectors, but criticized the CME because it did not calculate how Kyoto would also create jobs in other energy sectors. The CCPA calculated a net increase of 3,200 jobs over those lost by adapting to Kyoto, and concluded that the new jobs would be more satisfying than the existing environmentally offensive ones.

Social justice critics look at global warming issues somewhat differently. They argue that global environmental degradation is being caused by the overconsumption of the world's resources by developing countries. National ecological footprint analysis, for example, explicitly attributes environmental degradation at the global scale to overconsumption by rich countries. Mathis Wackernagel and colleagues (2001) show that the majority of the earth's surface is appropriated by the developed nations, whose overconsumption is disproportionately responsible for issues such as global warming, ozone depletion, ocean fisheries depletion, deforestation, and loss of biodiversity. Canada, for example, produces more greenhouse emissions per capita than most other developed and developing countries except the United States. Many Kyoto supporters believe that Canada has a global obligation to reduce its ecological footprint, and that those reductions can be achieved without major economic upsets. They believe the eductions are a social justice issue.

The Kyoto Protocol raises new challenges of global citizenship and global governance for Canadian governments, employers, workers, and citizens. Contemporary problem-solving around sustainability and global warming requires programs of education and action that work across many levels—local, national, international—at the same time.

NAFTA and hog farming

Intensive livestock operations (ILOs, also called confined feeding operations) are changing the Canadian farm landscape from one of small-size family farms to large-scale corporate operations. Specific structural economic factors have contributed to the problem of ILOs, which expanded from Quebec and Ontario to Manitoba and Alberta in the last decade in response to the Canada–United States Free Trade Agreement of the late 1980s and NAFTA, which went into effect in 1994. Under these trade negotiations with the United States, the Canadian government stopped supporting the transportation of wheat to coastal ports by withdrawing a subsidy called the Crow Rate. U.S. wheat began to outbid Canadian wheat in world markets (Novek 2003a). In Manitoba wheat production became unprofitable, and farmers moved into hog farming, especially in the 1990s (Ramsey and Everitt 2001). The shift to hogs by the independent grain farmer was paralleled, however, by increased corporate competition and investment in the industry. Corporations began funding mega-operations of up to 500,000 hogs.[3] A mega-barn pattern was set in place across Canada. Between 1976 and 1996 the number of hogs per Quebec farm increased from 178 to 1,113 (Mitchell, Gray, and Seguin 2000). At the same time the government of Alberta (the fourth-largest hog-producing province after Quebec, Ontario, and Manitoba) supported hog farming as an important growth sector of the provincial economy (Government of Alberta 2003). The government incentives and policies operated like a pull factor, attracting investment in the pork industry. Not everyone was happy. When the Taiwan Sugar Corporation proposed to construct an intensive hog operation in the Palliser Triangle near the town of Foremost in Southern Alberta, the local farmers successfully asked the county government to veto the proposal, despite the provincial government's push for the plan (Nikiforuk 2000a, 2000b).[4] Concerned farmers spoke about the economics and health issues of the proposal, not simply about pig barn odours.

7.2 The Alberta Advantage?

Beyond the Rocky Mountain Parks and the Highway 2 corridor, economic desperation has led a succession of communities to grasp at environmentally dubious schemes like hazardous waste treatment, strawboard manufacture, tire incineration, and mega-hog barns. Some advantage.

(Epp and Whitson 2001: xv)

At a public hearing into this issue, the National Farmers Union (NFU) explained how the pork industry is vertically integrated—that is, how the large industrial hog companies such as Maple Leaf Foods (a part of the McCain's conglomerate), Saskatchewan Wheat Pool, Mitchells, Premium Brand, and others control the system from the soil to the plate. These companies own grain farms that provide inputs such as feed; they control agricultural chemical businesses; and they are in charge of the killing and packing of hogs. This vertical integration places great pressure on independent farmers who raise pigs only for the marketplace. Industrial corporations make money even when pig prices are low—low pork prices mean higher producer profits because the costs of making bacon become cheaper. Integrated corporations always win. Conversely, when pig prices fall, independent farmers are caught with low returns. Moreover, allowing additional mega-barn hog operations furthers the control of the marketplace by these companies. For example, integrated slaughterhouses take hogs from their own farms first; this vertical buying from one wing of the company also allows the slaughterhouse to control "price discovery" and to further push down the price paid to independent hog producers. As the NFU spokespeople argued:

> Mega-barns are driving family farms out of the business, not because family farms cannot produce hogs as cheaply, but because, in an industry dominated by large sellers and buyers, small producers have trouble gaining market access. Those who wish a demonstration of this reality should attempt to supply their local supermarket with vegetables. (National Farmers Union 2000)

The net result across Canada has been a major drop in independent hog farms. Rejecting mega-barns, the NFU defended the role of the family farm in the local economy:

> Family farm hog production slows the extraction of wealth from rural areas.... Unlike corporate producers, when families produce hogs on farms they own, they receive the profits and they spend them in their local communities. When corporations produce hogs, the profits are quickly extracted from the area.
>
> Family farm production supports the local economy in other ways. Raising hogs requires feed, building materials, veterinary drugs, machinery, and other supplies. Small producers buy most of their supplies locally while large producers tend to stock many barns in many communities with supplies purchased in one location—usually a large and distant city.

The pressure on the family farm and the scale of change are enormous. In Manitoba the number of hogs increased from 870,000 in 1975 to 7.3 million in 2004. Hogs are now Manitoba's most valuable agricultural commodity. The industry employs 16,000 people and has an economic multiplier impact of about $2 billion (*Winnipeg Free Press* Oct. 6, 2004). Yet critics such as the National Farmers Union argue that intensive livestock operations break down the local community and that the interests of industrial hog farmers squarely oppose those of neighbours and family farmers who value odour free air and clean water. The critics are particularly concerned about the lack of regulations on livestock waste and the risk of hog wastes entering groundwater and drinking water in rural areas. Following the contaminated water incident in Walkerton, Ontario—which killed seven people because of E. coli, apparently from pig farm wastes infiltrating the groundwater and then the drinking water system—challenges to the expansion of intensive hog operations (called *megaporcheries* in Quebec) have increased (Mitchell, Gary, and Seguin 2000).

Over the last two decades the number of Canadians working in agriculture has declined to about 5 percent of the total workforce. Many rural towns are dying as youth move to the cities in search of work. Free trade agreements and large-scale corporate cattle and hog operations have increased wealth for some people, but at the cost of local communities, jobs, and environments.

Roger Epp and Dave Whitson (2001: xv) capture the contradictions across Western Canada:

> On the Canadian Prairies, cities like Calgary, Edmonton, and Saskatoon thrive, even as the farm crisis decimates rural communities around them. The countryside, meanwhile, is coming to serve two new and very different purposes—playground and dumping ground—as the traditional rural economy declines. In some fortunate regions, those accessible to urban vacationers and retirees, and having the right kinds of opportunities for mountain or marine recreation, "nature" is coming to mean clean and scenic environments for upscale ski and golf resorts, for various forms of back-country recreation, and for holiday homes. In more remote or less obviously scenic locations, meanwhile, where land is cheap and city people seldom come, rural communities are becoming dumping grounds: sites for the messes created by city garbage, by massive resource developments, by low-wage industry, and by intensive livestock production.

7.3 Pig Manure

On average, a pig produces 3.5 litres of manure per day. A 150,000 hog per year barn complex creates as much effluent as a 135,000-person city. Although hogs and people share much the same physiology and many of the same diseases, hog manure is not treated. Manure, highly concentrated and in huge quantities, becomes a potential toxin. As it is handled in most mega-barn complexes—liquefied and put in earthen pits with neither liners nor covers—the manure gives off terrible odours, lowers the quality of life for miles around, lowers property values, and threatens to poison surface and ground water. Liquefying manure greatly increases its tendency to move—both horizontally and vertically.

(National Farmers Union website, "Hog Barn")

Each of our three stories—logging, the Kyoto Protocol, and hog farming—demonstrates key structural aspects of capitalism that have a large impact on Canadians and the choices we can make about jobs and environmental integrity. Living within an economy that is putting great

7.4 The Meatrix

Manitoba now has nearly three times as many pigs as humans. It is impossible to expand and intensify livestock production without similarly expanding and intensifying waste production. That's a lot of hog waste! Have you seen "The Meatrix"? With the help of Moo-pheus, Leo the pig confronts the truth of corporate farming: <www.themeatrix.com/canada>.

Sources: StatsCan, Qualman in Epp and Whitson 2001; Global Resource Action Center for the Environment (GRACE) 2004; (accessed Nov. 14, 2004).

stress on our ecosystems and is increasingly integrated with the U.S. economy, Canadians have begun to question the economy's impact on nature and to question the economy itself. Is capitalism too contradictory, too voracious? Is the capitalist system, driven by a need to accumulate and expand into new areas to make profit, with little consideration for jobs or ecological overconsumption, the tyrant that must be overthrown? Or can it be harnessed and reined in? Can we adapt capitalism to environmental demands, and can we do so without job loss? Will Canadians accept a no-growth or slow-growth economy as part of their duty to protect the planet and act in solidarity with the poorest of the world's population? To answer these larger questions, we need to place these contemporary Canadian conflicts against the backdrop of capitalism's political and environmental history.

A Very Short History of Humans, Work, and the Environment

Humans are parasites on nature. Without extracting nutrients from plants and animals, they cannot survive. At the same time natural forces such as earthquakes, hurricanes, typhoons, tsunamis, and severe weather mean that humans are subject to natural "selection." Humans have also been repeatedly subject to microparasites that cause widespread death.[5] From being subjects of nature to its manipulators, humans now have the capacity to eliminate ourselves as a species by destroying those aspects of Earth's ecosystems that support human life. Some critics argue that capitalism has the ability to destroy the very natural systems that provide for the planet's survival. Others argue that Earth will survive—but simply without us humans.

No matter, to get to this point in history, there have been several breakthroughs in human interaction with nature. Examples are the agricultural revolution dating from 6,000–7,000 years BCE, and the industrial revolution from the late eighteenth century. For thousands of years after the birth of *Homo sapiens*, humans were hunters and gatherers whose livelihood depended on plants and animals in the wild. Early humans migrated from one place to another to secure food sources, and the human population was constrained by natural limits. Survival was based on people's knowledge of animal behaviour and plant biology (whether plants were edible or not, a plant's medicinal attributes), and human work (gathering and hunting) was inseparable from the natural environment.

Life was often short, nasty, and brutish, although anthropologist Marshal Sahlins (1972) argues that pre-agricultural societies enjoyed more leisure time than those since.

As their understandings of the world around them deepened, humans started "domesticating" both animals and plants in order to provide a steady food supply. They replanted fruit- and nut-bearing trees and bushes and tamed milk-bearing animals such as goats and cows, all of which led to large-scale grain-planting and field cultivation in the birthplaces of the four major civilizations: Egypt, Mesopotamia, India, and China. Accumulated surpluses became the foundation of these now class-based societies. In Egypt and China the majority of people were "owned" by ruling classes, while in later feudal societies (as in Medieval Europe) the majority were bound to the land as serfs obliged to render service in labour or rent to the lord. While still subject to extreme weather and epidemics, human activities began to alter the natural environment through soil erosion and desertification. Colin Duncan (1996: 18–24) illustrates how a vicious cycle of ecological collapse was put in motion by the spread of early extensive agricultural practices as vegetation was stripped by livestock, soil was eroded by tilling, and natural waterways were clogged with silt from farming. Initial boosts in food production led to increases in population, which in turn caused peasants to move onto less productive lands and more vulnerable ecosystems and soils. Their activities broke down ecosystems and induced cycles of socio-political collapse "in many parts of the world, notably China."

Later, in the mercantilist stage of capitalism (the sixteenth through eighteenth centuries), control over unequal exchange with regions of the extra-European world brought raw materials from outside ecosystems for fabrication in Britain and Europe; manufactured products, especially luxury goods and durables, were sold for high profits to the wealthy European ruling and bourgeois classes, as well as to ruling classes in the so-called developing or extra-European countries. With the emergence of the capitalist organization of work and production in Europe beginning in the late sixteenth century, a new economy driven by the motivation of endless accumulation of profit started. Capitalist farmers and sheep grazers who provided material for textile industries began to constantly reinvest in land and improvements. The state and the ruling classes intervened militarily on behalf of these yeoman farmers (early agrarian capitalists) to drive peasants off the land and enclose and privatize communal lands. Peasants resisted but quickly found themselves with little means of production for food or livelihood. They became urban migrants who entered the growing cities with only their labour power to sell for wages in order to live—forming the working classes of the early industrial period. The Industrial Revolution, the machine production system, the growth of factories, and wage labour created new industrial cities, and new wealth.

In this early industrial period the damage done to was readily portrayed in paintings, literature, and social commentary. Charles Dickens's *Hard Times*, for example, described the poverty and deprived living conditions of the working classes. Other social commentators and critics portrayed the open sewers and foul streets of cities, the smoke-choked atmosphere, dark satanic textile mills and factories, and the destruction of the English countryside by acid rain. Foster (1994: 52–55) notes how those who witnessed this new age of industrial factories, and its increased production and wealth, were shocked by the "contrast between the enormous riches produced by this system and the deterioration of environmental conditions"—as well as by the opulent living conditions of the rich and the destitution of the poor or working classes.

Within Europe a regional division of labour formed; Western Europe supplied products manufactured by industrial workers, and Central and East Europe (east of the Elbe River) supplied wheat and other agricultural goods produced by peasants still under feudal bondage. Surpluses in the West were realized through the **surplus value** generated when employers paid workers less for their labour than the price the company received for the commodities the workers produced. The ability to extract more surplus value from wage workers was maintained through a variety of mechanisms designed to keep to an absolute minimum the costs of social reproduction (that is, the amount of money workers needed to maintain the health and strength of themselves and their families). These mechanisms included the provision of cheap food from Eastern Europe, produced by exploited and unfree peasant classes, which allowed industrial worker families to eat despite the low wages paid by capitalists. This pattern of uneven development and inequality has persisted between Eastern and Western Europe, and the developed world and the countries of the global South, even today.

Trade and corporations

Trade played a key role in both the mercantilist period and the Industrial Revolution. Through trade in timber, cereals, and artisan goods with Hanseatic League towns (1200–1600) along the Baltic Sea, surpluses accumulated in Western Europe, especially in Amsterdam and London, giving merchants resources to compete with Spain and Portugal in global colonization. Surpluses were accumulated through direct exploitation (theft of gold and unequal exchange with weaker nations) or through the development of colonies. At this time the chartered joint stock company emerged. Two famous companies, the Hudson's Bay Company (founded 1670) and the Dutch East India Company (founded 1600) were granted the right by their monarchies to represent their states, and they became instruments of the military and economic conquest of non-European peoples and territories worldwide. The Dutch East India Company was the richest firm in the world by the mid-seventeenth century, and key to Dutch power. It was the British East Indian Company, however, that dominated trade with

India from the seventeenth century onwards and proved fundamental to the British trade monopoly and rise of British global power. By the mid-nineteenth century the East India Company controlled India, Burma, Hong Kong, and Singapore. U.S. corporations rose to prominence much later, in the 1890s, but they have dominated the last century of exploitation of the tropics by, for example, controlling sugar production in the Caribbean, Hawaii, and the Philippines, bananas in the Central American lowlands, coffee in the Central American and South American highlands, and rubber, mahogany, and other valuable woods in the rainforests of Latin America, Asia, and Africa. In the process these U.S. corporations crippled local food systems, degraded lands and ecosystems, and drew on the U.S. State Department and U.S. marines to overthrow local political regimes that threatened their monopolies (Tucker 2000).

Corporations in the nineteenth century were promoted by strong states, such as Great Britain, the United States, France, Germany, Italy, and Japan. These countries fought to establish exclusive access to resources in Asia and Africa in the form of empires, resulting in two world wars during the twentieth century. Between the late 1890s and 1945 most nations and peoples of Africa, Asia, and Latin America fell under the direct or indirect imperialist rule of one of the European powers or Japan. Many of the African countries we know today were created by European powers that divided up the resources and peoples of the continent.

In the post-World War II period the United States and its allied countries established a new world economic order called the Bretton Woods System, which was guided by the principle of free trade. Under this new system of trade rules, the value of the U.S. dollar was fixed to the price of gold (dollar=gold convertibility) and the value of other national currencies was pegged to the U.S. dollar (called a fixed exchange rate system). The International Monetary Fund (IMF), a global agency, was established so that member countries could borrow from it for development purposes or when they faced balance of payment deficits. This appeared to be a fair economic arrangement, but U.S. corporations were soon able to gain unbalanced access to the natural resources and markets of developing countries. Surplus continued to flow from the poorer borrower countries to the richer lender countries. Critics use the term **ecological imperialism** to describe how colonial powers and then global corporations altered ecosystems to extract supplies of raw materials, ripped apart local environments to plant export crops such as sugar cane and cotton, poisoned ecosystems and humans in their efforts to mine gold and silver, or simply exhausted the Earth as they extracted tin, bauxite, iron ore, and oil for European and North American factories.

Through independence struggles the people in the colonized regions achieved national independence in the 1940s and 1950s. These newly created countries launched national economic development projects using bilateral aid from the developed countries or multilateral aid from the

World Bank (officially the International Bank for Reconstruction and Development, or IBRD) and other regional development banks. The objective of many of these projects was to follow the development path of Europe and the United States through industrialization, but such projects were often unsuccessful and accompanied by a heavy burden on the environment. Japan, for example, did develop its economy, but also became known as "a museum of pollution," with heavy smog in Tokyo, heavy metal poisoning in Minamata and Niigata, paper mill waste-water pollution in Shizuoka, and more. In the global South, World Bank-funded projects created huge dams and power plants to support agriculture and mining activities, causing displacement of millions of people and widespread ecological damage (see chapter three). These ecological impacts are often not recognized by mainstream historians and development economists. Critics recently introduced the concept of metabolic rift to draw our attention to this conceptual blindness, indicating the ecological underpinnings of the capitalist economy and how capitalism has destroyed lands, nutrients, genetic diversity, and ecosystem services globally in the service of profits for a few.

Globalization: Capitalism into the 21st century

The post-World War II framework of economic development under the Bretton Woods arrangement went through fundamental changes after the mid-1970s. These changes—within a process referred to as globalization—have had significant implications for the possibilities of achieving sustainability. The increase in the U.S. prime rate from 6 percent in 1977 to 18 percent in 1979 created Third World debt problems of gigantic proportions. Many developing countries had previously borrowed money, at low interest rates, from U.S. and European banks. The sudden increase in interest rates amplified Third World payment obligations. Meanwhile, export earnings plummeted as prices for raw materials and goods declined. The first major debt crisis occurred in Mexico in 1982. Instead of forgiving the interest on the debt, and in order to save the U.S. banks that had loaned money to Mexico, the U.S. government pressured the IMF and World Bank to extend new loans with stringent conditions attached. These were called structural adjustment loans. The World Bank (and its controlling partners, the United States and European countries) told sovereign states how to run their economies, and to avoid bankruptcy and social crises these countries acceded to the demands. As each developing country experienced financial crises, the IMF and the World Bank imposed on them similar conditions, known as **Structural Adjustment Programs** (SAPs). Governments were required to raise interest rates, devalue currency exchange rates, liberalize trade and finance, and reduce government spending. The stated aim of the policy was to attract foreign investment, eliminate a so-called inefficient public sector, and remove so-called market distortions caused by policies to promote domestic industries. The end result was massive unemployment, recession due to higher interest rates, increased prices of imported goods including foods, foreign takeover of the national corporations and banks, removal of many environmental regulations and controls, and impoverishment and hunger among the poorest social classes.

Third World economies—with their exports of cheap raw materials, agricultural products, and manufactured goods—were transformed to service the global market. Structural adjustment policies played their part in this, allowing global corporations access to a country's natural resources and its labour force; and as if that weren't enough, the creation in the early 1990s of the World Trade Organization (WTO) further promoted free trade, opening up Third World natural resources even more to the global corporations. The pace of resource extraction and environmental degradation in the global South accelerated rapidly. As Perry Grossman (2002: 136) points out, not only did free trade increase access to raw materials by global corporations, but it also limited federal and state government controls over resource sectors and inhibited sustainable resource management. Free trade also had negative effects on a staples economy such as Canada's, which relies on forestry and agricultural production. Global agricultural corporations promote large-scale food production for exports that are heavily dependent on chemicals, fertilizers, and genetically modified plants, all of which threaten the ecosystem (see chapter four). Some Northern firms (and some desperate governments in the South) have even used free-trade agreements to justify shifting dirty industrial operations overseas and shipping toxic wastes from the industrial countries to the global South for treatment (Leonard 1993).

Globalization has expanded the flow of goods, services, investment, and information between national economies. Daily life in the global North (so-called industrial, developed countries, which enjoy higher living standards) has become dependent on clothes, foods, electronics, and

7.5 Hunger and the Global Debt Trap

The basic connections between hunger and debt are pretty straightforward. One of them is related to the IMF demand for exports. When you export more, that means that you are going to neglect food crops, because the state will usually give you a decent price for an export crop but not necessarily for a food crop. That isn't always the case, but usually that's what happens. Not everybody is necessarily going hungrier, but certainly people in the city are. Increasing exports mean the prices for local staple food crops go up in the cities. Now in many cases the peasant doesn't get a fair price, and there's no slow transition to higher prices. Many people just have to pay double or triple food prices immediately, and they can't absorb that kind of a shock in one go.

The IMF also wants to curb consumption. They want to restrict demand, and that includes demand for foodstuffs. That is part of a policy they call "demand management." As a result, food becomes more expensive. Food subsidies are wiped out because the IMF considers them to be too big a drain on government budgets.

Source: Aurora Online website, interview with Susan George, 1990.

various materials produced, manufactured, and processed in the global South (the so-called developing countries). But these productive activities in the global South are controlled by the corporations from the global North either through subsidiary operations (the local company is owned by the foreign parent corporation) or subcontracting (local companies, not owned by the foreign company, produce for the foreign company). In *The Vulnerable Planet* Foster (1994: 35) summarizes how the question of the environment and capitalism has entered a new a stage over the last century:

> What distinguishes the ecohistorical period of capitalism from the ecohistorical period of precapitalism is not environmental degradation or the threat of ecological collapse.... Capitalism has been so successful over the last few centuries in "conquering" the earth that the field of operation for its destruction has shifted from a regional to a planetary level.... The exploitation of nature has increasingly been brought within the sphere of the economy and subjected to the same measure, that of profitability.

The environment and Canadian capitalism

In Canada the patterns of ecological exhaustion and capitalist development had one or two special differences. Harold Innis described the Canadian economy as a **staples economy**, with the country as a hinterland engaged in the production of raw material for export to countries in the industrialized centre in exchange for finished products. From the time of the fur trade to today's production of lumber and minerals, Canada's major trade partners have been Great Britain and the United States.[6] Early in the country's history attempts to create an integrated Canadian economy included the construction of the St. Lawrence Seaway, national railways, and trans-Canada highways. In the last half-century, efforts to promote "domestic" industries in Canada included the Auto Pact, which forced foreign corporations to build cars in Canada, and the promotion and protection of Canadian corporations during the Trudeau years. The federal government instituted a foreign investment review to maximize local hiring and investment by outside corporations, and it established national economic corporations, such as Petro-Canada, and policies that sustained the agricultural and transportation sectors. Much of this policy direction was reversed in the 1980s by Conservative government policies under Brian Mulroney, which sought to take the government out of the realm of business, worked to strengthen economic ties with the United States, and pushed for a free-trade deal. The Mulroney government struck the Free Trade Agreement with the United States in 1987, and that deal was expanded to NAFTA (to include Mexico) in 1993 by Jean Chrétien's Liberal government (which had won the 1993 election after vowing to repeal the FTA). Despite its name, there is much evidence that the "free trade" deal has been decisively favourable to the United States (McQuaig 1992; Merrett 1996). Many Canadian industries face unilateral trade restrictions by the U.S. government (CBC 1997), and free trade has also deepened Canada's dependence on the United States as an export market, import source, and investment outlet. As the examples of pigs, trees, and global warming make clear, Canadian jobs are increasingly geared towards external markets and heavily influenced by U.S. environmental politics around Kyoto.

A staples-based economy such as Canada's is inherently unsustainable, both economically and environmentally. To promote staple exports, the Canadian government uses taxpayer's money to build roads, railways, ports, pipelines, power plants, and communications systems—an approach that forecloses the opportunity to invest in the manufacturing sector (what economists call **opportunity cost**). The approach draws the economy further into the vicious cycle of a "staples debt trap," with bleak consequences for jobs and the environment. Canada's reliance on a staple economy is reminiscent of Ricardo's theory of comparative advantage (see chapter four). Taking this theory a step further, the factor-endowment theory of international trade, known as the Heckscher-Ohlin theorem, identifies a country's comparative advantage in certain goods as being based on that country being "relatively more" endowed with the factors of production (land, labour, capital) required for production of those goods. According to these international economic models, Canada should specialize in staple goods such as fish, fur, lumber, and minerals. The problem remains, however, that almost all of these sectors are in decline economically. Canadian jobs in the staple sectors are falling in numbers, and in most developing countries the workers in the staple sectors are not enjoying rising living standards (because commodity prices, with the exception of petroleum, have been declining for some decades).

The cycle of instability in staple economies is all too clear in the demise of many Canadian towns that depended on single resource industries, such as Uranium City, a mining town turned ghost town, and in many of the fishing outports of Newfoundland that declined with the collapse of cod stocks. Export statistics indicate that the manufacturing sector (the automobile-related portion in particular) has surpassed the resource and resource-processing sectors as the largest contributor to Canadian exports.[7] The percentage of workers in the resource-related and agricultural sectors has dropped to 5.5 percent, and most Canadians now live in urban centres (Wallace and Shields, 1997: 394). The staple economy has also had a bitter impact on the environment—and the harm done stays behind in local places while the products go overseas. After over three hundred years of resource extraction—and with resource extraction now speeded up—the Canadian economy is running out of staples, and the related industries are suffering from exhaustion, pollution, and transmigration out of Canada. The Atlantic cod fisheries have been exhausted, old-growth forests have declined, pollution of the Great Lakes has increased, and the food chain suffers from the **bioaccumulation** of toxins. Iain Wallace and Rob Shields (1997: 386) conclude:

> Canada's staple resource industries are in retreat. The east coast cod fishery has been overexploited to the verge of extinction. In British Columbia, the salmon fishery has been severely reduced by mismanagement and environmental degradation; the forest sector is encountering serious constraints on the availability of wood fibre; and the minerals industry has met with government refusals of projected developments.

Canada's dependence on foreign investment, its integration with the U.S. economy, and increasing U.S. influence over Canadian political decisions about our economy suggest that the ultimate trap of the Canadian staple economy may be our loss of sovereignty to the United States (Watkins 1997: 33–34).

The Treadmill of Production or Natural Capitalism?

Is it possible to achieve harmony with nature while pursuing economic growth? The notion of **natural capitalism** is based on the optimism of the theory of ecological modernization. Like ecological modernization, natural capitalism holds an optimistic view that economic growth can be adapted to meet environmental and employment goals. For example, ecological modernization is quite positive about the capacity of capitalism to transform itself to care for the ecological problems it has created. By creating incentives, such as tax breaks and subsidies, the profit-seeking corporation is expected to create innovative solutions to the ecological problems. Various liberal green social movements share EM's conviction that sustainable development is made possible through the use of technology to mimic natural processes rather than by simply tightening regulatory control on corporate behaviour; corporations themselves are selling their greenness to promote their agenda. Paul Hawken, Amory Lovins, and L. Hunter Lovins (1999) call natural capitalism the "next industrial revolution." Ecocentric critics note a tendency for arguments of natural capitalism and ecological modernization to ignore problems, such as protecting the intrinsic value of a forest or ecosystem, that cannot be readily measured numerically or "scientifically."

The **treadmill of production** theory is useful here. It maintains that the capitalist system of production (including natural capitalism or green capitalism) cannot be altered to meet environmental goals because it is designed to eliminate and automate jobs, not ensure secure employment. It thus draws attention to the nature of capitalism as being fundamentally incompatible with ecological sustainability. The secret of successful capital accumulation rests in restricted competition and the externalization of social and environmental costs—that is, uncosted uses of nature that sustain the economy, such as using the atmosphere to disperse pollutants. Under globalization these processes have expanded to an international treadmill (Schnaiberg 1980; Schnaiberg and Gould 1994).[8]

Those who support capitalism insist that competition promotes technological and material development and efficient resource allocation. They argue that competitive markets attain the best outcome and any interference in the market (by states to protect jobs or the environment, for example) will create distortions. The phrase "competitive market" and its neo-liberal synonym "free market" in reality mean freedom for global corporations, which are monopolistic (that is, they control their entire production sector) and often have a larger turnover than the Gross Domestic Product of many poorer nations. Such concentrated economic power makes a mockery of claims to free competition and make it near impossible for regulatory agencies to impose environmental protection measures. Nevertheless, the neo-liberal model is widely supported, despite intensifying inequalities in income and asset distribution.

Cost externalization means that the costs of producing and reproducing resources are not a part of the normal flow of business; they are separated off and thereby passed on to the environment. Profit is made at the expense of nature. At the same time wage costs are reduced by the unpaid work of women and other household members who grow food, cook, wash, clean, and raise children. Capitalist accumulation requires the existence of this extra-market "society" to provide uncompensated services to the capitalist market. Then too, societal ties that once provided "free" services within households are being increasingly commodified in the global North. Professional and rich classes rely on cheap immigrant labour for domestic work, and even cheap luxuries such as wines and fruits are subsidized by migratory or temporary labourers who come from Mexico and the Caribbean to take up seasonal work at rates below minimum wage in the Okanagan Valley and Niagara Peninsula. Middle-class households increasingly rely on prepared foods purchased in the market instead of home-cooked meals.

Once on this treadmill, workers need higher wages to purchase services from the market. This need puts pressure on employers, who, to lower costs, shift their operations from the global North to the global South, looking for government concessions, handouts, and new low-wage workers. This is the flexibility sought by corporations in the post-Fordist society. In the North, those who lose their jobs still engage in the market by accumulating debt and using credit cards. Those who have no choices in the South work in sweatshops and pesticide-soaked fields for wages far below the cost of reproducing their labour power.

As world material production expands and the rate of extracting nonrenewable resources accelerates, current usage becomes unsustainable

(Grossman 2002: 136). Pollution, such as the dumping of wastes and other "negative externalities," exhausts ecosystem services. Alienated workers, desensitized about the potential harm that their activities may cause to the environment, lose their sense of being connected and part of nature. Can this process continue?

What Can We Do?

Our opening three examples of logging, greenhouse warming, and industrial pig farming each brought to the surface the contradictions of the relationship between our economy and the ecosystems it depends upon. Each showed how growth in the economy was seriously altering, even destroying, ecosystems and eliminating jobs. Each also showed the concentration of power and control in the hands of corporations, governments, and those who have power over international trade agreements, and how this power limits the sovereignty of nations, let alone local communities looking for alternatives. These three stories also showed a range of views about the ways out of these traps. They spanned from business as usual or growing our ways out of the problem, to efforts to control corporations, promote conservation, reverse free trade, and convert to small-scale economic and socially sustainable solutions. Placing contemporary issues in historical context, our short history of the changes in human economies also concluded that we are on a treadmill of exhaustion and that it is necessary to reverse directions, lower the level of production, and convert our economy towards ecological sustainability in order to avoid both environmental and social collapse.

How might this conversion economy come about, especially given the constraints placed on the national government by free-trade agreements and the IMF? For some green thinkers, the solution is to improve the efficiency of resource usage. Although the expression "efficiency" resonates with business rhetoric, the pursuit of improved resource productivity will fundamentally transform the way in which business is conducted. Lakshmi Narasaiah (1998) proposes:

> This is where another view of profitability comes in. Business management would no longer focus on value added, but on maintenance value over longer periods based on the intrinsic value of a product.... How can products be made with as few raw materials and as little energy as possible and create a high benefit as pollutant-free as possible for as long as possible during their life-cycle?...
>
> The reason is that saving resources is based in principle on substituting energy by work, rather than the reverse as has been customary to date....
>
> So large-scale reconditioning and repair work increase the

7.6 Artists Against War end hunger strike against NAFTA, November 20, 2003, Vancouver.

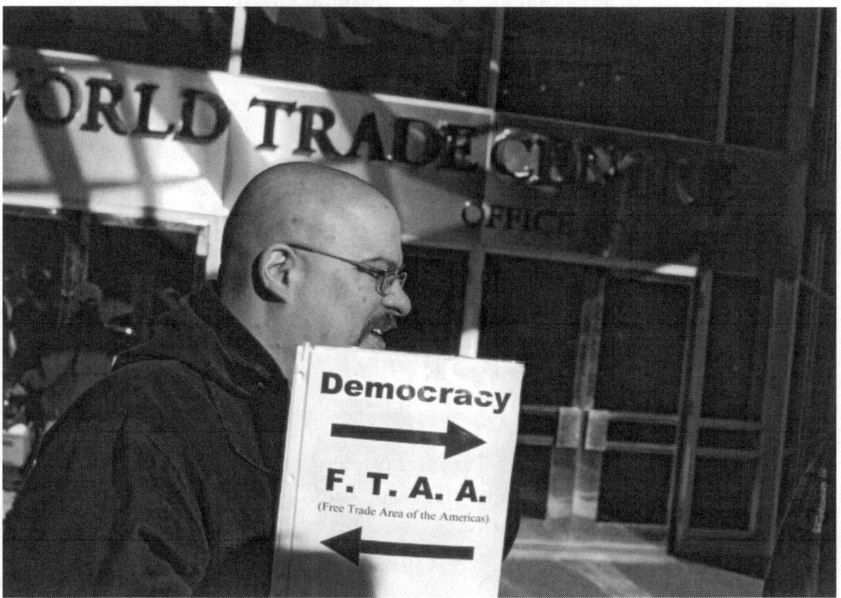

Photo: Colin Brown/Artists Against War

> number of skilled jobs and at the same time reduce the inflows of materials and energy.

The jobs created due to this kind of emphasis on efficiencies will reduce transportation and energy costs (see Hawken, Lovins, and Lovins 1999) because service-based industry tends to be based regionally rather than globally, and studies have shown that the transition to a society based on getting the most productivity out of the least amount of resources can be accomplished without costly unemployment (Spangenberg et al. 1999).

In principle the efficiency argument is powerful, yet it would be necessary to augment this approach by devising regulations or institutions to curb wasteful mass production and consumption. For example, to encourage ecologically sound activities, what is being called an "eco-tax" could be levied on environmentally offensive activities. Such taxes have been found to be effective for pollution reduction, according to the Organization for Economic Coooperation and Development (OECD) (Ember 1997), and they are being promoted by the B.C. Green Party (Heatherington 2000). Some critics argue that by combining eco-taxes with a carefully prepared fiscal policy that promotes ecological sustainability in spending, governments could guide the existing system in the proper direction.

These kinds of strategies assume that it is possible to work within the existing capitalist political and economic systems. Taking another approach, Anders Hayden (1999) argues that reductions in work hours and the introduction of job-sharing would provide the free time we need for significant reproductive work such as education. Sharing work not only creates jobs but also leads to better-balanced lives.[9] For Hayden, efficiency is a good, but limited, goal; we also need to develop new thinking around sufficiency. For him, a theory of limits to satisfaction offers another strategy for addressing global inequality: it involves changing our focus from means to goals. As European green thinker Wolfgang Sachs (1999: 41) writes, "An increase in resource efficiency alone leads to nothing, unless it goes hand in hand with an intelligent restraint on growth." For Sachs, the real question is not the efficiency of the toilet, but how many bathrooms are really necessary.

A similar criticism can be made of those who argue that we need to have more leisure time, and that this voluntary minimalism will allow for sustainability. Leisure, as Sharon Beder says, is supposed to be "time off the job," a means of "recovery from work," and yet it is "segmented and structured around work hours." In fact our leisure is increasingly not free time at all; it is leisure lost and time as "dictated by employers" (Beder 2000: 250–56). Juliet Shor, another advocate of leisure, argues that contradictions in capitalism make it near impossible to achieve free time within the current economic system. As she explains, "There are systemic pressures within the production process, coming from the profitability strategies of employers, which translate productivity growth into greater output and increased incomes rather than shorter hours of work." She argues that this "'output bias' is built into the very logic of capitalist market economies, and requires constantly escalating levels of consumption to absorb the expanding output of goods and services. Basically, this type of system funnels income to people without giving them the option to work less or consume less" (Schor 2004).

Faced with such structural constraints, some critics argue that we need to get beyond capitalism to create sustainable alternatives. The sustainable community movement (SCM) has attempted to create an alternative to the capitalist organization of the economy in various places over the world as a measure for community survival. One community in British Columbia initiated a local currency system after the closure of a plant that provided the bulk of employment in the area. The system of skill exchange and using local products provided job opportunities to unemployed people without relying on corporations, and the currency circulating in the local community created additional purchasing power. When a community makes its own decisions it will find that it is easier to make these decisions environmentally sound.

Like community groups, labour unions are examining other creative ways of protecting jobs and making new jobs available while taking measures to force corporations to adhere to environmental sustainability

7.7 Output bias of capitalism kills; from WorkLess Party action called Rat Race, October 23, 2004

Photo: Colin Brown/Artists Against War

(CAW website; NUPGE website). Considering matters on a more global scale, Kenneth A. Gould, Allan Schnaiberg, and Adam S. Weinberg (2001) promote citizen workers movements as federations of local movements against the treadmill of production. A pioneer in fair trade, George Monbiot, argues for a new world order based on fair trade—an order that would lead to a levelling of the world economy "founded on the conviction that one can lead a satisfactory life without having to ruin other people's" (Monbiot 2004: 181). His manifesto is practical. It makes good use of existing market mechanisms and progressive International Labor Organization standards to protect workers and environments. Monbiot even argues that corporations, properly regulated by a fair trade organization, are an effective means of organizing production.

Notes

1. See the website of environmentalist group Friends of Clayoquot Sound for the images of confrontation between the environmentalists and the loggers.
2. For the B.C. Government's Environmental Record, see BCFacts.org website. See also the Clayoquot Sound Central Region Board website and Friends of Clayoquot Sound (see Tofino Town Council website). In a similar confrontation between environmental protection and logging jobs, an Aboriginal community in Saskatchewan became split into two. The Sakaw-Aski elders council and a group of Natives called Protectors of Mother Earth staged a road-

block in May 1992 to stop logging activities pushed by the elected Meadow Lake Tribal Council. The protestors wanted to stop clear-cutting and protect their traditional way of life while the elected council supported a Native-run logging company that provided jobs for the local Cree people.

3. Elite Swine, a division of Maple Leaf Foods, operates hog systems that produce 500,000 hogs annually (Nikiforuk 2000a). See also the discussions in Qualman 2001 and Laidlaw 2003.
4. The CBC-TV special "Wild Hog" contains footage from the Foremost protest.
5. McNeill (1976) writes an excellent historical analysis of human interaction with microparasites.
6. Innis, a Canadian political economist, was the founder of staples theory. *Staples, Markets and Cultural Change* (Innis 1995) is a collection of his insightful articles about his work. "The Importance of Staple Products in Canadian Development" summarizes his contribution.
7. Ikeda (2004) argues that the Canadian economy shifted from the hinterland-staple economy to the hinterland-maquiladora economy with exports of staples and foreign-controlled manufacturing.
8. Novek (2003b) argues that intensive hog operations in Manitoba are an example of the international treadmill.
9. A calculation made by CAW research concluded that if each hour of overtime worked had to be offset by an hour of time off, and if legislated standards provided each worker with the right to one paid week of education/training, roughly half a million full-time job openings would be created. Whether or not the actual number is lower, the potential for job opportunities through the redistribution of work-time is great (CAW website).

8. Environmental Health Issues Related to Industrial Pollution

Ella Haley and Richard Tunstall

> If Martians took a look at planet earth... they'd be puzzled. For they'd see that we had polluted one fifth of the world's total water supply (the Great Lakes) with chemicals... and contributed to human disability and illness, including cancer. The Martians would say how could humans be so stupid.
> —Ross Hume Hall, International Joint Commission of the Great Lakes, 1999.

When someone is told that she or he or a family member or friend has cancer, the news hits with the force of a wrecking ball, altering their perception of life forever. The disease, not surprisingly, carries a great deal of weight on an individual level. Yet at the same time, the growing incidence of cancer in general around the world—the cancer epidemic—leads to a kind of numbness—which is a source of frustration for those searching for causes and new methods of treatment.

Breast cancer rates have been steadily increasing over the last fifty years, to the point that one in every eight women is subject to the illness (McCormick, Brown, and Zavestoski 2004: 3). Many other cancers (including thyroid, prostate, non-Hodgkin's lymphoma, melanoma, and women's lung cancer) increased in frequency by over 100 percent over the last thirty years. Based on incidence rates, 41 percent of Canadian men and 38 percent of Canadian women will develop cancer in their lifetimes (McCormick, Brown, and Zavestoski 2004: 3). Cancer, as most Canadians now know, is a leading cause of death. It places "a huge strain on the health-care system," cancer advocate Liz Armstrong (cited in *Canadian Environmental Law Association News* 1999) says—and the rates have increased even though "over the last 50 years cancer research budgets have ballooned into the billions" (Hall 1998: 62). What was once most often endured as a private illness has now become "a political experience." Yet few Canadians know, according to Armstrong, that "there has been an increase in many cancers that are linked to environmental and workplace causes."

Exposure to Industrial Pollutants

Since World War II industrialized nations have dramatically increased their production and application of chemicals, and with this has come an increase in health-related problems accompanied by rising citizen concern and activism. Although industrial societies have learned to avoid some of the more obvious toxins, we are still being exposed to a huge variety of chemicals. Of about 72,000 chemicals in use globally, only 10 percent have had any testing for potential toxicity, and a hundred new chemicals are introduced each year (Harper 2001). North Americans are exposed to various levels of toxins throughout our daily lives, but some of us are more susceptible than others: fetuses, children, the elderly, and those with compromised immune systems.

Recently the U.S. Center for Disease Control and Prevention tested 1,300 Americans for traces of thirteen pesticides and found at least one pesticide in 100 percent of those tested. DDT, a pesticide banned in North America since the late 1960s, was found in 99 percent of the subjects, including children (Mittelstaedt 2004d). Some people too young to have been directly exposed to DDT received DDE (a DDT derivative) from their mothers in utero and through breastfeeding, and from eating milk, meat, eggs, and fish (Steingraber 1997).

With environmental health problems related to industrial toxins in the workplace and the community on the increase, then, people who are exposed to these conditions face key obstacles: the narrow view of the biomedical model; scientific uncertainty; deceit within governments and industries; secrecy in the military; and, in general, environmental injustice. In all of this the public has faced difficulties in getting exposures to industrial toxins recognized and documented, in getting environmental health problems diagnosed and treated, and in receiving compensation. But times are changing—people are becoming politicized about toxic exposures in the home, at work, and in the community, and they are pressing for these issues to be dealt with both immediately and proactively. Communities are organizing themselves by exploring different health and social movements. In this work they are holding governments and industry accountable.

Here, following the lead of key researchers in the sociology of environment and health—people such as Brown (2000), Pellow and Park (2002), and Levine (1982)—we focus on environmental health issues related to industrial toxins, or, as Phil Brown puts it, "the health effects caused by toxic substances in people's immediate or proximate surroundings (soil, air, water, food, household goods)." As Brown points out, "These are chemical-related, air pollution-related, and radiation-related diseases and symptoms that affect groups of people in neighborhoods and communities." It is an area of environmental health that, he adds, "has engendered an enormous amount of conflict, policy-making, legislation, public awareness, media attention, and social movement activity. It puts into sharp relief a variety of disputes between laypeople and professionals, citizens and governments, and among professionals. It demonstrates an interesting example of social problem construction" (Brown 2000: 144).

People are growing increasingly concerned about toxins in their lives

8.1 Example of a Contested Illness: Multiple Chemical Sensitivity

The biomedical approach to illness has a profound impact on illness experiences. When we are ill and enter a formal health-care system, these institutions influence our perceptions of our disease. People who show the symptoms of Multiple Chemical Sensitivity (MCS) find it very difficult to get this illness diagnosed by mainstream medical doctors. Some who strongly believe that they have MCS become disillusioned with the medical system and sue insurance companies that deny them coverage. People with MCS have to find their own ways of avoiding chemical exposures in their daily lives in order to minimize their reactions and manage their symptoms. For example, some people with MCS must avoid certain paper reading materials, or wear a face mask when they read certain materials in order to avoid exposure to the chemicals in the paper.

MCS patients have become politicized because their accounts of their illness experience do not fit with the dominant epidemiological paradigm's (DEP) account of what constitutes a disease. Joel Thornton explains that paradigms are ways of seeing the world—lenses that determine "how we collect and interpret data, draw conclusions from them, and determine what kind of response, if any, is appropriate." The DEP is a belief system about what diseases actually exist and what their causes are.

MCS patients have used the Internet to learn about their illnesses and to share this knowledge with others. This networking has enabled them to build a "collective identity" from their shared illness experience and to challenge the medical establishment to learn more about how to prevent, diagnose, and treat the illness. MCS activism in Halifax has been particularly successful. City officials recently banned the use of fragrances in most indoor public places, declaring scented products hazardous to people's health.

Sources: Brown et al. 2004; Kroll-Smith and Floyd 1997; Potempa 2000; Thornton 2000: 7).

(Beck 1992) and taking a critical look at industrialized society. Environmental health problems are particularly contentious because of their links to the industrial foundations of Western economies. It is because they are "so centred in the daily life and economy." Phil Brown (2000: 144) says, that "the recognition of and action of these diseases is especially contested. The potency of these 'contested diseases' is so great that these diseases have become highly politicized and have engendered a very significant social movement."

Persistent Organic Pollutants

Even when we enter this world as babies we have already been affected by our parents' exposure to many chemicals. One group of chemicals—**Persistent Organic Pollutants** (POPs)—is particularly worrisome because of its ubiquitous presence throughout the world. POPs, a class of carbon containing chemicals with an affinity for fat, can in small concentrations "disrupt a whole slew of normal biological processes in ways that can promote cancer, suppress the immune system, and interfere with brain functioning, fertility, and fetal development" (Steingraber 2001: 137).

8.2 The Dirty Dozen: POPs banned under the Stockholm Convention (2004)

Aldrin—insecticide
Chlordane—insecticide
DDT—insecticide
Dieldrin—insecticide
Dioxins—industrial by-products
Eldrin—insecticide, rodenticide
Furans—industrial by-products
Heptachlor—insecticide
Hexachlorobenzene—fungicide, industrial by-product
Mirex—insecticide, fire retardant
Polychlorinated biphenyls—electrical insulators, other commercial uses
Toxaphene—insecticide
The European Union wants nine more chemicals added to this list.
Sources: Hogue 2000, Reuters News Service 2004.

POPs include chemicals such as dioxin, polychlorinated biphenyls (PCBs), and perfluorocarbons (PFCs), and pesticides such as DDT, aldrin, chlordane, and more. They also include aromatic amines and phthalates found in plastics, and brominated flame retardants (PBDEs). PFCs are an ingredient in Teflon, carpets, fast-food packaging, clothing, and more. In addition to flame retardant material, PBDEs are found in computer casings, televisions, furniture, cars, and rugs. POPs are persistent because they accumulate in the fat cells of our body and are stored there for a long time. They break down slowly and biomagnify, which means that they increase in concentration as they move up the food chain. We know little about the cumulative or synergistic effects of exposure to them. Children differ from adults in that they absorb toxins better and eliminate them more slowly, because human livers and kidneys do not fully develop until people are in their twenties. Studies show that compared to adults, children have twice the level of pesticides in their blood (Brooymans 2004).

PCBs are also spread through the atmosphere by what is called the grasshopper effect, which occurs when PCBs evaporate into the atmosphere and then in colder climates, where the PCBs condense and become part of the water droplets, drift back to Earth. This phenomenon explains why concentrations are so high among the Inuit in Canada, even though no POPs are produced in Northern Canada and are used very little there (United Nations Environment Programme, cited in People and the Planet 2004).

By May 2004 a number of countries had agreed, in a United Nations pact, to ban twelve of the most toxic chemicals—known as the "Dirty Dozen" and all containing chlorine (Doyle 2004b). DDT was still to be allowed in some countries to control malaria-carrying mosquitoes. The United States refused to sign the agreement, stating concerns that the

8.3 Circles of Poison

The *Multinational Monitor* reports:

> The persistence of the deadly [pesticide] trade is an international disgrace, a crime committed by the North against the South—and against itself. For the Third World, imported pesticides which are banned or restricted in Northern countries cause pesticide poisonings and severe environmental degradation. Consumers in Northern countries are also affected, as pesticides legally barred from appearing on their food slip through weak border inspection programs and show up on fruits and vegetables imported from countries which purchase the pesticides. The World Health Organization has recently estimated that Third World agricultural workers experience 25 million cases of acute occupational pesticide poisoning each year.... Tens of thousands die from workplace exposures, with many more undoubtedly suffering from pesticide-induced or -related diseases.... Many of the most toxic effects are caused by pesticides banned or restricted in industrialized countries. Northern countries have imposed restrictions on their use precisely because they are dangerous—but the restrictions do not apply to sales to the Third World.

Source: *Multinational Monitor* editorial 1991: 1.

language of the agreement could impede the future development of chemicals (World Wildlife Fund 2004).

The European Union wants PBDEs added to the Stockholm Convention's banned list of POPs (Reuters News Service 2004). Levels of PDBE in breast milk have increased by four times compared to levels in the early 1990s. The breast milk of Canadian mothers contains the second-highest PBDE levels in the world (Mittelstaedt 2004c). Animal experiments link it to learning and memory problems, and thyroid dysfunction. There is speculation that there may be a link between PBDEs, attention deficit hyperactivity disorder (ADHD), and thyroid disorders in humans (Mittelstaedt 2004c).

The Beginning of Life

There is a growing awareness of the reproductive impacts of toxic exposures for both men and women. Fathers are not innocent bystanders as toxic exposures affect sperm quality and quantity and therefore fetal health. Canadian scientists recently reported that male mice that breathed particulates in the air around an industrial area in Hamilton, Ontario passed on twice as many mutations through their sperm to their offspring as did male mice that breathed either filtered or country air (McIlroy 2004). A large-scale study of men working at the Sellafield nuclear reprocessing plant revealed that "the risk of a stillbirth increased with the father's exposure to radiation before conception" and "the risk of the stillborn babies having developed severe defects such as spina bifida in the womb was also higher" (BBC 1999).

A study of both breast-fed and bottle-fed babies showed that prenatal exposure to PCBs produces deficits. The higher the blood level of PCBs in the umbilical cord of the newborn, the poorer the neurological condition, the lower the psychomotor scores, the lower the cognitive abilities, the slower the reaction times, and the more signs of hyperactive behaviours and attention problems later in life (Steingraber 2001).

The breastfeeding dilemma

When a mother starts breastfeeding, the fat cells throughout her body are mobilized to become nourishment for the baby. The POPs become concentrated in the breast milk and the subsequent bioaccumulation, or storage, of POPs in the fat tissues of babies occurs at a time when the infants are at their smallest weight and in their fastest growth period. The livers of infants under six months of age are unable to detoxify these chemicals. Most POPs also affect the neurological system and can affect brain and nervous system development. A big concern is the long-term effects of POPs as probable carcinogens (National Research Council 1993). Writer and ecologist Sandra Steingraber (2001: 252–53) found:

> Those who had been breastfed at least six weeks as infants had nearly four times more PCB's in their blood serum than children who had been bottle-fed.... In addition to DDT and PCBs, common contaminants of breast milk include flame retardants, fungicides, wood preservatives, termite poisons, mothproofing agents, toilet deodorizers, cable-insulating materials, dry-cleaning fluids, gasoline vapours, and the chemical by-products of garbage incineration.

The good news is that for the last twenty years there has been a steady downward trend in the concentration of some POPs in breast milk, due to the banning of the most toxic POPs in many countries (Steingraber 2001). The bad news is that new POPs are being found in blood and woman's breast milk.

Although the statistics that show breast milk contains higher levels of POPs than bottled milk might seem to indicate that bottle-feeding is a superior choice for babies, the evidence still favours breastfeeding. Breastfed babies have higher IQs, fewer infections (including ear infections), fewer instances of sudden infant death syndrome, and better neurological cognitive and development scores. They are less likely to become obese, have fewer emotional problems, and are more likely to stay in school longer (Steingraber 2001).

Environmental Health Impacts of War

Many of the key industries that work with chemical toxins are part of the **military-industrial complex** (for example, pesticide, uranium, fluoride, and electronics industries). C. Wright Mills (1956) described this complex as a matter of interconnected power relationships among economic, political, and military elites. These elites basically converted the United States into a "private corporate economy" after World War II, perpetuating a "permanent war economy." After serving two terms as president of the United States, in his farewell broadcast former General Dwight Eisenhower called on citizens to recognize the "grave implications" of the development of the military-industrial complex and to "guard against" its "acquisition of unwarranted influence" (Word IQ 2004). Some forty years later that military-industrial complex is still very much with us, and Canada plays a key role in it, producing or providing the raw materials for weapons.

Canada provided uranium for the nuclear bombs that were dropped on Hiroshima and Nagasaki in Japan. The Elmira, Ontario-based Uniroyal Company was one of ten corporations that produced Agent Orange—the toxic defoliant that U.S. troops used during the Vietnam War. Canadian uranium is also used in weapons that contain depleted uranium (DU). A conservative estimate of the DU used in wars in the Middle East, Afghanistan, and Eastern Europe since 1991 is over 3,500 tons. The DU levels in Afghani citizens after the U.S. military intervention are the highest levels measured in a human population (Sherman 2004: 3). The Human Rights Tribunal in Geneva condemned the use of DU in warfare in 1996, calling the component "a weapon of mass destruction" (Bertell 1999). In 1999 initiatives by a UN subcommittee to ban DU were blocked, primarily by the

8.4 The End of Life

Edward Abbey urges us to "get the hell out of the way, with our bodies decently planted into the earth to nourish other forms of life." There are good reasons for this advice. Berton explains that crematoriums release toxins such as chromium, lead, nickel, and, "most significantly, mercury," primarily from mercury dental fillings in human bodies. Stowe, Schmidt, and Green add that with embalmed bodies, "Toxins, such as arsenic... formaldehyde, and gluteraldehyde, may leak from gravesites and pollute groundwater." Caskets and vaults may leach varnishes, preservatives, sealants and metals. In addition, many graveyards are routinely treated with pesticides.

There are better ecological alternatives. We can remember our loved ones by diverting money we would spend on toxic burials to "green burials" in designated reserves. Non-embalmed bodies can be buried in biodegradable caskets. California's first organic cemetery will be opening in 2004 with no embalming fluid, metal caskets, or floral arrangements allowed.

This thinking fits with Leopold's land ethic: "A thing is right only when it tends to preserve the integrity, stability, and beauty of the community, and the community includes the soil, waters, fauna and flora, as well as people."

Sources: E. Abbey in Stowe, Schmidt, and Green 2001; Leopold 1991: 345; Berton 2001; *Globe and Mail*, Aug. 12, 2004: A16; Loeffler 1989: 18.

United States (Johnson 2002).

Many of the veterans of the first Gulf War have health problems, and about one-third of them have been granted health claims by the U.S. Department of Veteran Affairs (Sherman 2004: 3). In addition, in Iraq, there is a sevenfold increase in childhood malignancies (compared to before the first Gulf War) (Caldicott 2002). Gulf-war-related illnesses represent another form of "contested illness," which means that there are major scientific disputes and public debates about their possible environmental causes (Brown 2003: 214).

Documenting Environmental Health Problems

> If you know where the chemical industry is, you know where the cancer hotspots are.... NCI (National Cancer Institute) researchers found higher death rates for all those living in the cancer hotspots—not just the workers in the offending plants.
> —Reiman 2001: 89.

Lay people and even empathic researchers have a hard time proving the existence of an indisputable causal link between environmental factors and disease. They also find it difficult to demonstrate that a specific disease is caused by exposure to specific environmental contaminants.

Disagreements about the health effects of exposure of industrial emissions and the responsibility of corporate and government officials frequently create internal tension in communities. Workers in contaminated areas are often reluctant to speak up about the pollution that they are exposed to at work and in their surroundings, for fear of losing their jobs or being ostracized by fellow workers. Working on environmental health issues in a neighbourhood takes a tremendous amount of energy. Women frequently head community-based groups (Pellow and Park 2002, Brown 2000), but may receive no support. In addition they may experience active opposition from their spouses or their neighbours, particularly if they work for the industry that is the source of the toxic emissions (see the movie *Erin Brockovich*, for example).

The people who lobby for action on environmental health problems frequently feel demoralized, particularly if they perceive that industry and government are unhelpful. Typically residents lose faith that the world is just, and they lose trust in government and in the economic and political systems because of the failure to help them (Brown, Kroll-Smith, and Gunter 2000).

Environmental health controversies are surrounded by uncertainties (Brown, Kroll-Smith, and Gunter 2000). Many doctors do not have any training in diagnosing environmental health problems, and few inquire into a patient's history of exposure to toxins. It is difficult to know when a specific level of exposure to a toxin will cause health problems, particularly in those who are most vulnerable (infants, children, and people with weak immune systems). We don't know the synergistic or cumulative effects of exposure to multiple environmental toxins.

8.5 Getting Diagnosed

A number of scientific uncertainties make it difficult to diagnose environmental health problems.

a) Patients may not know what toxin they have been exposed to.
b) There is a lack of data on the response to the dose of a specific toxin.
c) We don't know the combined (synergistic) effects of toxic exposure.
d) Etiological uncertainty—it is difficult to prove that a specific disease is caused by exposure to specific toxins.
3) Diagnostic uncertainty—many doctors have little or no training in the diagnosis of environmental health problems, or no access to specialized diagnostic laboratories.

Sources: Brown et al. 2004; Epstein 1998.

Most medical doctors and scientists working within mainstream medicine adhere to the biomedical model, which is scientifically based and focuses on physical causes and treatments, adhering to a single cause-effect explanation for cancer. This model is more like a "tinkering service" that involves experts repairing clients (Marshall 1998: 406). With cancer, the onus is placed on individuals to avoid cancer exposures (through healthy diets and lifestyles, for example) and to seek early detection (using mammography to detect breast cancer, or a blood test to detect prostate cancer). The research itself becomes largely focused on searching for the "magic bullet" to cure cancer.

In biomedical research cancer patterns become indicators of whether or not a particular substance is harmful, and this happens for several reasons: cancer is easily identifiable; animals, such as mice, have been genetically bred to be more susceptible to cancer; the research can be easily compared; and cancer is still a topic that attracts a lot of research money. But this biomedical model is problematic. For one thing it implies a "uniformity of medical ideas about causation and treatment" (Marshall 1998: 406). Another drawback is the usual lag or latency period between toxic exposure and the onset of health-related problems, which means that the illness takes a long time to show up, especially in humans. This characteristic makes it harder in real life to figure out exactly which toxin caused the cancer. Many changes occur in an organism before cancer manifests itself, and researchers are beginning to focus on earlier signs of dysfunction, such as changes in the immune system or liver function. Furthermore, toxins may cause other debilitating problems such as breathing difficulties, reproductive problems, inflammation, and arthritis.

The environmental and health movements are beginning to question why we wait until a disease such as cancer occurs before we address a problem. New studies are showing that exposure to toxins can also be linked to genetic mutations in specific genes. These biomarkers may help researchers to monitor human exposures to toxins and provide evidence of potential hazards—which could enhance risk assessments and "better inform regulatory decisions" (Markowitz and Rosner 2002: 295). The biomedical model also tends not to consider the social and political context of environmental health problems; it dismisses these as "confounding factors." Researchers who adhere to the biomedical model feel that confounding factors make it difficult for them to control for outside factors in establishing a single cause-effect relationship in medical experiments (Ali 2004). Environmental health movements seek a more holistic approach, stressing the importance of context.

Including context, however, leads to politicization, which government scientists and industry want to avoid altogether (Ali 2004). It is the context, after all, that creates inequities in the exposure of industrial chemicals—for example, locating factories that are known for releasing toxins to the air and water in minority neighbourhoods (Pellow and Park 2002) or within a specific industry assigning the most toxic tasks to minority workers. For example, electronics factories tend to locate in minority communities, contaminating the air, water, and land. Community health studies in Silicon Valley, California, indicate high rates of "birth defects, cancer, respiratory ailments and unexplained fatal illness" in both workers and nearby residents (Pellow and Park 2002: 2). Most computer assembly work in Silicon Valley is done by women of minority background, particularly East Asian and Mexican, and they have many reproductive problems related to toxic exposures.

The politicization of the toxins issue means that researchers who are knowledgeable about the health impacts of chemicals can be difficult to find. Industry-funded researchers are understandably wary of exposing the link between their industry's practice, government policy, and the production and emission of toxins into the environment. Establishing that link can mean "biting the hand that feeds them." Oppositional scientists—experts who are "willing to support communities in their efforts to seek recognition and assistance from industry or government" (Brown, Kroll-Smith, and Gunter 2000: 19)—often pay a price for their work, including industry lobbies that attack their research, the loss of grants, damaged reputations, and even being fired (for example, Health Canada scientists) (Haley 2000; Council of Canadians 2004a; Markowitz and Rosner 2002). As a result, many industry-funded studies are never published (Markowitz and Rosner 2003). Still, the work continues. As one group of researchers pointed out, "Activist involvement in science pushes scientists to examine why they ask certain questions and not others, why they use certain methodologies, and ... to examine how their research affects women with breast cancer" (McCormick et al., 2004: 6).

Increasingly, lay people are forming alliances with experts to provide clues about sources of exposures and the pattern of effects on vegetation, animals, and humans. Together they are sometimes carrying out a form of community-based research known as popular epidemiology—sometimes called environmental epidemiology—which builds upon people's personal knowledge of illness and considers the context of the environmental health problems in working to gain an understanding of the situation (Brown 2000). Oppositional scientists learn about the symptoms of affected people and benefit from citizens' insights on the possible paths of exposure. This collaboration enables lay people to document environmental exposures and have their health problems diagnosed and treated. Citizens and their advocates can then use this information as evidence in environmental inquiries or lawsuits, in seeking compensation, and in pressing for policies to hold corporations and governments accountable.

Popular epidemiology challenges some of the traditional assumptions of scientific research and medicine. It stresses the value of experiential knowledge and questions the neutrality of normal science. For example, the late Dr. George Waldbott and Dr. Lennart Krook, a veterinarian—both of them flouride specialists—worked with communities near phosphate and aluminum factories, helping them to document industrial fluorosis. They promoted the **precautionary principle**—protecting human health and preventing exposure to chemical toxins even before a pattern of fluoride poisoning is established in a community.

8.6 Love Canal's Oppositional Scientist: Beverly Paigen

Love Canal, N.Y., is one of the most famous cases of early environmental activism related to environmental contamination in the United States. During the 1940s and 1950s, Hooker Chemical Company dumped thousands of tons of highly toxic chemical waste into Love Canal, contaminating the neighbourhood. When Dr. Beverly Paigen became involved with documenting the health problems among the people in Love Canal, she reconsidered the implications of adhering to the biomedical model and its affiliated epidemiological model (also known as the dominant epidemiological paradigm).

> Before Love Canal, I also needed a 95 percent certainty before I was convinced of a result. But seeing this rigorously applied in a situation where the consequences of an error meant that pregnancies were resulting in miscarriages, stillbirths, and children with medical problems, I realized I was making a value judgment.... Whether to make errors on the side of protecting human health or on the side of conserving state resources.

Source: Brown and Mikkelsen 1997.

Doctors Waldbott and Krook differ from other health professionals who follow the dominant epidemiological paradigm (DEP), a belief system that dictates what diseases actually exist and what their causes are (Brown et al. 2003: 235). Like the biomedical model, the DEP has been criticized for being reductionist and seeing the world in mechanistic terms—for not being able to "account for complex interactions and social relationships that determine outcomes in complex systems" (Markowitz and Rosner 2002: 295). The DEP has prevented health researchers and officials from examining a health problem in a different light, and DEP studies have been

8.7 Steps in Conducting Popular Epidemiology

One of the most famous cases of popular epidemiology occurred in the small town of Woburn, Mass. Citizens who take part in popular epidemiology in contaminated communities tend to go through a number of stages, not necessarily in the following order.

1. Noticing health effects in themselves, their families, or neighbours.
2. Noticing pollutants.
3. Suspecting that something unusual is happening, usually that there is a connection between the health effects and the pollutants.
4. Sharing information with other members of their community and forming a common approach to the situation.
5. Becoming a more cohesive group, reading, asking questions, talking to government officials and scientific experts about the health problems and the suspected contaminants.
6. Organizing a residents' group to investigate further.
7. Pressuring government agencies to carry out official studies (of the contaminants, of the health problems). Typically these studies conclude that there is no link between the contaminants and the health effects.
8. Seeking their own experts for their community group to carry out a health study and to investigate the source of the contaminants, and any pathways of exposure.
9. Engaging in lawsuits and confrontation.
10. Pressing for acknowledgment of their popular epidemiological studies by scientific experts and government agencies.

Source: Brown 1993.

used to dismiss community concerns about exposures to industrial pollution. These studies have been criticized for failing "to make links between a contaminant, an iatrogenic treatment, or another problem of human/social action," which "results in inadequate recognition, treatment, and prevention" (Brown, Kroll-Smith, and Gunter 2000: 217). For example, Gulf war veterans reported that scientists, medical doctors, the U.S. government, and military agencies were reluctant to investigate health problems that the veterans believed were due to toxic exposures experienced on duty. The exposures included radiation from atomic testing and chemical exposure to the defoliant Agent Orange (Vietnam), Sarin, a neurotoxin (Shane 2004), and depleted uranium (Gulf Wars).

A Case Study of Popular Epidemiology in Action

In spring 2004 residents living near Fort Saskatchewan, Alberta, in Northeast Strathcona County—an area known as the province's Industrial Heartland, located just outside of Edmonton—entered into what became a series of official hearings related to the expansion of chemical factories in their neighbourhood. In a hearing of the Natural Resources Conservation

Board (NRCB), the residents challenged the multinational corporation Agrium Products, which produces fertilizers and other industrial products and wanted to expand its huge waste phosphogypsum piles (Kennedy, Powell, and Leggatt 2004). Alberta's Industrial Heartland was officially formed in 2001 to promote the processing of the bitumen from Alberta's tar sands and to promote any chemical spinoff industries related to this activity. The Northeast Strathcona County residents were worried about how the pollution from Agrium and other industries was affecting both the land around them and their health, including the health of their children, family pets and livestock. They became more and more alerted to what they found were the synergistic and cumulative impacts of their exposures to the many industrial chemicals emitted by the nearby chemical factories. (See Insert 8.9.)

They soon found out that Agrium Products was emitting huge volumes of airborne fluoride, in various forms. Fluoride, they learned, causes specific damage to vegetation, and to animal and human health. The residents also quickly learned that phosphate factories have a history of fluoride pollution, and they sought help from fluoride experts who were not funded by industry. They learned that the damage they were seeing on the land around them, including burn marks on crops and vegetables, was characteristic of fluoride pollution. They learned to recognize the stained teeth in their cattle as indicative of flourosis or flouride poisoning. In addition the residents began to correlate their own symptoms, such as bouts of gastro-intestinal problems, irritation of the respiratory track and of the eyes, and arthritic-like pains even in the young children, with symptoms of fluoride exposure (Kennedy, Powell, and Leggett, 2004).

Working closely with the experts, the residents learned how to take vegetation samples and digital photos of both their children's and their cattle's teeth. Lab analysis indicated fluoride damage in the crops and vegetation. Photo analysis indicated dental fluorosis—a key indicator of systemic fluoride exposure—in some of the children, and in the cattle. Armed

8.8 Open for Business

Alberta's Industrial Heartland, minutes away from Edmonton, is Canada's primary chemical alley. The website for the Industrial Heartland boasts that this area has the "largest petroleum and petrochemical processing network in Canada" and is Canada's largest centre for upgrading the petroleum, petrochemical, and chemical industries. Here bitumen from the tar sands feeds huge petrochemical factories and refineries, much of which is then distributed to the United States. Petrochemical and chemical corporations with factories in the Industrial Heartland include Dow Chemical, Shell Canada, Imperial Oil, Amoco, Chevron, Agrium, Sherritt International, BP Energy, Oxyvinyls Canada, and Nexen Chemicals, among others, with $11 billion invested. By 2007 another $47.2 billion will be invested here. The website states that Alberta provides a "business friendly environment with a minimum of red tape and regulatory hurdles," and lots of room to expand—the Heartland is approximately 75 square miles.

Source: Industrial Heartland website.

8.9 Locaton of the Northeast Strathcona County Residents group in the Industrial Heartland.

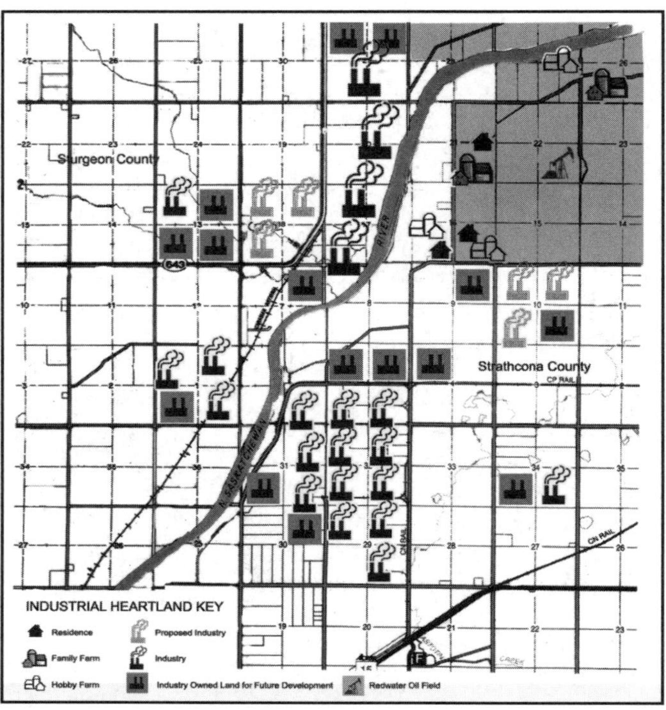

The factories on this map show only those factories in close vicinity to these families. They include oil refineries and upgraders (which process crude oil from bitumen from the tar sands in northern Alberta), a natural gas fractionation factory and underground natural gas storage. In addition there are spinoff industries of the petrochemical industry that produce fertilizers, styrene, pesticides, vinyl-chloride and hydrogen peroxide. There are many other emissions from factories located just beyond these factories.

Source: Adapted from the county maps for Strathcona and Sturgeon Counties. Graphics by C. M. Zuby, Ian Grivois, and Cheryl Henkelman.

with this evidence, the residents of Northeast Strathcona County began to pressure the government and local industry to relocate eight families who were now surrounded by the growing number of chemical factories in the Industrial Heartland and believed they had no choice but to move (Kennedy, Powell, and Leggett, 2004).

Learning from the past?

Alberta's Industrial Heartland might learn a few lessons from sick workers in Sarnia, Ontario, where the local "chemical valley" is a maze of petrochemical factories. According to reporter Martin Mittelstaedt, "The Sarnia area has 20 per cent of the country's refineries, hosts Canada's largest hazardous-waste dumps, produces about 40 per cent of the country's petrochemicals and... has some of the country's highest discharges into the environment of dangerous chemicals." As a result Sarnia has seen the "worst outbreak of industrial disease in recent Canadian history."

> The local occupational-disease clinic has in the past six years been contacted by 2,944 workers complaining of a bewildering and horrifying array of illnesses. Besides mesotheliomas [tumours of the lungs, or of the lining of the pleural or abdominal cavities, associated especially with exposure to asbestos], there are leukemias, lung cancers, brain cancers, breast cancers and gastrointestinal cancers, among other afflictions. (Mittelstaedt 2004b)

In Sarnia, as in other contaminated communities, industrial cancers are "family affairs," as women who washed their partners' clothes were also exposed to asbestos dust. Yet no one has conducted a detailed health study of Sarnia's blue-collar communities, and there is no national registry that tracks cancer cases by occupation (Mittelstaedt 2004b).

There will be many more cancers and health problems, given that there were many exposures in the 1980s, and asbestos-related diseases have a latency period of thirty to forty years. Sarnia industries have also had many toxic spills that compound toxic exposures to workers and nearby communities.

Holding government and industry accountable

Despite the uncertainty in linking environmental hazards and health impacts, there have been cases where such links were well known (for example, in the cases of lead and vinyl chloride). All too often such knowledge has been kept from full public view. It is tragic that the Sarnia workers were exposed to asbestos fibres, because asbestos disease was first reported in 1908, and by 1918 insurance companies in the United States and Canada were refusing to sell life insurance to people who worked with asbestos. Leading asbestos manufacturers knew the health dangers of asbestos fibres but covered up the information and failed to warn people of the hazards (Mokhiber 1988).

Industry has deep pockets, and governments often depend heavily on industry data to set standards, instead of doing their own monitoring and testing. Industry bodies play an influential role in the setting of "acceptable" standards (Markowitz and Rosner 2002). Many chemical companies

8.10 Workers Bear the Brunt of the Effects of Asbestos

Exposure to asbestos causes mesothelioma (cancer of the lung pleura) and asbestosis (a pulmonary disease). Asbestos mines in Quebec continue to receive provincial and federal subsidies and loan guarantees. Quebec men have one of the highest rates of mesothelioma in the world; Quebec women have the highest rate in the world. When France banned the import of goods containing chrysotile (a type of asbestos that is less dusty and crumbles less easily than some asbestos fibres), Canada challenged the ban, arguing that there was inadequate science to justify it. Joan Kuyek explains: "Canada's role in... discrediting those scientists who oppose asbestos exports is well documented, and is increasingly becoming a scandal in Europe and in the developing world.... Economic gains should never be an excuse for knowingly poisoning workers and their communities."

Source: Kuyek 2004: 2.

in Canada prefer self-monitoring to regulation and are involved in a program called Responsible Care, "a self-regulatory scheme to avert government regulation (Glasbeek 2002: 242).[1] Joel Bakan (2004: 110) considers Responsible Care to be hypocritical and immoral. He argues that it is a tactic by industry to prevent democratic society from acting through its government: "No one would seriously suggest that individuals should regulate themselves, that laws against murder, assault and theft are unnecessary because people are socially responsible. Yet oddly, we are asked to believe that corporations... should be free to govern themselves."

A root cause of many of our environmental and social problems is the "compulsion" of corporations to externalize their costs (Bakan 2004; Glasbeek 2002). For example, industries may avoid installing more expensive scrubbers for their waste stacks, or avoid proper disposal of their wastes in order to reduce costs. As Bakan (2004: 60) puts it, "Harms to workers, consumers, communities, the environment... tend to be viewed as inevitable and acceptable consequences of corporate activity—externalities in the coolly technical jargon of economics." Corporations externalize their costs because the benefits of doing so outweigh the costs, and they tend to be habitual offenders. "Risk/benefit analyses" are premised on the idea that a certain level of risk is "acceptable" given the advantages offered by industrial (and military) processes. For example, despite the lead industry's knowledge of the toxicity of lead, particularly with regard to children, for many years it promoted the benefits of adding lead to paint and putting lead in gasoline (Markowitz and Rosner 2002). This kind of thinking is based on a set of assumptions that are refuted by our growing knowledge about ecosystems and the synergistic reactions of chemicals.

Thornton (2000: 416) is highly critical of risk assessments, arguing that they protect the status quo and hide the politics regarding how decisions about toxic emissions are really made: "Risk assessment is a method designed to determine how to permit pollution sources, not whether they should be permitted." Many environmental health researchers and citizens argue that there is enough proof already that certain substances or groups of substances have been shown to be toxic. They are asking why these substances should not be banned, and they are pressuring industry to create environmentally benign substitutes.

Corporations also know given the dominant capitalist agenda of a liberal democracy, their behaviour will not be harshly sanctioned (Glasbeek 2002). Governments are often unwilling or unable to enforce laws that would hurt industries financially, in part because a political party that is too active in enforcing environmental standards will lose financial support from the industries in question. Industries can also always play the trump card of threatening to relocate to another country where the laws are lax and the labour is cheaper, an approach known as environmental blackmail (Bryant and Mohai 1997). Deborah Robinson (2000) states:

> Financial institutions and trade agreements have facilitated the movement of capital and goods across borders. Corporations have become more powerful than nation states and are not accountable to anyone except their shareholders. Their mobility has made it possible for them to seek the greatest profit, the least government regulations, and the best tax incentives, anywhere in the world. Workers are exposed to economic and environmental blackmail; they either accept low-paying, often non-unionized jobs with environmental health risks, or the jobs will move to another country.

In Sarnia one worker (who later died) described what the companies were doing as murder. His wife told a reporter: "You can't get away with it in private life, if you expose somebody or give them poison. You're going to be charged with murder. This is just legalized murder... he felt they killed him" (Mittelstaedt 2004b: F4).

In many cases corporations and their decision-makers take steps with full knowledge of the illegal or unethical nature of the activities. When corporations commit wrongs through carelessness, instead of premeditation, they often compound their guilt by "hiding, lying or falsifying" (Glasbeek 2002: 142). **Corporate crime** and **corporate deviance** tend to be systematic, with corporations committing crimes to help solve specific business problems. Researchers have documented rampant "lying and obfuscation" in the lead, vinyl chloride, tobacco, automobile, asbestos, fluoride, and nuclear power industries (Markowitz and Rosner 2002; Bryson 2004). "In this era of privatization, deregulation, and globalization," Markowitz and Rosner (2002) note, there is a particular concern that "the threat from unregulated industry is even greater. In fact, a deeper schism than ever separates the broader population's concerns about industrial pollution and the current political establishment's infatuation with market mechanisms and voluntary compliance."

Company employees who speak out against wrongdoing in their

workplaces are often stigmatized, especially in small, one-industry towns, where public "whistle blowing" can pit a worker against neighbours, friends, and even family members who earn their living in that industry (Brown and Mikkelson 1997; Pellow and Park 2002). Many industries are skilful at showing the face of a good corporate citizen by helping local charities and sports groups, for instance, and thereby fostering loyalty among their workers and communities (Markowitz and Rosner 2002).

Challenging occupational and environmental health problems caused by the military-industrial complex—with its power, influence, and secrecy— is particularly difficult. Environmental health advocate H. Patricia Hynes (2003) points out: "Worldwide, the military is the most secretive, shielded, and privileged of polluters; thus, in most cases, we lack the data for definitive health studies that enable us to attribute reproductive disorders, cancers, illness, and death in exposed populations to military pollution."

The documentary film *Fahrenheit 9/11* highlights the conflicts of interest involving the George W. Bush administration and weapons manufacturers. By early 2005, by one estimate, the war in Iraq, which began with the invasion in March 2003, had cost the United States over $150 billion—and rising—in congressional appropriations alone (Matsakis, Niko, and Elias Vlanton 2004). The "new" military-industrial complex is high-tech—with many of the industries (such as Lockheed Martin Corporation, Boeing Corporation, and Raytheon Corporation) tied to the Defense Department.

Resistance: Forming Social Movements

The growing incidence of environmental problems and the soaring cancer rates in industrialized societies are spawning a strong reaction. Social movements are addressing specific environmental health problems (breast cancer, Gulf War veterans' illnesses, toxic waste, genetically engineered food, for example). As a result these movements are making regulators, universities, and the industry take notice: "their protests and negotiations led to the commissioning of several health studies and the nationwide change in company policies regarding the use of certain toxins" (Pellow and Park 2002: 104–105).

Health social movements

Social movements—informal networks of people who share common beliefs and organize around difficult and usually contentious issues—adopt various tactics to achieve their goals (Della Porta and Diani 1999). Until recently, social movement researchers and sociologists have not paid much attention to health social movements, which involve people collectively challenging "medical policy and politics" (Brown et al. 2004). These movements range from concentrating on issues around toxic waste and environmental justice to issues of occupational health and safety, contested illness, and even peace.[2] One subset, the alternative health-care movement, challenges the biomedical model and promotes the prevention and investigation of environmental illnesses. Another subset, the organic, ecological, and humane food movement, addresses issues such as the McDonaldization of food and the industrialization of agriculture (see chapter four). These movements challenge various aspects of society that affect our health, including belief systems about the causes and treatments of health problems, the ways of doing scientific and medical research on these topics, the media coverage of health issues, and the management of organizations (formal and informal). Their ability to challenge the dominant epidemiological paradigm is influenced by factors such as scientific uncertainty, organizational barriers (and deceit), the degree to which an illness is stigmatized, and environmental injustice and environmental racism (Brown et al. 2000).

Health social movements challenge various forms of power (political, corporate, military, scientific, medical, media) and the personal and collective identities of people experiencing health issues.[3] The new movements embrace a new "public paradigm" influenced by Sheldon Krimsky's (2000) concept of a "public hypothesis," a stage that results when lay people demand to participate in scientific investigations and debates around issues that have a direct or personal impact on their lives (McCormick, Brown, and Zavestoski 2004). Health social movements address:

1. access to or provision of health-care services (for example, directing research funds to the study of environmental causes of their illnesses; getting diagnosed in order to qualify for disability pensions);
2. health inequalities and inequities (for example, greater toxic exposures to Black and minority workers in the workplace and in their communities); and/or
3. the actual illness and disability experiences of their members (Brown et al. 2004).

Environnmental justice movement

A new and broader environmental justice (EJ) movement is emerging that addresses how some "communities (and workers) are unfairly burdened with environmental toxics" (Pellow and Park 2002: 197). While the toxic waste movement addresses health problems in communities exposed to industrial pollution, and the occupational health and safety movement addresses the workplace, the EJ movement addresses "health inequality and inequities" based on race and ethnicity. Drawing members predominately from the environmental, labour, and civil rights movements, the EJ movement promotes sustainable production and "democratic decision-making structures that empower both community members and workers" (Pellow and Park 2002: 197).

The environmental justice movement has evolved from addressing the placement of toxic waste sites and polluting factories in minority communities to addressing gender and racial inequities in the workplace (Pellow and Park 2002). The movement has been particularly active in organizing electronics workers and communities near computer assembly factories in Silicon Valley and in forming international coalitions with movements in other countries. Among other things the EJ movement presses for the regulation of the global electronics industry to ensure that workers and communities are protected from toxic exposures. For example, environmental justice groups in Silicon Valley, California, also launched the Campaign to End the Miscarriage of Justice, urging the computer industry to phase out the use of ethylene-based glycol ethers, which may cause miscarriages (Pellow and Park 2002).

Embodied health movements

Embodied health movements (EHMs) are centred on actual lived experiences of disease, disability, and illness. The members, frustrated with the dominant epidemiological paradigm, collectively believe that the problems faced in their illnesses or by their disability group are due to social structures such as scientific bodies and the biomedical system and are unjust. Yet, unlike members of other social movements, members of EHMs are dependent on scientific and medical allies to help them get research funding, insurance coverage, and money for their support groups. For that reason they tend to form coalitions with scientists as a means of influencing scientific research, medical treatment, policy-making, and funding (Brown at al. 2004).

Social movement theories do not adequately address EHMs, for several reasons. The theories overlook how class influences access to health care and health outcomes. They do not address people's lived experiences of illness or disability or how a disillusionment with the biomedical model can propel people into collective action. In addition, social movement theories cannot account for how EHMs develop even without "political opportunities." Finally, while most other social movements challenge the state, EHMs mainly critique scientific and medical bodies. Their members question whether they can trust experts whose knowledge does not correspond with their lived knowledge of environmental health problems. Members of EHMS also tend to blur the boundaries between social movements by moving back and forth between them (for example, from the environmental to feminist, or civil rights), and between lay and expert roles. EHMs also "cross boundaries," with members working inside government units or voluntary health organizations (Brown et al. 2004: 10). These inside members empower lay members by facilitating the exchange of lay and expert knowledge. The Environmental Breast Cancer Movement (EBCM) and the Gulf War-Related Illness movement are examples of EHMs.

Environmental breast cancer movement

During the 1980s, women influenced by the feminist movement began to make public their personal stories of breast cancer. At first women only criticized the medical control of their bodies, without challenging the biomedical model. Later the environmental breast cancer movement (EBCM) emerged, influenced by the environmental movement's focus on the health impacts of exposure to toxins. According to one team of researchers, the Environmental Breast Cancer Movement "exemplifies social movement activity at the intersection of health and the environment, which is quite possibly the largest new arena of social movements, encompassing activism around lead poisoning, toxic wastes, nuclear power, food additives, biotechnology, genetically modified organisms, toxics reduction, and the precautionary principle" (McCormick, Brown, and Zavestoski 2004: 6).

The EBCM is a hybrid movement merging members and agendas from various movements: environmental, breast cancer advocacy, feminist, women's health, and AIDS—all of which reflect the "personal as political" philosophy. Insight from these different movements has enabled movement members to address the political economy of the causes of breast cancer. This includes the failure of governments to regulate industrial pollution or toxic products, to critique research directions and treatment options, and to challenge the dominant epidemiological paradigm (McCormick, Brown, and Zavestoski 2004: 4).

The movement's citizen–scientist alliances have played a key role in democratizing breast cancer research. Scientists not only make use of information about individual exposure to toxins but also empower lay activists by teaching them science. For example, through Project LEAD (leadership, education, and advocacy development programs), epidemiologists teach science to lay activists, enabling them both to dialogue with scientists and officials and to sit on federal research review panels (McCormick, Brown, and Zavestoski 2004). The training helps lay people to influence the direction of scientific research, to cross the boundary between lay and expert. The Silent Spring Institute[4] facilitates lay input at every level of the research process "to ensure lay participation is not overshadowed by scientists' knowledge" (Brown et al. 2004: 14). Women move from being subjects in research studies to being co-investigators.

The EBCM has been particularly vocal about shifting the focus of breast cancer research from lifestyle and genetic factors to the health impacts of "unregulated industrial processes." This movement puts the onus on corporations, science, and government institutions to prevent exposures to carcinogins (Brown et al. 2004: 15; McCormick, Brown, and Zavestoski 2004). It has effectively challenged routine exposure to synthetic estrogens—so much so that the U.S. Environmental Protection Agency must now screen and test endocrine disrupting chemicals by factoring in the "cumulative, additive or synergistic effects" (McCormick, Brown, and Zavestoski 2004: 21).

Gulf War Related Illness movement

Due to organizational barriers the Gulf War Related Illness (GWRI) movement is more fragmented and less effective than either the EJ movement or the Environmental Breast Cancer Movement. War-related illnesses are stigmatized because they tarnish the vision of the GI's body representing "the body of the nation" (Brown 2003: 236). Because of this stigma, Gulf War veterans find it difficult to form citizen–scientist alliances. Scientists fear being discredited for studying a topic that is not popular with the government or with funding bodies.

The veterans are challenging an entrenched system of power: scientific, medical, governmental, and military. These institutions block crucial data on exposures, deny exposures, and prevent Gulf War veterans from investigating possible environmental causes for their illnesses. Instead veterans are told that their problems are stress-related (Brown et al. 2003: 235). Many of the scientists studying GWRIs are in the military or the U.S. Department of Veteran Affairs, the very institutions that the veterans are challenging.

The Gulf War veterans have rejected that their health problems are simply stress related and are trying to hold the U.S. government and military responsible for their health problems. War veterans and civilians are increasingly turning to class-action suits against governments and corporations for occupational and environmental health damages related to the military use of weapons. For example, U.S. Vietnam veterans, and now a Vietnamese organization called Vietnam Victims of Agent Orange Association, have sued the companies that produced Agent Orange (Fawthrop 2004). The Vietnamese lawsuit alleges "war crimes against Monsanto, Dow Chemicals and eight other companies that produced Agent Orange and other defoliants used in Vietnam" (Fawthrop 2004).

What Can We Do?

What is at stake in this issue is the capacity of each of us to make decisions and take actions to ensure our own personal health and well-being. But who has control over health in our global system? The new global trade agreements enable corporations to roam the globe in search of the slackest environmental regulations, the cheapest resources, and the cheapest labour. This trend is particularly problematic because we now have to challenge new institutions that do not value human or ecological health. In reaction, broad coalitions such as health social movements are challenging the practices and policies of scientific, medical, government, and military bodies and industry.

Active and persistent social movements can play a key role in ensuring that environmental health issues such as "laws, government, and industrial policies and practices" are addressed (Park and Pellow 2002: 214). For example, corporate deviance is finally being criminalized, with chemical companies being charged for hiding information "that led to the deaths of workers and discharge of toxins that endangered public health" (Markowitz and Rosner 2002: 305). As Pellow and Park (2002: 217) argue, "Given the necessary political will and means, even the most toxic and polluting industries could substantially reduce their chemical inputs and outputs" (Pellow and Park 2002: 217). Markowitz and Rosner (2002) advocate forming international coalitions to prevent trade agreements that prioritize profit over ecology and environmental health. But there are other personal actions people can take:

- Take advantage of the scientific coaching that some of the embodied health movements offer so that you can partake in scientific discussions on toxics in your own life. This will enable you to sit at the table with scientists and hopefully be treated as an equal partner in research and policy making.
- Do research on the toxic releases in your neighbourhood.
- Avoid living near chemical factories.
- If you are a student, check to see if your student union is investing its funds in the very companies that now have class action law suits against them for environmental harm (for example, Dow, Union Carbide). If you have money in a pension fund, check these funds as well. Push to divest these funds.
- Try to avoid chemical exposures in your diet, around the home, and in the workplace. Speak out.
- Study the information on hazards in your workplace through the WHMIS (Workplace Hazardous Materials Information System). By law, manufacturers and employers must provide information on toxics in their products and in the workplace.
- Raise environmental health issues at election time.
- If you have a particular concern, see if there is an organization that you can join that can address this. If not, start one.
- Check Environment Canada's National Toxic Release Inventory (NPRI) at <www.ec.gc.ca/pdb/querysite/location_query_e.cfm> for specific chemical release from Canadian based companies in your area. To check local emissions, type in a postal code near where you live. For example, for the Northeast Strathcona Residents. Type "T8L". Type Edmonton under major urban centre. Under Community, Step Two, type Fort Saskatchewan to check the emissions from some of the other factories in the area[5]

Useful Websites

Environmental Working Group—report on fluoride
<www.ewg.org/reports/pfcworld/index.php>

Council of Canadians
<www.canadians.org/>

Silent Spring Institute
<www.silentspring.org/newweb/about/>

Silicon Valley Toxics Coalition
<www.svtc.org/>

Environmental Research Foundation
<www.rachel.org/home_eng.htm>

Military Toxics Project
<www.miltoxproj.org>

National Gulf War Resource Centre
<www.ngwrc.org>

Physicians for Social Responsibility
<www.psr.org//home.cfm?id=home>

Agent Orange website
<www.lewispublishing.com/orange.htm>

Notes

1. During the 1980s the Canadian Chemical Producers (CCP) promoted Responsible Care in response to the growing environmental movement. A 1994 standing committee of the Canadian federal legislature recommended that all persistent bioaccumulative and toxic substances be phased out. This move created panic in industry, and the CCP "used its influence with the heavyweights in government" to convince the government to drop these recommendations and to continue the "management of the release of toxic substances rather than the prohibition of their use altogether" (Glasbeek 2002: 243).
2. Addressing concerns about the environmental health hazards posed by militarism and promoting ethical investment that screens out weapons manufacturers.
3. Having illnesses dismissed as stress-related, for instance, or having possible environmental causes for illnesses dismissed without proper investigation.
4. Dedicated to addressing the environmental causes of breast cancer, this institute is named after Rachel Carson's famous book *Silent Spring.* Carson died of breast cancer.
5. Bear in mind that emission data is mainly produced by industry. Not all emissions are required to be reported, and the releases are often averaged over a period of time, thus huge periodic releases may be hidden by the averaging of this data.

9. Entropic Futures

Michael Gismondi and Debra J. Davidson

> Far out in the uncharted backwaters of the unfashionable end of the Western Spiral arm of the Galaxy lies a small unregarded yellow sun. Orbiting this at a distance of roughly ninety-eight million miles is an utterly insignificant little blue-green planet whose ape-descended life forms are so amazingly primitive that they still think digital watches are a pretty neat idea.
>
> —Douglas Adams, *The Hitchhiker's Guide to the Galaxy*.

Energy and Society

In October 2001 the popular newsmagazine *National Post–Business* devoted a special issue to energy, with the question "Are We Running out of It?" emblazoned across the cover. A front-page teaser offered: "On the coming oil crisis—Why it's good for Canada." Not everyone reads the *Post* or would agree with its pro-business perspective, but most Canadians would acknowledge that the relationship between energy and society can no longer be taken for granted. In fact, the role of energy in social organization has been central throughout history; each change in energy source has coincided with dramatic structural changes in our social systems.

The assertion that Canada is running out of fossil-fuel-based energy is certainly not new. Geologists have been saying as much for at least fifty years. But neither is it a universally accepted belief. Indeed, if we relied solely on the energy policies of Western nations as a guide we might conclude that our supplies of fossil fuels are limitless. Even in the midst of the energy "crisis" of 1973–74, when the Organization of Petroleum Exporting Countries (OPEC) scaled back production, the U.S. government responded not with conservation but by investing more money in domestic exploration in an attempt to achieve self-sufficiency in energy supplies.

According to one historian, by the 1990s the energy crisis had largely been forgotten by the U.S. public, the world's largest consumers of energy (Nye 1998). But after 2001 and the attack on the World Trade Center that attitude altered once again, and a new "fortress North America" attitude re-emerged, with new repercussions for energy issues, and for Canada: "Since 9/11, security has come to mean North American security," one Canadian critic of energy policy says, and what that also means is "American security of supply and how Canada can advance it" (Pratt 2004: 6).

9.1 Canadian Oil Production and Reserves

Canadian conventional oil and gas production as of 2001:

- 6.6 billion barrels conventional crude oil reserves
- 2.76 million barrels oil produced per day
- 3.6% of world oil production
- Alberta's conventional oil supplies will run out in less than 60 years
- 59.7 trillion cubic feet natural gas reserves
- 13.3% percent of world's natural gas supply
- 12% of U.S. natural gas supplies in 2000 were from Canada.

Oil Sands (crude bitumen) in Alberta and Saskatchewan:

- Tars sands and heavy oil production exceeded conventional oil in 2001
- 315 billion barrels recoverable oil estimated with given technologies
- Saudi Arabian reserves include 261.1 billion barrels
- At current production rates tar sands will last approximately 1,431 years
- This is equal to about 10 years of global demand.

Canada's role in the greenhouse:

- Canada emitted 726 megatonnes CO2 mt in 2000
- This represents a 19.6% increase over 1990
- 52% of emissions due to the production/consumption of petroleum.

Source: Brownsey 2003.

Feast or famine? Cornucopianism versus limits to growth

"Energy" refers to far more than how we heat our homes or fuel our cars. Energy is embodied in all the products we produce and consume, in the circulation of and trade in those products, and even in the culture and politics of that trade system. Coming to terms with how social systems use energy—how much, what kind—requires serious consideration of our economic systems, societal structures, and ways of life. But little agreement exists on how to proceed, or even on whether there is a need to proceed. While many of us would describe the current figures on energy supply and demand as a crisis situation, thinkers who tend to **cornucopianism**—the belief that resources are inexhaustible—argue that the last two millennia have been a time of continuous modernization, of human discovery and ingenuity that adeptly overcomes energy and resource obstacles and shortfalls. For these social critics, today's ecological modernization techniques are curbing pollution, creating efficiencies in production and consumption, and driving breakthroughs that will solve the energy crisis and the global environmental crisis.

Bjørn Lomborg (2001), for example, argues that consumption rates are not the issue: because we are always discovering more oil, which leads to rising predictions as to how many years it will last, then we must not be

9.2 Environmental Security: No Blood for Oil

In 1973 Arab sheiks painted a new Islamic face on the geopolitics of oil and wealth as they held Western ways of life to ransom with oil shortages and gas price hikes. In 2001 the fragile relationship between the world's largest oil exporters and the world's largest oil importers again came to blows, in this case leading to the tragic loss of several thousand lives on September 11. If one accepts the assertion by many geophysicists that the rivers of black gold may dry up in our lifetime, we can only expect global tensions to escalate. With the global economy dependent on oil, and the geographic distribution of oil concentrated in certain regions, the international movement of oil supplies creates political and economic conflicts as exporting countries vie for increased wealth and importing countries vie for influence or control. As the war in Iraq attests, guaranteeing the international flow of petroleum has become a rationale for power struggles and military conflict.

According to a new field of study by the same name, "environmental security" is the political construct being used to justify a number of measures, including military intervention (Dalby 2002). In the name of security, North American politicians have been promoting a continental oil and gas strategy that Canadian political economist Larry Pratt calls "Fortress North America." Encompassing exploration of Arctic oil in the Northwest Territories and Alaska, pipelines across Canada to the United States, and the North American Free Trade Agreement, this strategy describes a "deeper integration of the oil and gas industries in North America" (Pratt 2004: 3), in which Canadian interests are subsumed under the U.S. flag. The strategy shifts the Canadian east-west oil and gas infrastructure proposed by Prime Minister Trudeau in the name of self-reliance towards pipelines that move oil from the north down to U.S. consumers. As Pratt (2004: 5) explains, "Security proves a selling point for energy ventures whose true motive is commercial. Insecurity is prompting a rather predatory continentalism." In conclusion: "Security [used to mean] *security of supply for Canadian consumers*, and not security of the energy users of the continent of North America." Some years ago Jeremy Rifkin (1980) argued that historical energy crises were each met by increased centralization and control, and attempts by states to extend their domain geographically to obtain new sources of energy—a process called "earth hunger" by U.S. sociologist and anti-imperialist William Graham Sumner in 1913. Is Canada the pantry for America's Earth hunger?

running out. Lomborg also highlights our increased efficiency in exploiting resources and argues that furthermore, given the tremendous achievements of science and technology, we can count on scientists to come up with substitutes for resources that do become scarce. His arguments are premised on assumptions that have had long-standing historical preeminence in Western societies: that nature's bountiful resources are endlessly available for human use and accessible to scientific understanding, and that their beneficial use awaits the human development of tools for extraction and handling. Even if oil were scarce, that scarcity would catalyze human inventiveness, leading to innovative solutions, in much the same way that coal turned into a predominant heating source when wood became scarce in Britain in the nineteenth century.

At its core, cornucopian thinking relies upon the **human exemptionalism paradigm**, or the belief that nature poses no limits on human activity; due to our intellectual capacities, humans are in effect exempt from the ecological constraints faced by every other species. Even many social scientists have until recently abided by this notion, at least implicitly, by assuming that cultures, economies, and politics can be understood without the need to consider their interactions with the environment (Catton and Dunlap 1980).

In contrast to cornucopian thinking, a number of more critical scholars argue that no major deposits of oil remain to be uncovered. Drawing on geologist M. King Hubbert's work from 1956, contemporary analysts maintain that we have arrived at the age of peak oil production, that no new large discoveries of oil or natural gas remain to be made, and that oil estimates indicate that "the slowdown in oil production may already be beginning" (Deffeys 2001: 1). Richard Heinberg (2003) asserts that world oil production per capita peaked in 1979, and given our increasing global population, energy production per capita continues to decline. Furthermore, oil extraction rates will probably begin to decline sometime between 2006 and 2015. According to Heinberg, these conditions are likely to lead to military conflicts and eventually the collapse of the global economy, followed in turn by famines and massive depopulation. He and other critics of cornucopianism conclude that human ingenuity may be too late; we are simply not working aggressively enough to discover and implement energy alternatives.

Critical social analysis, though, calls for a certain wariness of debates over oil and gas facts, figures, and fictions. While ecological limits and biophysical evidence are important, what attracts our sociological attention are the broader questions about the place of humans and their economies in nature, and the social origins of most environmental problems. Social analysis moves beyond determining whether oil is running out or not to include a number of complex issues: global inequalities in the spatial distribution of energy supply and demand and the means by which these inequalities are perpetuated by powerful vested interests; the characteristics of political systems that regulate access and production; cultural and behavioural norms that favour particular forms of energy societies; and, most importantly, the political potential for consideration of proposed alternatives to a hydrocarbon society, and the relative benefits to society and the environment of each of those alternatives.

Some alternatives are viewed as ecologically friendly and may require the decentralization of energy management—a direction called "soft pathways." Some critics insist on small-scale alternatives because these approaches are presumed to be more sustainable and socially equitable.

Other alternatives, such as nuclear power, are "hard pathways" that may address issues of fossil-fuel dependency but pose other risks for sustainability and demand a centralized management system. These debates mirror discussions over appropriate systems of more general environmental governance, with some arguing that the complexity of environmental problems requires a global managerial class of experts to oversee global ecosystems and economics. Other social analysts, concerned about the undemocratic nature of such a system, propose a people's forum of global government based on principles of justice and equity, limited growth, a fair market economy, and a democratic approach to sustainability (Monbiot 2004).

Underlying the evolution of our energy histories, the emergence of energy alternatives, and energy politics is a broad social milieu that includes multiple interests vying for influence, each with its own socially constructed ideas about scarcity, plenty, power, and wealth. It is a milieu that includes both the structuralist (also known as realist) and social constructionist perspectives. Analyzing this social milieu will put us in a better position to acknowledge our personal role, address inequities in energy access and consumption, and envision alternative futures. The discussion also brings in the laws of thermodynamics that dictate energy's behaviour and its implications for the politics and sociology of sustainability.

Understanding thermodynamics

A primary interest of social scientists is social change. To explain change, many environmental social scientists have found it useful to turn to two fundamental laws more often cited in textbooks for the natural sciences: the first and second laws of thermodynamics. In brief, these two laws in combination say that, first, the total amount of energy in the universe is constant (it can neither be created nor destroyed; only its form can be changed)—which is known as the conservation law—and, second, that every time energy is transformed or converted, which is what we do whenever we expend energy in work or in heat production, the total amount of energy remains the same, but its availability for future work is reduced. **Entropy** is the measurement of this change in usefulness or availability (Suzuki 1997: 106).

Gas, oil, and wood are highly structured sources of available energy that we consume to drive machines or warm our homes. When we put these energy sources to use to heat our homes or power automobiles, the thermal energy contained in these resources is dissipated into the air, and recapturing that energy for future work becomes difficult to impossible. While the energy still exists, it becomes less structured. Similarly, our bodies store high-quality forms of energy taken from the food we eat. But when we go about our lives, doing our jobs or exercising, for instance, we convert that stored energy, in the form of sugars, into activity; the thermal heat given off during exercise becomes a low-quality form of energy. This change from more to less energy availability represents a shift from low to high entropy. High entropy means low availability; low entropy means high availability. What is most important to our understanding of energy and society is that all energy sources, when put into use, tend towards high entropy or disorder, and this process is irreversible.

Many social scientists and social critics have explored energy and societal change in terms of entropy. They do not all agree in their interpretations. In particular, two camps stand out: structuralist or realist analysts, who rely primarily upon empirical assessments of entropy in nature and scientific measurements of energy use to analyze changes in energy-society relationships; and social constructionists, whose analyses of entropy give primacy to particular historical, geographic, cultural, and political understandings of nature to explain the exhaustion of energy, and limit the types of energy alternatives available. The contrasting assumptions of these camps are of special interest.

Structuralist Explanations

Structuralism, also called realism, is a form of social scientific inquiry that focuses on identifying objectively what are presumed to be independent natural processes that are "out there," knowable, and identifiable. As in the natural sciences from which it emerged, the greatest benefit of this positivist form of social scientific inquiry is not only its ability to amass important information on the material requirements of social systems, but also its predictive power, particularly in regard to changes in the supply and demand of those natural resources upon which our growing human population depends (Burmingham and Cooper 1999). But a strictly structuralist point of view also has its weakness: a tendency to treat the human population in much in the same way as a physical scientist might treat bacteria in a petri dish—as a unified population of individuals whose behaviour can be predicted and undifferentiated. Such universal laws of action are highly unlikely to apply to even historical hunter-gatherer societies, and much less to complex contemporary social systems. Furthermore, the physical science conventions and concepts adopted by realists are themselves influenced by cultural assumptions that can influence their analysis (Latour and Woolgar 1986).

Despite the shortcomings of structural inquiry, several foundational works in this tradition can be credited with convincing sceptics that social facts can be ecological facts, which in turn justifies the emergence of social science fields, such as environmental sociology and human geography, that are committed to analysis of the society-environment relationship.

One of the most important of those works is now over fifty years old. In 1951, in the heyday of Western scientific optimism, Frederick Cottrell (1951: 2) argued, "The energy available to man limits what he *can* do and influences what he *will* do." By studying the history of our social systems, we know that if the energy available for use is high, the variety of human activities can increase. If more energy is produced than consumed, we have an energy surplus, which happens, for instance, in fertile regions in which a small amount of energy exerted can lead to the production of a large surplus of plant energy in the form of food grains. Surpluses can in turn lead to political conflict over claims made upon those surpluses; and can be used for, among other things, geo-political expansion; sacrifices to the gods; lavish consumption and waste among the rulers; or the establishment of a leisure class that can devote itself to the arts and sciences. Trade is also generally only undertaken if it leads to a surplus—if the energy stored in the item traded plus the energy required for transport is less than the energy represented by the item received in trade. These activities are not possible without surplus energy. In short, those features we associate with "civilized" society are made possible by energy surpluses. But crisis ensues in societies in which energy supplies have become depleted, in many cases leading to the abandonment of settlements and/or dramatic changes in the broader social order.

Still, the role of technology is central to our energy-society relationship, because it is through technology that we are able to discover, gain access to, and ultimately convert energy sources to human use. Thus the types of energy converters and fuels that a given society uses go a long way in determining the kind of societies that unfold. Even a structuralist theorist such as Cottrell acknowledges the extent to which the cultural and ideological characteristics of a social system can either encourage or constrain the adoption of new technologies and sources of energy. But the most important take-home message that structuralist analysis emphasizes is this: there are clear structural limitations to social development: "Man can exist only where he is able to replace the energy which he uses up in the process of living" (Cottrell 1951).

Consider the transition to a steam-powered society. Prior to the steam age, the geographic distribution of human settlement was established by trading routes dependent on wind patterns and sailing ships. In addition to wind power, these settlements made use of a variety of energy supplies, including wood, human and animal muscle power, and water-wheel power. Each of these energy sources has certain limitations. Many of them, such as water wheels, have limited capacity. Others have limited uses, and still others are unevenly distributed or subject to varying weather and climatic conditions. With the development of the steam generator, European societies could make use of a resource (coal) seemingly in ample supply as wood supplies became depleted. They had the ability to harness and convert energy for use more systematically, and at high output, with obvious benefits to industry and commerce. Steam generators, though, are enormously inefficient machines—requiring a high level of energy input in the form of coal per unit of work output—and the only way of increasing the efficiency of the machines was through increasing their size. Eventually the industrialists built enormous generators that could be used to power several activities at once. Those huge machines were not particularly mobile, and to avoid heavy expenditures on the transport of coal it made sense to build them as close to the source of energy as possible. It also made sense to concentrate those human activities requiring energy around the generators and, ultimately, to concentrate control over those energy supplies as well.

This need led to the establishment of dense population centres integrated with congested industrial areas. In North America especially, new settlements were patterned according to the needs of steam-based energy. The North American centres consequently had an enormous economic advantage in relation to the older social systems of Europe and Britain, which reflected settlement patterns established during a time when wind power ruled. Many of these countries consequently did not adopt steam-based energy nearly as rapidly as did the United States. Still, with the development of steam-powered railroads and river boats, some regions that were previously hindered in the former mercantile society because they lacked access to ship-based trade routes or ports, but happened to be located near coal supplies, suddenly found themselves in a position to compete with the formerly dominant seaport cities.

Other indirect social effects due to the development of steam generators quickly unfolded, as rapid expansion of railroads provided access to natural resources (minerals) that were not previously available in a mercantile system dependent upon sail. Later the energy regime of fossil fuels, especially oil, also brought changes to settlement patterns. As a liquid, oil is easily transported and stored, allowing for more dispersed and scattered settlement patterns, migration into harsher climates with long winters, and industrial expansion into the hinterlands.

These kinds of historical changes, then, can readily inspire cornucopian visions of human mastery over nature. Today, even though ecological facts may well constrain development, many of those ecological facts are characterized by the twin features of invisibility and escalating consequence. Older societies, for instance, quickly detected and responded to energy deficits, either through adaptation or social disintegration. In modern societies the indicators of deficit are less visible and the consequences are often exportable. The energy deficits can thus persist beyond the point at which social adjustment may be possible, raising the prospect of global system collapse, as Heinberg (2003) predicted. "Low-energy societies" were largely limited in geographic scope, defined by a stable local energy supply and a stable set of claims placed upon that supply. The introduction of high energy converters and the eventual transition to our modern high-energy society required the development of new social units, namely the nation-state system, which built, with public tax dollars, the needed energy infrastructure systems (pipelines, roads, electrical grids, dams). The system also required an international energy market to ensure the availability of supply for the growing centres of demand. In this global system the historic strategies of relocating societies to new energy sources, or importing those supplies to existing settlements, lose meaning because there is no "elsewhere" to which we can turn. In short, we may have overshot our Earth's carrying capacity—the maximum feasible load on the environment that the Earth could support indefinitely. William Catton (1980), in his book appropriately titled *Overshoot*, argues that we have indeed surpassed our carrying capacity, due to the reliance of our modern high-energy societies on imports from else*when*—energy from prehistoric fossil sources. These imports can be evaluated by employing the concept of ghost acreage. First coined by Georg Borgstrom (1965), ghost acreage refers to the number of additional acres of farmland that would be needed to grow organic fuels with energy content equivalent to the amount held in the fossil fuels on which we are dependent.

Catton employed that kind of analysis in evaluating the history of human development. As "prosthetic animals," humans have the ability to expand their habitat through the use of tools: clothing, transport vehicles, refrigerators, and more. Like some species, humans have used tools as a means of specialization that allows them to occupy previously unoccupied ecological niches and enlarge the carrying capacity available to them. The use of fire, for example, allowed humans to consume meat and inhabit colder climates, while the introduction of archery greatly expanded access to different varieties of meat. Prior to industrialization each of these events shared one thing in common: human carrying capacity was increased by the diversion of a portion of the Earth's carrying capacity away from supporting other kinds of life, a method Catton calls the **takeover method**. During the Industrial Revolution, however, increases in carrying capacity were largely achieved through the use of fossil fuels, or by what is called the **drawdown method**. Both methods ultimately face limits, but the transition from the takeover to the drawdown method also marked another crucial shift. Technology, which initially increased carrying capacity per capita, was now doing the reverse, by increasing per capita resource requirements for every unit of energy produced. Humans have in effect become **Homo Colossus**, with each generation drawing on more resources to sustain a single human life. For the most part, humans have been blind to this contradiction, because "by tapping fossil hydrocarbons, western societies freed themselves, at least for a time, from many of the complexities of interacting with ecosystems" (Norgaard 1997: 158–68), in large part through processes of distancing (see chapter two).

In essence, entropy explains our current Homo Colossus state. Because entropy always increases, each successive change in the energy system becomes more difficult to achieve (Rifkin 1989)—we consume a thousand times more energy per person on average today, in the age of machines and fossil fuels, than was true in the ancient times of wood and fire. As long as economic productivity continues to be measured in speed per unit of output, this trend will continue. Agrarian systems reliant upon human and animal power produced (and still produce in some parts of the world) ten calories for every calorie expended. In modern industrial agricultural systems this ratio is reversed: it takes ten fossil-fuel-generated calories to produce one calorie of food. This ratio increases if we include the energy required for the many other inputs that support modern agriculture, which are also manufactured with the use of fossil fuels. Again, distancing helps to hide this contradiction. Thus even though one farmer with an ox and plough produces more efficient yields per energy input than that same farmer can produce with the use of modern farming machinery and the use of chemical fertilizers, modern industrial agricultural systems have adopted the latter system because of the increase in economic yields that can be achieved.

The productivity expansion brought about by the use of fossil fuels was not solely limited to agriculture. The discovery of the means of employing fossil fuels directly fuelled industrial expansion in all sectors of the economy, particularly in the raw materials sectors. For example, the introduction of chainsaws in industrial forestry operations led to dramatic increases in yields in essential building materials and "changed social and ecological landscapes in North America and beyond, by unleashing the energy of fossil fuels in the forests. In an eon-straddling irony, the new machines allowed loggers to use energy derived from ancient vegetation (the source of oil) against modern forests" (McNeil 2001: 307).

The ready supply of fossil-fuel-based energy has fostered what Catton calls an Age of Exuberance, in which such contradictions seem irrelevant to many. But if these structuralist accounts are correct, this age cannot last forever. At some point our modern social systems will require more energy inputs than the system can afford. Most importantly, even though substitutes are theoretically available, the entropy law tells us that each new form of energy we "discover" will be less readily available for our use. In essence, it will cost a whole lot more to exploit that energy. Even the amount of energy required to continue on our current trajectory of dependence on oil is steadily increasing because the most readily available supplies have already been tapped. We now have to go further, dig deeper, and invest more energy and technology to gain access to fossil fuels. Other alternative energy sources such as wind and solar power do not have the same conversion efficiencies as do fossil fuels—meaning they simply cannot provide the high work output that fossil fuels do. The costs of producing the same level of energy output from renewable sources would require enormous expenditures in energy, infrastructure, technology, and administration.

Jeremy Rifkin (1989) reasons that we will be trapped in this pattern of declining energy efficiency combined with growing supply scarcity until humankind moves from a colonizing stage (emphasis on increasing flowthrough) to a climax stage of existence (minimizing energy

9.3 The Politics and Thermodynamics of the Alberta Tars Sands

The Klein government in Alberta has invested a tremendous amount of optimism, and resources, into the hodgepodge of clay, minerals, sand, water, and crude bitumen that make up the tar sands in the north of the province. The numbers look good; the oil reserves that can be extracted from the tar sands are on par with the vast reserves of Saudi Arabia. But numbers do not tell a complete story. The oil reserves of Saudi Arabia, and much of the Middle East, can be extracted without doing a whole lot more than inserting a long metal straw into the ground and sucking the oil out. In the tar sands, extracting the oil is energy-intensive. Most of the viable deposits are at least 200 feet under the surface, and the site must be prepped by removing all surface vegetation, diverting all waterways, and draining the muskeg common to the boreal region (Pratt 1976). Then the bitumen, not oil, must be mined, extracted from the other components of the sands, and processed into a usable form through coking, desulphurization, and hydrogenation (Pratt 1976). For example, two tons of sand are mined using a process that involves the injection of large volumes of water as steam into the ground, resulting in 2.5 barrels of liquid waste that is ultimately transferred to large open-air ponds, in order to produce one barrel of oil (Heinberg 2003). It takes the equivalent of two out of every three barrels of oil recovered to pay for the costs of extraction (Youngquist 1997). Given its location in the far north, an enormous infrastructure must also be built to transport people and resources to and from the site.

Is it all worth it? Here's what one researcher has to say:

> Back-of-the-envelope calculations show that the Athabasca oil sands could supply less than three years' worth of oil for the global economy. Three hundred billion barrels of oil (AEUB) gushing out of a pipe would only last 12 years at present World consumption of 70 million barrels a day. Oil sands would last just three years if we super-optimistically assume 25 percent net energy for the digging, etc. over the entire resource. (Hanson 1999)

The process is not only ecologically expensive in terms of entropy but also economically costly. In 1990 tar sands production led to 17 megatonnes of greenhouse gases. This is predicted to increase to 70 megatonnes of greenhouse gas emissions by 2010, or 9 percent of Canada's total. Critics also suspect that the Mackenzie Gas Project will be used to bring clean fossil fuel to the tar sands to supply energy to remove the dirtiest fossil fuels from the Earth, adding to the negative entropy balance (Wristen 2004). See as well the discussion of water uses in oil extraction in chapter four. In "the truth is stranger than fiction" category, the video *Nuclear Dynamite* (2000) shows how nuclear scientists planned to conduct some geographic engineering and explode a nuclear bomb in the Canadian tar sands to release the oil. See *Nuclear Dynamite* <www.bullfrogfilms.com/catalog/nd2.html>.

flowthrough), which will favour small decentralized institutions. In short, many structuralists have come to the conclusion that while energy is "the precondition of all commodities" (Schumacher 1973), we need to turn to human-scale technological alternatives such as small hydro dams and windmills, among other things. Unfortunately, our current emphasis on specialization and large-scale production has come at the cost of flexibility and sensibility to needs.

Unequal thermodynamic exchange

Structuralist theorists have been joined by many other advocates calling for limits on the use of nature. Many of these prescriptions have a clear logic to them and can lead to well-meaning policy. Simply asking individuals to adopt consumption limits is a naive policy approach, however, and while imposing personal limits may be necessary, particularly in high-consumption countries, it is certainly not sufficient. Most importantly, sturcturalist accounts that attempt to treat humans solely as ecological components tend to assume that we are all equally responsible for the problems of overshoot and drawdown, and they tend to ignore significant differences in consumption levels and political power. While ecological concepts help us to understand how our social systems are indeed integrated in fundamental ways with ecosystems, they do not sufficiently capture the numerous complexities of those social systems. Our carrying capacity limits have not been exceeded simply because we are overpopulated and consume too much.

Considerations for alternative energy futures consequently must account for the diverse and unequal social context within which such alternatives would take place. Historically, each new energy regime has created "arrangements by which energy is harvested, directed, stored, bought, sold, used for work or wasted, and ultimately dissipated" (McNeil 2001: 297). Whereas early societies, even coal-based societies, were locked into place, oil-based regimes are more spatially dispersed. Pipelines, ocean-going oil tankers, and storage tanks link distant oil wells with global centres of urban concentration and corporate and state political power. The reality that petroleum, considered since the 1920s to be "the bedrock of our hydrocarbon civilization" (Watts 2004: 177), is unevenly distributed geographically has generated a geopolitics of harvesting oil and gas that both reflects and reinforces global inequalities in the power of access, corporate exploitation, and dependence between nations. Alf Hornberg refers to this social and economic system as **thermodynamic imperialism**. His analysis links wealth in developed countries to the exchange of entropy between parts of the world:

> Calling world trade exploitative... is more than a value judgment. It is an inference based on the Second Law of Thermodynamics. If production is a dissipative process, and a prerequisite for in-

> dustrial production is exchange of finished products for raw materials and fuels, then it follows that industrialism implies a *social* transfer of entropy. (Hornberg 2001: 11)

Certain subsystems such as Europe and the United States have created wealth through the import of raw materials for the manufacture of finished products, and the export of certain industrial processes and wastes to other parts of the world, resulting in a decrease in entropy in those regions. But such decreases require increases in entropy in other subsystems (such as oil-exporting and natural-resource-exporting countries) that amount to an increase in the system as a whole. From this perspective, the social transfer of entropy is the very basis of capitalist economic growth and exploitation (Hornberg 2001). The increase in entropy in wealthy nations through transfers of resources is a process that Hornberg calls **exergy**, which describes an increase in the amount of available energy for industrial work and consumer lifestyles in the developed world and an associated decrease in available energy in the global South, all of which contributes to chronic poverty. The concept of exergy makes a critical connection between ecological vitality and social well-being: "the ecological and socioeconomic impoverishment of the periphery are two sides of the same coin" (Hornberg 2001: 11).

As a result, in the 1990s industrial market economies used eighty times the energy of sub-Saharan Africa countries, for example, on a per capita basis (de la Court 1990); and the Earth simply does not have sufficient resources to support extending those kinds of Western consumption levels to the rest of the world. The ecological footprint analysis (see chapter two) shows how lifestyles of residents in developed countries are supported by the carrying capacity of the global South. Addressing sustainability requires paying attention to critical notions such as social stratification, power, and social justice.

Structures of political power are as central to sustainability as are inequities in the geographic distribution of resources and consumption. Hornberg's "thermodynamic unequal exchange" describes how a core set of nations and corporations control access to resources and thereby also control the machines that are the centrepieces of modern industrial development. This control over access may even be more important to alternative energy futures than are shifts in technology: "Industrial technology.... Its power to conduct work 'in itself,' as it were, is a cultural illusion. It is the productive potential of fuels and other raw materials which is at work in our machines, not the machines 'in themselves'" (Hornberg 2001: 11). Those who control and direct the productive potential of energy and resources control industrialization processes, deploying them for their own trade interests, and limiting options for development by other countries and peoples.

Hornberg's approach confronts two powerful assumptions of the cornucopia model. The first assumption, also held by modernization theorists, is that capital accumulation in the core bears no relation to the poverty and environmental problems in the South. Clearly this is not the case. The attack on tropical forests provides just one example. Accelerating rapidly after World War II, tropical deforestation made way for large industrial agricultural enterprises that were controlled by Northern corporations and served Northern consumers (Tucker 2000: 345–415). The subsequent dislocation of resident rural populations led to migrations to urban centres that were already overpopulated. Those who remained in the deforested areas became the low-skilled labour-force for these foreign operations (see chapter four). The second assumption is that economic activity and environmental consequences tend to be confined to the same geographic space, much as in the case of the pollution over old London (see chapter six). Several social analyses of production systems have highlighted the extent to which the "production, distribution, and consumption of energy are always significant causes of pollution," but in our global economy, the pollution and other negative impacts are being geographically shifted to the developing world (Lutzenhiser, Harris, and Olsen 2002: 232).

Herein lies the rub of contemporary geopolitics: those countries with the political power to do so are capable of ignoring ecological limits by importing their energy shortfalls and exporting their ecological footprints, taking carrying capacity from somewhere or some*when* else. Even within countries we can see significant variations in energy use and conservation, varying by culture, class, income, gender, race/ethnicity, and lifestyles.

Applying Social Constructionism to Critical Analysis

Structuralism and social constructionism are two sides of the same coin, both equally necessary to critical social analysis. While we all confront the natural world "out there" in some form or another in our lives, environmental historians illustrate the dialectic relationship that exists between social constructions of the natural world and our very real impacts on the natural world, impacts that directly shape **second nature**—those landscapes and waterscapes that have been altered by human societies for several thousand years, leaving very little of the globe untouched by humans. Employing both perspectives provides us with a more comprehensive view of the interplay between humans and the ecosystems within which we live. By thinking of our actions as occurring within a "socially constructed adaptive landscape" (McLaughlin 2001), we are able to analyze not only how structural/environmental contexts limit the avenues available for social action, but also how that structural/environmental context is shaped in very particular ways, reflecting the socially constructed concepts of nature that predominate in particular places and times.

Even concepts such as carrying capacity can be subject to multiple socially constructed meanings. In exploring various definitions of carrying capacity employed in Australia, Sharon Beder (1993) first presents a construction of carrying capacity that is largely analogous with the one used by ecologists. Focusing primarily on the basic ecological survival needs of a species, and based on the presumption that Australians would be willing to follow a subsistence lifestyle, this analysis predicts that Australia's ecosystems could support fifty million people. Beder then contrasts this finding with a second, more culturally sensitive definition of carrying capacity, which proposes a quality of life that is both above basic subsistence and based on social equity and justice, while also recognizing the needs of other species. Employing this second definition, the carrying capacity of Australia is recalculated to seventeen million people. Crossing concepts and insights from ecology with a critical political economy opens up the discussion of the natural and social limits of ecosystems, and how we can allocate limited resources in a manner that allows people to thrive according to culturally defined standards for quality of life, in an equitable manner.

More broadly, social constructionism shows us how our behavioural choices are "patterned." Individualistic choices regarding energy use, for example, are shaped by choice patterns that are structured by the construction industry and housing developers "who limit choice and options or shape them in ways that limit conservation options or awareness" (Shove 1997: 261–73). Cultural practices and behaviours such as bathing frequency, expectations for comfort levels in our homes and for certain aesthetic features of our neighbourhoods, and the use of mass-produced convenience appliances all describe a system of **mundane consumption** that has a great impact on energy consumption and places considerable demands on ecosystems (Shove 1997).

One of the most important applications of a social constructionist approach involves analyses of the means by which power is manifested through **discourse**. In simple terms, discourse is a term used to describe what we say. But the term encompasses much more than simply speech or text; discourse describes our shared understandings of the world, expressing particular ways of thinking; it takes in the rules, norms, and behaviours that limit what we can see and say and that give certain individuals or groups power while taking away power from others (Mills 1997). Analyses of the use of concepts such as ecological modernization and sustainable development in contemporary environmental politics provide an important case in point. Ecological modernization has become an increasingly dominant policy discourse (Hajer 1995; Christoff 1996; Berger et al. 2001) that frames environmental issues in a manner that serves both to dissipate ecological dissent and promote the economic benefits of environmental reform. Ecological modernization creates a "success story" (Fisher and Freudenburg 2001), enabling government institutions to maintain legitimacy among publics who have expressed growing environmental concern, all the while continuing to pursue intensive economic development. This approach has been adopted by powerful industrial and state institutions in Alberta, where industrial development in the boreal forest becomes socially constructed as "sustainable development," while those organizations whose members insist on pointing out ecological limits and cumulative impacts of such development become marginalized in political debates (Davidson and MacKendrick 2004).

A Broader Understanding of Entropy

The entropy of the biophysical realm is also analogous to, and in many ways interrelated with, **social entropy**: the breakdown of social systems due to the disintegration of those structures that serve as foundations for the organization of society. Under these circumstances, social systems, or at least certain subgroups of those systems, are unable to persist in their current form. Emile Durkheim explored this concept over a century ago. Studying industrialization and urbanization in the late nineteenth century, Durkheim called this breakdown **anomie**, arguing that it resulted from rapid changes in society due either to growth and development that evolve too quickly for social organizations to adapt, or to the collapse and decay of those social organizations themselves. Both cases describe an inability of existing social organizations to function. Durkheim discovered that in these instances people experienced a sense of normlessness and despair in response and became unable to contribute to society in any meaningful way. This process describes the degeneration of a society from an ordered, functioning system into one characterized by disarray, in the same way that high entropy in physical systems describes the transformation of energy from an organized, usable form into a disorganized, unusable form.

Durkheim focused on the social anomie that resulted during periods of early rapid industrialization, but it is important to note that rapid industrialization continues to this day. Studies of rapid urbanization, for example, in the megacities of the global South—places such as Sao Paolo, Brazil, and Mombai, India—show how millions of people have been left to survive with few if any public services, how they struggle to make a living in what geographer Mike Davis calls a "planet of slums" (Davis 2004). Sociologist Peter Evans has introduced the term **livability** to capture this struggle by the poor for life itself. Evans is optimistic that a discourse of protest around livability will provide for a new politics of sustainability, with the deteriorating living conditions in cities adding an ecological component to debates about urban life. For Evans, the concept of livability provides for a politics of global solidarity between the poor in the developing world and those progressive social sectors in the richer Northern countries; it gives "the demands of subordinate groups a new claim to universality that can mobilize extra-local allies" (Evans 2000: 10, 17).

Many communities also experience social entropy when confronted by natural disasters or technologically induced environmental health disasters. Many sites of resource extraction have been locales for social entropy for centuries. Black lung disease and other respiratory diseases have decimated rural coal-mining towns in the Eastern provinces of Canada, and elsewhere across the globe. More recently, communities have been faced with more technologically complex disasters. Love Canal, a small suburb in New York, represented one of the earliest, and more publicized, cases of such a technological disaster. For the many residents living in adjacent communities the main thoroughfare connecting Baton Rouge to New Orleans, Louisiana, has come to be called Cancer Alley due to the serious toxic pollution associated with oil-refining, among other activities concentrated there. Studies have shown that the social impacts of ecological and especially technological disasters can persist for many years, contributing to anxiety, depression, loss of community participation, and an inability to mobilize the organizational resources needed for recovery—all of which describes conditions of high social entropy.

Social entropy in Canada: A case study of the Sydney Tar Ponds

In Sydney, Nova Scotia, twenty-six thousand residents live near 700,000 tonnes of contaminated sludge and 60 hectares of the carcinogen compound polycyclic aromatic hydrocarbon (PAH) contaminate, the residues from several decades of economic activity generated by the local steel company. The *Halifax Herald* (July 20, 2001) describes how these ponds, now known as the Sydney Tar Ponds, were generated: "a mixture of arsenic, lead and benzene was cooked with coal to make coke, a high burning fuel that powered the provincially owned Sydney steel plant. In one month in 1970, more than 500 tonnes of coal dust and other particles fell on every square mile of Sydney." Those working on top of coke ovens were exposed to PAHs equivalent to smoking thirty-five packages of cigarettes a day, and as early as the 1970s tests revealed that community children had developed lung problems. Other toxins, including arsenic, lead, and manganese, measured well above levels considered safe by the Council of Ministers of the Environment. A recent study in the vicinity of the plant identified "35 toxins in the Whitney Pier neighbourhood, including arsenic on Frederick Street, which is very close to the coke ovens, at 70 times the acceptable levels" (*Halifax Herald* Oct. 26, 2001).

Sydney residents have elevated levels of arsenic in blood and urine, and the area is known for high cancer rates, birth defects, and lifespans that are shorter than average. Many of these residents feel trapped, as if spectators, with limited power to change the situation (May and Barlow 2001). As is characteristic of entropy in general, the consequences of the events in question are not confined. The ensuing social entropy is defined not just by poor health but also by unemployment, lowered home values, loss of neighbourhood, social stress, and ultimately disempowerment in the face of intransigent governments and industries.

When the Sydney residents attempted to voice their concerns, they were marginalized by their former employer and public political representatives alike. Company owners retorted, “no smoke, no baloney” (*Toronto Sun* June 11, 2001), and their elected representative, Nova Scotia premier John Hamm, insisted, “The best scientific information available suggests there is no health risk to those living near the tar ponds.” Federal and provincial governments agreed, claiming in 2001 that the Sydney community was safe, although they were unwilling to share the results of soil samples with community residents.[1]

Families who for generations have been employed by the steel industry in Sydney now feel trapped, unable to leave yet unable to afford—emotionally or physically—to stay. A lack of alternative employment options for former steelworkers limits migration opportunities and offers residents little choice but to adapt to their living conditions. At the start of the June 2004 federal election, Prime Minister Paul Martin’s government promised $400 million to clean up the sites (CBC 2004), but residents are not likely to hold their breath, considering the response of federal and provincial officials so far.

Some would argue that these incidents are merely the necessary side effects of economic growth, “the price of progress,” or “the smell of money.” Over the last 150 years, however, the laws of entropy dictate a growing trend upward in what is already a very high price—a cost that is not distributed evenly. Those paying the environmental costs of economic progress are very rarely reaping any of the gains. Often the poorest classes and racially oppressed social groups are left to deal with the health and psychological effects of wastes and pollutants, as well as with the legal, economic, and political shocks that disrupt and disorganize their communities.

The Comeback Species?

We may be living in an era in which the Age of Exuberance is coming to an end, with increasing occurrences of energy shortages and carrying capacity deficits, with inevitable consequences for the human population, particularly underprivileged groups. Are we doomed to follow a path towards societal collapse? Societies have recovered from extraordinary disaster in the past. A quarter of Europe’s population was killed off by the Black Plague in the fourteenth century; some twenty million people are estimated to have died in Russia alone during World War II. Studies of community responses to natural disasters have catalogued the extraordinary resilience of human communities. The ability of people to overcome horrific crises, not only as individuals but also as communities, attests to their resilience, and to the steadfast will to survive in the human population. Ecologically, humans are also generalists, and with the use of technology they have proven remarkably adaptable to nearly every ecological niche that Earth has to offer.

Yet Heinberg (2003, 2004) predicts that it will be impossible for any nation to continue on an industrial path. Further, we are not yet in a position to make a smooth transition to alternative energy paths given our infrastructural dependence on fossil fuels, among other things. Joseph Tainter (1988: 91) argues that the benefits/energy investment ratio of sociopolitical complexity follows a classic economic marginal product curve: "Energy flow and sociopolitical organization are opposite sides of an equation. Neither can exist, in a human group, without the other, nor can either undergo substantial change without altering both the opposite member and the balance of the equation." More complex societies are simply more costly to maintain: the population as a whole must allocate increasing energy to maintaining organizational institutions. The management and regulatory apparatus required to maintain our highway system, not to mention nuclear power plants, require a level of investment that simply has no analogy to the organizational methods that characterized societies even a hundred short years ago.

Tainter argues that societies collapse because: 1) organizational complexity continues to increase; 2) sociopolitical systems require energy; 3) increased complexity carries with it increased per capita costs; and 4) just as is the case with energy extraction, investment in sociopolitical complexity is subject to the laws of entropy and inevitably reaches a point of declining returns. In other words, the amount of resources that must be invested just to maintain our social systems will increase. As reserves get used up and ecological entropy increases, so too does social entropy increase, and societies become vulnerable, less able to respond to the next calamity. Because of these central tendencies, the idea of societal collapse may in fact describe a return to a normal human condition. These tendencies have expressed themselves throughout history, but today, given the degree of integration of societies across the globe, the only real collapse in question in contemporary society is global.

What Can We Do?

What alternatives do we have? What choices? Is our fossil-fuel-based economy hopelessly "resource-dependent," or are we merely "culturally dependent" on fossil fuels? That is, are petroleum products our predominant source of energy because they are most economically and geographically rational? Or have we become culturally attached to oil, internal combustion engines, and everything these social constructs represent? Are we unconsciously, in our mundane consumption, hooked on the systems within which we exist, and unable to imagine a life characterized by alternative soft paths such as solar, wind, and water power? Are we therefore limiting ourselves to future hard path alternative energy sources such as large-scale hydroelectric dams and nuclear power?

We may have good reason to speculate that we are not dependent upon fossil fuels because we have no choice, but rather because of social "path-dependence"—our societies, economies, and most importantly political arrangements have evolved with the development of fossil-fuel consumption, and as is characteristic of all social institutions, these arrangements are resistant to change. Our settlement patterns have created several significant constraints to a switch away from private automobiles: our sites of work are physically separate from sites of residence, other community needs are no longer centralized, and popular recreation and leisure activities are frequently car-based (see chapter five). On a deeper level, other possibilities such as alternative fuels challenge our own sense of security within a social system that is familiar and predictable.

The ability to imagine a different future is only part of the obstacle we face. Many soft path options require a more decentralized management structure, which would mean fewer opportunities for concentrations of economic wealth and power. Alternative paths would thus challenge interest groups that are profiting from the current institutional infrastructure, groups that could be expected to bring their power and resources to bear in efforts to maintain the status quo.

Historical eras of rapid transition also describe a times of spectacular social dynamism, however, within which all forms of organization and behaviour have shown the ability to change. Today we must make the same leap to recognize the inherent limits posed by the laws of entropy, and because such transitory eras are historically associated with significant shifts in power structures, each of us can play a role in this transition (see chapter ten).

9.4 Free Enterprisers and the God-Given Right to Drill

Oil has moved beyond representing simply a carbon-based fuel. It has also become a powerful ideological force within the national and international politics of energy that cannot simply be explained by its physical properties, or ability to do work. Since the early decades of the twentieth century, popular images of wildcatting oil drillers tapping nature's bounty in the wilds of Canada, the fringes of the Arctic, the North Sea, or the jungles of Indonesia have filled our newspapers, history books, and even our music. Idyllic images of self-made, entrepreneurial men making oil fortunes overnight by releasing the bounty of nature persist through time, posing a formidable cultural challenge to states attempting to regulate energy management, and environmental organizations attempting to promote alternative energy paths; to do so is to challenge the very ideological premises of successful capitalism. As Keith Brownsey (2003) writes: "The oilpatch had a self-image of rugged individualism and any state incursion was resented as an unnecessary impediment on their God-given right to drill, produce and market oil and natural gas." For more discussion of ideology and oil development, see Foster 1979; House 1980.

9.5 Nuclear Power: A Low-Emissions Alternative?

Environmental historian John McNeill says that nuclear power "was unpopular and uneconomic innovation, less lethal than cars, but with mind-boggling ecological implications." He traces its emergence from the first civilian nuclear reactor in USSR in 1954 to the Chernobyl accident in 1986, which will be lethal for another 24,000 years—"the longest lien on the future that any generation of humanity has yet imposed." According to McNeil, "Nuclear did not replace other forms of energy production, as the car did the horse." Instead it complemented fossil fuels. Ironically, with the demise of fossil fuels, there has been a re-emergence of interest in nuclear power in Canada. The Manley Report argues for completing a nuclear plant in Ontario; see "Transforming Ontario's Power Generation Company"
<www.energy.gov.on.ca/index.cfm?fuseaction=electricity.reports_opgreview>.

Wolfgang Sachs, a long-time proponent of sustainability, is concerned that nuclear energy will allow the perpetuation of consumerism and delay the conservation ethic associated with the soft energy paths of wind, solar, and fuel cells, which will require innovations in efficiency and changes in lifestyles. See his discussions of anti-developmentalists in *Planet Dialectics* (1999).

Finally, who should consider the issues of risk associated with nuclear power (or other technologies such as GMOs or nanotechnology). Canadian sociologist Michael Mehta writes: "The public policy questions raised by the nuclear energy debate in Ontario are clear: What is the suitable balance between the influence of technical expertise and the influence of citizens in assessing and managing environmental risks? How much weight should public perceptions of risks have in regulating hazardous technologies like nuclear power?"

Source: Mehta 2004.

The work by past and future critical social analyses can play a central role in envisioning and working toward change. Two influential economists, Robert Costanza and Herman Daly, for example, have generated a reassessment of socio-economic development in light of the planet-wide decline of those ecological services that support contemporary societies (Costanza et al. 1997), suggesting that we need to employ moral/ethical arguments (ultimate ends) alongside material arguments about the second law of thermodynamics (ultimate means). As Herman E. Daly (1993) states: "Growth chestnuts have to be placed on the unyielding anvil of biophysical realities and then crushed with the hammer of moral argument. The entropy law and ecology provide the biophysical anvil. Concern for future generations and subhuman life, and inequities in current wealth distribution, provide the moral hammer." Bringing ecology to the foreground focuses attention on the ecological space in which development occurs—and reminds us that ecological equity requires analysis of social and material equity.

As other chapters in this book make clear, the options do exist for each of us to become more informed about our own individual ecological

9.6 There are energy alternatives. Greenpeace protest: E$$o—A company in denial. Vancouver, October 26, 2002.

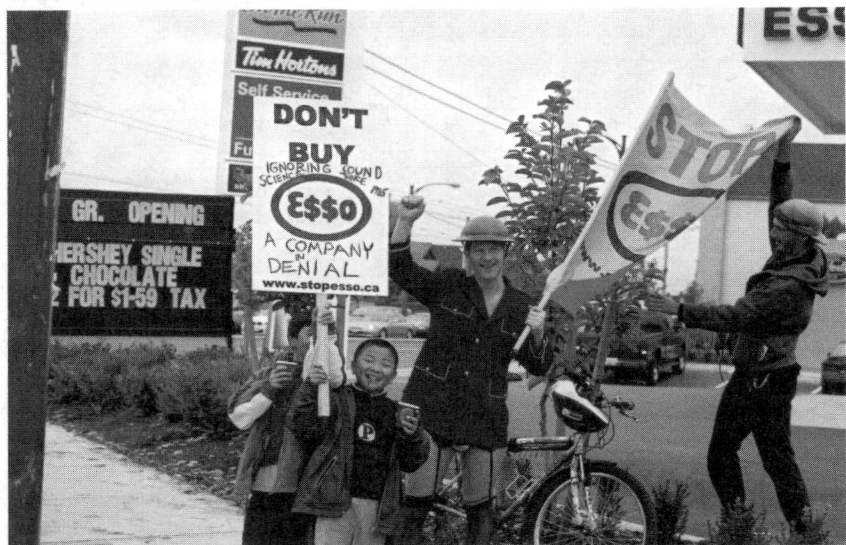

Photo: Colin Brown/Artists Against War

footprints, how to identify and utilize the alternatives available, and the opportunities for getting involved in existing organizations, or starting new ones. By making these activities a regular part of our lifestyles, we can minimize the potential for social entropy. The good news is that there are more opportunities to "power down" (Hienberg 2004: 163–86) and act on alternatives now than ever before in our recent past. Today regular features of Canadian politics include provincial and national initiatives to support green electricity providers, public assistance for families to make their homes more energy efficient, and a growing number of municipal initiatives to support the sustainable development goals established in international environmental treaties such as the 1992 Rio conference's Agenda 21. Job opportunities in the environmental sciences continue to increase in both government and industry, providing opportunities for influence in everything from national policy to corporate environmental responsibility. Most significantly, the number of non-governmental environmental organizations has exploded in the past ten years, providing concerned citizens with the opportunity to participate at the community, provincial, national, and global levels. In the end, adopting an entropy perspective will make clear that the actions of every individual count.

Useful Websites

National Energy Board
<www.neb-one.gc.ca/>
Nuclear Dynamite and the Nature of Things (October 2000)
www.bullfrogfilms.com/catalog/nd2.html>
The Coming Oil Crisis
<www.hubbertpeak.com/>
Thermodynamics
<www.iclei.org/EFACTS/THERMO.HTM>
Water and Oil: An Overview
<www.waterforlife.gov.ab.ca/html/technical_reports.html>

Notes

1. "Feds Won't Reveal Soil Tests, Officials Won't Say How Many Homes Exceed Federal Limits for Toxins," *Halifax Herald*, July 20, 2001; "Coke Ovens Report From '85 News to Hamm," *Halifax Herald*, June 9, 2001; "Toxic Cleanup Will Cost Taxpayers $10m," *Halifax Herald*, Dec. 5, 2001; "Pier Soil Tests Results Delayed," *Halifax Herald*, Oct. 26, 2001; "'Safe' Soil Report Called a 'Whitewash," Residents Won't Be Relocated from Toxic Hot Spot," *Toronto Star* Dec. 5, 2001: A3; "Sydney Soil Tests Find Most Home Safe," *Halifax Herald*, March 7, 2002.

10. Towards a Sustainable Future

Debra J. Davidson and Kierstin C. Hatt

> Any intelligent fool can make things bigger, more complex, and more violent. It takes a touch of genius—and a lot of courage—to move in the opposite direction.
> —Albert Einstein

While this book presents a diversity of perspectives, it also has one common theme linking them together: given the complexities of our relationship to the natural world, making the shift from a world with increasing ecological disruption towards a world of ecological renewal requires complex, and inevitably political, solutions. Multiple intellectual discussions are taking place in regard to what such a world might look like, but getting to that world depends on our collective ability—getting there requires changes in behaviours on the part of individuals and institutions alike, from the local to the global levels. Likewise, neither top-down nor bottom-up governance strategies will be enough on their own; we will need to employ the advantages of both types of strategies in combination. A comprehensive approach is necessary because activities at the local level and the larger social structures within which such activities occur serve to reconstitute each other continuously.

We end this book, then, with a discussion of where we should begin—a social-scientific understanding of social change.

Understanding Social Change

Despite a history of scholarly interest in social change that dates back over 2,500 years, social scientists are still not able to predict social change, which is why it is difficult to say exactly what actions must be taken to lead us to a future of healthy, vibrant communities and ecosystems. In the past some theorists, particularly historical figures such as Auguste Comte, optimistically postulated that social systems follow an evolutionary, linear path towards a more rational, civilized end point. Hints of this linear, or evolutionary, view are still apparent in more contemporary theories, such as modernization and Marxism. Other theorists have taken a similarly linear approach, although with a much more pessimistic outcome. The work of Joseph Tainter (chapter nine) is an example of that approach. Most evolutionary theorists attempt to point to a single causal variable to explain social change. For Marx it was class struggle; for the German social thinker Max Weber it was ideology. While these grand theories remain useful in our efforts to understand the world around us, such linear views rarely seem to hold up to empirical scrutiny; there are simply too many variables and anomalies throughout space and time.

Most evolutionary theories of social change are based on the presumption that periods of change are abnormal and that social continuity is the norm of human existence. Other social scientists, most notably Ralf Dahrendorf, posit the reverse: conflict and change are normal conditions, and no point of equilibrium is forthcoming. For the past fifty years, human scientists have certainly experienced far more dynamism than equilibrium. In fact, the pace of change since World War II is unprecedented throughout human history. This pace in itself is cause for alarm, because changes that occur too rapidly do not allow time for our cultures and social institutions to adjust. The rapid advances in technological development that have led to the ability to capture atomic energy, or to manipulate the DNA of our foods, are contemporary examples of changes that many people believe are ethically reprehensible; our regulatory institutions have not so far been able to establish a means of safely employing those technologies. The extraordinary pace at which the former Communist systems of the Soviet Union and Eastern Europe were dismantled is another example: in many of those countries the standards of living fell dramatically, and ethnic conflicts exploded.

As our lives become increasingly unpredictable, the institutions that have governed Western social systems, in particular the church and the state, are in a state of flux. At the same time each nation has become heavily interdependent upon other countries, and upon the global economic, political, and ecological systems themselves, so that rapid changes and uncertainties that emerge a long way off also have a strong impact close to home. But this dynamism is also cause for hope: times of rapid social change mean shifts in old power structures and opportunities for creativity and reform in otherwise rigid institutions. Like the Chinese yin-yang symbol, the character of crisis wears two faces, in this case the face of danger and the face of opportunity.

It comes down to power

One of the central variables that tends to get washed away in grand theories of social change is the role of power. To understand power, we need to move away from the macroscopic lens of grand theory and place our feet firmly on the ground, to see how power manifests itself in everyday life. A simple dictionary reference to power describes it as the ability to reach one's objectives despite resistance. But understanding power in social systems is far more complex than this definition suggests. Steven Lukes (1974) provides us with a three dimensional view of power. The **first dimension of power** describes the level of power that is most easily observed and experienced: individuals or organizations actively competing for influence; some win and some lose. Power also manifests itself at a much deeper level, though. Have you ever felt as though you don't even want to bother trying to assert your view, because you figure you'll never win anyway? If so, you have become subject to the **second dimension of power**: when certain groups or individuals feel so powerless that they don't bother to try to pursue their objectives. In this case, we say that those in power have the ability to set the agenda; only those issues of concern by people in power receive political attention.

The third level is the deepest, and most difficult to observe as a social analyst. The **third dimension of power** describes the tendency for members of oppressed groups to approve of the very power structure that is oppressing them. In this instance, we can say that the dominant ideology has become **hegemonic**. Women who come to believe that they aren't capable of doing the same jobs that men do or Aboriginal peoples who come to believe that the cultures and lifestyles of European descendents are superior to their own have become subject to the third dimension of power. This analysis of power is important; it tells us that only when a group of people come to believe that they deserve more, and also come to believe that they have the capacity to demand changes in society, do they actually do something about it.

Each of these dimensions has an impact on environmental sustainability. Environmental and community organizations are actively vying for influence in policy, and although they face formidable opponents, their numbers continue to grow. Nevertheless, many individuals are concerned about their exposure to toxins at work, for example, but opt not to voice those concerns for fear of losing their jobs. In addition, many communities across the globe have been exposed to images of opulent, consumptive Western lifestyles and come to covet those lifestyles and view their own, more modest lifestyles as inferior—due in no small part to the efforts of institutions that benefit from the increased consumption that comes from this exposure. The Western, individualized, mass consumer has become a hegemonic ideal the world over, with devastating ecological results.

New values for a new era

Even hegemonies have weaknesses. Indeed, the ideal of the Western lifestyle now appears to be teetering on its pedestal. Not only communities in developing countries, but also residents of high-income countries are opting for alternative lifestyles. These individuals have adopted what has come to be called the **new ecological paradigm** (NEP), or a worldview that prescribes new behaviours in recognition of ecological limits (Dunlap and Van Liere 1978). Emerging in affluent societies as a response to rising discontent with the rapid-paced, anonymous, and individualized lifestyles associated with contemporary industrial living, the NEP describes one of many components of the growing trend towards **post-materialist** values: emphasizing community and quality of life prerogatives, as opposed to materialist values that emphasize economic gain (Inglehart 1977). These trends are reflected in the dramatic growth in recent decades in vegetarianism and demand for organic foods, and the rise in popularity of ecotourist activities such as hiking and bird-watching.

Recent research indicates, however, that people do not necessarily need to have their material needs completely met before they begin to express concern about the environment: environmental values are not limited to the citizens of wealthy nations, but are being expressed the world over (Brechin and Kempton 1994). Indeed, a strong awareness of the ecological limits of our behaviours is sometimes even more apparent in societies and communities whose basic needs for heating supplies and safe food and water, for example, are not being met. In those contexts, however, the power to change individual behaviours is often most lacking.

In direct contrast to the human exemptionalism paradigm (see chapter nine), this growing value shift towards the NEP is characterized by a critical scepticism of science and industrial expansion (Masterson-Allen and Brown 1990) and by shifts in personal lifestyles towards more ecologically sensitive decision-making. This kind of shift in individual values and behaviours can have a tremendous impact on the trajectory of social change. Throughout history many revolutionary shifts in our social systems were not brought about by organized revolution, but rather by a gradual shift in cultural beliefs and values—the secularization that paved the way for the Industrial Revolution is a prime example. Ultimately, however, cultural shifts happen slowly, and are never uniform, given our pluralist social systems. A partial cultural shift does not in itself ensure the reform of institutions in our society that share a large proportion of the responsibility for ecological disruption; those who have been willing and able to make significant shifts towards less consumptive lifestyles still represent a tiny minority of citizens in Western countries, after all. To promote institutional reform, we need collective action.

Collective behaviour

Collective behaviour refers to any effort by individuals to engage in activities as a group. **Social movements** are one form of collective behaviour—and the one that has played the most significant role in social change throughout history. Social movements are sustained, organized activity that promotes or resists some dimension of social change. Modern movements can take several forms, based on the goals and tactics of their members. They include **alternative social movements**, which seek limited change in some small aspect of society (for example, some organic foods co-operatives); **reformative social movements**, which seek broad change in a social system by working within existing institutions (most of our established environmental organizations fall into this category); and **radical social movements**, which seek the basic transformation of society by working outside existing institutions, which are no longer seen as legitimate by movement participants (for example, Earth First!) In all instances, social movements represent a set of organized interests that are challenging the existing political (or social) agenda in some way.

Social movements have evolved historically with the development of capitalism and the capitalist state and especially with the introduction of the print media, which has provided a public forum for discussion of political matters among a wide audience and helped to build an understanding that each individual is part of a larger collective. As central decision-making mechanisms, nation-states provide a target for most social movements because they serve as bodies of social control and consequently are seen both as a threat and as the source of social goods.

In the past fifty years several theories have been posed about why movements emerge. Initially, in what is called **deprivation theory**, social movements were seen as natural reactions by those people in society who feel deprived relative to other members of society (Aberle 1966; Davies 1963). These were people who, perhaps due to exposure to new information regarding the rewards proffered to other groups, had come to expect more and were no longer satisfied with their current situations. They were presumed to organize automatically into social movements vying for change. As a variation on this theme, **structural strain theory** (Smelser 1962) posits that social movements are most likely to emerge when a given society is experiencing significant problems, such as a lagging economy or repeated food shortages. The likelihood of a movement emerging grows when that society's authority system is insufficient to stifle unrest.

More recently a number of scholars have pointed out that feelings of deprivation and periods of structural strain seem to happen far more often than social movements arise, and that therefore social movement activity is not nearly as automatic as originally assumed. According to **resource mobilization theory** (McCarthy and Zald 1977), social movements, particularly those that are successful, are the result of careful planning and the ability to acquire sufficient resources to initiate and sustain organized activity. Discontent and strain may exist for extended periods of time, but social movements will only emerge during narrow windows of opportunity in which the resources necessary to sustain the movement are available. Not surprisingly, many of our more successful social movements have originated in, or have at least had the support of, the middle classes, because lower classes rarely have sufficient resources on their own and must forge alliances with other groups. It stands to reason that the upper classes would never instigate a social movement, because they already have control. Once that control seems to be waning, however, members of the upper classes begin to engage in countermovements in an attempt to challenge the growing power of social movement organizations. One such countermovement that has been particularly effective is the "Wise Use Movement" in the western United States, instigated to defend the rights of private property owners against the growing tide of wildlife and wilderness protection policies that emerged in the 1970s. More recently, the organized actions of many corporations and their supporters to refute the claims of climate change scientists represent another countermovement that has had a significant role to play in environmental politics.

Finally, while movements prior to World War II, such as workers' movements to secure living wages, were predominantly geared towards improving material well-being, **new social movements** (NSM), which include the environmental movement, the civil rights movement, and the women's movement, for example, are more likely to take up quality of life issues (Offe 1985; Melucci 1980). More important perhaps than the hypothesized differences in the agendas of NSMs compared to their forebears are the differences in how these movements manifest themselves. Typically, while the values and vision of a particular social movement may remain constant, the specific battles or tactics used vary widely, depending on the needs at the time. NSMs tend to encompass a broader range of individuals from more diverse backgrounds (Brecher, Costello, and Smith 2002; Buechler 2000; Falk 1993), and as a result are in a position to override class or ideological boundaries and form alliances and coalitions with other groupings, as when environmental organizations ally with churches, trade unions, or even businesses in order to achieve common goals. These alliances can be temporary and issue-specific or ongoing. With the help of modern communications technology, NSMs also frequently reach beyond state borders, operating at the international level.

Given the extraordinary resources required to sustain a movement, and the often complex political actions or behavioural changes called for by contemporary social movement organizers, few social movements actually succeed in bringing about the changes they are pushing for. Participants who started with lots of enthusiasm become discouraged by the slow progress and the amount of menial tasks involved. Resources tend to dry up long before goals are reached. That is particularly true for small, community-level groups that face stiff opposition not only from powerful interests such as a forest company but also from friends and neighbours who are employees of that company. Many larger social movement organizations simply move into "compromise" mode to such an extent that they become "mainstream." Many established environmental organizations have been accused of entertaining such compromised positions—including, for instance, the groups that were willing to negotiate the North American Free Trade Agreement when many other more radical groups challenged the bases upon which the discussions were held. Most importantly, many modern social movements, including the environmental movement in particular, face an uphill battle simply because they attempt to assert simultaneous change in many institutions, including political, economic, cultural, and scientific institutions.

Those movements that do succeed rely on some combination of a number of advantages:

1) Timing—they emerge at a time when a given social system is particularly volatile and susceptible to change. Changes in political opportunities and constraints can create windows, or **political opportunity structures** (Eisinger 1973), within which a movement may succeed. An example could be the election into office of a sympathetic public official; or a recent event, like an oil tanker accident, that heightens the vigilance of other members of the public.
2) Getting the message out—simply having large geographic concentrations of people allows social movements to gain ground, but beyond this, **dense connecting networks** or **advocacy networks** across multiple organizations in society are needed to facilitate organization and information exchange in order to generate support, and to ensure that the concerns raised reach the ears of those organizations or institutions that are the targets of the movement. Local environmental justice groups, for example, often rely on the support of larger environmental organizations such as the Sierra Club to provide advocacy training, financial assistance with litigation, and lobbying. That is why we rarely observe successful social movements in contexts in which the basic infrastructure needed to bring together supporters and convey movement goals to other social institutions is lacking, such as in rural regions that have limited access to media and communications resources (Jackson et al. 1960; Freeman 1973; Keck and Sikkink 1998). The general public awareness of the struggles of communities in the southern, predominantly rural Mexican state of Chiapas to secure the protection of their land base is due in no small part to the ability of organizational leaders to make use of the Internet to broadcast their concerns and activities to a wide international audience.
3) Setting in place **collective action frames**, or a means of framing concerns—these not only need to be strong enough to bind together social movement participants who may come from diverse backgrounds, but also must be in alignment with the culture and beliefs of members of the broader society, something called **frame resonance** (Snow et al. 1986). An effort to frame the issue of sustainability in terms of democracy and equity, for example, may resonate with Western value systems, whereas posing sustainability in terms of humanity's spiritual linkage to other species may fall short.
4) Adopting novelty and flexibility in tactics taken and in alliances formed—this allows social movements to reach wide audiences, to mobilize resources in innovative ways, to take advantage of rapidly changing opportunity structures, and to respond to the ever-changing dynamics of governments, corporations, the media, and the economy (Rucht 1999; Keck and Sikkink 1998).
5) Gaining support from science and scientists—this is particularly critical for environmental movement organizations. Many environmental scientists and health scientists have become critical to the success of

environmental social movements and are beginning to instil an alternative paradigm in scientific institutions by recognizing the need for a shift towards the precautionary principle (see chapter eight), towards acknowledgement of the value of local, experiential knowledge, and towards recognition of the need to incorporate a broader set of information beyond traditional, quantitative data in decision-making.

6) Clearly recognizing, and not discounting, the means by which oppressive, non-democratic political systems can stifle movement activity due to the severe consequences for individual participants—environmental activists have been jailed or even killed in numerous countries, including Mexico, Brazil, Nigeria, and North Korea, to name a few examples.

Despite many obstacles, the environmental movement is one of the most successful movements of the past fifty years, covering a broad spectrum of concerns from rainforest depletion to nuclear disarmament. Most notably, in recent years the movement has been characterized by a simultaneous move towards global and local agendas.

The global agenda, taken up predominantly by non-governmental environmental organizations such as Greenpeace, is largely a response to emergent scientific information regarding pressing global environmental concerns such as ozone depletion, climate change, and loss of biological diversity. These international organizations are having a tremendous influence on the international environmental governance agenda. They place pressure on nation-states to undergo environmental reform, and they are spearheading the eco-labelling movement. Moreover, their influence has extended beyond the successful promotion of shifts in environmental policy to include influence in social, economic, and cultural realms—for example, by encouraging environmentally conscious consumption (Wapner 1996).

The growing number of local, grassroots movements reflects increases in awareness and concern about the environmental consequences faced by local residents who live near heavy industrial or technologically risky activities—such as the residents of southern Alberta who are living with sour gas wells in their communities (see chapter six). Local movements also reflect an increasing diversity of both values and political capacities that are brought to bear in community politics (see, for example, Lipschutz 1996). In many instances participants in these movements from below would not even describe themselves as "environmentalists." As several of our chapters here show, many local mobilizations come in response to a distrust of authorities who seem to disregard local sentiments. They arise from personal experiences with health problems, such as the increase in miscarriages or chronic headaches and nausea. They represent a response to problems of liveability among impoverished citizens who must survive

10.1 Citizens Fight Coca-Cola to Ensure Water Rights

In November 2004 citizens staged a massive protest against several Coca-Cola bottling facilities in India. While the protest march and rally centred on the Coca-Cola bottling plants in the communities of Ballia and Mehdiganj, both in the state of Uttar Pradesh, several communities organized across the country to fight other Coca-Cola plants. The protestors say the plants—there are twenty-five all across the country—cause water shortages and pollution. The plants use local water supplies and discharge their effluents on community lands, which are in many instances used for agriculture. Some communities have also contested the means by which plant owners have gained tenure to the land. Several communities have been successful in their fights against the plants. In December 2003 the Kerala High Court directed two local plants to find alternative sources of water. In another instance in that same state, a local village council refused to issue an operating licence to the local plant.

"Drinking Coke is like drinking farmer's blood in India," said march organizer Nandlal Master of the non-governmental organization Lok Samiti and the National Alliance of People's Movements. "Coca-Cola is creating thirst in India, and is directly responsible for the loss of livelihood and even hunger for thousands of people across India," Master said. "Water and land are essential to life, and challenging Coca-Cola is a fight for our survival. We have to shut it down." The protestors have been assisted by a number of NGOs, such as the India Resource Center, an organization that works with local groups in India to co-ordinate the campaign internationally.

Ironically, some reports indicate that farmers in India are using Coca-Cola as pesticide, with amazing success.

Source: *Environment News Service* 2004.

in degraded urban environments. Or they spring from anti-globalization sentiments among disenfranchised family farmers.

Despite their diversity—or more precisely because of it—these growing grassroots mobilizations promise to become central agents of change towards sustainability. Their concerns, after all, get to the very foundations of many of our ecological and environmental ills. Moreover, citizens who have come to feel alienated from politics at the national and international levels are now seeing very clearly the possibilities for change through combined efforts at the local level – and thus are becoming more and more engaged in that sphere.

Given that these movements are not rooted in strictly post-materialist values, and instead bring to the fore basic rights to natural resources, democracy, and equity, they also have an increased power to elicit response from some of our most rigid institutions. These new movements have shown us that sustainability can only be achieved if pursued in conjunction with two conceptual frames: **environmental justice**—demands for the equitable distribution of environmental resources and of the risks associated with certain technologies; and the closely associated concept of **ecological democracy**—the premise that equal opportunities to participate in environmental decisions that affect our lives and values will lead to better environmental management in the long run, ensuring that interest in sustainable livelihoods, not corporate profits, drive decision-making. Many social critics are optimistic that the incorporation of these concepts into environmental politics—rather than ambiguous concepts such as sustainable development—will lead a shift in our society-environment relationship. Using these frames, more appropriate decision-making will recognize ecological limits, endorse a shift towards the use of the precautionary principle in our scientific institutions, and also prioritize the need to make radical changes in our political and economic institutions.

The role of states

Ultimately, attempts to initiate changes in social systems depend upon the ability of social movements to encourage changes in our governance apparatuses. This is easier said than done: regardless of the sympathies of individual government employees to the cause, one of the greatest challenges in addressing environmental issues, from global climate change to the timber harvest to the safety of nuclear power plants, is simply the lack of an appropriate governance mechanism. This issue is so central that the world at large may well be facing a crisis in environmental governance (Elliott 1998). Canada certainly provides evidence of this as a federalist nation in which the provinces and territories hold a tremendous amount of political decision-making power. Before the government can act on certain national issues it needs to find, or achieve, a much greater degree of cross-country consensus than is the case in countries in which the federal government holds more power. The need for building consensus is particularly strong when it comes to policies that relate to the environment and natural resources, because responsibility for matters such as the regulation of energy production and timber harvest are explicitly in the hands of the provinces.

Canada is by no means a special case. Nation-states have served as our primary model of governance for several centuries and have evolved to perform certain functions in society, including the provision of basic infrastructure such as communications, transportation, education, law enforcement, and judicial systems. Nation-states are expected to provide a regulatory framework to control employment levels, distribute incomes, and protect local industries, and they are also in the business of regulating markets, fostering economic growth, and providing some level of protection against the volatile tendencies of modern economies. Our states are also called on to provide security to their citizens, particularly those who are most vulnerable, from various threats from military organizations, natural disasters, diseases, and other external sources. All of these roles are certainly not taken up in full by all, perhaps many, states across the globe, but at least they represent a yardstick by which we can measure the strength and effectiveness of a given nation-state.

Although the role of states in environmental protection is fairly new—only emerging in the late 1960s—states have been managers of land and natural resources for centuries. These assets have historically been important sources of power and wealth. The growth of **environmental states**, or states with apparatuses that assume responsibility for environmental well-being, has been attributed in large part to the growing ability of environmental movement organizations to exert political pressures on nation-states to establish national environmental ministries, parks and protected areas, and national environmental policies (Frank, Hironaka, and Schofer 2000; Frank 1999), and to sign international environmental treaties (Roberts 1996; Dietz and Kalof 1992). This argument is an international twist on a very old theme. At least until the 1960s, most scholars presumed that states functioned exactly how they were ideally meant to—with elected officials enforcing the wishes of the people. This view of state activity is called **pluralism**. A perfectly pluralist state is capable of implementing policies according to the agendas that are put forward by organizations in civil society (see, for example, Dahl 1961). Pluralism thus posits that environmental policy is a state's direct response to the concerns expressed by its (organized) citizenry.

Particularly since the 1970s, however, pluralism has come under attack by critical social scientists who highlight the tendency for states to favour the interests of the upper classes. In particular, **ecological Marxists** (see chapter one) argue that the traditional role of the state in protecting its citizenry from environmental degradation, or even ensuring the sustainability of vital natural resources, is seriously in question. In many instances, regardless of whether an organized environmental movement exists or not, states in industrial societies are constrained by the logic of capital, or the need to subsidize industry so that the companies can continue to make a profit, keep people employed, and in turn generate revenues for the state through taxation. The constraints placed on capitalist states are only exacerbated when the priorities of economic growth become codified in international trade agreements. The regulations of NAFTA, for example, make it much more difficult for states to protect natural resources, or to support locals in doing so (Schnaiberg and Gould 1994; O'Connor 1998, 1988; Roberts and Grimes 2002; Moore 2000; Chew 1995; Chase-Dunn 1989).

Ecological Marxism clearly parts ways with the ecological modernization perspective (chapter one), which suggests that nation-states have the ability to act according to an ecological rationality and implement effective reform by adopting less hierarchical, network approaches to management. Those approaches then enable state managers to gain access to the resources and expertise of organizations in civil society, and they ensure "reflexivity," or institutional learning, contributing to continuous improvements in our management capacities.

The reason as to why such seemingly incompatible views regarding nation-states can persist at the same time is because of the very diversity of state systems across the globe: in a given time and location cases can be found to support each of these theories. Individual nation-states have many central features in common, but they can also vary in size, power, relative priorities, and administrative structure. A given state's uniqueness is defined by its own history and context: when and under what circumstances it was formed, the size of the populace and economy within its realm, its position in the global economy, and the mix of cultures of its citizenry.

Not surprisingly, different nation-states can assume vastly differing degrees of responsibility for the environment. One of the keys to understanding this variation is the distinction between **legitimation** and **rationalization** (Frickel and Davidson 2004). The likelihood for significant growth in government responsibility for the environment is greatest when states come to view such responsibility as a component of their central roles. In other words, nation-states make environmental protection a basic goal by committing their institutional resources towards long-term environmental sustainability. Most state environmental activity to date, however, can be described as legitimation activity—doing the minimum necessary to reassure environmentally concerned citizens that their issues are being addressed. The more ambiguous our indicators of environmental well-being, the easier it is for a state institution to maintain legitimacy without actually addressing environmental problems (Beck 1999; Freudenburg and Pastor 1992; Freudenburg 1996). The key questions then become: under what conditions can we expect nation-states to adopt significant policies aimed, for instance, at reducing the level of greenhouse gas emissions, and what types of political conditions foster more symbolic measures that will have little impact on the level of emissions at all?

The answer may lie in the extent to which the dominant political discourse frames environmental concerns as issues that are key to the primary state roles. State efforts to promote energy efficiency and waste minimization, for example, may become a priority for states if those efforts are seen as being important to economic growth. Ensuring safe drinking-water supplies not only means healthy workers but also maintains internal order because threats to the drinking-water supplies can (and have) stir up a tremendous degree of social protest. At a deeper level, when environmental degradation comes to be recognized as an infringement on basic human rights, then ameliorating that degradation becomes an essential part of the core responsibilities of states and thus faces a much higher likelihood of receiving the attention of policy-makers and managers.

Attention is not always enough, however. State institutions also need the capacity to respond. Addressing some environmental dilemmas—such as the protection of endangered species, the reduction of greenhouse

10.2 New Delhi's Smog Success Story

New Delhi, India's second-largest city, has a population of about fourteen million people. It also has three million vehicles and airborne particulate matter that is frequently ten times India's legal limit. By the 1990s the black haze over New Delhi posed a serious health hazard. A public interest group in India, the Centre of Science and Environment, sued the Delhi State government, resulting in a court decision demanding that the government take action to clean up the air. In particular, the Supreme Court ruled in July 1998 that the diesel-fuelled bus fleet of New Delhi, along with all commercial autorickshaws (three-wheeled motor vehicles) and taxis, must be converted to Compressed Natural Gas (CNG) by March 31, 2001, or they would not be allowed to operate. The public transit system nearly collapsed soon after the deadline, with only eight hundred buses out of the two thousand owned by the public sector having been converted by that time. Another twelve thousand buses owned by private operators who had also not complied were prevented from operating as well.

Despite the immediate hardships, by 2003 compliance was nearly complete. People could breathe again and, some say, even see the stars. More than seventy-five thousand vehicles are now running on CNG, and over a hundred CNG filling stations are available. Other initiatives put in place include: sales tax exemptions for conversions to CNG; banning of taxis, buses, and autorickshaws older than fifteen years; lead-free gasoline; and restrictions on goods-carrying vehicles during daytime hours.

Source: *Gallon Environment Newsletter* 2004.

gases, or even the systematic testing of new chemicals for their potential carcinogenic effects—can be extraordinarily expensive. Many nation-states, particularly in developing countries, do not collect sufficient revenues to perform those activities. In other cases the education systems of a given country, or access to them, are so limited that bureaucratic organizations cannot find the skilled personnel they need to attend to the complexities of environmental monitoring and management. The nature of a given country's social system, then, also poses limits on state actions.

Global Environmental Governance

Our nation-state system is not solely premised upon the need for organized bodies to attend to certain domestic societal needs. It is also premised on the need for a system of agreed upon rules of interaction among ruling bodies. Central to these rules of international engagement is the ideal of national sovereignty—a national government, in other words, has the right to be free from external control. While designed to put a check on imperial ambitions, the concept of state sovereignty poses a paradox for the addressing of global environmental issues. When transboundary pollution problems emerged along the Canadian-U.S. border, the leaders of those countries negotiated some of the first modern international environmental policy agreements; but regulating transboundary pollutants, even among these two developed nations, has never been devoid of its problems. That task is inordinately more straightforward, furthermore, than is achieving binding agreements involving over one hundred nations, as is the case in many of our international environmental agreements. Given that our nation-state system has been in place for several centuries, introducing new mechanisms of governance that are more appropriately suited to global issues is not easy.

Consequently, although the global integration of national economies has flourished, particularly with the aid of electronic media, our political systems have not followed suit. The result is a fully integrated global system dominated by corporate actors (Paehlke 2003), while politics is still woefully entrenched in this centuries-old nation-state system. The emergence of international and global economic institutions diminishes state sovereignty and reduces the state's capacity to intervene in economic activities (Wapner 1996), while at the same time no new governing apparatus appears to be forthcoming anytime soon. As Lash and Urry (1994) put it, nation-states today are too big for the small problems and too small for the big (global, high-consequence) problems.

In the 1970s, the heyday of the environmental state, nearly all environmental managers and scholars saw no realistic alternative other than to rely upon nation-states to address environmental problems. More recently, after decades of state-led efforts that have fallen short of expectation, some critics have argued that we should simply do away with the nation-state system of environmental management altogether, particularly when it comes to the global commons resources of air and climate. The main alternatives to the nation-state approach to global (and other) environmental issues have been, on one hand, to foster a broad network of decentralized, autonomous local-level governance structures and, on the other hand, to organize at the global level.

Bioregionalism proposes the decentralization of environmental governance so that decisions are made entirely at the local level. First proposed by Kirkpatrick Sale in the mid-1970s, this radical approach emerged in direct opposition to the dominant centralized-state approach to environmental management. Sale (1974) argued that societies, economies, and politics should be organized around local bioregions, rather than the reverse. The bioregion, including the soil, watershed, climate, native plants, and animals of a local area, would then become the focal point for human activity and consciousness. This grounded (literally) "sense of place" is obtained as humans orient their lives and livelihoods to their local bioregion and its natural limits (Dobson 1991; Sale 1974, 2001).

The operating principles of bioregionalism include, first, a shift in economic interactions towards co-operation rather than competition and, second, basing the governance of development on respectful self-sufficiency rather than on expansionism. In addition, governance would be based on decentralization, whereby local residents become engaged in environmental politics in a participatory democratic framework. The values, knowledges, and experiences of local citizens would be employed in decision-making.

A shift to a bioregionalist political framework would be no small feat, given, for example, the degree to which current structures are oriented towards nation-states and the exploitation of natural resources (Dobson 1991; Sale 1974, 2001). More importantly, bioregionalism has been heavily critiqued for being unrealistically utopian. The implications of extreme decentralization also draw criticism. For example, there is no guarantee that decentralization will inevitably produce environmentally sound decisions; indeed, there is nothing to preclude a given local political system from being oppressive or exploitative (Dobson 1991). Many of today's environmental dilemmas, furthermore, require the co-ordinated effort of societies across the globe. Finally, and perhaps most importantly, because natural resources such as water, fertile soil, forests, and energy supplies are not distributed equally, some regions may find themselves to be quite capable of sustaining high standards of living, but others will not, leading to inevitable conflicts.

Nevertheless, the concept of bioregionalism continues to be popular. Among other things it provides for a new way of organizing human activity. As such it strikes a chord not just with environmentalists but also with those who feel alienated by social and economic systems. Still, as one critic says, because of difficulties with the details of its implementation and operating principles, people "are most likely to extract the spirit from the bioregional project without necessarily following it to the letter" (Dobson 1991: 77).

Organized environmental governance at the global level, on the other hand, has taken off since the 1980s (Mol and Buttel 2002). International organizations with a focus in environmental management have exploded in number, including non-governmental environmental organizations such as the Worldwide Fund for Nature and international scientific bodies such as the Global Environment Facility and Intergovernmental Panel on Climate Change. These organizations, which have become increasingly influential in international politics, serve as a set of voices that transcends the interests of nation-states. Some critics have pointed to the powerful position they enjoy, however, and their non-representative, non-democratic structures (Goldman 1998). As well, because their ranks are filled predominantly with scientists from Europe and the West, these organizations represent a set of interests and values, and establish scientific agendas, that do not necessarily include the priorities and concerns of people in developing countries. With over one hundred of its scientists on the Intergovernmental Panel on Climate Change, for example, Canada is certainly more than adequately represented; but numerous developing countries have only a small handful of scientists each on the Panel, and some have none at all. Indeed, many representatives of developing coun-

10.3 Environmental Standards in the European Union

As a means of harmonizing environmental conditions in all countries in the European Union, all industrial facilities operating there must first receive an authorization permit according to the Integrated Pollution Prevention and Control (IPCC) Directive, established in 1996. The permits must be based on the concept of Best Available Techniques (or BAT), which in many cases demands radical environmental improvements. Permits are also based on "integrated" assessments of industrial activities, which means that operators must take into account the whole environmental performance of the plant, including emissions to air, water, and land, generation of waste, use of raw materials, energy efficiency, noise, prevention of accidents, and risk management.

While such large-scale harmonization of standards implies a centralized regulatory apparatus, operators and permitting authorities must also take into account the technical characteristics of the installation, its geographical location and local environmental conditions, demanding a decentralized and site-specific approach to evaluation. To ensure continuous improvements in and harmonized implementation of BAT, the European Commission organizes an exchange of information between experts from the E.U. member states, industry, and environmental organizations. Finally, the directive prioritizes a transparent and participatory process by ensuring the availability of all relevant documents to the public. The active participation of the public at large is seen as essential in driving industrial environmental performance forward.

Source: Europa Environment 2004.

tries were vehement opponents of policies being proposed during the Kyoto negotiations, and that was because other concerns, including hunger and poverty reduction, take precedence in their countries. According to Vandana Shiva, the efforts of international scientific and environmental organizations to pressure developing countries to adopt Western-defined environmental and ecological standards, often in exchange for much-needed development aid, amounts to **green imperialism** (Shiva 1993).

International governmental organizations face their own challenges, however, and the number of actual governing bodies at the global level, such as the United Nations Environment Programme, remains small. Far more common are international bodies that represent a much smaller number of countries, the largest and most successful being the European Commission Environment Directorate. In all cases, these bodies consist of a constellation of nation-state representatives, each of them far more inclined to protect the interests of their own nation than to adopt an interest in the common global good. Oran Young (1997) describes international environmental governance systems in terms of regimes: social institutions that consist of agreed upon principles, norms, rules, decision-making procedures, and programs that govern the interactions of actors in specific issues areas. But this system is by definition premised first on the voluntary decision by nation-states to participate, and second on the willingness to agree upon the norms and rules that dictate governing actions. Given the vast differences in size, strength, stakes, and vulnerabilities among nations across the globe, international governance, at least in the near future, may be on a precarious footing.

The type of international governance apparatus needed to address global environmental problems effectively is simply not in place. As Lorraine Elliott (1998: 96) states, we need international agreements "which are not only precautionary and take into account often-incomplete but changing scientific information, but which also establish environmental standards and means by which those standards can be met and verified." These agreements, she says, will have "to account for the interests of a range of 'stakeholders' including environmental non-governmental organizations, grass-roots movements, indigenous peoples, industry, financial institutions, scientific bodies and intergovernmental organizations as well as states and governments. Environmental governance, therefore, must at minimum be co-operative and collective."

Many individuals, non-governmental organizations, and communities and cities, however, have proven themselves to be far more flexible, progressive, and creative in addressing environmental and ecological concerns than have our fledgling international governmental organizations. Even though international co-operation may ultimately be necessary to address many environmental concerns, these other actions at different levels are already having a significant impact, not least by offering options for resistance to the structural forces that foster the ecological crisis.

Starting Today

The ecological crisis can appear to take on the guise of an impenetrable web of corporate power, hegemonic ideologies, media influence, scientific uncertainty, conflicting social constructions, and even our own cultural propensities. Every web, however, is made up of single strands that are replete with weaknesses. The key to our own agency is to recognize and be prepared to act when those weaknesses cross our path. By this means we empower ourselves and ensure our own contribution to the reshaping of the web. Doing so requires first and foremost a new level of consciousness that evaluates the decisions we make every day with an eye towards minimizing our own ecological footprints and resisting dominant power structures. This consciousness can guide us through the grocery store and the rest of our lives as consumers. It can help determine our selection of classes and reading materials, how we decide to spend our free time, who we vote for, what technologies we adopt, what companies we support. If we only passively wander through our habitual lifestyles, uncritically accepting the dominant ideologies that speak to us every day, we are in effect passing on to others the power for change; we are at the mercy of their decisions and priorities. The more we take opportunities to penetrate the web rather than succumb to its whims, the greater will be the potential for social change.

Glossary

acceptable risk: a term used to define the limit of risk tolerance; grounded in the belief that biological and ecological systems can tolerate a certain level of pollution.

activist scientists: in environmental justice research, researchers dedicated to responding to communities' crises and needs.

advocacy or participatory research: with environmental justice research, "the theory and practice of making academic research more applicable, more sustainable, and more relevant to communities.

Agenda 21: developed at the 1992 United Nations Conference on Environment and Development in Rio de Janeiro, establishes sustainable development goals for communities."

alternative social movements: seek limited change in some small aspect of society.

anomie: Durkheim's description of social breakdown. Studying industrialization and urbanization in the late nineteenth century, Durkheim argued that anomie resulted from rapid changes in society, due either to growth that develops too quickly for social organizations to adapt or to the collapse and decay of those social organizations.

anti-corporate movement (anti-globalization; globalization from below): predominately local social movements and grassroots coalitions that contest the negative aspects of globalization.

bioaccumulation: the process whereby certain toxic substances (for example, POPs) collect in living tissues and pose a latent hazard to human health.

bioregionalism: a concept developed by Kirkpatrick Sale, it advocates an extreme decentralization of environmental governance, whereby all human activity (including social, economic, and political organization) would be based around local bioregions.

biotechnology: the application of elements of the principles of engineering and technology to the life sciences or to biological entities.

boom-bust cycle: an economic trend that is especially strong in remote resource-dependent communities. The emergence of a natural resource economy or industrial activity in a local area encourages rapid economic growth in local towns. Once the resource is exhausted or the industry moves elsewhere, the town is left in economic, and therefore social, disarray.

carrying capacity: the maximum feasible load on the environment that the Earth can support indefinitely.

civil society: those institutions, social movements, organizations, and voluntary activities that function in the realms between the state and our personal and business lives.

class-action suit: a lawsuit launched by members of a large group of people on behalf of all members of the group (for example, Vietnamese class-action suit against DOW Chemical).

cognitive science approach: large body of social-psychological research on how and why laypersons perceive risks associated with modern technologies.

collective action frames: the means by which social movement organizations discursively present their agendas to civil society.

colonization: in the context of rural communities, demographic shifts resulting from rural economic restructuring combined with a counter-urbanization movement in the middle class create incentives for residential real estate development on the urban-rural fringe.

commodification of nature: A process whereby the ecological services and products of nature are priced for exchange in the marketplace. Natural goods such as genes, water, and air that were formerly understood as part of the health and well-being of human species and societies are under pressure of privatization by capitalist corporations for profit and gain. This process is associated with globalization. **Decommodification** is the struggle by groups to return these public goods from private control and back to the commons, as common property.

commodity: according to the *Concise Oxford Dictionary*, simply a useful thing; an article of trade. In Marxist theory, the commodity embodies the change from production for use value (the useful thing), to production for exchange value (the article of trade). Hence a commodity is something that can be sold for profit in a marketplace. As a process this is referred to as **commodification**, which entails a transformation of relationships, formerly untainted by commerce, into commercial relationships of buying and selling.

commodity chain: a commodity chain is the series of linkages that contribute to the final product, from cultivation or production, marketing, and distribution to consumption.

common pool resource: a natural resource, such as a fishery, air, forest, groundwater aquifer, or gene pool from which it is hard to exclude other users. Unless some collective regulatory systems are in place, these common pool resources can be subject to degradation as a result of overuse or misuse. Many such resources have been managed through common property management systems throughout history.

commons: areas of social and natural life that remain under communal stewardship and responsibility; examples are genes, seeds, culture, health, air, and water. The ideal of the commons is both democratic and multifaceted. Commons operate across geographic and temporal scales and comprise both common rights and common property. A local commons can include groundwater and food, while a global ecological commons can include atmosphere and oceans. A civil commons means traditions of democratic participation, public service, and cultural heritage that serve to protect and regulate access to natural commons. The **global commons** crosses national boundaries.

comparative advantage: developed by British economist David Ricardo (1772–1823), refers to the ability of an individual or group to carry out an economic activity, such as production, at a lower cost and more efficiently than another entity is able to do. When implemented on a global scale, it refers to each nation specializing in and exporting what it can produce most efficiently (that is, cheaply), and importing those products that it cannot efficiently produce.

consumerism: an ideology, and practice, in which a progressively greater consumption of goods is seen as beneficial. In a culture and economy of production and consumption, especially in developed industrialized countries, goods are produced, purchased, discarded, and manufactured again (and purchased again) on a recurring basis in order to sustain capitalist profit. Consumption is often misperceived as being driven by personal gratification and self-expression or by the culture of marketing and shopping. Most cultural studies analysts erroneously delink it from production.

conversion economy: the socially planned redirection of the economy necessary to create a sustainable society (John Bellamy Foster).

core: in world systems theory, the core (or industrialized centre) is developed by exploiting the value from the underdeveloped **periphery**. Power and resources tend to flow from the periphery to the core because of **dependency** relations and global inequality.

cornucopianism: belief that natural resources are inexhaustible, and that human ingenuity will resolve all societal problems.

corporate crime: when corporate employees or owners commit a crime such as fraud, environmental pollution, manufacturing of unsafe products, and maintaining dangerous work environments, as a means of gaining a financial advantage.

corporate deviance: the violation by corporations of social and legal norms.

corporatization: see **privatization**.

costs of social reproduction: the minimum amount of money individual workers need to feed and clothe and maintain the health of themselves and their families.

debt-service ratios: the percentage of gross income used to pay interest and principal on loans; as interest rates increase, countries spend increasing amounts of money on interest and still do not cover their obligations, thus adding debt service. Third world countries are putting so much of their national earnings into paying the interest on their loans that they are unable to buy the food and agricultural inputs needed to strengthen their economies and societies.

decentralization: the distribution of the functions or powers of a state government among local authorities.

dematerialization: the claim that unsustainable uses of resources by capitalist societies and firms can be resolved by the development of new technologies that use and reuse material resources more efficiently. The thesis assumes that advanced capitalist societies will become dematerialized first, lessening environmental impacts on the globe, allowing resource capacity for less developed countries to grow and industrialize, thus solving social justice issues and inequalities. The idea has been much criticized in the literature.

dense connecting networks or **advocacy networks**: connections between individuals and organizations in society that are sufficiently integrated to allow for regular communication and exchange. Seen as a necessary feature of social movement mobilization (Jackson et al. 1960; Freeman 1973).

dependency/dependent: lack of independence or self-sufficiency. For world systems theory, dependency relations are an expression of global inequality with respect to power.

deprivation theory: a theory that attributes the emergence of social movements to the tendency for people in society to feel deprived relative to other members of society; particularly when they are exposed to new information regarding the rewards proffered to other groups, which means that they thus come to expect more for themselves (Aberle 1966; Davies 1963).

deregulation: the removal or easing of regulations such as pollution laws, aiming at as few restrictions as possible in order to let corporations pursue profit.

diagnostic uncertainty: uncertainty in diagnosing environmental health problems. Often doctors do not have the training or knowledge to tie exposures to specific health conditions.

discourse: the communicative practices through which meaning is assigned to the world.

distancing: the separation of production from consumption decisions, which displaces ecological and social costs over space and time and severs the cycle of ecological and social feedback; the greater distance between production and consumption increases the likelihood of environmental and human exploitation.

dominant epidemiological paradigm (DEP): a belief system that sees diseases as existing in a simple cause-effect relationship. It is criticized for not being able to address the complexities of environmental health problems.

drawdown method: technology, which initially increased carrying capacity, has since the Industrial Revolution been doing the reverse by increasing per capita resource requirements for every unit of energy produced under a fossil fuel-dependent regime.

eco-labelling: a voluntary method of environmental performance certification, based on life-cycle consideration.

ecological democracy: the equitable distribution of environmental goods and risks.

ecological footprint: the environmental impact of one human being on the ecosystem, measured by the variety of material goods consumed in day-to-day living; the concept includes the area of productive land and water (ecosystems) required on a continuous basis to produce the resources consumed and to assimilate the wastes produced by a defined population, wherever on Earth that land is located.

ecological imperialism: the biological expansion of European plants, diseases, and animals that accompanied European colonialism and imperialism across the globe with a consideration of how these elements altered local ecosystems, sometimes with drastic affect. Contrast with **green imperialism**.

ecological Marxism: a body of theory positing that capitalism will ultimately reach a crisis in production as the lands and resources upon which production depends become used up and polluted.

ecological modernization: a contemporary social theory proposing that incremental reforms to existing industrial and political systems can bring about ecological sustainability, without the need for fundamental structural or revolutionary social change. Considered a technocentric ideology by its critics, it assumes that ecological problems can be resolved by technological ingenuity and that natural limits can be overcome without threatening current ways of economic life.

economies of scale: a reduction in the cost of production due to the large number of items produced. It is contested as a universal principle.

ecosystem services: the free ecological services provided in nature, such as soil formation, nutrient cycling, climate moderation, pollination, habitat, and more, all of which are fundamental to maintaining the basic building blocks of life on Earth; they are usually ignored in our thinking about environment and society because they are free.

entropy: associated with the second law of thermodynamics, which states that every time energy is transformed or converted, which is what we do whenever we expend energy in work or in heat production, the total amount of energy remains the same but its availability for future work is reduced. Entropy is the measurement of this change in usefulness or availability.

environmental justice: democratic decision-making that empowers both community members and workers to participate in environmental decisions that have an impact on their lives and values, regardless of race, ethnicity, citizenship, income level, or place of residence.

environmental justice movement: a movement dedicated to the principles of environmental justice.

environmental racism/environmental injustice: the tendency for minorities of all types to face unfair treatment, discrimination, and oppression, resulting in greater risks of pollution and other forms of environmental risk, often regardless of their socio-economic status.

environmental risks: also called modernization risks, they encompass the unintended side effects of technological development (see, for example, Beck 1992, 1999).

environmental states: states with apparatuses that have primary responsibility for environmental well-being.

epidemiology: determination of the incidence and distribution of a particular disease (for example, by age, sex, or occupation), which may provide information about the cause of the disease.

etiological uncertainty: uncertainties about the cause (of an environmental illness).

exergy: process by which certain subregions increase in entropy through transfers of resources that serve to increase the amount of available energy for industrial work and consumer lifestyles in the developed world, and poverty in the global South; a term coined by Hornberg (2001).

externalization (of costs): The tendency by producers (particularly corporations) to push the costs associated with production onto others, either knowingly or through ignorance of the real costs of production. Such costs may come in the form of, for example, social welfare, pollution, or ecological disruption. For example, industries may avoid installing more expensive scrubbers for their waste stacks, or avoid proper disposal of their wastes in order to reduce costs.

Fordism: named for Henry Ford's automobile assembly line, with a detailed division of labour broken down into step-by-step construction, and the flow of work and organization of the workers drawing from the time and motion efficiencies suggested by industrial psychologist Frederick Taylor.

fossil acreage/ghost acreage: the number of additional acres of farmland that would be needed to grow organic fuels with energy content equivalent to the amount held in the fossil fuels on which we are dependent (Catton 1980).

frame resonance: when a social movement's collective action frame is in alignment with the culture and beliefs of members of the broader society (Snow et al. 1986).

framing: attempts to present an argument in a manner designed to persuade listeners to see that argument in a particular way.

free-rider problem: refers to the tendency for people not to act to protect or remediate natural resources held in common, based on the presumption either that someone else will act, or that no one wants to be solely responsible for the costs of a benefit that everyone will enjoy. When assumed, the concept implies that human nature is naturally competitive and self-interested, and that when a common good is maintained by the collective, some individuals will take advantage and not contribute their fair share. As an assumption, it is debated and controversial.

gender bias: the separation of gender in a way that, because of cultural ideals and stereotypes of masculinity and femininity, favours one sex over the other.

genetically engineered (GE), genetically modified (GM), genetically modified organism (GMO): any alteration of genetic material in a plant or animal to make it capable of producing new substances or performing new functions. Often involves cutting parts of DNA out of one organism and inserting them into another. Highly controversial because of the tendency to be associated with **commodification** of organisms or biological materials.

global assembly line: a global arrangement of nations whereby every nation specializes in its **comparative advantage** such that every nation plays its specialized role in an increasingly complex and interdependent world trade system. Related to **globalization** and **commodity chains**.

globalization: like the term modernization, globalization is a contested concept; some proponents see it as the positive extension of capitalist firms, trade, and flows of capital into all regions of the world, unifying economic systems and facilitating freer trade in goods, knowledges, and peoples. Critics see it as the domination of nation-states and national regulatory protections by powerful corporate and international interests, which are breaking down national democratic rights from without and at the same time commodifying the common property resources of the globe (sometimes called neo-liberal globalism or the Washington Consensus). See also **anti-corporate movement**.

green consumerism: an approach that avoids buying products that harm the environment, or that buys products that have a lesser impact on the environment. It is controversial because of its tendency to substitute for more substantial critiques of consumerism in general.

green imperialism: the efforts of international scientific and environmental organizations to pressure developing countries to adopt Western-defined environmental and ecological standards, often in exchange for much-needed development aid (Shiva 1993). Contrast with **ecological imperialism**.

hegemony: a term used by Gramsci to describe how ideology is imposed to perpetuate the dominance of the ruling class, by winning the passive consent of those dominated and thereby minimizing the need for coercive force.

heuristics: mental "shortcuts" that individuals tend to employ in their assessment of new phenomena. Kahneman and Tversky (1979) attributed the heightened risk perceptions of laypersons (when compared to scientific experts) to the use of heuristics, which serve as a means of associating the risk to other experiences that may be more familiar.

Homo Colossus: societal condition in which humans draw on more resources per capita than did each previous generation (Catton 1980).

human exemptionalism paradigm (HEP): belief that nature poses no limits on human activity; humans are in effect exempt from the ecological constraints that all other species face. HEP until very recently has contributed to the lack of consideration among social scientists for environmental phenomena (Catton and Dunlap 1980; Dunlap and Catton 1994).

hydrosphere: refers to all the water on or near the earth's surface that is part of a self-sustaining system of water circulation. See **waterscapes**.

imperialism: the policy of extending a nation's power and authority by increasing its territory or by establishing economic and political hegemony over other nations.

individualization: a process by which the focus of an issue is increasingly on the individual rather than on a collective entity or entities. The **individualization of responsibility** is a response to environmental degradation that understands the problem as the product of individual shortcomings that is best countered by individual, consumer-based action.

job blackmail: term developed by Kazis and Grossman (1982) to describe the threat by corporations of layoffs, closures, or pulling investment out of their community because workers or communities complain of health or environmental impacts from an industry's production processes. This tactic ensures that labour will defend the interests of the company in environmental disputes.

land ethic: Aldo Leopold argues: "The land ethic simply enlarges the boundaries of the community to include soils, waters, plants, and animals, or collectively: the land.... [It] changes the role of *Homo sapiens* from conqueror of the land-community to plain member and citizen of it. It implies respect for his fellow-members, and also respect for the community as such" (Leopold 1949).

landscape: refers to both the physical makeup of particular parts of the Earth's surface and its social constructions associated with economic, cultural, and political systems.

legitimation: activities undertaken by an organization or institution in an attempt to maintain legitimacy and avoid outside challenge.

life cycle analysis: the systematic evaluation of the environmental aspects of a product or service system through all stages of its life cycle.

liveability: term used to explain the struggle by the poor for life itself. Coined by Peter Evans (2002: 10): "In cities the coin of livability has two faces. Livelihood is one ... ecological sustainability ... the other." Evans is optimistic that a discourse of protest around liveability will provide for a new politics of sustainability.

military-industrial complex: refers to the interlocking power relationships between economic, political, and military elites to establish the United States as a "private corporate economy" after World War II, and perpetuate a "permanent war economy." The new military-industrial complex relies heavily on a high-tech arsenal.

modernization theory: posits that impoverishment in countries of the South is the result of internal factors, and all countries are potentially capable of the level of capital accumulation that is now enjoyed by wealthy countries—if those poor countries follow the path of industrial modernization.

morbidity/mortality: morbidity measurements produce information on the incidence of illness, while mortality measurements provide data on death rates.

mundane consumption: coined by Elizabeth Shove (1997) to describe how cultural practices have shifted in ways that demand increasing natural resources, such as bathing frequency, expectations for comfort levels in our homes, and the cultural adoption and use of mass-produced convenience appliances.

NAFTA (North American Free Trade Agreement): a trilateral trade agreement signed in 1993 by Canada, Mexico, and the United States; it promotes trade between nations based on free-market principles, without tariffs, import quotas, or other restrictive regulations. Its proponents argue that it provides economic benefits to all countries, whereas its critics argue that it has exacerbated economic and social dependency relations resulting in exploitation in Canada and Mexico, and a decrease in sovereignty over national policies and resources.

natural capital: the economic value of water, land, air, soil, and ecosystem services that are typically outside the market. Some analysts would like to place value on these elements. Critics argue that by valuing nature as "capital," natural systems are drawn into the money economy and commodified.

negative externalities: when market exchanges have negative spillover effects that have impacts on others and the environment that are not considered in economic theory; those causing the damage are not responsible for it financially. This connection is sometimes referred to as "privatizing the benefits and socializing the costs" (Beder 1993: 44). Negative environmental externalities occur when economic activities alter the proper functioning of ecosystems. Positive externalities are the non-market (unpaid for) environmental services used by firms for economic benefit.

neo-liberalism: an ideology regarding development that became predominant during the late twentieth century, which is premised, first, on the theory that social wellbeing is best addressed through economic development, and second, that economic development can proceed most efficiently if we rely on market forces themselves to allocate resources. Neo-liberalism is pursued through economic policies that favour free trade, state deregulation, and global competition.

new ecological paradigm (NEP): describes an ecological worldview in which humans are part of the web of life and must respect environmental limits. Dunlap and VanLiere (1978) hypothesized it to be emerging among citizens of Western countries in recent decades. These researchers developed an attitudinal scale that is still in use to measure individual ecological/environmental attitudes in surveys.

new social movements (NSM): describes modern social movements that are more likely to focus on quality of life issues rather than on efforts to improve material well-being (Offe 1985; Melucci 1980; Buechler 2000).

NIMBY: acronym for Not-In-My-Backyard movements, describing community responses to environmental risks.

opportunity cost: the value of goods and services that we give up or forgo in order to produce a specific product or service. Critics argue that we forgo certain futures when we choose pulp mills over tourism, for example.

overshoot: a societal condition in which humans have exceeded the Earth's carrying capacity (Catton 1980).

periphery (hinterland, satellite): in **world systems theory**, the periphery is actively underdeveloped by the core through systematic disorganization, exploitation, and the flow of power and resources from the periphery to the core; it is caught in exploitative dependency relations, particularly with respect to the political economy.

persistent organic pollutants (POPs): a class of chemicals that accumulate in the fat cells of the body, where they are stored for a long time.

pesticide cycle: occurs when illegal pesticides from the North are sold to the South and used on crops, which are then exported to Northern countries for consumption.

pluralism: a theory of political structure positing that societies are made up of diverse interests that organize to compete for political favour; within this system no individual set of interests has any structural advantage over another (for example, see Dahl 1961).

political ecology: the notion that physical and social systems are integrated and that we need to study the politicized aspects of the environment, and human uses of nature, in order to understand global environmental issues.

political opportunity structures: refers to how changes in political opportunities and constraints—which can describe times in which coercive forces are weak, or when there may be greater levels of public support for movement goals—can create windows of opportunity within which a movement can have a greater chance of success (Eisinger 1973).

pollutant sink: biospheric trajectories, such as airsheds or watersheds, into which pollutants tend to be emitted with the assumption that the biosphere will absorb them so that they pose no harm to humans.

popular epidemiology: involves citizens and experts documenting environmental health problems in a community (see **epidemiology**).

post-Fordist economy: a complex of economic and organizational changes to work and the economy starting in the mid-1960s, when capital investment shifted geographically to set up new workplaces in developing countries and regions like the U.S. sunbelt. Machinery and computers captured workers' skills and expertise, reducing the need for specialists and tradespeople; firms could hire green or unskilled labour at cheap rates; work was reorganized to accommodate just-in-time production, flexible contracted out workforces instead of unions, and small-batch production to lower inventories. All of this increased profits and reduced turnover times.

post-materialism: a value system that has purportedly emerged in modern, affluent, industrial societies that promote community integrity and personal quality of life. Post-materialism is viewed as a reaction to the dissatisfaction of many with the fast-paced, economic-dominant lifestyles promoted by modern Western societies (Inglehart 1977).

power, first dimension of: describes that level of power that is most easily observed; a number of individuals or organizations actively compete for influence, and some win and some lose (Lukes 1974).

power, second dimension of: when certain groups or individuals feel so powerless that they don't bother to try to pursue their objectives. In this case, we say that those in power have the ability to set the agenda (Lukes 1974).

power, third dimension of: describes the tendency for oppressed groups to approve of the very power structure that is oppressing them. See also **hegemony** (Lukes 1974).

precautionary principle: preventing exposure even before there is a definite causal link to health.

principle of non-discrimination: the idea that goods should trade freely and that no nation can prejudice the trade of any goods or services regardless of their country of origin. This principle is promoted by the WTO (World

Trade Organization) as the basis of all bilateral, multilateral, and international trade agreements. Critics believe that the policy is used to undermine national sovereignty.

privatization: a process where the state sells publicly run services to private interests. It is usually justified by governments and business with the argument that privately run companies manage and use resources more efficiently than their public counterparts, but this argument has been heavily criticized, particularly by scholars who study common pool resource management systems.

psychometric paradigm: based on an approach developed by Kahneman and Tversky (1979), this describes research in which the focus is on the expressed risk preferences of individuals, through analysis of the factors that shape an individual's risk perceptions.

public-private partnerships (P3s): collaborations between public bodies and private companies; government-directed P3 programs are used to attract privately raised capital to fund and manage services and areas that were previously public services, such as health, water treatment, and electrical provision. Critics question their accountability to the public.

quantitative risk assessments: tools used to generate the information employed in risk management, involving calculations to quantify the chance of an undesirable event, usually expressed in terms of mortality.

radical social movements: seek a fundamental transformation of society by working outside existing institutions, which movement participants see as no longer being legitimate.

rationalization: the systematic reorganization of goals and actions in order to respond to new or changing situations. Nation-states that undergo fundamental reform in response to the need to assume responsibility for environmental well-being can be said to have undergone environmental rationalization (Frickel and Davidson 2004).

realism/structuralism: also called essentialism, is a form of social scientific inquiry that focuses on identifying what are presumed to be independent natural processes that are empirically "out there," knowable, and identifiable in universal patterns of change. As in the natural sciences from which it emerged, the greatest benefit of this positivist form of social-scientific inquiry is its ability to provide scientists with predictive power, and the ability to respond to environmental problems.

recreancy: the failure of institutions to abide by the duties or responsibilities expected of them by society (see Freudenburg 1993).

reformative social movements: seek broad change in a social system by working within existing institutions to promote such changes.

regulatory capture: the outcome when corporations use various tactics to ensure that standards are removed or made more lenient.

resource mobilization theory: posits that social movements, particularly the successful ones, are the result of careful planning, and have the ability to acquire sufficient resources to initiate and sustain organized activity (McCarthy and Zald 1977).

risk paradigm: the view that biological and ecological systems can tolerate a certain level of toxic exposures, that environmental hazards are safe until proven otherwise, and that there is a certain amount of "acceptable" risk.

risk society: a term coined by Ulrich Beck to describe the centrality of risk in contemporary societies. This centrality is due both to an increase in the complexity and catastrophic potential of real risks, such that all members of society become victims, and to a shift in individual and societal perceptions of phenomena in terms of a heightened awareness of their risk potential.

rural restructuring: a process of social, cultural, and economic change taking place in rural Canada that is associated with increased employment diversification associated with a decline in the traditional agricultural community resulting from global economic changes.

scales: social, economic, political, and cultural processes can occur at multiple levels (or scales), usually signified at the level of individual, community, region, national, and international.

scientific uncertainty: the inability of scientists to know the health effects of chemicals.

second nature: describes those components of ecosystems that have been altered by human societies.

semi-periphery (see also **core** and **periphery**): in **world systems theory**, the semi-periphery shares aspects of the developed, core countries and of the underdeveloped, periphery countries. Canada is argued to be a semi-peripheral state because it has not only achieved high levels of economic and social development, but has also been involved in dependency relations because of its relations with the United States, **NAFTA**, and its heavy dependency on **staples**.

sense of place: people, through experience with a particular locale, may develop an emotional connection or bond with that locale. A sense of place is socially constructed and may vary depending on the type of experience an individual has with the place.

sexism: a system of discrimination based on **gender bias**.

slapp (strategic lawsuits against public participation): lawsuits by corporations claiming damages from people who have challenged that corporation (for pollution damages, for example).

social constructionism/socially constructed: a school of thought introduced in 1966 by Peter Berger and Thomas Luckman in their book *The Social Construction of Reality.* Social constructionists view reality through the lens of social experience and interaction.

social entropy: the breakdown of social systems due to changes in those structures that serve as foundations for the organization of society, to such an extent that those social systems, or at least certain subgroups of systems, are unable to persist in their current form.

social movements: sustained, organized activity that promotes or resists some dimension of social change, usually targeted at states.

social spatiality: refers to how space is intertwined with social practices and social processes, such that social practices and social processes are impacted by and impact space. This interplay between the social and the spatial is known as social spatiality.

space: a social construct, which is ultimately embedded in the materiality of the world. Our ability to construct space is embedded within our culture (through language and beliefs, for instance). Being a social construct, however, does not imply personal subjectivity. The view of space (and time) as objective relates to the view in society that these concepts are universal and foundational to all other notions in a manner that is pervasive, though not imposed (Harvey 1996).

staples economy: in what became known as "Staples Theory," Canadian economist Harold Innis examined Canada's reliance on the export of natural resource "staples" for economic development. The "staples trap" is the tendency to become economically dependent on more powerful countries when the economy is based on staples or primary resources.

structural adjustment programs (SAPs): an approach based on neo-liberal principles of free trade and free market competition; supporters in the World Bank and IMF argue that it will reduce world poverty. In order to receive an IMF loan, a country must follow a number of policies: devaluation of currencies, privatization, liberalization of markets, removal of public subsidies on food or local goods, cuts in social programs.

structural strain theory: a theory of social movement emergence positing that social movements are most likely to emerge when a given society is experiencing significant problems, such as a poor economy or repeated food shortages. This likelihood grows when that society's authority system is insufficient to stifle unrest (Smelser 1962).

structuration: a concept developed by Anthony Giddens (1993) to stress the interrelationship between societal structures and agency. Individuals are neither hapless pawns in a world defined by larger, immutable structures and institutions, nor are they completely immune to the influences of those institutions.

subpolitics: political activity that occurs outside the traditional political institutions of modernity and is associated with grassroots organizing and direct action.

subtractability: when common pool resources are overused or degraded (by one person, group of persons, or through agricultural and/or industrial use), the benefits of that resource for others is reduced and becomes less available for future uses.

suburbanization: the movement of a population (usually the more affluent members) from the city to the suburbs (areas on the outskirts of cities). Suburbanization is said to occur as a result of a number of push and pull factors. Push factors include the decline of cities, higher city taxes, and higher urban crime. Pull factors include the perception that the suburbs offer more space for raising families, less crime, less taxes, and a greater sense of community.

surplus value: the source of profit in a capitalist economy, generated by paying workers less for their labour than the price that can be received for the commodities they produce.

sustainability/sustainable development: economic activity or growth that balances current interests without reducing or depleting the resources available to future generations. Sustainable development as a term was popularized in *Our Common Future*, the 1987 Report of the World Commission on Environment and Development. It is a highly contested concept. Many in the environmental movement reject the term, fearing its meaning has been co-opted "as being merely to preserve the environment to the extent that it is necessary for the maintenance of the economic system" (Beder 1993). Since its first usage, the differences between corporate visions of sustainability and those of environmental organizations, social movements, and the poor countries of the South have become sharper.

sustainable ecosystem management: some theorists suggest that humans can exploit ecological systems sustainably if they work within natural systems, using only the natural growth and redundancy within the ecosystem. In order to minimize disturbance, it is suggested that corporations mimic the normal ranges of disturbance in ecosystems, so that now clear-cuts are designed to emulate the natural disturbances caused by forest fires, for example.

sweatshop: originally used in the nineteenth century to describe a subcontracting system in which the contractors earned their profit from the margin between the amount they received for a contract and the amount they paid the workers to whom they subcontracted. This margin was said to be "sweated" from the workers because they received minimal wages for excessive hours under unsafe conditions (Source: UNITE Canada website.)

symbolic politics: the use by politicians of political symbols and rituals designed to ensure citizens of democratic societies that their values and concerns are being addressed, while concealing that in actuality politics serves only a narrow set of special interests (Edelman 1964).

takeover method: describes the means by which humans increased carrying capacity prior to industrialization, by diverting a portion of the Earth's carrying capacity away from supporting other kinds of life, in order to support human life (Catton 1980).

thermodynamic imperialism: Hornberg (2001) coined the term to describe the politics and economics of our current energy regime, linking wealth accumulation in developed countries to the trade in social entropy from underdeveloped countries.

time-space compression: the process by which space is reorganized in such a way that it reduces the constraints of time and decreases the notion of space. Technologies, like the automobile, are said to shorten time and decrease distance, thus contributing to time-space compression.

transnational corporations (TNCs/transnationals); multinational corporations (multinationals): corporations whose sales and production are carried out in many different nations. As a result of their multinational reach these corporations are often thought to be beyond the political control of any individual nation-states.

treadmill of production: the process of capitalist accumulation in which the unlimited expansion of markets and production includes a drive to displace workers, to increase the scale of use (withdrawals) of resources, and to increase the amount of additions of pollutants to the ecosystem—all with the goal of increased throughput and economic profitability for shareholders but not for the local communities in which the industries are located.

urban sprawl: the spreading out of urban development (in the form of residential areas and businesses) from the inner city to its outskirts, thereby dispersing the space over which the urban area is located. (See also **suburbanization.**)

urbanization: the demographic shift towards an increased proportion of the population living in urban centres. In Canada this shift has occurred in association with **rural restructuring**, where declining employment opportunities in rural sectors is driving a **youth exodus** into different, more often urban, occupations.

waterscapes: a term to used describe human alterations of natural water flows and systems designed over time for moving water into and out of human settlements and human bodies. Few of the Earth's water resources remain untouched by human activity, therefore our perceptions of water as "natural" or "independent" of human activity is mistaken, according to critical theorists.

world systems theory: derived from the work of Karl Marx and developed by Immanuel Wallerstein, the theory is based on the idea that capitalism must be seen as involving relationships among nations; these relationships are based on inequality and exploitation whereby the periphery is actively underdeveloped because of dependency relations with the core. See **core, periphery, semi-periphery**.

youth exodus: a cultural phenomenon occurring in rural areas, where economic incentives outside of the agricultural sector are attracting the younger generation away from rural regions.

Contributors

Josh Evans is a graduate student in human geography in the Department of Earth and Atmospheric Sciences at the University of Alberta. His research centres on resource development conflicts with a focus on topics such as risk, local politics, and resistance.

Debra J. Davidson is Associate Professor of Environmental Sociology, with a joint appointment between the Department of Rural Economy and the Department of Renewable Resources, at the University of Alberta. Areas of research and teaching include natural resource politics and environmental risk/justice. She has published several papers, including recent articles in the *Canadian Review of Sociology and Anthropology*, *International Sociology*, and *Journal for Risk Research*.

Mike Gismondi, a sociologist, writes on local environmental politics, environmental assessment, public hearings, and globalism. He co-authored an insider's account of environmental reviews in *Winning Back the Words: Confronting Experts in an Environmental Public Hearing* (Garamond 1993). Upcoming work (with Josee Johnson and James Goodman) examines the commons as a counterpoint to economic globalization in *Nature's Revenge: Sustainability in an Age of Corporate Globalism* (Broadview 2005). He is Director, Master of Arts—Integrated Studies at Athabasca University, Canada's Open University, and a two-term municipal councillor in the Town of Athabasca in northern Alberta.

Ella Haley is Assistant Professor in the Centre for Global and Social Analysis at Athabasca University. She researches environmental health issues and is active in helping communities organize around pollution concerns.

Kierstin C. Hatt teaches in the Augustana Faculty of the University of Alberta in the Sociology Department. Her areas of research and teaching are gender, development, environment, and Latin America. Her dissertation was a holistic analysis of the banana industry in Costa Rica. She is also interested interdisciplinarity and alternative education. These are all implemented, in part, through her work with the Canada-Mexico Rural Development Exchange.

Satoshi Ikeda is Associate Professor of Sociology at the University of Alberta. He received a Ph.D. in economics from Michigan and a Ph.D. in sociology from the SUNY-Binghamton. While teaching globalization and social inequality, he has ventured into environmental sociology as a part of his research on globalization. His other areas of interest include world-system studies, political sociology of Japan and East Asia, and methods of historical sociology.

Ineke Lock is a Ph.D. candidate in the Department of Sociology at the University of Alberta. Her interests are in sustainable development, globalization, and corporate social responsibility.

Jeff Masuda is a Ph.D. candidate in human geography at the University of Alberta, Department of Earth and Atmospheric Sciences. His dissertation focuses on a case study investigation of the social impacts of proposed industrial development in a rural community in Alberta. Through such research he is interested in exploring the social construction of risk, place, and community as they occur in the globalized new rural economy.

Stephen Speake is a graduate student in the Department of Sociology at the University of Alberta. His research interests include globalization as it relates to the global food economy and environmental sociology.

Richard Tunstall is a naturopathic doctor who practises in Edmonton. He has also taught health studies at Athabasca University and supervised student clinicians at the Canadian College of Naturopathic Medicine.

Jeji Varghese has recently completed her Ph.D. in rural/resource sociology in the Department of Rural Economy at the University of Alberta. Her dissertation involves a comparative case study of six Canadian local buyouts of a forest product mill/tenure to identify the ex-post social impacts of local ownership as part of an examination of the relationship between local ownership, community sustainability and community learning. She is also interested in the sociology of space.

References

Aberle, D. 1966. *The Peyote Religion among the Navajo*. Chicago: Aldine.

Aboriginal Pipeline Group (APG). 2004. "Maximizing Ownership and Benefits of a Mackenzie Valley Pipeline." Available at <www.aboriginalpipeline.ca> (accessed on November 7, 2004).

Achbar, J., and B. Simpson (Producers). 2003. *The Corporation.* [film]. Vancouver: Big Picture Media Corporation.

Adams, F. 1914. *Conquest of the Tropics*. New York: Doubleday, Page and Company.

Agriculture and Agri-Food Canada, 2004. "Exports—Agri-Food for January to September 2004." Available at <ats-sea.agr.ca/stats/3684_e.pdf> (accessed on January 23, 2005).

_____. 2001. "The Canadian Bottled Water Industry." Available at <www.agr.gc.ca/food/profiles/bottledwater/bottledwater_e.html#Issues> (accessed on June 17, 2004).

Alberta Energy and Utilities Board. 2003. *Public Safety and Sour Gas Annual Progress Report*. Calgary: Alberta Energy and Utilities Board

_____. 1994. *Report and Recommendations to the ERCB on Public Safety and Sour Gas*. Calgary: Energy and Resources Conservation Board.

_____. 1990. "GASCON2: A Model to Estimate Ground-level H2S and SO2 Concentrations and Consequences from Uncontrolled Sour Gas Releases." Prepared by E. Alp et al. *Concord Environmental Corporation*. Calgary: Alberta Energy and Utilities Board.

Ali, H. 2004. Personal communication, October 21.

Ali, S. 1997. "Trust, Risk and the Public: The Case of the Guelph Landfill Site." *Canadian Journal of Sociology* 22, 4.

Allison, L. 1979. "Who Hates Hypermarkets?" *New Society* 48 (April).

Amin, S. 1974. *Accumulation on a World Scale: A Critique of the Theory of Underdevelopment*. New York: Monthly Review Press.

Angelico, I. 1998. *The Cola Conquest*. Produced by A.J. Neidik, DLI Productions: Montreal. Available at <www.dliproductions.ca/orderfrm.html> (accessed on March 1, 2005).

Association of Canadian Manufacturers and Exporters. 2004. "Kyoto Alert." Available at <www.cme-mec.ca/kyoto/documents/KyotoAlert.pdf> (accessed on November 10, 2004).

_____. 2002. "Pain without Gain: Canada and the Kyoto Protocol." Available at <www.cme-mec.ca/kyoto/index.html> (accessed on November 10, 2004).

Baird, S. 1993. "Energy Educators of Ontario Fact Sheet: The automobile and the environment." Available at <www.iclei.org/EFACTS/AUTO.HTM> (accessed on July 17, 2004).

Bakan, J. 2004. *The Corporation: The Pathological Pursuit of Profit and Power*. Toronto: Viking Canada (Penguin Group).

Baran, P. 1957. *The Political Economic of Growth*. New York: Monthly Review Press.

Baran, P., and P. Sweezy. 1966. *Monopoly Capital: An Essay on the American Economic and Social Order*. New York: Modern Reader Paperbacks.

Barkin, D. (ed.). 2001. *Innovaciones Mexicanas en el Manaejo Del Agua*. México City: Centro de Ecologia y Desarollo.

Barlett, D., and J. Steele. 2000. "Big Money and Politics: Who Gets Hurt?" *Time* (Canadian Edition), February 7.

Barlow, M., and T. Clarke. 2002. *Blue Gold: The Battle against Corporate Theft of the World's Water*. Toronto: Stoddart.

Barndt, D. 2002. *Tangled Routes: Women, Work, and Globalization on the Tomato Trail*. Toronto: Garamond Press.

Baudrillard, J. 1994. *Simulacra and Simulation*. (S. Glaser, Trans.). Ann Arbor: University of Michigan Press.

Bauman, Z. 1998. *Work, Consumerism and the New Poor*. Philadelphia: Open University Press.

Baumgarten, S. 2002. "Alberta eyes legal challenge to Canada's Kyoto approval." *Chemical Market Reporter* 262, 8 (September 9).

Baxter, J. 1998. "Scientists 'Pressured' to Approve Cattle Drug: Health Canada Researchers Accuse Firm of Bribery in Bid to OK 'Questionable' Product." *Ottawa Citizen,* October 23.

Beanery Franchisees Association. 2005. "Spice Kit Workshop." Available at <www.alternatives.com/bfa/index.php?module=pagemaster&PAGE_user_op=view_page&PAGE_id=3&MMN_position=3:3> (accessed January 24, 2005).

Beck, U. 1999. *World Risk Society*. Cambridge: Polity Press.

_____. 1995. *Ecological Politics in an Age of Risk*. Cambridge: Polity Press.

_____. 1992. *Risk Society: Towards a New Modernity*. London: Sage.

Beckenbach, F. 1989. "Social Costs in Modern Capitalism." *Capitalism, Nature, Socialism* 3, 1.

Beder, S. 2000. *Selling the Work Ethic: From Puritan Pulpit to Corporate PR*. London: Zed Books.

_____. 1993. *The Nature of Sustainable Development*. Newham, Australia: Scribe Publications.

_____. 1989. *Toxic Fish and Sewer Surfing*. Sydney: Allan and Unwin.

Belitt, B. (ed.). 1961. *Selected Poems of Pablo Neruda*. New York: Grove Press.

Bello, W. 2003 "The Future in the Balance." Acceptance speech for Right Livelihood Award. Swedish Parliament, Stockholm (December 8). Available at <www.rightlivelihood.se/speeches/bello.htm> (accessed on August 23, 2004).

Bendix, R. 1967. "Tradition and Modernity Reconsidered." *Comparative Studies in Society and History* 9, 3 (April).

Benton, T. 1994. "Biology and Social Theory in the Environmental Debate." In M. Redclift and T. Benton (eds.), *Social Theory and the Global Environment*. London: Routledge.

Berger, G., A. Flynn, F. Hines, and R. Johns. 2001. "Ecological Modernization as a Basis for Environmental Policy: Current Environmental Discourse and Policy and the Implications on Environmental Supply Chain Management." *Innovation* 14, 1.

Berger, T. 1983. "Resources, Development, and Human Values." *Impact Assessment Bulletin* 2, 2.

_____. 1978. *Northern Frontier, Northern Homeland: The Report of the Mackenzie Valley Pipeline Inquiry* (Volume II). Ottawa: Publishing Centre, Supply and Services Canada.

_____. 1977. *Northern Frontier, Northern Homeland: The Report of the Mackenzie Valley Pipeline Inquiry*. (Volume I). Ottawa: Publishing Centre, Supply and Services Canada.

Bergman, B. 1999. "The Hidden Life of Computers." *Sierra Magazine* (July-August). Available at <www.sierraclub.org/sierra/199907/computers.asp> (accessed on November 11, 2004).

Bertell, R. 1999. Speaking at a meeting, "An Unjust and Illegal War: Leading Opponents of the War against Yugoslavia Speak out," Toronto, May 6. The Canadian Centres for Teaching Peace. Available at <www.peace.ca/depleteduranium.htm> (accessed August 5, 2004).

Berton, J. 2001. "Vocal Sunnyvale Residents Say New Crematorium Will be Responsible for the Stink in Their City." *Metro, Silicon Valley's Weekly Newspaper* August 30–September 5.

Best, J. 1993. "But Seriously Folks: The Limitations of the Strict Constructionist Interpretation of Social Problems." In J. Holstein and G. Miller (eds.), *Reconsidering Social Contructionism: Debates in Social Problems Theory*. New York: Aldine de Gruyter.

_____. 1989. "Extending the Constructionist Perspective: A Conclusion—and an Introduction." In J. Best (ed.), *Images of Issues: Typifying Contemporary Social Problems*. New York: Aldine de Gruyter.

Biro, A. 2002. "Wet Dreams: Ideology and the Debates over Canadian Water Exports." *Capitalism, Nature, Socialism* 13, 4.

Blair, A. 1979. "Leukemia among Nebraska Farmers: A Death Certificate Study." *American Journal of Epidemiology* 110, 3.

Bollman, R., and R. Beshiri. 2000. *Rural and Small Town Canada: A Demographic Overview.* Paper presented at the Conference on the New Rural Economy, Alfred, ON.

Bomke, A., and W. Temple. 2001. "Bioregional Approach to Agricultural and Community Development." Available at <www.naturalists.bc.ca/fbcn_bn/bn0105-3.htm> (accessed on May 31, 2004).

Bond, P. 2004. "Water Commodification and Decommodification Narratives: Pricing Policy and Policy Debates from Johannesburg to Kyoto to Cancun and Back." *Capitalism, Nature, Socialism* 15, 1.

Borgstrom, G. 1965. *The Hungry Planet: The Modern World at the Edge of Famine*. New York: Macmillan.

Boseley, S. 2003. "Sugar Industry Threatens to Scupper U.S. Funding of WHO." *Guardian Weekly* April 24.

Bourgois, P. 1994. *Banano, Etnia y Lucha Social en Centro América*. San José, Costa Rica: Editorial Departamento Ecuménico de Investigaciones (DEI).

_____. 1989. *Ethnicity at Work: Divided Labor on a Central American Banana Plantation*. Baltimore: Johns Hopkins University Press.

Boyens, I. 2004. "Do Burgers Fry Your Brain?" *Globe and Mail*, May 8.

Brecher, J., T. Costello, and B. Smith. 2002. *Globalization from Below: The Power of Solidarity*. Cambridge: South End Press.

Brechin, S., and W. Kempton. 1994. "Global Environmentalism: A Challenge to the Postmaterialism Thesis?" *Social Science Quarterly* 75, 2.

British Broadcasting Corporation (BBC). 2004. "Vietnamese File Agent Orange Suit." Available at <www.news.bbc.co.uk/2/hi/health/3459277.stm> (accessed on July 4, 2004).

_____. 1999. "Radiation Link with Stillbirths." Available at <www.news.bbc.co.uk/1/hi/health/481875.stm23> (accessed on July 4, 2004).

British Columbia Ministry of Sustainable Resources. 2003. "Clayoquot Sound Watershed Plans." Available at <www.gov.bc.ca/rmd/specialprojects/

clayoquot/watershed.htm> (accessed on November 8, 2004).

Brockerhoff, M. 1996. *Population Today* 24 (3) (Monthly newsletter of the Population Reference Bureau).

Brooymans, H. 2004. "New Standards Studied for Bottled Water: Guidelines Tougher on Chemicals, Bacteria." *Edmonton Journal* April 10.

_____. 2003. "Landowners Not Convinced that Methane Extraction Process Safe." *Edmonton Journal* February 27.

Brown, Phil. 2002. "Preface." In P. Brown (ed.), *Health and the Environment, Volume 584 of the Annals of the American Academy of Political and Social Science*. Thousand Oaks, CA: Sage.

_____. 2000. "Environment and Health." In C. Bird, P. Conrad, and A. Fremont (eds.), *Handbook of Medical Sociology*. Fifth Edition. Upper Saddle River, NJ: Prentice-Hall.

_____. 1993. "Popular Epidemiology Challenges the System—Citizen Action in Stopping Toxic Waste Pollution of Water Supply." *Environment* (October). Available at <www.findarticles.com/p/articles/mi_m1076/is_n8_v35/ai_14546653> (accessed November 14 2004).

Brown, P., S. Kroll-Smith, and V. Gunter. 2000. "Knowledge, Citizens, and Organizations: An Overview of Environments, Diseases and Social Conflict." In S. Kroll-Smith, P. Brown, and V. Gunter (eds.), *Illness and the Environment: A Reader in Contested Medicine*. New York: New York University Press.

Brown, P., and E. Mikkelsen. 1997. *No Safe Place: Toxic Waste, Leukemia and Community Action*. Berkeley: University of California Press.

Brown, P., S. Zavestoski, S. McCormick, B. Mayer, R. Morello-Frosch and R. Altman. 2004. "Embodied health movements: New approaches to social movements in health." *Sociology of Health and Illness* 26, 1 (January).

Brown, P., et al. 2003. "Chemicals and Casualties—The Search for Causes of Gulf War Illnesses." In Monica J. Casper (ed.), *Synthetic Planet: Chemical Politics and the Hazards of Modern Life*. New York: Routledge.

Brownell, K., and K. Horgan. 2004. *Food Fight: The Inside Story of the Food Industry, America's Food Crisis, and What We Can Do about It*. New York: McGraw Hill.

Brownsey, Keith. 2003. "The Best of Times? Petroleum Politics in Canada." Paper presented at the Canadian Political Science Association Meetings, Halifax, NS.

Brubaker, E. 2002. *Liquid Assets: Privatizing and Regulating Canada's Water Utilities*. Toronto: University of Toronto.

Bryant, B., and P. Mohai. 1997. *Race and the Incidence of Environmental Hazards: A Time for Discourse*. Boulder, CO: Westview Press.

Bryson, C. 2004. *The Fluoride Deception*. New York: Seven Stories Press.

Buchholz, R., and S. Rosenthal. 1998. "Toward an Ethics of Consumption: Rethinking the Nature of Growth." In L. Westra and P. Werhane (eds.), *The Business of Consumption: Environmental Ethics and the Global Economy*. New York: Rowman and Littlefield.

Buechler, S. 2000. *Social Movements in Advanced Capitalism: The Political Economy and Cultural Construction of Social Activism*. New York: Oxford University Press.

Bueckert, Dennis. 2004. "Health Canada Ignored Its Own Scientists on Mad Cow, Report Says." Available at <www.healthcoalition.ca/bse-whistleblowers.pdf> (accessed July 4, 2004).

Bullard, R. 2000. *Dumping in Dixie: Race, Class and Environmental Quality*. Boulder, CO: Westview Press.

_____. 1994. "Environmental Justice for All." In R. Bullard (ed.), *Unequal Protection*. San Francisco: Sierra Club Books.

_____. 1993. *Confronting Environmental Racism: Voices from the Grassroots*. Boston: South End Press.

Bulmer-Thomas, V. 1987. *The Political Economy of Central America Since 1920*. New York: Cambridge University Press.

Bunker, S. 1985. *Underdeveloping the Amazon: Extraction, Unequal Exchange, and the Failure of the Modern State*. Urbana: University of Illinois Press.

Burdge, R. 2004. *A Community Guide to Social Impact Assessment*. Third Edition. Middleton, WI: Social Ecology Press.

Burmingham, K., and G. Cooper. 1999. "Being Constructive: Social Constructionism and the Environment." *Sociology* 33, 2.

Buttel, F., and P. Taylor. 1994. "Environmental Sociology and Global Environmental Change: A Critical Assessment." In M. Redclift and T. Benton (eds.), *Social Theory and the Global Environment*. London: Routledge.

Caldicott, H. 2002. *The New Nuclear Danger—George W. Bush's Military-Industrial Complex*. New York: The New Press.

_____. 1992. *If You Love This Planet: A Plan to Heal the Earth*. New York: W.W. Norton.

Campbell, C. 2004. *The Coming Oil Crisis*. Brentwood, U.K.: Multi Science Publishing.

Canadian Arctic Resources Committee (CARC). 2001. "Special Issue." *Northern Perspectives* 27, 1.

Canadian Broadcasting Corporation (CBC). 2004. "Sydney Tar Ponds Get $400-Million Cleanup." Available at <www.cbc.ca/stories/2004/05/12/canada/tarponds_20041012> (accessed on June 17, 2004).

Canadian Federation of Humane Societies. 1999. "rBST Illegal But Used." Available at <www.cfhs.ca/AWIF/AWIF1999-1/AWIF99-1p11.htm> (accessed on November 8, 2004).

Canadian International Development Agency (CIDA). 1991. *Policy for Environment and Development*. Ottawa: Canadian International Development Agency Publication.

_____. 1987. *Sharing Our Future*. Ottawa: Canadian International Development Agency Publication.

Canadian Tourism Commission. 2004 (January 28). Available at <www.travelcanada.ca/travelcanada/app/en/ca/experiences.do?catId=12>.

Cardoso, F., and E. Faletto. 1979. *Dependency and Development in Latin America*. Berkeley: University of California Press.

_____. 1969. *Dependencia y Desarrollo en América Latina: Ensayo de Interpretación Sociológica*. México City: Siglo XXI Editores, S.A.

Catton, W. 1980. *Overshoot: The Ecological Basis of Revolutionary Change*. Urbana, IL: University of Illinois Press.

Catton, W., and R. Dunlap. 1980. "A New Ecological Paradigm for a Post-exuberant Sociology." *The American Behavioural Scientist* 24, 1.

Center for Media and Democracy. 2004. *Military-Industrial Complex*. Available at <www.disinfopedia.org/wiki.phtml?title=Military-industrial_complex> (accessed July 4, 2004).

Cerdas Mora, J. 1976. "La Huelga Bananera de 1934: Anécdotas y Enseñazas de uno de sus Principales Dirigentes." *ABRA* 1980, 2.

Chacón R., L. Fernando, S. Hernández, and A. Luis. 1994. "Estudio de Manejo de Desechos del Banano y Calidad de Vida." Unpublished thesis: Universidad de Costa Rica, Escuela de Ingeniería Industrial.

Chase-Dunn, C. 1989. *Global Formation*. Cambridge, MA: Blackwell.

Chavez, Cesar. 1969. "Viva Cesar E. Chavez!" *Engage* 2, 5 (November 11).

Chew, S. 1995. "Environmental Transformations: Accumulation, Ecological Crisis, and Social Movements." In D. Smith and J. Borocz (eds.), *A New World Order? Global Transformations in the Late Twentieth Century*. Westport, CT: Praeger Publishers.

Chiquita Brands. 2004. "Discover: Our Story: Chiquita History." Available at <www.Chiquita.com> (accessed on June 7, 2004).

Choudry, A. 2003. "Miami Vice: The FTAA returns to Florida. Nov. 11, 2003." Available at <www.stopftaa.org/article.php?id=155> (accessed on August 25, 2004).

Christensen, B. 1995. *Too Good To Be True: Alcan's Kemano Completion Project*. Vancouver: Talonbooks.

Christoff, C. 1996. "Ecological Modernisation, Ecological Modernities." *Environmental Politics* 5, 3.

Clarke, L. 1993. "The Disqualification Heuristic: When do Organizations Misperceive Risk?" *Research in Social Problems and Public Policy* 5.

Clarke, R. 1993. *Water: The International Crisis*. Cambridge, MA: MIT Press.

Clarke, T., and B. Inouye. 2002. "Galloping Gene Giants: How Big Corporations are Re-organizing their Push for a Biotech Future and What Can be Done to Challenge this Agenda." *Polaris Institute Report*. Available at <www.polarisinstitute.org/polaris_project/bio_justice/corp_biotech/ggg_report.pdf> (accessed on May 25, 2004).

Clayoquot Sound Central Region Board. 2004/02/05. "Clayoquot Sound Watershed Plans." Available at <www.island.net/~crb/> (accessed on November 16, 2004).

Clement, W., and G. Williams. 1997. "Resources and Manufacturing in Canada's Political Economy." In W. Clement (ed.), *Understanding Canada: Building on the New Canadian Political Economy*. Montreal and Kingston: McGill-Queen's University Press.

Clow, M. 1991a. "Economy and Ecology: Why Sustainable Development Can't Sustain Our Economy." Discussion paper for International Development Studies, Saint Mary's University, Halifax, NS.

_____. 1991b. "Greening Political Economy: Linking an Analysis of the Economy and the Environment." Draft for presentation at Atlantic Canada Studies Ecology Seminar at Saint Mary's University, Halifax, NS.

_____. 1989. "The Political, Economic, and Bio-physical Options to Sustainable Development." *Canadian Journal of Public Administration* (November).

Coalition to Oppose the Arms Trade (COAT). 2004. "Stop Canada Pension Plan Investments in War!" Available at <www.coat.openconcept.ca/> (accessed on July 3, 2004).

Cobb, John B. 1992. *Sustainability: Economics, Ecology, and Justice*. Maryknoll, NY : Orbis.

Cole, L., and S. Foster. 2001. *From the Ground Up: Environmental Racism and the Rise of the Environmental Justice Movement*. New York and London: New York University Press.

CONSAD Research Corporation. 1998. "The Kyoto Protocol: A Flawed Treaty Puts America at Risk." Available at <www.consad.com/reports/kyoto.html> (accessed on February 26, 2004).

CORBANA (Corporación Bananera Nacional). 1990–1997. *Costa Rica: Informe Anual de Estadísticas de Exportación de Banano*. San José, Costa Rica.

_____. 1992. *La Actividad Bananera en Costa Rica*. San José, Costa Rica.

Cortese, A. 2004. "Teflon Issue May Stick to DuPont." *Hamilton Spectator* August 9.

Costanza, R., J. Cumberland, H. Daly, R. Goodland, and R. Norgaard. 1997. *An Introduction to Ecological Economics*. Boca Raton, FL: St. Lucie Press.

Cottrell, F. 1951. *Energy and Society: The Relation between Energy, Social Changes, and Economic Development*. New York: McGraw Hill.

Couch, S., and J. Kroll-Smith. 1985. "The Chronic Technical Disaster: Toward a Social Scientific Perspective." *Social Science Quarterly* 66, 3.

Council of Canadians. 2004a. "Canadians demand independent investigation into Health Canada firings." July 15. Available at <www.canadians.org> (accessed January 23, 2005).

_____. 2004b. "Ask Questions and Press Candidates to Make Real Promises." Press Release, May 13. Available at <www.Canadians.org.>

_____. 2003. "Planting Seeds of Doubt: GE Wheat Trial Set at Public Meeting." February 26. Available at <www.canadians.org/display_document.htm?COC_token=:COC_token&id=556&isdoc=1&catid=304>

Covello, V., and J. Mumpower. 1985. "RISK Analysis and Risk Management: An Historical Perspective." *Risk Analysis* 5, 2.

Cox, C. 1998. "Glyphosate Factsheet." *Journal of Pesticide Reform* 108, 3 (Fall). Available at <www.mindfully.org/Pesticide/Roundup-Glyphosate-Factsheet-Cox.htm> (accessed on June 22, 2004).

Crawford, J. 2002. *Carfree Cities*. Utrecht, The Netherlands: International Books.

Cresswell, T. 1996. *In Place/Out of Place: Geography, Ideology, and Transgression*. Minneapolis: University of Minnesota Press.

Cristol, S., and P. Sealy. 2004. "Is Your Brand a Nuisance?" Available at <www.brandchannel.com/papers_review.asp?sp_id=31.html> (accessed on April 13, 2004).

Crosby, A. 1986. *Ecological Imperialism: The Biological Expansion of Europe, 900–1900*. Cambridge: Cambridge University Press.

CUPE. 2002. "New Brunswick's P3 Graveyard." Available at <www.cupe.ca/www/ARP2002Moncton/4446> (accessed on January 21, 2005).

Czerny, M., and J. Swift. 1988. *Getting Started on Social Analysis in Canada*. Second Edition. Toronto: Between the Lines.

Dahl, R. 1961. *Who Governs?* New Haven, CT: Yale University Press.

Dalby, S. 2002. *Environmental Security*. Minneapolis: University of Minnesota.

Dalmeny, K. 2003. "Sugar and Spin." *The Ecologist* 33, 9.

Daly, H. 1993. "Introduction to Essays toward a Steady–State Economy." In H. Daly and K. Townsend (eds.), *Valuing the Earth: Economics, Ecology, Ethics*. Cambridge MA: MIT Press.

Daly, H., and J. Cobb. 1989. *For the Common Good: Redirecting the Economy Toward Community, the Environment, and a Sustainable Future*. Boston: Beacon Press.

Davidson, D., and N. MacKendrick. 2004. "All Dressed Up with Nowhere to Go: The Discourse of Ecological Modernization in Alberta, Canada." *Canadian Review of Sociology and Anthropology* 41, 1.

Davies, J. 1963. *Human Nature in Politics: The Dynamics of Political Behavior*. New York: John Wiley.

Davis, M. 2004. "Planet of Slums." *New Left Review* 26 (March-April). Available at <www.newleftreview.net/NLR26001.shtml> (accessed on October 29, 2004).

_____. 1994. "House of Cards: Las Vegas: Too Many People in the Wrong Place, Celebrating Waste as a Way of Life." Available at <www.rut.com/mdavis/housecards.html> (accessed on June 22, 2004).

de la Court, T. 1990. *Beyond Brundtland: Green Development in the 1990s*. London: Zed Books.

de Villiers, M. 2000. *Water: The Fate of Our Most Precious Resource*. Boston: Houghton Mifflin Company.

Deffeys, K. 2001. *Hubbert's Peak: The Impending World Oil Shortage*. Princeton: Princeton University Press.

DeJuan, J., and J. Seater. 2003. "The Sensitivity of Consumption to Income Innovations: Evidence from Canadian Provinces." Available at <www4.ncsu.edu/~jjseater/PDF/WorkingPapers/CanadianCrossSection.pdf> (accessed on March 5, 2004).

Della Porta, D., and M. Diani. 1999. *Social Movements: An Introduction*. Malden, MA: Blackwell.

Dembo, D. 1989. "Bhopal: Settlement or Sellout?" *Global Pesticide Monitor*. Available at <www.panna.org/resources/pestis/PESTIS.burst.135.html> (accessed on July 4, 2004).

Diamond, J., and E. Diamond. 2002. *The World of Fashion*. Third Edition. New York: Fairchild Publications.

Dickens, Charles. 1997 (1881). *Bleak House*. New York: Penguin Books.

Dickens, P. 1996. *Reconstructing Nature: Alienation, Emancipation and the Division of Labour*. London: Routledge.

Dicum, G., and N. Luttinger. 1999. *The Coffee Book: Anatomy of an Industry from Crop to the Last Drop*. New York: New Press.

Dietz, T., and L. Kalof. 1992. "Environmentalism among Nation-states." *Social Indicators Research* 26, 4 (June).

Dobbin, M. 1998. *The Myth of the Good Corporate Citizen: Democracy under the Rule of Big Business*. Toronto: Stoddart.

Dobson, A. 1991. *The Green Reader: Essays toward a Sustainable Society*. San Francisco: Mercury House.

Douglas, M. 1992. *Risk and Blame: Essays in Cultural Theory*. London: Routledge.

_____. 1986. *Risk Acceptability According to the Social Sciences*. London: Sage.

Douglas, M., and A. Wildavsky. 1982. *Risk and Culture*. Berkeley: University of California Press.

Doyle, A. 2004a. "'Dirty Dozen' Toxins are Banned by U.N. Pact." *The Guardian*, May 17. Available at <www.guardian.co.uk/waste/story/0,12188,1218182,00.html> (accessed on July 6, 2004).

_____. 2004b. Reuters News Service. "U.N. Chemical Blacklist from May 17 Said Too Short." Available at <www.planetark.com/dailynewsstory.cfm?newsid=25124&newsdate=17=May-May-2004> (Nov. 17)

Drache, D. (ed.). 1995. *Staples, Markets and Cultural Change: Selected Essays*. Centenary Edition. Montreal: McGill-Queens University Press.

Duffy, William. 2003. "Sweet Death." *Ecologist* 22 (9): 44–37.

Duncan, C. 1996. *The Centrality of Agriculture: Between Humankind and the Rest of*

Nature. Montreal: McGill-Queens Press.
Dunk, T. (ed.). 1991. *Social Relations in Resource Hinterlands*. Thunder Bay, ON: Centre for Northern Studies, Lakehead University.
Dunlap, R. 1998. "Lay Perceptions of Global Risk: Public Views of Global Warming in Cross-national Context." *International Sociology* 13, 4.
Dunlap, R., and W. Catton, Jr. 1994. "Struggling with Human Exemptionalism: The Rise, Decline and Revitalization of Environmental Sociology." *American Sociologist* 25 (Spring).
Dunlap, R., and K. Van Liere. 1978. "The 'New Environmental Paradigm': A Proposed Measuring Instrument and Preliminary Results." *Journal of Environmental Education* 9.
Dunn, K., P. McGuirk, and H. Winchester. 1995. "Place Making: The Social Construction of Newcastle." *Australian Geographical Studies* 33, 2.
Ecologist. 2004. "Interview: Carlo Petrini." 34, 3 (April).
Edelman, M. 1964. *The Symbolic Uses of Politics*. Urbana: University of Illinois Press.
Edelman, M., and J. Kenen (eds.). 1989. *The Costa Rica Reader*. New York: Grove Weidenfeld.
Edelstein, M. 1988. *Contaminated Communities: The Social and Psychological Impacts of Residential Toxic Exposure*. Boulder, CO: Westview Press.
Edelstein, M., and A. Wandersman. 1987. "Community Dynamics in Coping with Toxic Exposure." In I. Altman and A. Wandersman (eds.), *Neighborhood and Community Environments*. New York: Plenum Press.
Edmonton Journal. 2004. "Delay Approvals for Coalbed Wells." Editorial, April 12.
Eisenstadt, S. 1966. *Modernization: Protest and Change*. Englewood Cliffs, NJ: Prentice-Hall.
Eisinger, P. 1973. "The Conditions of Protest Behavior in American Cities." *American Political Science Review* 67.
EIU (The Economist Intelligence Unit). 1999. *Country Reports: Costa Rica*. New York: *The Economist*.
Elliot, S., S. Taylor, S. Walter, D. Stieb, J. Frank, and J. Eyles. 1999. "Modeling Psychosocial Effects of Exposure to Solid Waste Facilities." *Social Science and Medicine* 37, 6.
Elliott, Lorraine. 1998. *The Global Politics of the Environment*. Washington Square, NY: New York University Press.
Ember, L. 1997. "Ecotaxes Reduce Pollution, OECD Report Finds. (Organization for Economic Co-operation and Development Findings on the Implications of Ecotaxes on Pollution Control)." *Chemical and Engineering News* 75, 22 (June).
Enloe, C. 1990. *Making Feminist Sense of International Politics: Bananas, Beaches and Bases*. Berkeley and Los Angeles: University of California Press.
Environment Canada. 2004. "Freshwater Website." Available at <www.ec.gc.ca/water/en/manage/use/e_agri.htm> (accessed April 14, 2004).
_____. 1987. "Fresh Water Policy." Available at <www.ec.gc.ca/water/en/info/pubs/fedpol/e_fedpol.htm> (accessed on June 15, 2004).
Environment News Service. 2004. "Indian Marchers Protest Coca-Cola Pollution, Water Use." November 15.
Epp, Roger, and Dave Whitson. 2001. "Introduction: Writing Off Rural Communities?" In Roger Epp and Dave Whitson (eds.), *Writing Off the Rural West: Globalization, Governments and the Transformation of Rural Communities*. Ed-

monton: Parkland Institute and the University of Alberta Press.

Epstein, S. 1998. *The Politics of Cancer Revisited*. Fremont Center, NY: East Ridge Press.

Esteva, G. 1992. "Development." In W. Sachs (ed.), *The Development Dictionary: A Guide to Knowledge as Power*. London: Zed Books.

Europa Environment. 2004/07/27. "The IPCC Directive." Available at <http://europa.eu.int/comm/environment/ippc/index.htm> (accessed on November 17, 2004).

Evans, P. 2002. *Liveable Cities? Urban Struggles for Liveability and Sustainability*. Berkeley: University of California Press.

_____. 2000. "Fighting Marginalization with Transnational Networks: Counter-Hegemonic Globalization." *Contemporary Sociology* 29, 1.

Falk, P. 1993. *Global Visions: Beyond the New World Order*. Boston: South End Press.

Fallas, C. 1995. *Mamita Yunai*. San José, Costa Rica: Editorial Costa Rica.

_____. 1954. "Reseña de la intervención y penetración Yanquí en Centro America," *ABRA* 1980, 5–6.

Fawcett, B. 2003. *Virtual Clearcut: Or, The Ways Things are in My Hometown*. Toronto: Thomas Allan Publishers.

Fawthrop, T. 2004. "Vietnam's War against Agent Orange." *BBC News*. Available at <www.news.bbc.co.uk/2/hi/health/3798581.stm> (accessed July 4, 2004).

Fearnside, P. 1994. "The Canadian Feasibility Study of the Three Gorges Dam Proposed for China's Yangzi River: A Grave Embarrassment to the Impact Assessment Profession." *Impact Assessment* 12.

Featherstone, M. 1991. *Consumer Culture and Postmodernism*. London: Sage.

Fischoff, B., S. Lichenstein, P. Slovic, S. Derby, and R. Keeney. 1981. *Acceptable Risk*. Cambridge: Cambridge University Press.

Fischoff, B., P. Slovic, S. Lichenstein, S. Read, and B. Combs. 1978. "How Safe is Safe Enough? A Psychometric Study of Attitudes towards Technological Risks and Benefits." *Policy Sciences* 9.

Fisher, D., and W. Freudenburg. 2001. "Ecological Modernization and Its Critics: Assessing the Past and Looking Toward the Future." *Society and Natural Resources* 14.

Fortin, M., and C. Gagnon. 1999. "An Assessment of Social Impacts of National Parks on Communities in Quebec, Canada." *Environmental Conservation* 26, 3.

Foster, J. Bellamy. 2002. *Ecology against Capitalism*. New York: Monthly Review Press.

_____. 1994. *The Vulnerable Planet: A Short Economic History of the Environment*. New York: Monthly Review Press.

_____. 1993 "Lessons from the Ancient Forest Struggle of the Pacific Northwest." Available at <www.iww.org/unions/iu120/local-1/EF/JBFoster5.shtml#top> (accessed on October 29, 2004).

_____. 1978. *Working for Wildlife: The Beginning of Preservation in Canada*. Toronto: University of Toronto Press.

Foster, P. 1979. *The Blue-Eyed Sheiks: The Canadian Oil Establishment*. Don Mills, ON: Collins Publishers.

Fowler, H.W., and F.G. Fowler (eds.). 1964. *The Concise Oxford Dictionary of Current English*. Fifth Edition. Oxford: Oxford University Press.

France, A. 2004. "Coke's Bottled Water Recall 'Disastrous Setback': Cancer-causing Chemical Discovered." *National Post*, March 20.

Frank, A. 1971. *Lumpenburguesía: Lumpendesarollo*. México City: Ediciones Era, S.A.

_____. 1969. *Capitalism and Underdevelopment in Latin America*. New York: Monthly Review Press.

Frank, D. 1999. "The Social Bases of Environmental Treaty Ratification, 1900–1990." *Sociological Inquiry* 69, 4.

Frank, D., A. Hironaka, and E. Schofer. 2000. "The Nation-state and the Natural Environment over the Twentieth Century." *American Sociological Review* 65 (February).

Franklin, U. 1999. *The Real World of Technology*. Revised Edition. Toronto: House of Anansi Press.

Freeman, J. 1973. "The Origins of the Women's Liberation Movement." *American Journal of Sociology* 78, 4.

Freudenburg, W. 1997. "Contamination, Corrosion and the Social Order: An Overview." *Current Sociology* 45.

_____. 1996. "Risky Thinking: Irrational Fears about Risk and Society." *Annals of the American Academy of Political and Social Science* 545 (May).

_____. 1993. "Risk and Recreancy: Weber, the Division of Labor, and the Rationality of Risk Perceptions." *Social Forces* 71, 4.

_____. 1992. "Heuristics, Biases, and the Not-So-General Publics: Expertise and Error in the Assessment of Risks." In S. Krimsky and D. Golding (eds.), *Social Theories of Risk*. Westport, CT: Praeger.

_____. 1988. "Perceived Risk, Real Risk: Social Science and the Art of Probabilistic Risk Assessment." *Science* 242.

Freudenburg, W., and S. Pastor. 1992. "Public Responses to Technological Risks: Toward a Sociological Perspective." *Sociological Quarterly* 33, 3.

Freund, P., and G. Martin. 1996. "The Commodity That Is Eating the World: The Automobile, the Environment, and Capitalism." *Capitalism, Nature, Socialism* 7, 4.

_____. 1993. *The Ecology of the Automobile*. Montreal: Black Rose Books.

Frickel, S., and D. Davidson. 2004. "Building Environmental States: Legitimacy and Rationalization in Sustainability Governance." *International Sociology* 19, 1.

Friends of Clayoquot Sound. 2003. "Tofino Takes A Stand Against Working Forest." Available at <www.focs.ca/1newsreleases/031024.htm> (accessed on November 8, 2004).

Fröbel, F., J. Heinrichs, and O. Kreye. 1980. *The New International Division of Labour: Structural Unemployment in Industrialized Countries and Industrialization in Developing Countries*. New York: Cambridge University Press.

Furtado, C. 1971. *La Economía Latinoamericana: Formación Histórica y Problemas Contemporáneos*. México City: Siglo Veintiuno Editores.

_____. 1964. *Development and Underdevelopment*. Berkeley: University of California Press.

Gale, F. 2002. "Caveat Certificatum: The Case of Forest Certification." In T. Princen, M. Maniates and K. Conca (eds.), *Confronting Consumption*. Cambridge, MA: MIT Press.

Gallagher, M., and C. McWhirter. 1998. "Chiquita Secrets Revealed." *Cincinnati Enquirer*, May 3.

Gallon Environment Newsletter. 2004. 9, 12, June 24.

Gamble, D. 1978. "The Berger Inquiry: An Impact Assessment Process." *Science*

199, 3.

Garcia, Deborah Koons. 2003. *The Future of Food*. [Film]. Mill Valley, CA: Lily Films, C. Butler (producer). Available at <www.thefutureoffood.com/index.htm> (accessed on November 10, 2004).

García D., E. Guillermo, and V. Chacón and M. Isabel. 1995. *Panorama Ecológico: Problemática y Perspectivas en Costa Rica*. San José, Costa Rica: ABC Ediciones.

García Márquez, G. 1970. *One Hundred Years of Solitude*. (G. Rabassa, trans.). New York: Harper and Row.

Gardner, G., and P. Sampat. 1998. "Mind over Matter: Recasting the Role of Materials in Our Lives." Washington, DC: Worldwatch, Paper 144.

Geller, Leah. 2004. "Pesticide Use Spawns Market for Organic Cotton." *Edmonton Journal* March 2: E1.

Gephart, R. 1997. "Hazardous Measures: An Interpretive Textual Analysis of Quantitative Sense-making during Crisis." *Journal of Organizational Management* 18.

_____. 1993. "The Textual Approach: Risk and Blame in Disaster Sense-making." *Academy of Management Journal* 36, 6.

Gibson, G., E. Higgs, and E. Hrudey. 1998. "Sour Gas, Bitter Relations: Poor Communication between Unocal and the Lubicon Cree about Sour Gas Risks Fostered Distrust rather than Communication." *Alternatives Journal* 24, 2.

Giddens, A. 1993. *New Rules of Sociological Method*. Cambridge: Polity Press.

_____. 1991. *Modernity and Self-Identity: Self and Society in the Late Modern Age*. Cambridge: Polity Press.

_____. 1990. *The Consequences of Modernity*. Cambridge: Polity Press.

Gieryn, T. 2000. "A Space for Place in Sociology." *Annual Review of Sociology* 26.

Gill, S., and D. Law. 1988. *The Global Political Economy: Perspectives, Problems and Policies*. Baltimore: Johns Hopkins University Press.

Gindin, S. "The Canadian Auto Workers: The Birth and Transformation of a Union." Available at <www.caw.ca/whoweare/ourhistory/cawhistory/ch10/p4c10_4.html> (accessed on October 29, 2004).

Glasbeek, H. 2002. *Wealth by Stealth: Corporate Crime, Corporate Law and the Perversion of Democracy*. Toronto: Between the Lines.

Gleick, P. 1998. *The World's Water 1998–1999: Annual Renewable Water Resources*. Washington, DC: Island Press.

Glenn, J. 2000. *Once Upon an Oldman: Special Interest Politics and the Oldman River Dam*. Vancouver: University of British Columbia Press.

Global Forest Watch: "Canada: An Overview." Available at <www.globalforestwatch.org/english/canada/> (accessed on November 8, 2004).

Global Resource Action Center for the Environment (GRACE). 2004. *The Meatrix Information Center*. Available at <www.themeatrix.com/homepage.html> (accessed on November 9, 2004).

Globe and Mail. 1998. "Oil Producer Opposes Climate-change Treaty: Don't Ratify Kyoto Deal, Imperial tells Ottawa." November 12.

_____. 1995. "Clayoquot Panel Urges End to Clear-cutting." May 30.

Goldman, M. 1998. "Introduction: The Political Resurgence of the Commons." In M. Goldman (ed.), *Privatizing Nature: Political Struggles for the Global Commons*. New Brunswick, NJ: Rutgers University Press.

Gomberg, Tooher. 1996. "Having Your Car and Eating It Too," CarSharing Library. Available at <www.caa.ca/e/automotive/pdf/drivingcosts-04.pdf>.

Goodman, T. 2002. "Thirsty for Power." *The Salt Lake Tribune*, August 13. Available at <www.active.com/print.cfm?category=activeparks_index&story_id=9238> (accessed on June 24, 2004).

Gorz, Andre. 1993. "Political Ecology: Expertocracy versus Self-Limitation." *New Left Review* No. 203.

Gould, K. 1991. "The Sweet Smell of Money: Economic Dependency and Local Environmental Political Mobilization." *Society and Natural Resources* 4, 2.

Gould, K., A. Schnaiberg, and A. Weinberg. 2001. *Local Environmental Struggles*. New York: Cambridge University Press.

Gouldson, A., and J. Murphy. 1996. "Ecological Modernization and the European Union." *Geoforum* 27, 1 (February).

Government of Alberta. 2003. "Alberta's Pork Production Industry." Available at <www1.agric.gov.ab.ca/$department/deptdocs.nsf/all/agdex3016?opendocument> (accessed on November 8, 2004).

_____. 2002. "Alberta will Continue to Defend Economy from Kyoto Implementation." Available at <www.gov.ab.ca/home/kyoto/display.cfm?id=15&lkfid=321> (accessed on March 10, 2004).

Government of Canada. 2004. "Canada Announces Coming into Force of Amendments to International Boundary Waters Treaty Act." Available at <www.webapps.dfait-maeci.gc.ca/minpub/Publication.asp?FileSpec=/Min_Pub_Docs/105776.htm&Language=E> (accessed on April 14, 2004).

_____. 1996. *The State of the Environment*. Ottawa: Environment Canada.

Government of Canada, National Forest Strategy. 2003. "Toward the Sustainable Forest." Available at <http://nfsc.forest.ca/strategies/strategy5.html> (accessed on November 8, 2004).

Gray, T. 1997. "Politics and the Environment in the U.K. and Beyond." In M. Redclift and G. Woodgate (eds.), *The International Handbook of Environmental Sociology*. Cheltenham, UK: Edward Elgar.

Greenberg, M. 1991. "American Cities: Good and Bad News about Public Health." *Bulletin of the New York Academy of Medicine* 67: 17–21.

Greenpeace. 2004. "How to Avoid Genetically Engineered Food: A Greenpeace Shoppers Guide." Second Edition. Available at <www.greenpeace.ca/shoppersguide/download.php> (accessed on November 11, 2004).

Greenspon, E. 1997. "Provinces Let Down at Kyoto, Klein says: Deal on Emissions 'not Acceptable.'" *Globe and Mail*, November 12.

Greer, J., and K. Singh. 2000. "A Brief History of Transnational Corporations." *Global Policy Forum*. Available at <www.globalpolicy.org/socecon/tncs/historytncs.htm#bk2_ft1> (accessed on October 29, 2004).

Griffiths, M., and D. Woynillowicz. 2003. "Oil and Troubled Waters: Reducing the Impact of the Oil and Gas Industry on Alberta's Water Resources." Drayton Valley, AB: The Pembina Institute. Available at <www.pembina.org/pdf/publications/OilandTroubledWaters.pdf> (accessed on October 29, 2004).

Grimes, P., and J. Kentor. 2003. "Exporting the Greenhouse: Foreign Capital Penetration and CO2 Emissions 1980–1996." *Journal of World Systems Research* 9, 2.

Grossman, Perry. 2002. "The Effects of Free Trade on Development, Democracy, and Environmental Protection." *Sociological Inquiry* 72, 1 (Winter).

Hagmann, Michael. 2003. "Nutritionists Unimpressed by Sugar Lobby's Outcry." *Bull World Health Organ* 81, 6.

Hajer, M. 1995. *The Politics of Environmental Discourse: Ecological Modernization and the Policy Process*. Oxford: Oxford University Press.

Haley, E. 2002. Interview (Former Worker at a Phosphate Processing Factory). July 30.

_____. 2000. "Methodology to Deconstruct Environmental Inquiries Using the Hall Commission as a Case Study." Ph.D thesis, Department of Sociology, York University, Toronto.

Hall, R.H. 1998. "The Medical-Industrial Complex." *Ecologist* 28 (2): 62.

Halweil, Brian. 2002. "Home Grown: The Case for Local Food in a Global Market." *Worldwatch, Paper 163*. Available at <www.worldwatch.org/pubs/paper/163/> (accessed on May 30, 2004).

_____. 2001. "How Now, Mad Cow?" March 8. Available at <www.worldwatch.org/press/news/2001/03/08/> (accessed on March 2, 2005).

Hannigan, J. 1995. *Environmental Sociology: A Constructionist Perspective*. London: Routledge.

Hansen, Karen Tranberg. 2000. *Salaula: The World of Second-Hand Clothing and Zambia*. Chicago: University of Chicago Press.

Hanson, Jay. 1999. "Energetic Limit to Growth." Available at <www.oilcrash.com/energetic/htm>.

Haraway, D. 1991. *Simians, Cyborgs, and Women: The Reinvention of Nature*. New York: Routledge.

Hardin, G. 1968. "The Tragedy of the Commons." *Science* 162.

Hare, W., C. Hull, and D. Pritchard. 1999. "Report on CPT Fact-Finding Mission to Asubpeeschoseewagong Netum Anishnabek (Grassy Narrows First Nation)." Available at <www.cpt.org/canada/grassyffm.php> (accessed on May 8, 2004).

Harper, C.L. 2001. *Environment and Society: Human Perspectives on Environmental Issues*. Second edition. Toronto: Prentice-Hall.

Harper, C., and B. LeBeau. 2003. *Food, Society, and Environment*. Upper Saddle River, NJ: Prentice Hall.

Harvey, D. 1999. *The Condition of Post Modernity*. Cambridge, MA: Blackwell.

_____. 1996. *Justice, Nature, and the Geography of Difference*. Cambridge, MA: Blackwell.

_____. 1990. "Between Space and Time." *Annals of the Association of American Geographers* 80, 3.

Hatt, K. 2000. "Development, Transnational Power, and Environmental Degradation: A Case Study of the Costa Rican Banana Industry." Ph.D thesis, McGill University, Montreal.

Hattam, J. 2004. "Biotech Fails the Test." *Sierra* 89, 3 (May/June).

Hawken, Paul, Amory Lovins and L. Hunter Lovins. 1999. *Natural Capitalism: Creating the Next Industrial Revolution*. Boston: Back Bay Books.

Hayden, A. 1999. *Sharing the Work, Sparing the Planet: Work Time, Consumption and Ecology*. Toronto: Between the Lines.

Health Canada. Office of Nutrition Policy and Promotion. 2005. "What Is Canada's Food Guide to Healthy Eating?" Available at <www.hc-sc.gc.ca/hpfb-dgpsa/onpp-bppn/using_food_guide_e.html> (accessed January 24, 2005).

Health Canada Online. 1999a. "Health Canada Rejects Bovine Growth Hormone in Canada." Available at <www.hc-sc.gc.ca/english/media/releases/1999/99_03e.htm> (accessed on October 29, 2004).

_____. 1999b. "Report of the Royal College of Physicians and Surgeons of Canada

Expert Panel on Human Safety of rbST." Available at <www.hc-sc.gc.ca/english/protection/rbst/humans> (accessed on November 14, 2004).

Heatherington, T. 2000. "Green Economic Policy." *The Progress Report*. Available at <www.progress.org/archive/shift19.htm> (accessed on March 10, 2004).

Hecht, S., and A. Cockburn. 1990. *The Fate of the Forest: Developers, Destroyers, and Defenders of the Amazon*. London: Penguin Books.

Heinberg, Richard. 2004. *Powerdown: Options and Actions for a Post-Carbon World*. Gabriola Island, BC: New Society.

_____. 2003. *The Party's Over: Oil, War and the Fate of Industrial Societies*. Gabriola Island, BC: New Society.

Helwig, S. n.d. "The Push for a Pipeline through Canada's Northern Frontier." *CBC Radio News*. Available at <www.cbc.ca/news/radionews/context/pipeline/#change> (accessed on May 1, 2004).

Hemispheric Social Alliance. 2001. "Alternatives for the Americas: Discussion Draft #3." Expanded and Revised Edition. Prepared for the 2nd Peoples Summit of the Americas (Quebec City, Canada, April 2001). Available at <www.asc-hsa.org/pdf/altering2.pdf> (accessed on August 25, 2004).

Henson, D. 2002. "The End of Agribusiness: Dismantling the Mechanisms of Corporate Rule." In A. Kimbrell (ed.), *The Fatal Harvest Reader: The Tragedy of Industrial Agriculture*. Washington, DC: Island Press.

Henton, Darcy. 2002. "Concerns over Water Resources Rising: Province Consulting Albertans on Issues." *Edmonton Journal* April 22: A7.

Hernández, C. 1997. *A Systems Method for Evaluating the Sustainability of Ag-Production: An Evaluation of Banana Production in Costa Rica*. Ph.D. Thesis, Michigan State University.

Heyman, D. 2004. "Soft Drink Industry Pulling its Sodas out of Schools." *Calgary Herald*, January 6.

Hilije, L., E. Luisa, M. Castillo, L. Thrupp, and I. Wesseling. 1987. *El Uso de los Plaguicidas en Costa Rica*. San José, Costa Rica: Editorial Heliconia and Editorial Universidad Estatal a Distancia.

Hinrichsen, D., B. Robey, and U. Upadhyay. 1998. "Solutions for a Water-Short World." Population Reports, Series M, No. 14. *Population Reports* XXVI (1). Available at <www.infoforhealth.org/pr/m14/m14print.shtml> (accessed on April 14, 2004).

Hofmann, N. 2001. "Urban Consumption of Agricultural Land." *Rural and Small Town Canada Analysis Bulletin* 3, 2.

Hogue, C. 2000. "Toxics Pact Down to the Wire." *Chem. and Eng. News* 28(48). Nov. 27.

Hood, G. 1994. *Against the Flow: Rafferty-Alameda and the Politics of the Environment*. Saskatoon: Fifth House.

Hornberg, A. 2001. *The Power of the Machine: Global Inequalities of Economy, Technology and Environment*. Lanham, MD: Altamira Press.

House, J. 1980. *The Last of the Free Enterprisers: The Oilmen of Calgary*. Toronto: MacMillan.

Huber, J. 1982. *Die verlorene Unschuld der Okologie. Neue Technologien und Superindustrielle Entwicklung*, Fisher Verlag: Frankfurt am Main.

Hynes, P. 2003. "Ten Reasons Why Militarism is Bad for Women's Health" April 10. Available at <www.peacewomen.org/resources/Health/Hynes.html> (accessed January 23, 2005).

Ikeda, S. 2004. "Zonal Structure and Trajectories of Canada, Mexico, Australia, and Norway under Neoliberal Globalization." In Stephen Clarkson and Majorie Cohen (eds.), *Governing under Stress*. London: Zed Books.

Independent Television Service. 2004. *The Democratic Promise: Saul Alinsky and His Legacy*. [Film]. Available at <www.itvs.org/democraticpromise/alinsky2.html> (accessed on July 2, 2004).

Industrial Heartland. 2004. *Heartland: Connect.Net.Work*. Available at <www.industrialheartland.com/execsummary.html> (accessed on July 12, 2004).

Inglehart, R. 1977. *The Silent Revolution: Changing Values and Political Styles among Western Publics*. Princeton, NJ: Princeton University Press.

_____. 1930. *The Fur Trade in Canada: An Introduction to Canadian Economic History*. New Haven: Yale University Press.

Innis, H. 1995. *Staples, Markets, and Cultural Change: Selected Essays*, edited by Daniel Drache. Montreal: McGill-Queen's University Press.

_____. 1930. *The Fur Trade in Canada: An Introduction to Canadian Economic History*. New Haven: Yale University Press.

Inouye, K. 2003. "Unpacking the Agro Biotech Engines: How the Leading Seed and Agrochemical Corporations Are Driving the Biotech Agenda." Ottawa: Polaris Institute. July. Available at <www.polarisinstitute.org/polaris_project/bio_justice/corp_biotech/unpacking_agro.pdf > (accessed January 24, 2005).

Insight Column. 2004. "Bottling Hype." *NOW Magazine Online Edition* 22, 5. Available at <www.nowtoronto.com/issues/2002-10-03/news_insight.php> (accessed on November 12, 2004).

Inuvialuit Regional Corporation (IRC). 2002. *September/October Newsletter*. Available at <www.arcticgaspipeline.com/Delta%20Route.htm#Mackenzie%20Valley%20Pipeline%20News> (accessed on May 1, 2004).

Irwin, A. 1997. "Risk, the Environment and Environmental Knowledge." In M. Redclift and G. Woodgate (eds.), *The International Handbook of Environmental Sociology*. Northampton, MA: Edward Elgar.

Jackson, M., E. Peterson, J. Bull, S. Monson, and P. Richmond. 1960. "The Failure of an Incipient Social Movement." *Pacific Sociological Review* 31.

Jackson, W. 1994. *Becoming Native to This Place*. Lexington: University of Kentucky Press.

Janicke, M. 1997. "The Political System's Capacity for Environmental Policy." In M. Janicke and H. Weidner (eds.), *National Environmental Policies: A Comparative Study of Capacity-Building*. Berlin: Springer.

Jansen, L. 1998. *Explaining Rural Calm and Rural Unrest in Costa Rica: The Coffee and Banana Export Sectors*. Ph.D. thesis, University of Washington.

Janzen, D. (ed.). 1983. *Costa Rican Natural History*. Chicago: University of Chicago Press.

Johnson, J. 2003. "Who Cares About the Commons?" *Capitalism, Nature, Socialism* 14, 4 (December).

Johnson, J., M. Gismondi, and J. Goodman. 2005. (Forthcoming). *The Revenge of Nature: Reclaiming Sustainability in an Age of Corporate Globalism*. Peterborough: Broadview Press.

Johnson, L. 2002. "Iraqi Cancers, Birth Defects Blamed on US Depleted Uranium." *Seattle Post-Intelligencer*. Available at <http://seattlepi.nwsource.com/national/95178_du12.shtml?searchpagefrom=2&searchdiff=606> (accessed on July 4, 2004).

Johnson, S. 2004. "Young Canadian Social Entrepreneurs." *New Academy Review*

2, 4 (Winter).
Kahneman, D., and A. Tversky. 1979. "Prospect Theory: An Analysis of Decision under Risk." *Econometrica* 47 2.
Kasarda, J. 1989. "Urban Industrial Transition and the Underclass." *Annals* 504, 40.
Kaur, S. 2000. *A Call to Women: The Healthy Breast Program and Workbook*. Kingston, ON: Quarry Health Books.
Kazis, R., and R. Grossman. 1982. *Fear at Work: Job Blackmail, Labor and the Environment*. New York: Pilgrim Press.
Keck, M., and K. Sikkink. 1998. *Activists beyond Borders: Advocacy Networks in International Politics*. Ithaca, NY: Cornell University Press.
Keeling, A. 2001. "The Rancher and the Regulators: Public Challenges to Sour-Gas Industry Regulation in Alberta, 1970–1994." In R. Epp and D. Whitson (eds.), *Writing off the Rural West: Globalization, Governments and the Transformation of Rural Communities*. Edmonton: Parkland Institute and University of Alberta Press.
Kennedy, B., R. Powell, and S. Leggett. 2004. "Natural Resources Conservation Board with Respect to Application 03/01, Filed by Agrium Product Inc." Held at Fort Saskatchewan, Alberta, February 23–March 12. Available at <www.tscript.com/> (accessed January 23, 2005).
Kilburn, K. 1997. "Exposure to Reduced Sulphur Gases Impairs Neurobehavioral Function." *Southern Medical Journal* 90, 10.
Kilpatrick, K. 1999. "Farmers near Lake Huron Raising Stink over Pollution from Large Pig Farms." *Globe and Mail*, September 28.
King, Jr., M. 1986. *A Testament of Hope*. New York: HarperCollins.
Klein, Naomi. 2000. *No Logo: Taking Aim at the Brand Bullies*. Toronto: Knopf Canada.
Kleiss, K. 2004. "Canola Ruling 'Abominable' says Sturgeon County Farmer." *Edmonton Journal*, May 22.
Kneen, B. 2004. Personal Interview. Nov. 10.
_____. 1999. *Farmageddon: Food and the Culture of Biotechnology*. Gabriola Island, BC: New Society Publishers.
Krimsky, S. 2000. *Hormonal Chaos: The Scientific and Social Origins of the Environmental Endocrine Hypothesis*. Baltimore: Johns Hopkins University Press.
Kroll-Smith, S., and H. Floyd. 1997. *Bodies in Protest: Environmental Illness and the Struggle over Medical Knowledge*. New York: New York University Press.
Kuyek, J. 2004. "Asbestos and Canada." Available at <www.sierraclub.ca/national/programs/health-environment/toxics/asbestos-amiante-canada.pdf> (accessed on May 5, 2004).
Laidlaw, S. 2003. *Secret Ingredients: The Brave New World of Industrial Farming*. Toronto: McClelland and Stewart.
Laird, G. 2002. *Power: Journey across an Energy Nation*. Toronto: Penguin Books.
Lang, G. 2002. "Forests, Floods, and the Environmental State of China." *Organization and Environment* 15, 2.
Lappé, F., and A. Lappé. 2003. *Hope's Edge: Tthe Next Diet for a Small Planet*. New York: Jeremy P. Tarcher.
Lappé, F.M., and J. Collins with C. Fowler. 1977. *Food First: Beyond the Myth of Scarcity*. Boston: Houghton-Mifflin.
Lash, S., and J. Urry. 1994. *The Economies of Signs and Space*. London: Sage.
Latour, B., and S. Woolgar. 1986. *Laboratory Life: The Construction of Scientific*

Facts. Second Edition. Princeton, NJ: Princeton University Press.

Lazarus, R., and S. Folkman. 1984. *Stress, Appraisal and Coping*. New York: Springer.

Lee, S., C. Liffman, and C. McCulligh. 2002. *The New and Improved Supermarket Tour*. Hamilton, ON: Ontario Public Interest Research Group (OPIRG) McMaster University.

Lefebvre, H. 1991. *The Production of Space*. (D. Nicholson-Smith, Trans.) Cambridge, MA: Blackwell.

Leibman, D., and A. El-Eini. 1996. "The Sustainability Movement: Rhetoric or Reality?" *Friends of the Earth*, Sept/Oct. Available at <www.sustainable.doe.gov/articles/rhetoric.shtml> (accessed on November 8, 2004).

Leiss, W. 2004. "BSE Risk in Canada, Part 3: Two Stinking Cows—And the Way Forward for Canada." Available at <www.leiss.ca/bse/143?download> (accessed on November 12, 2004).

Leiss, W., and C. Chociolko. 1994. *Risk and Responsibility*. Montreal and Kingston: McGill-Queens University Press.

Leonard, A. 1993. "South Asia: The New Target of International Waste Traders." *Multinational Monitor*. Available at <http://multinationalmonitor.org/hyper/issues/1993/12/mm1293_08.html> (accessed on November 8, 2004).

Leopold, A. 1991. "The Ecological Conscience." In S. Flader and J. Callicott (eds.), *The River of the Mother of God and Other Essays by Aldo Leopold*. Madison: University of Wisconsin Press.

_____. 1949. *A Sand County Almanac and Sketches Here and There*. New York: Oxford University Press.

Levant, V. 1999. "Canada and the Vietnam War." *The 1998 Canadian and World Encyclopaedia*. Toronto: McClelland and Stewart. Available at <www.geocities.com/Athens/Rhodes/1588/> (accessed on July 4, 2004).

Levidov, L. 1999. "Regulating BT Maize in the United States and Europe." *Environment* 41, 10.

Levine, A. 1982. *Love Canal: Science, Politics and People*. Toronto: Lexington Books.

Lewis, H., and J. Gertsakis with T. Grant, N. Morelli and A. Sweatman. 2001. *Design + Environment: A Global Guide to Designing Greener Goods*. Sheffield, UK: Greenleaf Publishing.

Lin, J. 2003. "A New Look: Retail Clothing Sales in Canada." *Statistics Canada Analytical Paper* (Catalogue no. 11-621-MIE, No. 006). Ottawa: Statistics Canada.

Lindsey, R. 1993. "Cesar Chavez, 66, Organizer of Union for Migrants." *New York Times* April 24. Available at <www.maineaflcio.org/cesar%20chavez%20biography.htm> (accessed on July 2, 2004).

Linton, J. 1997. *Beneath the Surface: The State of Water in Canada*. Kanata: Canadian Wildlife Federation.

Lipschutz, R. 1996. *Global Civil Society and Global Environmental Governance*. Albany: SUNY Press.

Lodziak, C. 2002. *The Myth of Consumerism*. London: Pluto Press.

Loeffler, J. 1989. *Headed Upstream: Interviews with Iconoclasts*. Tucson, AZ: Harbinger House

Lomborg, B. 2001. *The Skeptical Environmentalist*. Cambridge, UK: Cambridge University Press.

López, J. 1988. *La Economía del banano en Centroamérica*. San José, Costa Rica:

Editorial Departamento Ecuménico de Investigaciones (DEI).
Losch, P. 1990. "Green Consumerism and Eco-labels." *Earth Island Journal* 5, 2 (Spring).
Luginaah, I.N., S.M. Taylor, S.J. Elliot, and J.D. Eyles. (2002). "Community Responses and Coping Strategies in the Vicinity of a Petroleum Refinery in Oakville, Ontario." *Health and Place* 8.
Lukes, S. 1974. *Power: A Radical View*. London: MacMillan Press.
Lundholm, J. "Place Jamming with Guerrilla Gardening." Available at <www.animana.org/tab3/32lundholm-placejamming.shtml> (accessed on June 1, 2004).
Lupton, D. 1999. *Risk*. New York: Routledge.
Lush, P. 1995. "B.C. Moves Fast to Save Clayoquot: Environmentalists Surprised and Delighted but Unions Worried about Potential Job Losses." *Globe and Mail*, July 7.
Lutzenhiser, L., C. Harris, and M. Olsen. 2002. "Energy, Society and Environment." In R. Dunlap and W. Michelson (eds.), *Handbook of Environmental Sociology*. Westport: Greenwood Press.
Machum, S. 2001. "De-prioritizing Agriculture: Lessons from New Brunswick." In R. Epp and D. Whitson (eds.), *Writing Off the Rural West*. Edmonton: Parkland Institute and University of Alberta Press.
MacKenzie, D. 2000. "You Can Still Shop to Save the World." *New Statesman* 129, 4468 (Special Supplement).
MacKinnon, M. 2000. "Halve Greenhouse Gases Soon, Easily, Suzuki Says: Reduction Does not Mean Economic Disruption, Study Argues." *Globe and Mail*, April 18.
MacQueen, K. 2002. "The Anti-Retailer." *Maclean's* 115, 17 (April 29).
Magdoff, F., J. Foster, and F. Buttel. 2000. "An Overview." In F. Magdoff, J. Foster and F. Buttel (eds.), *Hungry for Profit: The Agribusiness Threat to Farmer, Food and the Environment*. New York: Monthly Review Press.
Malkia-Pykh, I., and Y. Pykh. 2003. *Sustainable Water Resources Management*. Southampton, Boston: WIT Press.
Mallet, J. 2004. "Our Water and the Law." *Law Now* 28, 6 (June/July).
Maniates, M. 2002a. "Individualization: Plant a Tree, Buy a Bike, Save the World?" In T Princen, M. Maniates, and Ken Conca (eds.), *Confronting Consumption*. Cambridge, MA: MIT Press.
_____. 2002b. "In Search of Consumptive Resistance: The Voluntary Simplicity Movement." In T. Princen, M. Maniates, and K. Conca (eds.), *Confronting Consumption*. Cambridge, MA: MIT Press.
Maquiladora Solidarity Network (MSN). "The Labour Behind the Label: How Our Clothes are Made." Available at <www.maquilasolidarity.org> (accessed on November 12, 2004).
_____. "No Sweat Organizers Guide." Available at <www.maquilasolidarity.org> (accessed on November 12, 2004).
Marchak, P. 1995. *Logging the Globe*. Montreal: McGill-Queen's.
Markowitz, Gerald, and David Rosner. 2002. *Deceit and Denial: The Deadly Politics of Industrial Pollution*. Berkeley: University of California Press.
Marr-Laing, T., and C. Severson-Baker. 1999. *Beyond Eco-Terrorism: The Deeper Issues Affecting Alberta's Oil Patch*. Drayton Valley, AB: Pembina Institute for Appropriate Development.
Marshall, D. 2002. "Making Kyoto Work." *Canadian Centre for Policy Alternatives*.

Available at <www.policyalternatives.ca/bc/making-kyoto-work.pdf> (accessed on November 1, 2004).

Marshall, G. (ed.). 1998. *Oxford Dictionary of Sociology*. Toronto: Oxford University Press.

Martin, G. 2002. "Grounding Social Ecology: Landspace, Settlement, and Right of Way." *Capitalism, Nature, Socialism* 13, 1.

Martinez-Alier, J. 1999. "The Social-ecological Embeddedness of Economic Activity: The Emergence of a Transdisciplinary Field." In E. Becker and T. Jahn (eds.), *Sustainability and the Social Sciences: A Cross-disciplinary Approach to Integrating Environmental Considerations into Theoretical Reorientation*. London: Zed Books.

Massey, D. 2004. "Geographies of Responsibility." *Geographiska Annaler* 86, 1.

Masterson-Allen, S., and P. Brown. 1990. "Public Reaction to Toxic Waste Contamination: Analysis of a Social Movement." *International Journal of Health Services* 20, 3.

Mata, L., and A. Mata. 1993. "Efectos de la Expansión bananera sobre la Salud Humana y el Sistema Ecológico." In N. Rodrigues (ed.), *Comunicación y Ambiente*. San Pedro de Montes de Oca, Costa Rica: Fundaciones Iriria Tsochok y Friederich Naumann Stiftung.

Matas, R. 1993a. "Clayoquot Ruling Satisfies No One: Environmentalist Want Logging Banned; Industry Upset over Job Loss." *Globe and Mail*, April 14.

_____. 1993b. "Natives Vow to Stop Logging on Clayoquot Sound: B.C. Tribes Insist on having Voice in Land Use Decisions that could Affect Claims." *Globe and Mail*, May 1.

Mateu, E., and M. Martin. 2001. "Why Is Anti-Microbial Resistance a Veterinary Problem as Well?" *Journal of Veterinary Medicine. Series B* 48, 8. Available at <www.blackwellsynergy.com/links/doi/10.1046/j.14390450.2001.00475.x/abs/;jsessionid=kBKRENLgWD-c> (accessed January 23, 2005).

Matsakis, N., and E. Vlanton. 2004. "The War in Iraq Cost the United States." Available at <http://costofwar.com/> (accessed on July 4, 2004).

Mawhinney, M. 2002. *Sustainable Development: Understanding the Green Debates*. Oxford: Blackwell Science.

May, E., and M. Barlow. 2001. "The Tar Ponds." *Alternatives Journal: Canadian Environmental Ideas and Action* 27, 1.

McCarthy, J., and M. Zald. 1977. "Resource Mobilization and Social Movements: A Partial Theory." *American Journal of Sociology* 82, 6.

McCormick, S., P. Brown, and S. Zavestoski. 2004. "The Environmental Breast Cancer Movement." *The Ribbon* 9, 2 (Spring). Available at <www.envirocancer.cornell.edu/Newsletter/General/v9i2/movement.cfm> (accessed on November 14).

McCutcheon, S. 1991. *Electric Rivers*. Montreal: Black Rose Books.

McDaniels, T., J. Axelrod, and P. Slovic. 1996. "Perceived Ecological Risks of Global Change." *Global Environmental Change* 6, 2.

McDonough, W., and M. Braungart. 2002. *Cradle to Cradle: Remaking the Way We Make Things*. New York: North Point Press.

McIlroy, A. 2004. "Researchers in Hamilton Find that Particles of Soot and Dust Cause Genetic Mutations in Sperm That Affect Offspring." *Globe and Mail*, May 14.

McIntyre, L. (writer), and N. Docherty (director). 2004. "Dead in the Water." [Television]. *The Fifth Estate*. Canadian Broadcasting Corporation.

ɹcKenzie, J. 2002. *Environmental Politics in Canada: Managing the Commons into the Twenty-First Century*. Toronto: Oxford University Press.

McKinley, N. 1999. "Ideal Weight/Ideal Women." In J. Sobal and D. Maurer (eds.), *Weighty Issues: Fatness and Thinness as Social Problems*. New York: Walter de Gruyter.

McLaughlin, P. 2001. "Toward an Ecology of Social Action: Merging the Ecological and Constructivist Traditions." *Human Ecology Review* 8, 2.

McMichael, Philip. 2000. *Development and Social Change: A Global Perspective*. Thousand Oaks, CA: Pine Forge Press.

McNamee, K. 1993. "From Wild Places to Endangered Spaces: A History of Canada's National Parks." In P. Dearden and R. Rollins (eds.), *Parks and Protected Areas in Canada: Planning and Management*. Toronto: Oxford University Press.

McNeil, J. 2001. *Something New under the Sun: An Environmental History of the Twentieth Century*. New York: W.W. Norton.

McNeill, W. 1976. *Plagues and Peoples*. New York: Anchor Books.

McQuaig, Linda. 1992. *The Quick and the Dead*. Toronto: Penguin.

Meadows, D., D Meadows, J. Randers, and W. Behrens. 1972. *The Limits to Growth: A Report for the Club of Rome's Project on the Predicament of Mankind*. New York: New York University Press.

Mehta, M. 2004. "Re-licensing of Nuclear Facilities in Canada: The Risk Society in Action." Available at <http://www.sociology.org/content/vol003.001/mehta.html> (accessed on June 15).

Meier, G., and D. Seers. 1984. *Pioneers in Development*. New York: Oxford University Press.

Meléndez, C. (ed.). 1978. *Documentos Fundamentales del siglo XIX*. San José, Costa Rica: Editorial Costa Rica.

Melucci, A. 1980. "The New Social Movements: A Theoretical Approach." *Social Science Information* 19.

Merrett, C. 1996. *Free Trade: Neither Free nor About Trade*. Montreal: Black Rose Books.

Michaels, L., and the Agriculture Project at Corporate Watch. 2002. "What's Wrong with Supermarkets?" *Corporate Watch*. Available at <www.corporatewatch.org.uk> (accessed on August 23, 2004).

Middendorf, G., M. Skladany, E. Ransom, and L. Busch. 2000. "New Agricultural Biotechnologies." In F. Magdoff, J. Foster and F. Buttel (eds), *Hungry for Profit: The Agribusiness Threat to Farmer, Food and the Environment*. New York: Monthly Review Press.

Mies, M. 1986. *Patriarchy and Accumulation on a World Scale: Women in the International Division of Labour*. London: Zed Books.

Miller, D. (ed.). 1995. *Acknowledging Consumption: A Review of New Studies*. London: Routledge.

Mills, C. Wright. 1956. *The Power Elite*, New York: Oxford University Press.

Mills, K.. and P. Mills. 2000. *C. Wright Mills: Letters and Autobiographical Writings*. Berkeley: University of California Press.

Mills, S. 1997. *Discourse*. New York: Routledge.

MIRENEM (Ministerio de Recursos Naturales, Energía y Minas). 1990. *Estrategía de Conservación para el Desarrollo Sostenible de Costa Rica*. San José, Costa Rica.

MIRENEM (Ministerio de Recursos Naturales, Energía y Minas) and Unión Mundial para la Naturaleza (UICN). 1992. *Diagnóstico del Impacto Socioambiental de la*

Expansión Bananera en Sarapiquí. Tortuguero y Talamanca, Costa Rica. Preliminary Technical Report.

Mitchell, A., J. Gray, and R. Seguin. 2000. "Fear of Farming: The Deadly Water of Walkerton has Canadians Wondering about the Rapid Rise of the Massive Livestock Operation. Is it safe? Now Even the People Running the Factory Farms Are Saying: 'We Want Some Answers Too.'" *Globe and Mail*, June 3.

Mittelstaedt, M. 2004a. "Blayne Kinart 1946–2004. The Voice of Sick Workers: Sarnia Millwright Hoped to Increase Public Awareness of the Plight of Employees Poisoned on the Job." *Globe and Mail*, July 10.

_____. 2004b. "Dying for a Living." *Globe and Mail*, March 13. Available at <www.ohcow.on.ca/clinics/sarnia/docs/globeandmailstory.html> (accessed on July 4, 2004).

_____. 2004c. "Flame Retardant in Breast Milk Raises Concern." *Globe and Mail*, June 7.

_____. 2004d. "13 Pesticides in Body of Average American." *Globe and Mail*, May 21.

_____. 2000. "Companies Seek to Delay Emissions Reduction: Lobby Group Says Targets Set by Kyoto Protocol Cannot be Met Without 'Substantial Impairment' to the Canadian Economy." *Globe and Mail*, January 24.

_____. 1999. "Bottlers Free to Drain off Groundwater." *Globe and Mail*, July 3.

Modavi, N. 1991. "Environmentalism, State and Economy in the United States." *Research in Social Movements, Conflicts, and Change* 13.

Mohai, P., and B. Bryant. 1992. Environmental Injustice: Weighing Race and Class as Factors in the Distribution of Environmental Hazards. *University of Colorado Law Review* 63, 4.

Mokhiber, R. 1988. *Corporate Crime and Violence: Big Business Power and the Abuse of the Public Trust*. San Francisco, CA: Sierra Club Books.

Mol, A. 2001. *Globalization and Environmental Reform: The Ecological Modernization of the Global Economy*. Cambridge, MA: MIT Press.

_____. 1996. "Ecological Modernization and Institutional Reflexivity: Environmental Reform in the Late Modern Age." *Environmental Politics* 5, 2.

Mol, A., and F. Buttel. 2002. "The Environmental State under Pressure: An Introduction." In A. Mol, F Buttel and H. Frederick (eds.), *The Environmental State Under Pressure*. Amsterdam: JAI.

Mol, A., and G. Spaargaren. 2000. "Ecological Modernization Theory in Debate: A Review." In A. Mol and D. Sonnenfeld (eds.), *Ecological Modernization around the World: Perspectives and Critical Debates*. London: Frank Cass.

Molotch, H. 1970. "Oil in Santa Barbara and Power in America." *Sociological Inquiry* 40.

Monbiot, G. 2004. *The Age of Consent: A Manifesto for a New World Order*. London: Harper Perennial.

Moore, B. 1966. *Social Origins of Dictatorship and Democracy*. Boston: Beacon.

Moore, J. 2000. "Environmental Crises and the Metabolic Rift in World-historical Perspective." *Organization and Environment* 13, 2.

Multinational Monitor. 1991. "Deadly Exports." Editorial. 12, 7and8 (July/August). Available at <www.multinationalmonitor.org/hyper/issues/1991/07/mm0791_02.html> (accessed November 16 2004)

Munn, R.E., and A.R. Maarouf. 1997. "Atmospheric Issues in Canada." *The Science of the Total Environment* 203: 1–11.

Murillo Chaverri, C. 1995. *Identidades de Hierro y Humo*. San José, Costa Rica:

Editorial Porvenir.

Myers, N. 2000. "Sustainable Consumption: The Meta-Problem." In B. Heap and J. Kent (eds.), *Towards Sustainable Consumption: A European Perspective*. London: The Royal Society.

Narasaiah, L. 1998. "Employment and Promoting Ecology: How a Service Culture could put People back to Work." *Co-op Dialogue* 8, 3 (October/December).

National Breast Cancer Coalition (US). 2004. "Project Lead: NBC's Innovative Science Program for Breast Cancer Activists." Available at <www.natlbcc.org/bin/index.asp?Strid=483&btnid=4&depid=7#subjects> (accessed on August 28, 2004).

National Dairy Council. 2005. "Nutrition and Product Information—Dairy Food Safety." Available at <http://www.nationaldairycouncil.org/nutrition/safety/foodSafetyfactsheet.asp> (accessed January 24, 2005).

National Energy Policy Group (NEPD). 2001. "Reliable, Affordable, and Environmentally Sound Energy for America's Future." Available at <www.whitehouse.gov/energy> (accessed on November 6, 2004).

National Farmers Union. 2004. "Submission to the Dairy Farmers of Ontario." Available at <www.nfu.ca/on/briefs/Brief%20to%20Dairy%20Farmers%20of%20Ontario%20-%20May%2026%202004.pdf> (accessed on November 10, 2004).

_____. 2000. "The Effects of Hog Mega-Barns on Communities, the Environment, and Independent Hog Producers." A brief presented to the Flagstaff County Appeal Board. Available at < http://www.nfu.ca/hogbarn-brief.htm>.

National Film Board. 1995. T. Nash (Director). *Who's Counting? Marilyn Waring on Sex, Lies and Global Economics*. [Film]. Bullfrog Films.

National Forest Strategy Coalition. 2004. "National Forest Strategy 2003–2008." Available at <http://nfsc.forest.ca/strategies/strategy5.html> (accessed on November 14, 2004).

National Research Council. 1993. *Pesticides in the Diets of Infants and Children*. Washington, DC: National Academy Press.

Natural Resources Canada. 2002. "Our Water." (January 23). Available at <www.adaptation.nrcan.gc.ca/posters/articles/on_05_en.asp?Category=wr&Language=en&Region=onNatural Resources> (accessed on March 24, 2004).

_____. 2001 "Land and Freshwater Areas." (July 7). Available at <atlas.gc.ca/site/english/learningresources/facts/surfareas.html>.

National Union of Public and General Employees (NUPGE). "National Union Focus on the Environment: Sustainability Must Become Our Way of Life." Available at <www.nupge.ca/issues/environment%5Fold.htm> (accessed on March 7, 2004).

Nelson, P. 2001. "Rural Restructuring in the American West: Land Use, Family and Class Discourses." *Journal of Rural Studies* 17, 4.

Neumann, Roderick P. 1998. *Imposing Wilderness: Struggles over Livelihood and Nature Preservation in Africa*. Berkeley: University of California Press.

Neville, G. 2004. "Lamentable Landmark." *Globe and Mail*, May 22.

Niezen, R. 1993. "Power and Dignity: The Social Consequences of Hydro-electric Development for the James Bay Cree." *Canadian Review of Sociology and Anthropology* 30, 4.

Nikiforuk, A. 2001. *Saboteurs*. Toronto: McFarlane Walter and Ross.

_____. 2000a. "County Kills Hog-factory Plan." *Globe and Mail*, July 12.

_____. 2000b. "The Price of Bringing Home the Bacon: Hog Farming: Intensive Pig Farming may be the Future on the Prairies, but There can be a High Environmental Cost for Pork Factories." *Globe and Mail*, June 12.

Norberg-Hodge, H., T. Merrifield, and S. Gorelick. 2002. *Bringing the Food Economy Home*. Halifax: Fernwood.

Norgaard, R. 1997. "A Coevolutionary Environmental Sociology." In M. Redclift and G. Woodgate (eds.), *The International Handbook of Environmental Sociology*. Cheltenham, UK: Edward Elgar.

Norman, A. 1999. *Slam-dunking Wal-Mart! How You can Stop Superstore Sprawl in Your Hometown*. Atlantic City, NJ: Raphael Marketing.

Novek, J. 2003a. "Intensive Livestock Operations, Disembedding, and Community Polarization in Manitoba." *Society and Natural Resources* 16.

_____. 2003b. "Intensive Hog Farming in Manitoba: Transnational Treadmills and Local Conflicts." *The Canadian Review of Sociology and Anthropology* 40, 1.

Nye, D. 1998. *Consuming Power: A Social History of American Energies*. Cambridge MA: MIT Press.

O'Connor, J. 1998. *Natural Causes: Essays in Ecological Marxism*. New York: Guilford Press.

_____. 1988. "Capitalism, Nature, Socialism: A Theoretical Introduction." *Capitalism, Nature, Socialism* 1.

Off, C. 1997. "The Deal of the Decade. Canadian Broadcasting Corporation Archives." Available at <archives.cbc.ca/IDC-1-73-536-2804/politics_economy/free_trade/clip11> (accessed on November 11, 2004).

Offe, C. 1985. "New Social Movements: Challenging the Boundaries of Institutional Politics." *Social Research* 52, 4.

Olsen, G. 2004. "The Deadly Spins: Gluttony." *Common Ground*, Issue 155 (June).

O'Malley, M. 2002. "Backgrounder: The Mackenzie Valley Pipeline." Available at <www.cbc.ca/news/features/mackenzievalley_pipeline.html> (accessed on May 1, 2004).

Ontario Public Health Association (OPHA). 2005. "A Systemic Approach to Community Food Security: A Role for Public Health." Available at <www.opha.on.ca/foodnet/cfs/summary.html> (accessed January 24, 2005).

Organic. 2003. "What's News in Organic." *Organic* Issue 24 (Spring).

Organic Consumers Association. 2003. "Genetically Engineered Wheat Article: All-Out Attack on Genetically Engineered Wheat Launched." Available at <www.organicconsumers.org/wheat/canada_ge_wheat.cfm> (accessed on May 31, 2004).

Paehlke, R. 2003. *Democracy's Dilemma: Environment, Social Equity, and the Global Economy*. Cambridge, MA: MIT Press.

Parkins, J., J. Varghese, and R. Stedman. 2001. "Locally Defined Indicators of Community Sustainability in the Prince Albert Model Forest." *Information Report NOR-X-379*. Edmonton: Natural Resources Canada, Northern Forestry Centre.

Parks Canada. 2004a. "The Parks Canada Charter." Available at <www.pc.gc.ca/agen/chart/chartr_E.asp> (accessed on November 8, 2004).

_____. 2004b. "Frequently Requested Alberta Tourism Statistics." Available at <www.alberta-canada.com/statpub/pdf/frequentTourismQuestions.pdf> (accessed on June 21, 2004).

_____. 2003. "Banff National Park: State of the Park Report." Available at

<www.pc.gc.ca/pn-np/ab/banff/docs/rap-rep/chap1/rap-rep1_e.asp> (accessed on June 1, 2004).

Pearce, P. 1974. *The Mackenzie Pipeline: Arctic Gas and Canadian Energy Policy*. Toronto: McClelland and Steward.

Pellow, D.N., and L.S. Park. 2002. *The Silicon Valley of Dreams: Environmental Injustices, Immigrant Workers, and High-Tech Global Economy*. New York: New York University Press.

Pengelly, D., M. Campbell, S. Ennis, F. Ursitti, and A. I-Muller (Toronto Public Health). 2000. *Air Pollution Burden of Illness in Toronto*. Toronto: City of Toronto.

People and the Planet. 2004. "'Dirty Dozen' Chemicals Banned at Last." May 17. Available at <www.peopleandplanet.net/doc.php?id=2148> (accessed on January 23, 2005).

Perrow, C. 1984. *Normal Accidents: Living with High Risk Technologies*. New York: Basic Books.

Pesonen, P. (director). 2004. *Victims of Cheap Coffee* [Film]. Finnish Broadcasting Co. New York: Filmmakers Library

Pesticide Action Network North America. 2004a. "Alert: Demand Protection for California Farmworkers." Available at <www.panna.org/resources/documents/fieldsAlert.dv.html> (accessed on July 2, 2004).

_____. 2004b. "PAN Pesticides Database—Chemicals: Cadmium." Available at <www.nowtoronto.com/issues/2002-10-03/news_insight.php> (accessed on May 31, 2004).

Petrella, R. 2001. *The Water Manifesto: Arguments for a World Water Contract*. London: Zed Books.

Petroleum Communication Foundation. 2000. *Flaring*. Calgary: Petroleum Communication Foundation.

Phillips, P. 2004. "Seeds of Doubt over the Monsanto Decision." *Globe and Mail*, May 12.

Postel, S. 2000. "Groundwater Depletion Widespread." In L. Brown, M. Renner and B. Halwell (eds.), *Vital Signs 2000*. New York: W.W. Norton.

Potempa, A. 2000. "Trouble in the Air: Sensitivity to Common Fragrances Brings Isolation." *Anchorage Daily News*. Available at <www.eisc.ca/trouble_in_air.html> (accessed on November 14, 2004).

Pratt, L. 2004. "Pipelines and Pipe Dreams: Energy and Continental Security." Unpublished paper, Edmonton, Alberta.

_____. 1976. *The Tar Sands: Syncrude and the Politics of Oil*. Edmonton: Hurtig.

Prebisch, R. 1964. *Integración de América Latina*. México City: Fondo de Cultura Económica.

Pretty, J. 2001. "Some Benefits and Drawbacks of Local Food Systems." November 2. Available at <www.ruralfutures.org/frame.htm> (accessed January 24, 2005).

Princen, T. 2002a. "Distancing: Consumption and the Severing of Feedback." In T. Princen, M. Maniates and K. Conca (eds.).

_____. 2002b. "Conclusion: To Confront Consumption." In T. Princen, M. Maniates and K. Conca (eds.).

Princen, T., M. Maniates, and K. Conca. 2002. *Confronting Consumption*. Cambridge, MA: MIT Press.

Project for Public Places. "Issue Paper: Streets." Available at <www.pps.org/info/placemakingtools/issuepapers/issuestreets> (accessed on November 1, 2004).

Qualman, D. 2001. "Corporate Hog Farming: The View from the Family Farm." In R. Epp and D. Whitson (eds.), *Writing Off the Rural West: Globalization, Governments, and the Transformation of Rural Communities*. Edmonton: Parkland Institute and University of Alberta Press.

Radford, T. 2003. "GM Cotton Doubles Yield in India Trials." *The Guardian*, February 7.

Ram's Horn. 2003–2004. "Corruption." *Ram's Horn* 17. Available at <www.ramshorn.ca/archive2003/217.html#part1> (accessed on July 15, 2004).

Ramsey, D., and J. Everitt. 2001. "Post-Crow Farming in Manitoba: An Analysis of the Wheat and Hog Sectors." In R. Epp and D. Whitson (eds.), *Writing Off the Rural West: Globalization, Governments and the Transformation of Rural Communities*. Edmonton: Parkland Institute and University of Alberta Press.

Ransom, D. 1999. "Banana Split." *New Internationalist* 317 (October).

Red Deer Chamber of Commerce. "Why You Should Vote No on Ratification of the Kyoto Protocol." Available at <www.reddeerchamber.com/memberdb/PDF/021128NotoKyoto.pdf> (accessed on March 10, 2004).

Redclift, M. 1991. *Environment and Development in Latin America: The Politics of Sustainable Development*. Manchester, NY: Manchester University Press.

_____. 1988. "Sustainable Development and the Market: A Framework for Analysis." *Futures* 20, 6.

_____. 1987. *Sustainable Development: Exploring the Contradictions*. New York: Routledge.

_____. 1984. *Development and Environmental Crisis: Red or Green Alternatives?* London: Methuen.

Redclift, M., and G. Woodgate. 1997. "Sustainability and Social Construction." In M. Redclift and G. Woodgate (eds.), *The International Handbook of Environmental Sociology*. Cheltenham, UK: Edward Elgar.

Reed, M. 2003. *Taking Stands: Gender and the Sustainability of Rural Communities*. Vancouver: University of British Columbia Press.

Rees, W. 1998. "Reducing the Ecological Footprint of Consumption." In L. Westra and P. Werhane (eds.), *The Business of Consumption: Environmental Ethics and the Global Economy*. New York: Rowman and Littlefield Publishers.

Reeves, M., K. Schafer, K. Hallward, and A. Katten. 1999. "Fields of Poison: California Farm Workers and Pesticides: Executive Summary." *Pesticide Action Network North America*. Available at <www.panna.org/resources/documents/fieldsSum.dv.html> (accessed on November 10, 2004).

Reiman, J. 2001. *The Rich Get Richer and the Poor Get Prison: Ideology, Class and Criminal Justice*. Needham Heights, MA: Pearson.

Relph, E. 1976. *Place and Placelessness*. London: Pion.

Rempel, S. 2004. "Letter to the Editor." *Edmonton Journal*, May 16.

Reuters News Service. 2004. "EU Wants to Expand 'Dirty Dozen' Chemicals List." August 12. Available at <www.planetark.com/dailynewsstory.cfm/newsid/26553/ story.htm> (accessed on January 23, 2005).

Ribas, M. (producer), C. Guardia, and R. Valles (directors). 2004. *Sugar: The Rules of the Game*. [Film]. New York: Filmmakers Library.

Rifkin, J. 1980. *Entropy: Into the Greenhouse World*. New York: Bantam.

Ritzer, G. 2000. *Enchanting a Disenchanted World: Revolutionizing the Means of Consumption*. Thousand Oaks, CA: Pine Forge Press, Sage.

_____. 1996. *The McDonaldization of Society*. Revised Edition. California: Pine

Forge Press.
Robb, D. 2004. Introduction to Global Visions Film Festival, Edmonton, Alberta. November 7.
Robbins, R. 1999. *Global Problems and the Culture of Capitalism*. Toronto: Allyn and Bacon.
Roberts, J. 1996. "Predicting Participation in Environmental Treaties: A World-System Analysis." *Sociological Inquiry* 66, 1.
Roberts, J., and P. Grimes. 2002. "World System Theory and the Environment: Toward a New Synthesis." In R. Dunlap, F. Buttel, P. Dickens and A. Gijswijt (eds.), *Sociological Theory and the Environment: Classical Foundations, Contemporary Insights*. New York: Rowman and Littlefield.
Roberts, J., P. Grimes, and J. Manale. 2003. "Social Roots of Global Environmental Change: A World-systems Analysis of Carbon Dioxide Emissions." *Journal of World Systems Research* 9, 2.
Robinson, D. 2000. "Environmental Racism: Old Wine in a New Bottle." *Echoes: Today's Faces of Racism* 17. Available at <www.wcc-coe.org/wcc/what/jpc/echoes/echoes-17-02.html> (accessed on November 14, 2004).
Rodriguez, M., and J. Silva (writers), L. Thielen (director). 1988. *Love, Women and Flowers (Amor, Mujeres y Flores)*. [Film] Available at <www.wmm.com/catalog/pages/c71.htm> (accessed on November 12, 2004).
Rollings-Magnusson, S. 2000. "Canada's Most Wanted: Pioneer Women on the Western Prairies." *Canadian Review of Sociology and Anthropology* 37, 2.
Rosegrant, M., W. Cai, and S. Cline. 2002. *Global Water Outlook to 2025: Averting an Impending Crisis*. Washington, DC: International Food Policy Research Institute.
Ross, A. (ed.). 1997. *No Sweat: Fashion, Free Trade, and the Rights of Garment Workers*. New York: Verso.
Rostow, W. 1960. *The Stages of Economic Growth: A Non-Communist Manifesto*. London: Cambridge University Press.
Rothfeder, J. 2001. *Every Drop for Sale: Our Desperate Battle over Water in a World About to Run Out*. New York: Penguin Putnam.
Rucht, D. 1999. "The Transnationalization of Social Movements: Trends, Causes and Problems." In D. della Porta, H. Kriesil, and D. Rucht (eds.), *Social Movements in a Globalizing World*. New York: Macmillan.
Ruddick, S. 1989. *Maternal Thinking: Towards a Politics of Peace*. Boston: Beacon.
Ryan, J.C., and A. Durning. 1997. *Stuff: The Secret Lives of Everyday Things*. Seattle: Northwest Environment Watch.
Sachs, W. 1999. *Planet Dialectics: Explorations in Environment and Development*. London: Zed Books.
_____. (ed.). 1992. *The Development Dictionary: A Guide to Knowledge as Power*. Atlantic Highlands, NJ: Zed Books.
Sahlins, M. 1972. *Stone Age Economics*. Chicago. Aldine Atherton.
Sale, K. 2001. "There's No Place like Home: Bioregionalism." *The Ecologist* 31, 2 (March).
_____. 1974. "Mother of All." In S. Kumar (ed.), *The Schumacher Lectures, Volume 2*. London: Abacus.
Sapsford, D. 2002. "Smith, Ricardo and the World Marketplace." In D. Sapsford, V. Desai and R. Potter (eds.), *The Companion to Development Studies*. New York: Oxford University Press.
Satterfield, T. 2002. *Anatomy of a Conflict: Identity, Knowledge and Emotion in Old-*

Growth Forests. Vancouver: University of British Columbia Press.

Sault Star. 2004. "Water Users Should Pay." Editorial, May 13.

Savitz, J., T. Hettenbach, and R. Wien. 1998. *Factory Farming: Toxic Waste and Fertilizer in the US*. Washington: Environmental Working Group/The Tides Center.

Schindler, D., and S. Bayley. 1990. "Fresh Waters in Cycle." In C. Mungall and D. McLaren (eds.), *Planet under Stress*. Toronto: Oxford University Press.

Schlosser, E. 2001. *Fast Food Nation: The Dark Side of the American Meal*. New York: Houghton Mifflin.

Schmit, J. 2000. "Countries Consider Joint Study of Agent Orange." *USA Today* March 16.

Schnaiberg, A. 1980. *The Environment*. New York: Oxford University Press.

Schnaiberg, A., and K. Gould. 1994. *Environment and Society: The Enduring Conflict*. New York: St. Martin's.

Scholte, J. 2000. *Globalization: A Critical Introduction*. New York: St. Martin's.

Schor, J. 2004. "The Politics of Consumption." *Aurora Online Journal*. Available at <aurora.icaap.org/2004Interviews/JulietSchor.html> (accessed on January 21 2005).

_____. 2002. "Cleaning the Closet: Toward a New Fashion Ethic." In J. Schor and B. Taylor (eds.), *Sustainable Planet: Solutions for the 21st Century*. Boston: Beacon Press.

_____. 2000. "Postmodern Markets." In J. Schor (ed.), *Do Americans Shop Too Much?* Boston: Beacon Press.

Schrecker, T. 1996. "Of Cars, Sustainability and Equity: A Canadian Case Study." *Capitalism, Nature, Socialism* 7, 4.

Schumacher, E. 1973. *Small is Beautiful: Economics as if People Mattered*. London: Blond and Briggs.

Scott, H. 1998. *Effects of Air Emissions from Sour Gas Plants on the Health and Productivity of Beef and Dairy Herds in Alberta, Canada*. Guelph, ON: University of Guelph.

Sexton, S., and Banana Link. 1997. "Going Bananas." *The Ecologist* 27, 3 (May/June).

Shane, S. 2004. "Chemicals Sickened '91 Gulf War Veterans, Latest Study Finds." *New York Times* October 15.

Sharratt, L. 2002. "Regulating Genetic Engineering For Profit: A Guide to Corporate Power and Canada's Regulation of Genetically Engineered Foods." *Ottawa: Polaris Institute*. Available at <www.polarisinstitute.org/polaris_project/bio_justice/canadian_regulation/regulating_paper.pdf> (accessed on May 24, 2004).

Sheik, Yasmin. 1999. "Has the Clothing Industry Adapted to the Changing Economic Environment?" *ClothingIndustries*. Available at <www.statcan.ca:8096/bsolc/ english/bsolc?catno=34-252-X>.

Sheller, M., and J. Urry. 2000. "The City and the Car." *International Journal of Urban and Regional Research* 24, 4.

Sherman, J. 2004. "Gulf War Illnesses—At Home and Abroad." August 9. Available at <www.dissidentvoice.org> (accessed January 23, 2005).

Sherman, J., and M. Gismondi. 1997. "Jock Talk, Goldfish, Horselogging, and Star Wars." *Alternatives Journal* 23, 1.

Shi, D. 1985. *The Simple Life: Plain Living and High Thinking in American Culture*. New York: Oxford University Press.

Shiva, V. 2002. *Water Wars: Privatization, Pollution, and Profit*. Cambridge, MA: South End Press.

_____. 1993. "The Greening of Global Reach." In W. Sachs (ed.), *Global Ecology: A New Arena of Political Conflict Global Ecology*. London and Atlantic Highlands, NJ: Zed Books.

_____. 1991. *The Violence of the Green Revolution: Third World Agriculture, Ecology and Politics*. Atlantic Highlands, NJ: Zed Books.

Shove, E. 1997 "Revealing the Invisible: Sociology, Energy, and the Environment." In M. Redclift and G. Woodgate (eds.), *The International Handbook of Environmental Sociology*. Cheltenham, UK: Edward Elgar.

Shutt, H. 1998. *The Trouble with Capitalism: An Enquiry into the Causes of Global Economic Failure*. London and New York: Zed Books.

Sierra, S., and L. Eduardo. 1993. *El Cultivo del Banano: Producción y comercio*. Medellín, Colombia: No publisher listed.

Simonsen, K. 1996. "What Kind of Space in What Kind of Social Theory?" *Progress in Human Geography* 20, 4.

Singelmann, J. 1996. "Will Rural Areas Still Matter in the 21st Century? (or) Can Rural Sociology Remain Relevant?" *Rural Sociology* 61, 1.

Skoggard, I. 1998. "Transnational Commodity Flows and the Global Phenomenon of the Brand." In A. Brydon and S. Niessen (eds.), *Consuming Fashion: Adorning the Transnational Body*. New York: Berg.

Slater, D. 1997. *Consumer Culture and Modernity*. Cambridge: Polity Press.

Slovic, P., B. Fischoff, and S. Lichenstein. 1980. "Facts and Fears: Understanding Perceived Risk." In R. Schwing and W. Albers, Jr. (eds.), *Societal Risk Assessment: How Safe is Safe Enough?* New York: Plenum.

Smelser, N. 1962. *Theory of Collective Behavior*. New York: Free Press.

Smith, E., and M. Marquez. 2000. "The Other Side of NIMBY." *Society and Natural Resources* 13.

Smith, J. 2003. "Against the Grain." *The Ecologist* 33, 9.

Smith, N. 1984. *Uneven Development: Nature, Capital and the Production of Space*. Oxford: Blackwell.

Snow, D., E. Rochford, Jr., S. Worden, and R. Benford. 1986. "Frame Alignment Processes, Micromobilization, and Movement Participation." *American Sociological Review* 51 (August).

Soja, E. 1996. "The Trialectics of Spatiality." *Osterreichische Zeitschrift fur Soziologie* 21, 2.

Soto Ballestero, M. 1992. *Bananos: Cultivo y Comercialización*. San José, Costa Rica: No publisher listed.

South Coast Liveable Communities. 2002. "Transportation Outline for Liveable Communities." Available at <www.southcoastlivablecommunities.org/transoutline.html> (accessed on April 14, 2004).

Spaargaren, G., and A. Mol. 1992. "Sociology, Environment, and Modernity: Ecological Modernization as a Theory of Social Change." *Society and Natural Resources* 5.

Spangenberg, J., I. Omann, and F. Hinterberger. 1999. "Sustainability, Growth and Employment in an Alternative European Economic Policy: Theory, Policy and Scenarios for Employment and Environment." Paper presented at the 5th Workshop on Alternative Economic Policy for Europe, Brussels, Belgium, October 1–3.

Spears, Tom. 2004. "Rising Oceans Threaten Millions, Experts Warn." *Edmonton*

Journal November 10: A1.

Spector, Malcolm, and John I. Kitsuse. 1987. *Constructing Social Problems*. New York: Aldine de Gruyter.

Spurlock, M. (director and producer) 2004. *Supersize Me: A Film of Epic Proportions*. [Film]. Los Angeles: Samuel Goldwyn Films.

Standing Senate Committee on Agriculture and Forestry. 1999. "rBST and the Drug Approval Process: Interim Report." Available at <www.parl.gc.ca/36/1/parlbus/commbus/senate/com-e/agri-e/rep-e/repintermar99-e.htm> (accessed on November 10, 2004).

STAT Communications. 2004. "Can Africa Succeed Under GM Farming." Available at <www.Statpub. com/open/77671,html> (accessed on January 23, 2005).

Stauber, J., and S. Rampton. 1995. *Toxic Sludge is Good For You: Lies, Damn Lies and the Public Relations Industry*. Monroe, ME: Common Courage Press and Center for Media and Democracy.

Steger, M. 2002. *Globalism: The New Market Ideology*. New York: Rowman and Littlefield Publishers.

Steingraber, Sandra. 2001. *Having Faith: An Ecologist's Journey to Motherhood*. Cambridge, MA: Perseus.

_____. 1997. *Living Downstream: An Ecologist Looks at Cancer and the Environment*. Reading, MA: Addison-Wesley.

Stern, P. 1997. "Toward a Working Definition of Consumption for Environmental Research and Policy." In P. Stern et al. (eds.), *Environmentally Significant Consumption: Research Directions*. Washington, DC: National Academy Press.

Stowe, J., E. Schmidt, and D. Green. 2001. "Toxic Burials: The Final Insult." *Conservation Biology* 15, 6 (December).

Strange, S. 1998. *Mad Money: When Markets Outgrow Governments*. Ann Arbor: University of Michigan Press.

Strange, S., S. Smith, T. Biersteker, C. Brown, P. Cerny, J. Grieco, and A. Groom. 1996. *Retreat of the State: The Diffusion of Power in the World Economy*. Cambridge: Cambridge University Press.

Strassoldo, R. 1987. "The Sociology of Space: A Typological Framework." Discussion Paper Series #90. New York: Syracuse University, Department of Geography.

Strosher, M. 1996. *Investigations of Flare Gas Emissions in Alberta*. Edmonton: Alberta Research Council.

Stroud, E. 2003. "Reflections from Six Feet under the Field: Dead Bodies in the Classroom." *Environmental History* 8, 4. Available at <www.historycooperative.org/journals/eh/8.4/stroud.html> (accessed on July 6, 2004).

Struzik, E. 2003. "Agreement Will Set Stage for Mackenzie Valley Oil, Gas Work; Nahanni Expansion." *Edmonton Journal*, April 17.

_____. 1990. Stopping the River's Flow: Can Wild Rivers Survive our Government's Love Affair with Dams? *Nature Canada* 19, 1.

Sunkel, O., and P. Paz. 1979. *El Subdesarrollo Latinoamericano y la Teoría del Subdesarrollo*. México City: Siglo Veintiuno Editores.

Sustain/Elm Farm Research Centre Report. 2001. "Eating Oil: Food in a changing climate." Available at <www.sustainweb.org/chain_fm_eat.asp> (accessed on November 11, 2004).

Suzuki, David, and A. McConnell. 1997. *The Sacred Balance: Rediscovering Our Place in Nature*. Vancouver, BC: Greystone Books.

Swyngedouw, E. 2004. *Social Power and the Urbanization of Water: Flows of Power*. Oxford: Oxford University Press.

_____. 2003. "Modernity and Production of the Spanish Waterscape, 1890–1930." In K. Zimmerer and T. Bassett (eds.), *Political Ecology: An Integrative Approach to Geography and Environmental Studies*. New York: Guilford Press.

Szasz, A. 1994. *EcoPopulism: Toxic Waste and the Movement for Environmental Justice*. Minneapolis: University of Minnesota Press.

Tainter, J. 1988. *The Collapse of Modern Societies*. Cambridge: Cambridge University Press.

Taras, H., J. Sallis, T. Patterson, P. Nader, and J. Nelson. 1989. "Television's Influence on Children's Diet and Physical Activity." *Journal of Development and Behavioural Paediatrics* 10.

Taverne, D. 2004. "How Science can save the World's Poor." *The Guardian*, March 3.

Terhune, C. 2004. "Coke CEO Says Obesity Is a Challenge." *Wall Street Journal*. June 18.

Thompson, R., Y. Olsen, R. Mitchell, A. Davis, S. Rowland, A. John, D. McGonigle, and A. Russell. 2004. "Lost at Sea: Where is all the Plastic?" *Science* 304, May 7.

Thornton, Joe. 2000. *Pandora's Poison: Chlorine, Health, and a New Environmental Strategy*. Cambridge, MA: MIT Press.

Tibbetts, J. 2004. "Canola Grower Loses Battle with Monsanto: Supreme Court Rules that a Gene can be Patented and that Saskatchewan Farmer Should Pay for Seeds." *Edmonton Journal* May 22.

Transfair Canada. 2004. "Fair Trade Criteria." Available at <www.transfair.ca/tfc/criteria.html> (accessed on May 31, 2004).

Tropical Science Center. 1982. *Costa Rica Country Environmental Profile: A Field Study*. San José, Costa Rica: Tropical Science Center, US Agency for International Development.

Tuan, Yi-Fu. 1974. *Topophilia: A Study of Environmental Perception, Attitudes and Values*. New York: Prentice-Hall.

Tucker, R. 2000. *Insatiable Appetite: The United States and the Ecological Degradation of the Tropical World*. Los Angeles: University of California Press.

Tulip, K., and L. Michaels. 2004. "A Rough Guide to the UK Farming Crisis." *Corporate Watch*. Available at <www.corporatewatch.org.uk> (accessed on August 23, 2004).

Unión Mundial para la Naturaleza (UICN) and the Nature Conservancy. 1995. *Proyecto Corredor Biológico Talamanca-Caribe*. San José, Costa Rica: NeoGráfica.

Union of Concerned Scientists. 1992. "World Scientists' Warning to Humanity." Available at <www.ucsusa.org/ucs/about/page.cfm?pageID=1009>.

United Farm Workers of America, AFL-CIO (Producer). 1989. *The Wrath of Grapes*. [Videocassette]. Keene, CA

United Nations Development Program (UNDP). 2004. *Stockholm Convention on Persistent Organic Pollutants (pops) to Enter into Force on 17 May 2004*. Available at <www.empa.ch/plugin/template/empa/*/27216/—/l=1> (accessed on July 6, 2004).

_____. 1998. *Human Development Report 1998*. New York: Oxford University Press.

_____. 1992. *Human Development Report 1992*. New York: Oxford University Press.

United Nations Educational, Scientific and Cultural Organization (UNESCO). 2004. "The UN World Water Development Report: Water for People, Water for Life." Available at <www.unesco.org/water/wwap/wwdr/pdf/chap1.pdf> (accessed on June 15, 2004).

United Nations Environment Programme (UNEP). 2002. *Global Environment Outlook 3.* New York: United Nations Environment Programme.

US Public Interest Research Group. 2004. "Super Polluters: The Top 25 Superfund Polluters and their Toxic Waste Sites: Executive Summary." *Campaign to Clean Up Toxics*. Available at <www.pirg.org/reports/enviro/super25/page1.htm> (accessed on November 14, 2004).

Van Sickle, K., and P. Eagles. 1998. "Budgets, Pricing Policies and User Fees in Canadian Parks Tourism." *Tourism Management* 19, 3.

Vandermeer, J., and I. Perfecto. 1995. *Breakfast of Biodiversity: The Truth about Rain Forest Destruction*. Oakland, CA: Food First.

Vaughan, D. 1990. "Autonomy, Interdependence, and Social Control: NASA and the Space Shuttle Challenger." *Administrative Science Quarterly* 35, 2.

Veblen, T. 1899. *The Theory of the Leisure Class*. New York: MacMillan.

Verburg, R., and V. Wiegel. 1997. "On the Compatibility of Sustainability and Economic Growth." *Environmental Ethics* 19 (Fall).

Vevatne, J., and S. Olmos. 2000. "Canada on the Brink: From Frontrunner to Laggard?" *Cicerone* (June).

Wackernagel, M., D. Deumling, C. Monfreda A. Linares, I. López Falfán, and M. Sánchez. 2001. *Ecological Footprint of Nations: December 2001 Update*. Oakland, CA: Redefining Progress. Available at <www.redefiningprogress.org/publications/1997_efoot.pdf> (accessed on November 14, 2004).

Wackernagel, M., B. Niels, D. Schulz, A. Deumling, A. Linares, M. Jenkins, V. Kapos, C. Monfreda, J. Loh, N. Myers, R. Norgaard, and J. Randers. 2002. "Tracking the Ecological Overshoot of the Human Economy." Paper presented at the National Academy of Sciences of the United States, July 9.

Wackernagel, M., and W. Rees. 1996. *Our Ecological Footprint: Reducing Human Impact on the Earth*. Gabriola Island, BC: New Society.

Wada, Y., W. Rees, and M. Wackernagel. 1993. "Assessing Progress in Agriculture: The Ecological Footprint of Hydroponic Tomato Production." Paper presentation at the National Conference of the International Society for Ecological Economics (Canadian Chapter), Ottawa, Canada.

Wakefield, S., and S. Elliot. 2000. "Environmental Risk Perception and Wellbeing: Effects of the Landfill Siting Process in Two Southern Ontario Communities." *Social Science and Medicine* 50.

Wakefield, S., S. Elliot, D. Cole, and J. Eyles. 2001. "Environmental Risk and (Re)Action: Air Quality, Health, and Civic Involvement in an Urban Industrial Neighborhood." *Health and Place* 7.

Waldbott, G.L, A.W. Burgstahler, and H.L. McKinney. 1978. *Fluoridation: The Great Dilemma*. Lawrence, Kansas: Coronado Press.

Wallace, Iain, and Rob Shields. 1997. "Contested Terrains: Social Space and the Canadian Environment." In W. Clement (ed.), *Understanding Canada: Building on the New Canadian Political Economy*. Montreal and Kingston: McGill-Queen's University Press.

Wallerstein, I. 1979. *The Capitalist World Economy*. Cambridge: Cambridge University Press.

_____. 1974. *The Modern World System, Voume 1*. New York: Academic Press.

Wapner, P. 1996. *Environmental Activism and World Civic Politics*. Albany: SUNY Press.

Waring, M. 1999 *Counting for Nothing: What Men Value and What Women are Worth*. Second Edition. Toronto: University of Toronto Press.

_____. 1988. *If Women Counted: A New Feminist Economics*. New York: Harper Collins.

Watkins, M. 1997. "Canadian Capitalism in Transition." In W. Clement (ed.), *Understanding Canada: Building on the New Canadian Political Economy*. Montreal and Kingston: McGill-Queen's University Press.

Watson, P. 1995. "Agent Orange Still Maims Vietnam's Unborn." *Toronto Star* April 27.

Watts, M. 2004. "Natural Resources." In S. Harrison, S. Pile and N. Thrift (eds.), *Patterned Ground: Entanglements of Nature and Culture*. London: Reaktion Books.

Weale, A. 1992. *The New Politics of Pollution*. Manchester: Manchester University Press.

Weiner, M. 1966. *Modernization*. New York: Basic Books.

Weiss, E. 2004. "'Big-Box' Stores Leave More Than a Void." *Washington Post* January 20.

Whitson, D. 2001. "Nature as Playground: Recreation and Gentrification in the Mountain West." In R. Epp and D. Whitson (eds.), *Writing Off the Rural West: Globalization, Governments and the Transformation of Rural Communities*. Edmonton: Parkland Institute and the University of Alberta Press.

Wilkinson, I. 2001. *Anxiety in a Risk Society*. London: Routledge.

William, D., and S. Stewart. 1998. "Sense of Place: An Elusive Concept that is Finding a Home in Ecosystem Management." *Journal of Forestry* 96, 5.

Williams, C. 2000. "100 Years of Income and Expenditures." *Canadian Social Trends*. Ottawa: Statistics Canada (Catalogue 11-008, Number 59).

Wilson, D. 2002. *Fateful Harvest: The True Story of a Small Town, a Global Industry, and a Toxic Secret*. New York: Harper Collins.

_____. 1993a. "Clayoquot Protesters Predict Arrests: Trained Activists Plan Blockade to Keep Loggers out of BC Rain Forest." *Globe and Mail* July 3.

_____. 1993b. "Mass Arrests in Logging Protest: RCMP Round Up More than 250 Men, Women, and Children in BC." *Globe and Mail* August 10.

_____. 1993c. "Defenders of Clayoquot Sound call Dr. Seuss: Anti-logging Activists, Most of Whom have Never Met a Lawyer Before, Create a Curious Trial as They Face Contempt Charges." *Globe and Mail* October 2.

_____. 1993d. "Clayoquot Protesters Jailed 45 Days for Violating Court Order: Judge Cites Need to Deter Illegal Demonstrations." *Globe and Mail* October 15.

Wilson, J. 1998. *Talk and Log: Wilderness Politics in British Columbia*. Vancouver: University of British Columbia Press.

Winnipeg Free Press. 2004. "Expert Warns of Hog Farm 'Disaster': Booming Industry Lacks Regulation." *October 6.*

Winson, A., and B. Leach. 2002. *Contingent Work, Disrupted Lives*. Toronto: University of Toronto Press.

Wolf, Naomi 1995. "The Beauty Myth." In M. L. Anderson and P. H. Collins (eds.), *Race, Class, and Gender: An Anthology*. Belmont: Wadsworth.

World Commission on Dams. 2000. *Dams and Development: A Framework for Decision-Making*. London and Virginia: EarthScan Publications.

World Commission on Environment and Development. 1987. *Our Common Future*. Oxford: Oxford University Press.

Word IQ. 2004. "Military-industrial Complex." Available at <www.wordiq.com/definition/Military-industrial_complex> (accessed on July 4, 2004).

World Social Forum. 2004. "Charter of Principles." Available at <www.wsfindia.org/charter.php> (accessed on August 24, 2004).

World Trade Organization. 2003. "WTO Public Symposium 2003: Ecolabelling." Available at <www.cid.harvard.edu/cidtrade/geneva/ecolabelling.html> (accessed on November 10, 2004).

World Wildlife Fund (WWF). 2004a. "Stockholm Convention on Persistent Organic Pollutants: Promoting International Control on Toxic Chemicals". Available at <www.worldwildlife.org/toxics/projects/project2.cfm> (accessed on July 4, 2004).

_____. 2004b. "Living Planet Report 2000: Needed—Two More Planets." Available at <www.panda.org/news_facts/publications/general/livingplanet/lpr00.cfm> (accessed on November 14, 2004).

Wood, O. 2002. "Water Facts and Figures." Available at <www.cbc.ca/news/indepth/background/groundwater2.html> (accessed on March 25, 2004).

WorldWatch Institute. 2004. *State of the World 2004. Special Focus: The Consumer Society*. New York: W.W. Norton.

Wristen, K. 2004. "Adding Fuel to the Fire: The Mackenzie Gas Project." *The Parkland Post* 8, 2 (Summer).

Wynne, B. 1992. "Risk and Social Learning: Reification to Engagement." In S. Krimsky and D. Golding (eds.), *Social Theories of Risk*. London: Praeger.

_____. 1982. *Rationality and Ritual: The Windscale Inquiry and Nuclear Decisions in Britain*. Chalfont St. Giles: British Society for the History of Science.

Yanz, L., B. Jeffcot, D. Ladd, and J. Atlin. 1999. *Policy Options to Improve Standards for Women Garment Workers in Canada and Internationally*. Toronto: Maquiladora Solidarity Network.

Young, O. (ed.). 1997. *Global Governance: Drawing Insights from the Environmental Experience*. Cambridge, MA: MIT Press.

Youngquist, W. 1997. *Geodestinies: The Inevitable Control of Earth Resources over Nations and Individuals*. Portland, OR: National Book Company.

Yussuff, H. 2000. "No Jobs on a Dead Planet: The Future of Work is Green, says a Vice-President of the Canadian Labour Congress." *Globe and Mail* February 15.

Zaretsky, N. 1996. "Bananas: A New Spin on an Old Argument." *Caribbean Studies Newsletter* 23, 1.

Zygmunt, B. 1998. *Work, Consumerism and the New Poor.* Philadelphia: Open University Press.

Website References

Aurora Online website. "Interview with Susan George." Aurora.icaap.org/archive/george.html>

B.C. Facts.org. "Government Overrules Clayoquot Resource Board." <www.bcfacts.org/index.cfm>

Calorie Counter. <www.calorie-counter.net/donuts-calories.htm>

Canadian Auto Workers (CAW). <www.caw.ca>

Car Free Day. "Car Free Day September 22." <www.carfreeday.ca>

CBC News website. <www.cbc.ca/news/national/magazine/kyoto/index.html, 08/08/2002>

Clayoquot Sound Central Region Board. <www.island.net/~crb>

Consumer Reports. "Dry Cleaning Alternatives 2/03." <www.consumerreports.org/main/detailv2.jsp 0>

Critical Mass. <www.critical-mass.org>

Economic Research Service, United States Department of Agriculture. "Briefing Room: Cotton." <www.ers.usda.gov/briefing/cotton/>.

Fluoride Action Network. <www.flouridealert.org>

Global Ecolabelling Network (GEN). "What is Ecolabelling?" <www.gen.gr.jp/eco.html 7>.

Government of Alberta. "Customer Choice in Plain Talk." <http://www.customerchoice.gov.ab.ca/>

LEAD (Leadership for Environment and Development). "Ecological Footprint Calculator." <www.lead.org/leadnet/footprint/intro.htm>.

Mackenzie Gas Project website. <www.mackenziegasproject.com/the Project/regulatory Preocess/EISInBrief/EISInBrief.htm/>

The Manley Report argues for completing a nuclear plant in Ontario; see "Transforming Ontario's Power Generation Company" <www.energy.gov.on.ca/index.cfm?fuseaction=electricity.reports_opgreview>

Monsanto. "Products and Solutions." <www.monsanto.com/monsanto/layout/products/default.asp>.

Mountain Equipment Co-op. "Social and Environmental Responsibility: Ecological Footprint." <www.mec.ca>.

National Union of Public and General Employees (NUPGE). <www.nupge.ca/default.htm>

Parmalat. "About us: History." <www.parmalat.ca/>.

STAT Communications. 2004. "Can Africa Succeed under GM Farming?" <www.Statpub.com/open/77671.html> (access January 23, 2005).

Sustainable Cotton Project website, "Pesticides." <www.sustainablecotton.org/PESTICIDES/index.htm>

TerraChoice. "Eco-logo Program." <www.terrachoice.ca>.

Tofino Town Council. <www.foc.ca/1newsreleases/031024>.

Toronto Environmental Alliance. "Waste reduction." <www.toronto environment.org>.

UNEP. 2004. Production and Consumption Branch, Sustainable Consumption (SC), Lifecycle Initiative. <www.uneptie.org/sustain/lcinitiative0>